Number Ten Downing Street and the Cabinet Office are at the apex of power in British government, but relatively little is known about the day-to-day functioning of these great institutions of state. With an unprecedented level of access, and wide-ranging interviews from former ministers, senior civil servants and special advisers, Patrick Diamond examines the administrative and political machinery serving the prime minister, and considers how it evolved from the early years of New Labour to the election of the Coalition Government in 2010.

Drawing on previously unpublished material, Diamond provides a unique analysis which considers the continuing power of the civil service, the tensions between permanent officials and political aides, and the hard grind of achieving policy change from the centre in Whitehall. By exploring the ideological beliefs underpinning the policy-making process and illuminating the importance of the British Political Tradition in shaping the institutions and practice of state-craft, this book reveals the contemporary realities of government and democracy in practice.

Patrick Diamond is Lecturer in Public Policy at Queen Mary, University of London and Gwilym Gibbon Fellow at Nuffield College, Oxford. He was formerly Head of Policy Planning in 10 Downing Street and Senior Policy Adviser to the Prime Minister. He is the co-author of *Beyond New Labour*; *Social Justice in the Global Age*; *After the Third Way*; and *Global Europe, Social Europe*.

D0223632

In the series:

After the Third Way: The Future of Social Democracy in Europe
Edited by Olaf Cramme and Patrick Diamond
ISBN: 978 1 84885 992 0 (HB); 978 1 84885 993 7 (PB)

Europe's Immigration Challenge: Reconciling Work, Welfare and Mobility
Edited by Elena Jurado and Grete Brochmann
ISBN: 978 1 78076 225 8 (HB); 978 1 78076 226 5 (PB)

Left Without a Future? Social Justice in Anxious Times
Anthony Painter
ISBN: 978 1 78076 660 7 (HB); 978 1 78076 661 4 (PB)

Progressive Politics after the Crash: Governing from the Left
Edited by Olaf Cramme, Patrick Diamond and Michael McTernan
ISBN: 978 1 78076 763 5 (HB); 978 1 78076 764 2 (PB)

Governing Britain: Power, Politics and the Prime Minister
Patrick Diamond
ISBN: 978 1 78076 581 5 (HB); 978 1 78076 582 2 (PB)

The Europe Dilemma: Britain and the Challenges of EU Integration
Roger Liddle
ISBN: 978 1 78076 222 7 (HB); 978 1 78076 223 4 (PB)

policy network

Patrick Diamond

Governing Britain

Power, Politics and the Prime Minister

I.B. TAURIS

LONDON · NEW YORK

Published in 2014 by I.B.Tauris & Co. Ltd
6 Salem Road, London W2 4BU
175 Fifth Avenue, New York NY 10010
www.ibtauris.com

Distributed in the United States and Canada Exclusively by Palgrave Macmillan
175 Fifth Avenue, New York NY 10010

ISBN: 978 1 78076 581 5 (HB)
ISBN: 978 1 78076 582 2 (PB)

A full CIP record for this book is available from the British Library
A full CIP record is available from the Library of Congress

Library of Congress Catalog Card Number: available

Typeset in Minion by 4word Ltd, Bristol
Printed and bound in Great Britain by T.J. International, Padstow, Cornwall

'This is an excellent account of New Labour's governing philosophy. Patrick Diamond's "four phases of governance reform" are especially insightful in understanding New Labour's management of the state and public services. He rightly highlights deep continuities in respect of England's tradition of centralised politics and policy-making, while acknowledging the variations on that theme.'
Andrew (Lord) Adonis

'Patrick Diamond's informed and perceptive study of changes in the pattern of government under New Labour raises big questions now in the coalition era about the traditional, and enduring, centralist Whitehall model, and about adapting ministerial/civil service relations. He is right that we may be witnessing only an initial phase in the reconstruction of the British state.'
Peter Riddell, Director of the Institute for Government

'Patrick Diamond has provided a groundbreaking book. Through detailed research with the key actors, he has provided a sophisticated understanding of how government worked in the Blair and Brown administrations. His analysis undermines many of the myths of the era and provides an incisive insight into how government really works.'
Martin Smith, Professor of Politics, University of York

Contents

Figures and Tables

Figures

Tables

Glossary of Abbreviations

AES	Alternative Economic Strategy
APM	Asymmetric Power Model
BIS	Business, Innovation and Skills
BoE	Bank of England
BPT	British Political Tradition
CASE	Centre for the Analysis of Social Exclusion
COBRA	Cabinet Office Briefing Room A
CPRS	Central Policy Review Staff
CPS	Centre for Policy Studies
CSR	Comprehensive Spending Review
CTC	City Technology College
DCLG	Department for Communities and Local Government
DCSF	Department for Children, Schools and Families
DEA	Department of Economic Affairs
DES	Department of Education and Science
DfEE	Department for Education and Employment
DfES	Department for Education and Skills
DoE	Department of Education
DoH	Department of Health
DPM	Differentiated Polity Model
DSS	Department of Social Security
DTI	Department of Trade and Industry
EAZ	Education Action Zone
EDS	Economic and Domestic Secretariat
ERM	Exchange Rate Mechanism
FNP	Family-Nurse Partnership
FSA	Financial Services Authority
FSU	Forward Strategy Unit
HAZ	Health Action Zone
HMT	Her Majesty's Treasury

HRA	Human Rights Act
IEA	Institute of Economic Affairs
IfG	Institute for Government
IFS	Institute for Fiscal Studies
ILP	Independent Labour Party
IMF	International Monetary Fund
IPPR	Institute for Public Policy Research
LEA	Local Education Authority
LMS	Local Management of Schools
MPC	Monetary Policy Committee
MSC	Manpower Services Commission
MTFS	Medium-Term Financial Strategy
NDPB	Non-Departmental Public Body
NEB	National Enterprise Board
NEC	National Economic Council
NEDC	National Economic Development Council
NOMS	National Offender Management System
NPM	New Public Management
Ofsted	Office for Standards in Education
PASC	Public Administration Select Committee
PCT	Primary Care Trust
PFI	Private Finance Initiative
PISA	Programme for International Student Assessment
PIU	Performance and Innovation Unit
PMDU	Prime Minister's Delivery Unit
PMPD	Prime Minister's Policy Directorate
PMPU	Prime Minister's Policy Unit
PMSU	Prime Minister's Strategy Unit
PPP	Public–Private Partnership
PSA	Public Service Agreement
PSB	Public Service Bargain
SCU	Strategic Communications Unit
SEU	Social Exclusion Unit
SETF	Social Exclusion Task Force
TARP	Troubled Assets Relief Programme

Acknowledgements

I am especially grateful to colleagues at the University of Manchester and Nuffield College, Oxford, for the series of seminars, workshops and informal discussions that have influenced the preparation of this book. In particular, I would like to thank Professor David Richards, Professor Martin Smith, Professor Colin Hay, Professor Michael Kenny, Dr Helen Thompson, Professor Kevin Theakston and Dr Felicity Matthews for their substantive comments which shaped and influenced this account of continuity and change in Whitehall and the core executive. Many former colleagues in the Blair and Brown administrations helped to develop my understanding of the policy-making process in central government, alongside the relationship between politicians and the permanent bureaucracy in the British political system.

I am deeply grateful to those who gave up their time to be interviewed for this study and to colleagues in the Department of Politics at the University of Sheffield for their practical assistance. The staff at I.B.Tauris and Policy Network, particularly Joanna Godfrey and Michael McTernan, were always helpful and encouraging. Hannah Jameson read and commented incisively on successive drafts, making this an immeasurably better book. Finally, profound thanks go to my family for their forbearance as this work was completed.

Patrick Diamond
May 2013

Introduction

Governance, Power and Politics in the Contemporary British State

No unbiased observer who derives pleasure from the welfare of his species can fail to consider the long and uninterruptedly increasing prosperity of England as the most beautiful phenomenon in the history of mankind. Climates more propitious may impact more largely the mere enjoyment of existence, but in no other region have the benefits that political institutions can confer been diffused over so extended a population; nor have any people so well reconciled the discordant elements of wealth, order and liberty.

Hallam (1818)[1]

The tradition of all the dead generations weighs like a nightmare on the brain of the living.

Marx (1852)

Civil servants propose. Ministers decide. Civil servants execute.

(*The Times* editorial, quoted in Campbell & Wilson, 1995: 23)

Introduction

This book is principally concerned with New Labour's governing strategy: its approach to the central state as a means of governing effectively. The focus is New Labour's statecraft, the art of operating the levers of governmental power at the centre, as adopted by the Blair and Brown administrations between 1997 and 2010. The former progressive Democratic governor of New York, Mario Cuomo, famously quipped that political actors 'campaign in poetry. But when we're elected, we're forced to govern in prose. . .' . Cuomo was depicting the arduous grind that governments face in translating the promises that politicians make during election campaigns into changed outcomes in the daily lives of citizens. The New Labour governments sought to turn a multitude of manifesto pledges and electoral commitments into tangible delivery on the ground.

The Labour administration made 'modernising' state services one of its pre-eminent goals, but in pursuing reform the party fashioned a distinctive conception of the role of government and the legitimate exercise of state power within the British political system. According to Peters (2004), political leaders have been searching for ways of governing more effectively from the centre over the last thirty years, taking into account fundamental changes in society, the nature of governance, and public administration. The focus of the volume is the dynamics of continuity and change in the core executive, in a context where institutional capacity at the centre of the state has been continuously reformed, modified and adapted. The book addresses how far New Labour's approach to governing through Whitehall and the core executive was *new*, and whether it represented a fundamental challenge to what had gone before. Moreover, this approach to the governing process had implications that go beyond the central state. Most prominently, it led to the cascading down of a target-driven, audit culture throughout Britain's public services.

The Labour Party's determination to rebuild the strategic centre of government had a bold purpose. It was intended not just to improve governmental performance, but to transform the nature of society by accruing power at the centre of the state. Nonetheless, in time both Tony Blair and Gordon Brown came to realise that pulling levers at the centre does not necessarily lead to the anticipated outcomes being delivered on the ground. After the initial euphoria of gaining office following eighteen years in the wilderness of opposition, ministers became frustrated that the policy ambitions they were pursuing in Whitehall were not necessarily achieving what they intended. As the Labour administration progressed, there was a growing sense of disenchantment, of energy dissipating and momentum being lost: a widening gap between the government's promise and its performance.

Labour ministers practised the art of governing in an era where political systems are widely believed to have ceded the capacity to govern (Peters, 2004): the scope for government to ensure that the formulation and implementation of policy fitted seamlessly together was perceived to have weakened. This is an environment where for political agents, power is discernibly, 'harder to use, and easier to lose' (Naim, 2013). Those who posit the 'hollowing-out' of the state insist that an age of 'governance' has replaced 'government': the governing process is dominated by actors beyond the central state and its institutions, and political leaders no longer possess the tools to govern authoritatively. In today's world, ministers rely on the tacit support of their officials, professional interest groups, public service managers and, increasingly, the active involvement of civil society. The most intractable issues, from anti-social behaviour and crime to obesity, alcohol addiction and teenage pregnancy, are influenced by factors beyond the direct control of central government. More than anything, the structure and capacities of Whitehall and the core executive necessitate a debate about the role of the state: what central government can, and should, do in the contemporary era.

A core theme of this book is that despite structural challenges to the state's legitimacy and authority, British governments have not been denuded of power. Rather it is the continuous and unremitting search for levers that enable political actors to govern, 're-centring' the state, which is at the heart of this volume. That means addressing New Labour's relationship with Whitehall and the core executive between 1997 and 2010; the core executive refers to 'all those organisations and procedures which co-ordinate central government, and act as the final arbiters of conflict between different parts of the government machine' (Rhodes, 1995: 12). As we shall see, this theme is not without controversy. The process of re-centring government has meant that, over time, the central state has taken responsibility for achieving outcomes without having the means to deliver them. Moreover, pertinent trends such as politicisation and presidentialisation are refashioning British governance, leading to growing tensions in the central executive territory of the British state.

New Labour and Whitehall

At the outset, Labour's view of the Whitehall machine was apparently contradictory and ambiguous. Like previous prime ministers, Blair and Brown came to office with a commitment to uphold the inherited traditions and conventions of the British state. The civil service was a revered institution guaranteeing British government's professionalism, integrity and competence, the product of a stable tradition of constitutional monarchy and representative government. New Labour self-consciously sought acceptance of the party as a trusted custodian of the British state and constitutional settlement, rejecting the dissenting voices of an earlier generation of politicians such as Richard Crossman and Tony Benn who argued that Whitehall and the civil service were an impediment to political change. Blair, in particular, had no intention of weakening the Northcote-Trevelyan principles of Whitehall neutrality and public service. The then Prime Minister proclaimed: 'A neutral civil service is one of the great assets of our political system and we will not put it at risk' (cited in Blunkett & Richards, 2011: 183). What is more, Whitehall mandarins, while remaining neutral and non-partisan, keenly anticipated New Labour's election, which they saw as heralding a new era of influence and prestige for the civil service. As a result, any far-reaching reform of the constitutional convention governing the relationship between ministers and civil servants was strictly off-limits. New Labour's view was that officials played 'a vital role at the fulcrum between politics and administration by virtue of their expertise in making the system work' (Theakston, 1999: 58).

The paradox, however, is that apparent respect for the traditional Whitehall model went hand in hand with growing frustration at the capacities and capabilities of the modern civil service. Within months of arriving at the Treasury in May 1997, Gordon Brown removed a number of senior officials, most prominently his permanent secretary, Sir Terry Burns, who the new Chancellor believed had grown too close to the previous Conservative administration, and was unsympathetic to Labour's aspirations for economic and social reform (Rawnsley, 2006). In the initial months of the New Labour administration, seven top officials were eased out from across central government (Seldon, 2006). Having anticipated the Rolls-Royce service of popular myth, the new administration discovered an institution apparently ill-equipped to deal with the demands and pressures of the modern world (Blair, 2010; Hyman, 2004).

Not only was the civil service perceived as either unwittingly or deliberately obstructing ministers from carrying out their reforms. It was judged to be weak at identifying and defusing political 'time-bombs' that have the potential to destroy ministerial careers, making governments appear incompetent and directionless. In the postwar years, the British civil service gained a reputation for complacency and fatalism about Britain's relative decline. Economic failure and the weakening of the Keynesian welfare state produced a ferocious backlash against corporatist strategies and institutions, most prominently the civil service, exemplified by Martin Wiener's polemic *English Culture and the Decline of the Industrial Spirit 1850–1980*. This burgeoning decline literature was applied to every corner of British national life, 'to Britain's underperforming capitalism, its anachronistic *ancien regime*, and its underfunded and failing public services' (Gamble, 2003: 133).

From New Labour's perspective, the British system of government had been infected by a culture of resignation and powerlessness. Michael Barber, one of Blair's most senior advisers, railed against 'the shambolic amateurism that used to characterise public service policy-making' (2007: 268). Departments were plagued by 'excessive risk aversion, exaggeration of the likely difficulties, refusing to believe that what the politicians want is what they really want, slowing down or watering down implementation, and last but not least, simple incompetence' (2007: 313). The former head of the Downing Street Policy Unit, Andrew Adonis, complained that Whitehall was incapable of leading change since officials changed jobs too frequently, rarely developing the expertise and project management capability to implement key policy programmes (Adonis, 2012). Ministers believed the civil service was characterised by insufficient focus on delivery, a slow speed of response, and poor innovative capacity. While the New Labour governments were perceived as 'control freaks', Blair and his ministers insisted the reality was very different.[2] The dominant feeling was of impotence rather than being all-powerful.

As a consequence, on the eve of New Labour's second victory in 2001, the Prime Minister argued 'the modus operandi has to change dramatically', in Whitehall, 'to expand our capacity to act':

> We need a team focused on delivery, day to day management of departments, the operational management of getting the job done. This should combine the Policy Unit and No.10. In each area, we should have the people who can chase up, prod, push and monitor delivery by departments [...] We should have a special unit focused particularly on forward policy thinking and strategy. This is separate from the day to day. Of course, forward thinking and the intermediate should interchange but we require [...] far clearer definition on policy; and real policy development in a far more fundamental sense than achieved so far: what is the role of the private sector in the NHS? What should the university system look like in ten years? What are the principles governing the tax system? At the moment, we are capable of brilliant pushing of departments, some development of existing policy positions but not, I feel, of radical rethinking.[3]

The Prime Minister's 'instruction to deliver' led to a significant strengthening of institutional capacity: the creation of the PM's Delivery Unit, the PM's Strategy Unit and an expanded Number Ten Policy Unit, reshaping Whitehall and the core executive. In response to Blair's edict, however, senior civil servants developed an increasingly cynical view of the New Labour administration, caricatured in the popular television satire, *The Thick of It*: modern governments are run by political apparatchiks whose motivation is to manage the 24-hour news cycle to benefit their minister, not to come up with sound policy in the public interest. These advisers see their role as concealing ministerial and governmental incompetence with lies and deceit in order to gain party political advantage (Johnston, 2009). Malcolm Tucker, the leading protagonist in *The Thick of It* and the Prime Minister's director of communications, apparently had more power and influence than Cabinet ministers.

Whereas an earlier popular television series, *Yes, Minister* emphasised that civil servants were able to cynically dupe their political masters, by the late 1990s commentators were complaining that the power of the Whitehall mandarins had been eroded to the point where officials' advice was no longer valued, and traditional lines of accountability were increasingly redundant (Johnston, 2009). Blair was determined to bolster the centre of the state, believing that only a firm grip over the machinery of government would enable his party to achieve its governing ambitions, avoiding the damaging policy failures which had characterised Labour governments in the past. As a consequence, it was widely assumed that the relationship between ministers and civil servants was undergoing fundamental change: ministers were less dependent on the civil service for policy and delivery advice than ever before.

The conundrum which forms the centrepiece of this book, however, is that while there was much about Whitehall that irritated Blair and his colleagues, they remained hugely dependent on, and loyal to, the traditional institutions and processes of the Whitehall machinery. Officials had resources, expertise, institutional memory and tacit knowledge, crucial for an incoming government that had been out of power since 1979. New Labour was driven by the imperative of *governing competence*, overhauling the management capacities of the state in order to restore their reputation for fiscal responsibility and prudent macro-economic management (Blair, 2010; Bulpitt, 1986; Powell, 2010; Seldon, 2006). New Labour's aim was *political*, demonstrating that unlike the 1960s and 1970s, the party had the capacity to deliver in office (Driver & Martell, 2004; Giddens, 1998; Smith, 2010). Ministers were locked in a relationship of mutual dependency with civil servants and their departments from the early days of Blair's premiership, a pattern reinforced throughout the duration of Brown's tenure in Number Ten.

'Governing Britain': Addressing Gaps in the Literature

This core insight about mutual dependency in the core executive is the product of a somewhat unusual academic study, in that the author was once a practitioner at the heart of British government.[4] *Governing Britain* offers a distinctive approach to practising political science: the author is a political analyst, while having been a participant in the day-to-day events with which this work is directly concerned. This can be potentially fruitful in building a bridge between politics 'in theory' and politics 'in practice'. There is no rigid distinction between 'outsiders' and 'insiders' in the study of public administration and governance: it is important to acknowledge the flow of ideas and concepts back and forth. Both academic researchers and political practitioners draw on the same raw material of ideas and understandings, constructing distinctive 'images' of the political system (Tivey, 1999).

This book is arguably the first of its kind to examine and assess the New Labour period from 1997 to 2010 by addressing structural change in Whitehall and the core executive. The analysis addresses *informal* relationships, as well as *formal* structures in the central state machinery. The starting-point of this study of the core executive is how policy-making is practised by ministers and officials. The development and implementation of policy is an inherently *political* exercise. Policy delivery is never straightforward: there is a 'primeval policy soup' in which ideas are continuously circulated and exchanged. Ultimately, policy matters in determining who gets what, when and how.[5]

Research that explores how actors perceive, understand and interpret policy-making within the core executive is relatively scarce. There are certain exceptions (Heclo & Wildavsky, 1981; Marsh et al., 2001; Rhodes, 2012; Thain & Wright 1995). Nonetheless, few studies have addressed the politics of institutional relationships, the structure of policy-making, and the nature of power relations between the centre and departments.

A Theoretical Approach to Public Administration: The British Political Tradition, the Whitehall Paradigm, and the Core Executive

The field of British public administration has been notorious for its predominantly atheoretical approach (Elgie, 2011; Gamble, 1990; Marsh et al., 2003). Initially, the academic study of UK government, particularly Whitehall departments, was overly descriptive lacking any rigorous theoretical underpinning (Chester & Wilson, 1968; Elgie, 2011; Hood & Dunsire, 1981). The discipline was dominated by a long-running and ultimately irresolvable dispute about the relative power of the prime minister and Cabinet. This led more recently to vigorous questioning of the ontological and epistemological assumptions underpinning research, and an attempt to broaden the debate (Bevir & Rhodes, 2006b; Bevir & Richards, 2009; Hay, 2011; Marsh, 2011; McAnulla, 2006; Rhodes, 2012). The ontological disagreement relates to whether there is a 'real' world out there which can be uncovered; epistemology, in turn, concerns whether social phenomena exist as anything other than agents' interpretations and how knowledge is mediated. This raises a number of fundamental questions for political science: can British government be understood through empirical research, and if so, what kind? What motivates actors and how far are they constrained by institutions? To what extent is power hermetically sealed at the centre of the state?

There are a range of accounts which aim to break out of the arid confines of prime ministerialism, emphasising the fluid and relational nature of power, and the complexity of continuity and change in the central executive territory (Bevir & Rhodes, 2006b; Elgie, 2011; Hay, 2011; Marsh et al., 2001; Rhodes, 2011):

- Richardson and Jordan (1979) map decision-making in British government based on interviews with officials. They focus on the rules of the game in Whitehall, and the system's underlying conservatism.
- Heclo and Wildavsky (1981) made pioneering use of interviews to depict the culture of Whitehall, focusing attention on its 'village life'.[6] The policy process is defined as a 'trial of personalities' from which the Treasury emerges as the dominant player.
- Dunleavy and Rhodes (1990) change the terms of debate about the central state by coining the phrase 'core executive'. They draw attention to the organisations and structures that serve to 'pull together and integrate' central government policy.
- Marsh, Richards and Smith (2001) develop a case study approach across Whitehall departments, comparing and contrasting how change occurs by examining the interaction between structure and agency.
- Page and Jenkins (2005) assess the role of 'middle-ranking' officials in policy-making. They draw on rational choice accounts which emphasise the role of officials as utility-maximising agents, while making extensive use of interviews alongside quantitative data.
- Rhodes (2011) harnesses the ethnographic method mapping 'everyday life in British government' through the interpretations of actors. This builds on previous work concerning the differentiated polity, alongside the 'hollowing-out' of the state.
- Gains and Stoker (2011) examine the role of ministerial special advisers in transmitting ideas drawn from social science into the process of governmental policy-making.

So there is a substantial and compelling body of research on which to build. This book draws on an eclectic literature analysing the cumulative impact of New Labour on the organisational shape and day-to-day functioning of the British core executive. In so doing, it examines the dynamics of politics and power in British central government. The focus is not merely the constitutional status of the prime minister and the Cabinet, but the role of actors and institutions throughout the policy-making arena of the central state.[7] The research addresses 'the assemblage of ministers and senior civil servants who preside over the work of Cabinets and departments' in a 'marketplace exchange of an agreed culture, day after day and year after year' (Heclo & Wildavsky, 1981: 9). This approach bypasses constitutional and legally focused conceptions of the state in favour of 'a person-centred insider notion of the real dynamics of government' (Parry, 2003: 15).

The British Political Tradition

As such, this volume analyses the 'real dynamics' of Whitehall and the core executive, while being rooted in an explicit theoretical framework. The literature on the British Political Tradition (BPT) provides an exacting 'meta-theoretical orientation', addressing the interaction between institutions and ideas. As an organising perspective, the BPT offers 'a map of how things interrelate and leads to a set of research questions' (Bache & Flinders, 2004: 33). The literature focuses on the institutional practices of the British polity, namely the ideas that underpin and inform institutions and processes. This provides a vital starting-point in assessing patterns of continuity and change in Whitehall. The most prolific authors in the 'classical' BPT literature – A.H. Birch, W.H. Greenleaf, and Samuel Beer – represent a generation of political scientists who argued that the 'English model' based on liberal constitutional government created an effective and representative state, an exemplar of institutional continuity and political stability, and an object of imitation for other nations (Gamble, 2003).

Birch, Beer and Greenleaf's interpretive analysis is rejected by the 'modernist empiricist' tradition in political science, emphasising the importance of measuring, comparing, classifying and categorising political institutions (Rhodes, 2012). The BPT is viewed as outdated and anachronistic, underlining how far the study of British politics was implicitly attached to a 'Whig' conception of history. The literature on the BPT has nonetheless proved decisive in moving away from the descriptive study of institutions towards an interpretive approach, which examines how institutions and practices are underpinned by ideas about power, governance and the state. Furthermore, modernist empiricism is inherently ahistorical, treating institutions as atomised objects that are divorced from any wider social, economic and ideological context – an inadequate basis on which to analyse patterns of continuity and change in the central British state.

The BPT approach has shaped the empirical research on which the volume is based. The BPT provides an organising perspective which informs subsequent chapters: the British polity is constituted by a 'limited' liberal concept of representation and a 'strong' conservative idea of responsibility (Birch, 1964). The BPT literature emphasises that the British political system is shaped by contrasting views: the 'liberal' perspective drawing on a participative and inclusive model of representative democracy, which is in practice outweighed by the 'Whitehall' view focused on stability, order and strong government (Birch, 1964; Flinders, 2010). The contested role of ideas and traditions illuminates why the relationship between continuity and change is a dialectical one: any proposal for reform is challenged by the existing framework of institutions and norms, underpinned by the dominant tradition in British politics. Moreover, the BPT does not make change impossible, but reinforces incremental, evolutionary and ad hoc patterns of institutional change in Whitehall and Westminster.

The Whitehall Paradigm

The dominant tradition in the British polity is manifested in the Westminster model and the 'Whitehall paradigm' (Campbell & Wilson, 1995). The Westminster model has been criticised for offering an outdated conceptualisation of the British state (Bevir & Rhodes, 2006b; Marsh et al., 2001). Nonetheless, the Westminster model provides crucial benchmarks for assessing continuity and change, characterised by:

- parliamentary sovereignty;
- accountability through 'free and fair elections';
- 'majority party control' over the executive;
- strong Cabinet government;
- 'central government dominance';
- a doctrine of ministerial responsibility;
- a neutral and non-political permanent bureaucracy (Gamble, 1990: 404).

The Westminster model defines the interaction between civil servants and ministers, where classically mandarins advise and ministers decide. This offers criteria to assess whether the traditional constitutional rules of the game still apply in Whitehall. As a sub-set of the Westminster model, the Whitehall paradigm comprises core elements of the civil service and permanent bureaucracy (Campbell & Wilson, 1995; Flinders, 2002; Page, 2010):

- a bureaucratic state of politically neutral officials;
- a generalist cadre of civil servants;
- Whitehall as a 'career for life';
- officials as the 'monopoly provider' of ministerial policy advice.

While a number of topical debates are touched upon including accountability, devolution, agencification, Europeanisation and freedom of information, the book does not seek to provide a comprehensive overview of the Whitehall paradigm. Crucial topics such as the changing pay, rewards and occupational structure of the UK civil service are not considered in any depth. The research addresses pertinent trends during the New Labour era, particularly the extent of the politicisation and pluralisation of policy-making in Whitehall, as the institutional power resources of the core executive have been greatly modified and extended. From Attlee to Thatcher, the civil service mandarinate commanded prestige and power as the pre-eminent conduit of policy advice to ministers. After 1997, however, an infusion of policy 'tsars', task forces, thinktanks, appointees and political advisers appeared to weaken and demoralise the British civil service.

This study examines structural change in the core executive and Whitehall model by addressing a set of empirical questions:

- How far did the centre in Number Ten seek to bypass departments in the policy-making process?
- To what extent was the Whitehall model reshaped by the imposition of politicisation and pluralisation, and how did that influence patterns of continuity and change in the central state?
- How far has the British state been characterised by path dependency: do modernising practices such as 'evidence-based policy' and 'joined-up government' challenge or merely reinforce the traditional, hierarchical 'power-hoarding' model?

Conceptualising the Whitehall Model

Governing Britain takes seriously the edict of Raadschelders and Rutgers: 'In order to understand the development of civil service systems, the social context – ideas of authority, sovereignty, public service, the nature of functionaries, public ethos, politics and economy – has to be taken into account' (1996: 70). There are several key themes that contextualise and inform the analysis of the Whitehall model undertaken in this volume.

The first relates the machinery of government to the role of the state in British politics. Keynes wrote in his seminal essay on *The End of Laissez-Faire*: 'The important thing for government is not to do things which individuals are doing already, and to do them a little better or a little worse; but to do those things which at present are not done at all' (Keynes, 1926). The civil service must respond to structural challenges, from the impact of changing demography to the threat posed by climate change. Austerity and retrenchment have meant the distinction between the 'agenda' and 'non-agenda' of government is being more explicitly defined. In the context of a debate about the decline of public trust, it is important to address the limits, as well as the possibilities, of central government intervention avoiding where possible the damaging cycle of unrealistic expectations and disillusionment (Flinders, 2012; Gamble, 2003; Stoker, 2004).

This means addressing what role and capabilities central government ought to have. By the time of the 2010 election, civil service headcount had reached its lowest level since World War II, less than 2 per cent of total employment in the UK. The dramatic down-sizing of the civil service, combined with the loss of implementation capacity at the centre through agencies and contracting-out, has raised concerns about the permanent bureaucracy's capability and performance. These vulnerabilities have been highlighted by 'policy fiascos' in Whitehall such as the ill-fated franchise renewal of the West Coast mainline (Glaister, 2013). While headcount is not necessarily the most suitable indicator of effectiveness, former Chancellor of the Exchequer Alistair Darling complained of lack of institutional memory and expertise in the Treasury, compromising the quality of policy advice in the wake of the 2008–9 financial crisis (Darling, 2011). The fracturing of governance capacity has implications for the authority and legitimacy of the state (Milmo & Topham, 2012).

That alludes to a second major theme in this volume, namely the comparative dimension of public administration addressing how far alternative models of civil service organisation in other countries have influenced the Whitehall model. Britain has traditionally been parochial and insular in reforming its governing arrangements. As dissatisfaction with the Whitehall model has increased since the 1970s, however, there has been growing interest in what might be learned from other countries, particularly 'Westminster-based' systems such as Australia, New Zealand and Canada. New Labour had also been influenced by the Clinton administration's strategy of 'reinventing government', with its ethos of 'steering not rowing': governments are less concerned with providing services, more focused on overseeing delivery (Osbourne and Gaebler, 1990). While cross-national learning is potentially valuable, it is nonetheless essential to examine the institutional tensions that emerge in exporting initiatives from one country to another.

The final theme alludes to the relationship between the civil service at the centre, and public services at the 'front-line'. As the governance literature reveals, the modern-day civil service does not operate in isolation, delivering policy in an ordered hierarchy, top-down from the 'commanding heights' of Whitehall. The policy-making and implementation process is undertaken through a myriad of institutions and actors outside the authority of the central state (Bell & Hindmoor, 2009; Bevir & Rhodes, 2006b). While accounts alleging the 'hollowing-out' of the state should be treated cautiously, policy implementation occurs through a variegated assemblage of public, private and third sector agencies.

As such, the relationship between Whitehall and front-line delivery is mediated by exchange relations and bargaining games where policy goals are redefined and interpreted by actors. Power is not a zero-sum game: the central state depends on other agents to enact its goals (Smith, 1999). While policy delivery can be understood as a linear process of transmission from central government to local agencies, scores of ministers voiced their frustration at discovering 'rubber levers' not connected to anything outside. Actors' control over institutions beyond the central state is inevitably circumscribed.

Paradoxically, the perceived loss of control over implementation has led political elites to strengthen their grip over the governing instruments of the state (Le Gales, 2012; Peters, 2004). The contemporary state retains its modernist ambitions encapsulated in the grandiose, hubristic values of the post-1945 settlement, reinforced by New Labour's zeal for bureaucratic reform and its search for new 'technologies of power' (Smith, 2009). While operating from the centre has become increasingly arduous over the last three decades, central government has continued to search for new ways of reforming Britain's society and economy to achieve the elusive ambition of governing hegemony.

The UK Core Executive: A Case Study in Path Dependency?

New Labour's approach to the core executive reflected its view of activist government, implying a determination to intervene systematically in society and the polity (Gamble, 1984; Moran, 2003; Newman, 2005). After 1997, Labour acquired greater responsibility for the delivery and management of public services, redrawing the parameters of state activity. The belief was that 'a suitably modified state could improve people's lives and that, without such intervention, many would suffer' (Fielding, 2003: 114). New Labour's purpose was to rebuild governance capacity within the state, 're-centring' British government while strengthening the role of political actors in initiating policy (Peters, 2004). This meant recasting the government machinery around the core executive augmenting the capability to orchestrate policy through 'joining-up' departments and streamlining co-ordination; enhancing prime-ministerial authority and expanding the strategic capacities of Number Ten and the Cabinet Office; and reshaping the civil service and public administration in accordance with the goals of national efficiency and modernisation (Burnham & Pyper, 2008). New Labour's approach implied the re-casting of the Whitehall model:

> A smaller strategic centre; a civil service with professional and specialist skills; a civil service open to the public, private and voluntary sector and encouraging interchange among them; more rapid promotion within the civil service and an end to tenure for senior posts; a civil service equipped to lead, with proven leadership in management

and project delivery; a more strategic and innovative approach to policy; government organised around problems, not problems around government.

(Blair cited in Hennessy, 2005: 8)

Labour's rhetoric emphasised the scale and extent of change, reinforced by the judgement of numerous Whitehall commentators. Kavanagh (2001: 13) argues that New Labour sought to make departments more responsive to the centre: 'In the first four, let alone eight years of his premiership, [Blair] presided over more change around Number Ten than had been achieved over the previous fifty years.' Another observer insisted: 'In Tony Blair's first year as Prime Minister, a new entity was invented in Britain's infinitely flexible constitution. It was called "the centre"' (Rentoul, 2009: 5). More tellingly, one of Britain's most eminent 'Whitehall watchers' averred:

> Power has been draining out of Whitehall for years. Top civil servants have seen themselves usurped by spin doctors, political advisers, quangos, management consultants and unelected so-called experts. All too often officials have been cowed into becoming mere courtiers telling ministers what ministers want to hear [...] Modern politicians are not prepared to be told the truth and nor do they recognise any division between civil servants and political advisers.
>
> (Cameron, 2009: 7)

Similarly, *The Economist* argued that Whitehall had been subject to far-reaching reforms:

> The Prime Minister's sole experience of leadership has been in the Labour party, where he had achieved his aim – making the party electable – by ruthlessly imposing his will from the top. It is no surprise, therefore, that Mr Blair wanted to replace the percolator with a cafetiere: strong pressure from above, infusing the policies and actions of the departments below. Cabinet committees have not been abolished. But the big decisions are no longer hammered out around committee tables. They are settled from Mr Blair's sofa and often communicated to other ministers by mobile phone.
>
> (*The Economist*, 1999)

This view is endorsed by a plethora of retired officials criticising the scale, intent and allegedly dysfunctional nature of managerial reforms of Whitehall, foreseeing 'a revolution in how we are governed, with an outcome as yet too unstable to last' (Foster, 2005: 8).[8] Restructuring the centre of government to institutionalise New Labour's style of administration has stirred controversy. According to Hennessy (2005: 11):

> Number Ten [...] in the eyes of some Whitehall veterans, is behaving as if it were a White House without the numbers or competencies involved in Washington. Having

degraded the old collective Cabinet committee system, Blair's centre is left trying to operate the worst of both worlds.

Although Whitehall by the end of New Labour's tenure was markedly different from that which served the Wilson and Callaghan administrations in the 1960s and 1970s, there has been a tendency both among practitioners and academic commentators to overstate and exaggerate the extent of change in the core executive (Foster, 2005; Hennessy, 2000). In contrast, the concept of 'political tradition' draws attention to the weight of long-standing historical conventions and practices in the contemporary British state. The BPT literature, in keeping with the essence of historical institutionalism, demonstrates that programmes and policies are implemented within boundaries established by laws, rules, norms and institutions inherited from the past (Wrisque-Cline, 2008). This creates a tendency towards inertia and institutional path dependency in the central state machinery. Structural change has to be contextualised within the wider history of public management reform, state institutions and Whitehall modernisation (Wrisque-Cline, 2008). As such, the central claims of this study are the following:

- The Whitehall paradigm and Westminster model continue to influence how actors operate.
- Whitehall is built around departments and retains a federal structure.
- Policy making is no longer monopolised by civil servants, but the civil service still dominates the policy process.
- The pattern of careers in the senior civil service has not been radically altered, despite more external appointments.
- Numerous 'modernising' reforms such as 'joined-up' government and 'evidence-based policy' largely reinforce the traditional power-hoarding model and the dominant tradition in British politics.

Theoretical Approach and Research Methodology

Illuminating the dynamics of continuity and change in Whitehall requires a theoretical framework, as well as empirical investigation. The approach adopted in this work is anchored in critical realism: power is understood as concentrated and hierarchical, rather than diffused throughout society and the state. This view of power acknowledges the interaction between structure and agency, and how one shapes the other in a dialectical process. Agents are affected by structural change, but political actors are 'resource-rich', having the capacity to adapt and modify institutions. The focus is the policy-making process within the machinery of government: how ideas, norms and traditions shape the attitudes and actions of agents. Descriptive accounts address only what can be seen, in keeping with the behaviourist tradition in political science; however, it is important to focus attention on what is *unobservable* in the institutions and practices of British governance:

- Actors are conditioned by their institutional setting and structural context: a *critical realist ontology*. The state is a material reality and structures matter; however, reflexive agents are able to modify and shape outcomes (Fawcett, 2011; Jessop, 2007; Marsh, 1999). As such, institutional settings are 'autonomous' of human agency but actors are purposive agents who reproduce their institutional context: structures enable *and* constrain agents.
- Social phenomena amount to more than just the interpretations of actors; moreover, structures exist that are not directly observable. That said, how actors interpret their social context affects outcomes: a *critical realist epistemology* (Archer, 1995; Giddens, 1984). The agent's knowledge is mediated through concepts and theories that are developed in order to understand the world. Judge (2006) attests to how theories of representative and responsible government are used by actors to negotiate the British political system, shaping the roles and responsibilities of ministers and civil servants, becoming hardwired into the institutions and processes of the British state.
- This approach emphasises the interpretations of agents and their understanding of power, drawing on a qualitative methodology.

The research involved 52 hour-long semi-structured interviews. The interviewees were selected on the basis of a 'process-tracing method' (Appendix I contains a breakdown of those interviewed) (Bennett & George, 2005; Tansey, 2007). The 'Chatham House rule' protects anonymity, while certain participants agreed to have remarks attributed. Other sources included unpublished papers, as well as diaries, Select Committee reports and memoirs. Gamble (2012: 494) insists political biographies are 'valuable sources on the inside story but often have less to say on [...] the wider context in which governments operate, in particular the structures of power that shape British society and the British state'. Even so, memoirs offer insight into the changing institutions and practices of the British system of government.

The limitations of qualitative research are obvious enough. The tendency of respondents to conceal the truth, their propensity for selective recollection, and their inclination to tell the interviewer what it is they believe he or she wants to hear pose a number of challenges (Dowding & James, 2004). Political actors may be tempted to promulgate myths about their pre-eminent role and status.

Then there is the distinction between 'revealed' and 'actual' preferences: how agents behave may contradict what they say their preferences are. Nonetheless, there is no freely available source of uncontaminated and reliable data: even official government records are subject to the 30-year rule (Tansey, 2007). The notion of a 'value-free' political science is, in any case, dubious: observation is selective, always influenced by prior assumptions (Johnston, 1998). Critical realism seeks to address the power relations that exist between officials and ministers, departments and the centre.

In addition, interview material has meaning only in so far as it is interpreted. The participants were made aware of the researcher's prior role within central government. This may affect what interviewees are prepared to disclose.[9] An interviewer familiar with the 'hidden wiring' of the British state has an advantage in evaluating the responses given by interviewees: tacit knowledge of the 'inside story' bridges the gap between 'actual' and 'revealed' preferences. Nevertheless, this study quotes extensively from the interview transcripts so that others may draw their own conclusions about the interpretations placed on the data.

According to Van Maanen, 'There is no way of seeing, hearing or representing the world of others that is absolutely, universally valid or correct' (1988: 10). The challenge is to interpret any political context through the eyes of the observed, without sacrificing a critically detached analytical perspective. Furthermore, there is an inherent synergy between practitioners and political scientists. Actors work from a background of 'historically informed practices'; analysts rely on the interpretations of agents. For both, 'narratives of the past and traditions play a key role in framing debate and choices in the present' (Adcock and Bevir, 2005: 3). There is an influential tradition of political 'insiders' drawing on theoretical insights from the academic literature to inform their accounts of political leadership in British government (Gains, 2013). Like Tivey (1998: 1) the study addresses the 'operative ideals' that emerge from the interaction between political scientists and practitioners.

Structure of the Book

This book is divided into two sections. Part 1, The Theory of Governing Britain, reprises key debates in the literature, outlining the theoretical framework informing this account of how actors in the central state have sought to rebuild governing capacity. Chapter 1 addresses the literature on the BPT: accounts of the dominant political tradition examine the case for stability and path dependency, and the norms and beliefs which shape the context in which power operates, reflecting a centralising and top-down conception of British democracy. The literature on Whitehall and the Westminster model is assessed in Chapter 2, addressing the nature of power in British government, particularly how power relations structure the policy-making process.

While Chapters 1 and 2 analyse the conceptualisation of power and democracy within the British state and the BPT, Chapter 3 examines Labour's approach to the state and the party's willingness to adhere to an elitist model of statecraft. This provides further evidence of stability and path dependency, as Labour has historically deferred to the BPT and the Westminster model. These initial chapters are concerned with the weight of tradition and path dependency, but Chapter 4 considers a body of literature which theorises the nature of continuity alongside change. The Anglo-Governance School and the Differentiated Polity Model (DPM) emphasise discontinuity, while the Asymmetric Power Model (APM) ascribes weight to institutional inertia and path dependency.

Part 2, The Practice of Governing Britain, addresses the empirical context of politics and public administration in the British state. Chapter 5 maps the case studies of academy schools, Family-Nurse Partnerships (FNPs), and the National Economic Council (NEC), illuminating the character of the policy-making process. Chapter 6 outlines findings of how far the centre has bypassed departments in formulating policy. The cases are atypical given Number Ten's particular determination to intervene from the centre. However, the research demonstrates that even where the centre is involved, departments retain relative autonomy. Chapter 7 addresses the over-arching process of continuity and change, relating to key developments including the politicisation and pluralisation of policy-making. The chapter builds a typology of continuity and change, understanding and explaining institutional path dependency in the contemporary British state.

In the light of the evidence for path dependency, Chapter 8 assesses the role of the dominant political tradition in fashioning Labour's governing strategy. The chapter examines the influence of the BPT in shaping the beliefs and actions of ministers and officials, defining broader patterns of continuity and change. The central conclusion of the chapter is that the exercise of power within the core executive takes place in a structured context infused by the BPT. Finally, Chapter 9 gauges the wider implications of the research for the nature of governance, power and the state. The study emphasises the interaction between traditions, beliefs and norms, relating Greenleaf's (1983a) concern with theory and 'cognate developments' in political thought to the institutional practices of democracy, Whitehall and the machinery of British government in the contemporary world.

Part I
The Theory of Governing Britain

CHAPTER 1

The British Political Tradition and Whitehall Reform

One sure symptom of an ill-conducted state is the propensity of the people to resort to theories.

Burke (1981: 274)

Happy is the country in which consensus and conflict are ordered in a dialectic that makes of the political arena at once a market of interests and a forum for debate of fundamental moral concerns.

Beer (1965: 390)

The people's representatives require to have a large measure of discretion and autonomy in decision-making 'on behalf' of the people and in their ultimate interests [...] In this view, government is a specialised vocation; government must therefore be unfettered, free and independent, in order to make sometimes difficult decisions on behalf of the people.

Tant (1993: 4)

Introduction

This chapter argues first and foremost that there is a dominant British Political Tradition (BPT), predominantly based around a centralised and hierarchical understanding of power. The chapter's principal claim is that there is a governing code in the British polity which underpins the traditional 'power-hoarding' model of Whitehall and the core executive. The chapter considers leading contributors to the literature on the British Political Tradition, namely the 'classical' wave of Beer, Birch and Greenleaf, followed by the 'critical' accounts of Marsh, Tant and Evans (Hall, 2011; Marsh & Hall, 2007). The aim is to examine the defining role of *political traditions*, assessing the strengths and weaknesses of critical realist, and latterly interpretive, approaches. The chapter seeks to offer a nuanced understanding of Whitehall reform which recognises the conflicting influence of ideas, traditions and institutional norms.

In so doing, this chapter interrogates the wide-ranging and eclectic literature on the BPT. The argument is that structural reform in Whitehall and the core executive occurs within an institutional context underpinned by the BPT, constraining the extent of radical change in the permanent bureaucracy. The literature on the BPT alludes to stability and path dependency within the British state, where particular norms and beliefs are inscribed into governing institutions as 'the set of values, and meanings prescribing legitimate government and how state power should be apportioned and operate' (Judge, 2006: 387). The BPT literature emphasises structural continuity, in contrast to subsequent theories of governance which reinforce a dynamic, path-breaking conception of the central state.[1] Marquand in the *History of Britain Since 1918* attests: 'The British Political Tradition, and the memories and understandings it encapsulates, loom in the background throughout, like the Chorus in a Greek play' (2008: 6), affirming a role for the BPT as a break on institutional change.

The 'classical' account of the BPT alludes to the exceptionalism of Britain's political development, reinforced by the enduring stability of British political institutions. The roots of the British tradition predated universal suffrage, as Britain's governing institutions were fashioned prior to the emergence of mass democracy. The British political system adjusted to a period of rapid social and economic change during the nineteenth and twentieth centuries, acquiring an unwritten but essentially 'pre-democratic' set of normative understandings of where power lies and how it should be exercised. Above all, the BPT gave legitimacy to the notion of a strong executive accountable, in theory, to a sovereign Parliament. According to critics, the BPT concealed how dominant interests in society sought to keep politics within acceptable limits, incorporating oppositionalist forces such as the organised working class within the Westminster model and the British state. As it is, for more than half a century the BPT has shaped and influenced the literature on how the British system of government operates. An understanding of the BPT is necessary to analyse and assess the institutions and ideas underpinning the British system of government and the changing core executive.

The Conservative Tradition School

The tradition school and the work of the idealist philosopher Michael Oakeshott provide an important starting-point, alluding to how tradition operates as a force for institutional continuity in the institutions of the British polity. According to Oakeshott, traditions are organic and evolutionary: that is to say, a tradition is non-rational, non-ideological and indigenous, reflecting a unique national inheritance anchored in political institutions marking Britain out from continental Europe. The tradition of *parliamentary government* in Britain where power is accrued at the centre is long established, as is the restraint on arbitrary rule through the courts (Judge, 2006). As Bulpitt attests (1983: 83), 'Parliament, in fact was the lynchpin of the whole structure. It was the essential intermediary [...] and it was on its brokerage and socialisation capacities that the whole operation depended.' This reverence for continuity in the life of political institutions is encapsulated in Norton's more recent account of *The British Polity*: 'There is a strong case to be made for the existing constitutional framework [...] attachment to parliamentary government remains a strong feature of the political culture' (1999: 373–4).

Oakeshott understands tradition as a richly intertwined fabric of custom embedded in the political culture of the nation. As McAnulla attests: 'Tradition is considered by conservatives to consist of the accumulated wisdom that supposedly emerges organically from years of experience and trial and error' (2007: 3). This alludes to Oakeshott's scepticism about rationalism in politics and the role of ideology. The British tradition is concerned with addressing social problems in a pragmatic fashion, eschewing rationalist doctrines while upholding the commitment to 'the rule of law', emphasising the importance of vibrant 'civic associations' (Kenny, 1999). According to Oakeshott, these attributes are embodied in the everyday practice of political institutions and actors. Actions and beliefs are mediated through 'traditions of practice' (MacIntyre, 1985), shaping political life as a set of recurring values buried within deeper structures of custom and ritual (Gamble, 1990; Kenny, 1999). This reflects a conservative view of tradition: continuity and stability are integral to the political system, legitimating historical conventions such as an uncodified constitution and the concentration of legislative power in Parliament (Judge, 1993; McAnulla, 2007; Tant, 1993).

Kenny (1999) examines a range of contributions to the literature on tradition, distinguishing between tradition as the 'habitual' force of history and culture from tradition as the set of enduring ideological conflicts in British politics. This illuminates 'a philosophical division between an authentic political culture as an expression of the national psyche, and the ideological paradigms that are imported into political life' (1999: 275). As such, Oakeshott's critics question the conservative tradition's tendency to implicitly 'naturalise' social practices, concealing structured hierarchy and inequality. First, traditions that appear to arise organically are more often the product of struggle and contingency (Bevir, 1999; Evans, 2003; McAnulla, 2007; Tant, 1993). Moreover, the discourse of tradition is used to construct ideologies through which the status quo can be defended and legitimised (Kenny, 1999; McAnulla, 2006). Despite these criticisms, Oakeshott's concern with interpretation, context and meaning ought to be central to the analysis of stability and change in the institutions of British governance, inspiring a wider literature on the BPT.

The British Political Tradition: The 'Classical' and 'Critical' Wave

Gamble defines the BPT as 'a constitutional doctrine, a conception of the state, and an interpretation of British history' (1990: 406). Marsh and Hall (2007) offer a framework to assess the 'classical' and 'critical wave' in the BPT literature.[2] Marsh and Hall distinguish between several distinctive conceptions of tradition:

- the BPT as the dominant overarching narrative about the British political system and British institutions (Birch, 1964);
- the BPT as synonymous with political culture, permeating governing elites and the wider electorate (Beer, 1965);
- the BPT as a framework of ideas hard-wired into the institutions and practices of British government (Greenleaf, 1983a, 1983b).

While political scientists have concentrated on assiduously mapping the institutional characteristics of the British polity, these authors draw attention to the ideas underpinning institutions and practices (McAnulla, 2006). Marsh and Hall argue that there is a dominant tradition in British politics which inevitably reinforces the preferences of ministers and officials: challenges occur within the framework of institutions and procedures shaped by the BPT, underpinning the status quo. Their account points firmly towards continuity. Marsh and Hall insist the BPT does not lead inexorably to path determinism, however: the BPT shapes, but does not determine, agency: outcomes are not foreordained. While core ideas and practices constrain actors, agents have the capacity to adapt, modify and reinterpret traditions. Critical realists seek to locate actors within the context of the dominant political tradition mediated through the relationship between institutions and ideas.

The Classical Wave: Birch, Beer and Greenleaf

This section of the chapter examines the 'classical' accounts of the BPT developed by Birch, Beer and Greenleaf (Hall, 2011), illuminating how authors use the BPT to emphasise stability and continuity in the British political system. The 'classical' wave is distinguished by its normative commitment to Britain's constitutional and political settlement renowned for providing continuity, stability and legitimacy, apparently superior to the trajectory of political development on the European continent. The maintenance of a characteristically 'power-hoarding' polity is construed by BPT authors as distinctively 'British', embedded deep within the political culture.

Birch: Doctrines of Representation and Responsibility

Birch defines the BPT in terms of rival theories of representation and responsibility. There is a strong emphasis on continuity given the apparent virtues of the British constitution. For instance, Birch states: 'Fresh theories have not replaced the old, but have tended to take place alongside old ones as strands in the British Political Tradition' (1964: 227). Birch's focus is the divergent conceptions of democracy within the BPT, exploring how ideas of representation and responsibility inform the institutions and practices of the British polity (McAnulla, 2006). In *Representative and Responsible Government* (1964), Birch defines the essential characteristics of the BPT:

> The people have some power to choose their rulers and various kinds of influence over what their rulers do, but the people neither have nor expect to have any direct control over questions of government policy. If democracy were defined as government by the people, it would not be possible to regard the British political system as democratic.
>
> (Birch, 1964: 265)

As such, the British political system is composed of a hierarchy of procedures and practices:

> First, consistency, prudence and leadership, second, accountability to Parliament and the electorate and third, responsiveness to public opinions and demands [...] It is this tradition [...] that explains the system of disciplined party government that the country now enjoys.
>
> (1964: 245)

The importance of Birch's work relates to the attention given to key ideas in British politics (McAnulla, 2006). Birch argues that although the liberal ideal of representative government was dominant in the mid-nineteenth century, it was increasingly displaced by other elements within the BPT, particularly notions of responsibility and strong government. Birch insists: 'The responsibility for governing the country rests with the Queen's Ministers; effective decision-making power in Britain rests with "the government", who do not share their power with Parliament or with the people' (1964: 266). Birch's interpretation of the BPT centres on the overwhelming virtues of authoritative and decisive government. The strength of an elitist, 'power down (to the people)' view is emphasised, rooted in customary tradition tacitly informing the development of British political institutions and practices. As Birch (1964: 267) remarks:

> It is based [...] on confidence: confidence that the government will keep to the rules of the political game and confidence that it will in practice be open to the influence

of public opinion through a wide variety of channels. Conformity to the rules of the game is guaranteed by the almost universal acceptance of constitutional traditions. It is these rules, traditions and practices that constitute the essence of British democracy.

Birch insists elected governments must be sensitive to underlying currents of public opinion, alluding to the dialectical relationship between representation and responsibility. Although ministers have the capacity to act independently through the unhindered exercise of royal prerogatives, from declaring war to exercising powers of patronage without direct reference to Parliament, they must always take some account of the electorate's views. The imperative of mobilising electoral support acts to constrain executive discretion. Nevertheless, there were few formal limits to ministerial authority in the British polity. As a consequence, Birch averred that the dominant tradition ensured competent, decisive government. This conception of democracy accorded neither with radical nineteenth-century liberalism, nor abstract constitutional doctrine. Instead:

> It meets the various criteria of good government that are implicit in the British political tradition and the general values of British society. It ensures political stability; it protects the liberties of the subject; it satisfies British ideas about justice and fair play; it provides strong (if unimaginative) leadership.
>
> (Birch, 1964: 278)

Birch insisted that the BPT attained wider legitimacy since it encapsulated the values governing British citizens and British society. There was a natural harmony between the ideas informing the BPT and the wider institutions and practices of the British political system. In explaining the persistence of a 'Whitehall' and 'liberal' view of British democracy, Birch addresses the relationship between institutions and ideas. In a similar fashion to Birch, Beer focuses on theories of representation and responsibility, placing them in the wider context of Britain's political culture.

Beer: The British Political Tradition as Political Culture

Beer's analysis of the BPT emphasises tradition as political culture conditioning and shaping the behaviour of actors, while reinforcing stability and path dependency in the British political system. For Beer: 'Political culture is one of the main variables of a political system [...] the distinctive system of political ideas informs the decisions of individuals and political formations', distilled into 'men's visions of legitimate authority and the common good' (1965: 390). 'Culture' is fundamental to Beer's writings:

I lay great stress on the political culture as one of the main variables of a political system and a major factor in explaining the political behaviour of individuals, groups, and parties. Specifically, it is in the political culture of the time that I have found the most useful clues to the prevailing type (or types) of political behaviour.

(Beer, 1965: x)

The emphasis on political culture enables Beer to closely interrogate the relationship between institutions and ideas. Tradition is a source of tension and conflict around which key debates in politics are elaborated: 'Politics is not just a market of interests, but a forum for the debate of fundamental moral concerns.' Beer insisted: 'The political culture of a country is rarely monolithic' (1965: 162). For instance, the post-1945 consensus in British politics should not imply an absence of disagreement about the legal and constitutional fundamentals of the state. Beer recalls Lionel Trilling's claim in *The Liberal Imagination* (1954) that 'a culture is nothing if not a dialectic'. British politics is understood as a continuous debate between opposing theories of representation and responsibility.

This dialectic is played out in two distinct arenas. The first concerns the normative commitment to economic equality and social justice, whatever the apparent agreement between the political parties about the legitimate role of government and the welfare state after World War II. Issues of redistribution, egalitarianism and rival conceptions of justice have informed key debates in British party politics. The second aspect of the dialectic relates to conceptions of how party democracy ought to function, as traditional Tory authoritarianism has adapted to modern views of liberalism and representative democracy.

As such, parties have distinctive ideas about how power ought to be exercised within the British state. The Labour Party promulgated a theory of representation predicated on socialist democracy. The guild socialism of G.D.H. Cole and R.H. Tawney necessitated an attack on liberal representative democracy for ignoring the economic dimensions of political legitimacy, emphasising the need for effective representation of working-class interests. In contrast, 'Tory democracy' gave primacy to the art of governing, requiring a governing class that emphasised the strength and stability of Britain's political institutions. As Beer avers:

Tory democracy accepts class rule – this derives from its essential and ancient Toryism: 'Hierarchy is the order of nature', as a Conservative writer put it recently. But Tory democracy is also democratic in its own way. Although it is not, in Amery's words, government by the people, it is nevertheless government with the people.

(Beer, 1965: 101)

Moreover, Beer cites an influential passage by Hearnshaw on postwar Conservatism:

> Its very genius affirms on the one hand, the solidarity of the nation and the unity of all classes in the whole; on the other hand, the propriety of leaving predominant political control in the possession of those who are by descent, by character, by education, and by experience, best fitted to exercise it.
>
> (Beer, 1965: 102)

The Conservatives sought to define British politics in terms of which party was considered competent and fit to rule. The BPT and Tory democracy were indistinguishable: the British Conservatives were in Harold Macmillan's terms, 'the national party' (Beer, 1965: 102). The creed of nineteenth-century Tory authoritarianism may have dissipated in an era of mass suffrage. Nonetheless, the tradition of strong government integral to Tory democracy based on a paternalistic conception of the national interest permitted the gradual expansion of state power. The British political system experienced a natural evolution towards collectivism over the course of the twentieth century.

The collectivist ethos was assimilated within the BPT as prevailing notions of authority were adapted to an age of universal suffrage. As Beer insists:

> This pre-capitalist, pre-individualist, pre-liberal creed ought surely to have died out in the nineteenth century. Yet not only has it survived into the era of the Welfare State and the Managed Economy, it can also claim credit for having helped create them.
>
> (Beer, 1965: 69)

According to Beer, while Tory and socialist philosophies are informed by conflicting ideals of parliamentary democracy, there is underlying agreement about the merits of strong government. This led to the accommodation of the Labour Party within the British constitutional settlement. Indeed, conceptions of Tory and socialist democracy centred on antagonistic theories of representation share important underlying presuppositions: 'Old traditions of strong government, paternalism and the organic society have made easier the massive reassertion of state power' (Beer, 1965: 69). To demonstrate the strength of the commitment to existing political institutions, Beer cites common acceptance of dominant institutional and legal structures in which Tory and socialist views 'agree on how political power is to be organised within this legal and constitutional framework' (Beer, 1965: 70).

Beer's claim is that the BPT is entrenched within Britain's political culture, accepted by all mainstream political parties and politicians. The capacity of the BPT to incorporate ideologies such as British socialism and the advance of collectivism ensured the political class was committed to the notion of 'strong government' integral to the BPT. The BPT operates as a force for continuity, as postwar Labour and Conservative governments adhered to an elitist model of statecraft. Greenleaf's comprehensive, three-volume account of *The British Political Tradition* (1983a; 1983b; 1987) provides a further interpretation of how tradition reinforces the link between past and present, ensuring stability in the institutions of the British polity.

Greenleaf: The BPT and the Rise of Collectivism

Greenleaf addresses how the British political system is shaped by the dialectical relationship between competing, even diametrically opposing ideas recurring in the institutions and discourses of government. In examining how ideas are hard-wired into institutions, Greenleaf diverges from Beer and Birch by anchoring his account of the BPT in relation to more explicit political ideologies. Greenleaf draws on the idealist philosophy of T.H. Green,[3] developing a conception of tradition as:

> A complex amalgam of different forces and opposing choices, and therefore of internal tensions, which is at the same time in a continual state of flux and development but which nevertheless constitutes a recognisable and acknowledged whole.
>
> (Greenleaf, 1983a: 13)

In Greenleaf's account of *The Rise of Collectivism* (1983a), the BPT is viewed as a dialectic between the conflicting ideologies of 'libertarianism' and 'collectivist social democracy', which together constitute the framework in which political activity in Britain occurs. The concept of libertarianism has four key characteristics:

- The importance of individualism, namely the rights of the individual to be free of 'arbitrary' political control, is emphasised.
- The role of government is limited in order not to interfere with the sphere of 'individuality'.
- Any 'concentration' of power is dangerous since it intrudes on individual choice and activity; there should be a diffusion of decision-making and authority.
- Libertarianism demands the 'rule of law', while ensuring that there is no arbitrary power of constraint (1983a: 17–19).

In Greenleaf's work, libertarian ideology is explicitly contrasted with the rise of collectivism in twentieth-century British politics:

- The dominant concern is the 'public good' alongside the interests of the community.

- Collectivism creates 'uniform conditions' of equality and security of at least a minimum or basic kind.
- Decentralisation is regarded as dangerous, weakening the pursuit of social justice and equality of opportunity.
- Individual liberty entails more than an absence of legislative and social restraint, requiring social organisation so all can live 'a complete and reasonable life' (1983a: 21–23).

Both libertarianism and collectivism lead to distinctive models of economic and political organisation. These apparently irreconcilable tendencies nevertheless create a common framework encompassing key governing practices and institutions. Like Beer, Greenleaf highlights that the BPT readily accommodated an expansion in the role of the state. Greenleaf acknowledges that for Dicey, the changing role of government amounted to a transformation in Britain's social and economic order: 'A more fundamental revolution in the beliefs, in the habits, and in the life of England has taken place than has ever been achieved within so short a period' (1983a: 24). The most significant feature of British politics in the twentieth century has been the extension of government's role into numerous arenas of civic and associational activity.

Greenleaf considers how a liberal, laissez-faire society premised on limited government was dislodged by a 'positive state' enacting interventionist programmes in the name of social justice and a more equal society. Although Oakeshott's study, *Rationalism in Politics* (1962), was a key influence in Greenleaf's writings, Oakeshott was sceptical that the BPT would survive the transition towards the collectivist society. Only gradual, evolutionary change preserved Britain's distinctive political identity and heritage. In contrast, Greenleaf averred that the BPT had the capacity to accommodate the transition from libertarianism to collectivism. The British political system was premised on the concentration of power at the centre of government, together with an absence of formal restraint on executive authority. Neither libertarianism nor collectivism weakened an elitist model of statecraft as the key pillar of constitutional government.

In Dicey's terms: 'The sovereignty of Parliament is (from a legal point of view) the dominant characteristic of our political institutions' (Greenleaf, 1983a: 195). The centrality of parliamentary sovereignty meant: 'There was to hand a means of securing radical change by legislation that could not be effectively challenged in the courts or in any other formal way and which was thus available for the purposes of substantial reform (Greenleaf, 1983a: 200). Over time, British socialism became increasingly amenable to the basic precepts of the BPT and its institutional manifestation in the Westminster model.

Greenleaf's interpretative approach examines how the ideas underpinning the institutions and practices of British government adapted and evolved, drawing attention to patterns of continuity and change. In so doing, Greenleaf develops an argument for continuity in Britain's political institutions, demonstrating how collectivism and libertarianism are absorbed within the BPT while emphasising the commitment to centralising, top-down government within the political class.

The 'classical' wave literature on the BPT confirms the extent to which power in Britain is exercised within the context of norms, traditions and beliefs widely shared across generations, alluding to stability and continuity in Whitehall and the British polity. This literature depicts the BPT not merely as an ideational construct, but as a normative justification for Britain's system of responsible government inscribed and embedded in political institutions.

The Critical Wave: Marsh, Tant and Evans

A recurrent theme in the 'classical' literature on the BPT is the superiority and adaptability of Britain's governing institutions. The political system accommodated the rise of socialism and collectivism, further reinforcing institutional stability and continuity. As such, Birch, Beer and Greenleaf adopt an explicitly ideational perspective, a core feature of 'classical' wave accounts. This focus on the relationship between institutions and ideas is invariably absent from the literature on British government and Whitehall. Nonetheless, critics insist 'classical' BPT authors have a tendency to exaggerate the formative role of ideas (Bulpitt, 1986; McAnulla, 2006).

In that context, Beer, Birch and Greenleaf's writings ought not to be conflated: important distinctions remain in the positions adopted by these authors. Greenleaf emphasises how the BPT is hard-wired into the institutions and practices of the British state; attention is given to the interaction between institutions and ideas. For Beer, the BPT encapsulates Britain's political culture, establishing norms and beliefs through which political discourse is mediated. In contrast, Birch emphasises how notions of representation and responsibility at the core of the BPT have shaped the dominant 'narrative' about democracy in Britain (Hall, 2011). The constitutional doctrine of responsible and representative government has continued to influence changing forms of governance and statecraft.

Nevertheless, Beer, Birch and Greenleaf collectively emphasise the unique character of Britain's political institutions, locating the tradition of responsible government within the framework of a 'balanced constitution' (Gamble, 1990). This is an interpretation of history widely promulgated by Whig historians, emphasising institutional continuity in the British political system since the 'Glorious Revolution' of 1688 (Gamble, 1990: 407; Kenny, 1999; Mackintosh, 1963). As Gamble remarks: 'The leading practitioners of political science were convinced that change needed to be evolutionary and gradual and that there were strict limits to what could be achieved through political action' (1990: 408). Britain's relative success in sustaining economic development, civil stability and Empire was attributed to the 'excellence' of its political institutions, predicated on parliamentary sovereignty and strong, decisive government (Collini et al., 1984; Gamble, 1990).

As a result, the efficacy of the British polity was praised by authors operating within the parameters of the BPT's 'classical wave'. For example, Keir celebrated how government in Britain was 'conducted by [...] men sharing a common political tradition', affirming the way in which 'institutions the world over [...] testify to the resilience and continuity of the British tradition' (Keir, 1989). The 'classical' literature on the BPT had an abiding faith in the superiority of the British political system:

> The English Tradition has been empirical, reformist, and collectivist, a combination which has placed political scientists both conceptually and practically within the limits set by the present order, rather than with both feet, or even one foot, outside them.
>
> (Barker cited in Gamble, 1990: 411)

Inevitably, there are weaknesses in 'classical wave' BPT accounts. For example, Greenleaf's interpretation of libertarianism and collectivism is anchored in narrow, rigidly defined categories which exclude the rise of contemporary political ideologies such as feminism and environmentalism (Barker, 1994b; Kenny, 1999). Moreover, political doctrines are generally cross-cutting, porous and interwoven; there has been a great deal of interchange between collectivist and libertarian ideologies over the course of the twentieth century (Freeden, 1999; Gamble, 1994). Similarly, authors such as Birch adopt a narrow and elitist conception of governmental responsibility, which does not address how in practice liberal constitutional norms have sought to justify untrammelled executive authority (Judge, 2006). The twin roles of representation and responsibility are more intertwined than is commonly considered in the 'classical' BPT literature.

As Hall (2011) reiterates, 'classical' accounts of the BPT have provoked a more 'critical' literature associated with Marsh (1980); Marsh and Tant (1989);

and Evans (2003; 2008). While Marsh's work emphasises the top-down, 'power-concentrating' model of British democracy, Tant provides a powerful counter-argument to the interpretation of the BPT associated with the 'classical' literature. Tant exposes the narrow and elitist nature of the British political system, including the system's capacity to ardently defend itself against the radical ambitions of participatory democracy. The 'critical wave' offers a further approach to path dependency, emphasising that the contours of the BPT reinforce a centralising, hierarchical system of government.

Tant: British Government and the Triumph of Elitism

Birch, Beer and Greenleaf take Britain's 'balanced constitution' as their starting-point.[4] The internal dynamics of British government are inherited from a past where political debate was a matter for elites, and the role of the populace was essentially 'passive and legitimating' (Tant, 1993: 12). A.P. Tant takes issue with the claim of Beer, Birch and Greenleaf that the BPT was consensual and widely supported.[5] These authors believed that parliamentary sovereignty and the absence of a written constitution were favourable to collectivism and postwar social democracy, ensuring there were few restraints on executive authority. Both the Conservatives and the Labour Party could confidently uphold the existing legal and constitutional framework.

Tant diverges from the consensual view of 'classical' BPT authors, insisting that the 'content' of collectivism should be separated from the 'system' in which it has developed (1993: 89). While collectivist programmes rely on government intervention and a positive role for the state, the political system was underpinned by a nineteenth-century doctrine premised on atomised economic individualism. This meant that the institutional roots of collectivism and the developmental state in Britain were shallow, assisting the return to a liberal 'laissez-faire' state under Thatcherism. The institutional framework was compatible with classical liberalism and a limited role for government, reinforced by its residual hostility towards collectivism (Tant, 1993).

According to Tant, 'classical' wave literature on the BPT is predicated on a pluralist view of power and the relationship between institutions and ideas. This leads Birch, Beer and Greenleaf to interpret ideas in terms of their intrinsic merit rather than analysing the asymmetries of power through which ideas are mediated. Tant insists that British government operates in a context marked by a narrow and top-down view of British democracy. Centralising, 'power-hoarding' practices are favoured by the dominant political culture which performs an 'active, inhibitive role' (Tant, 1993: 94). This ensures that a power-concentrating governing code is entrenched within the British political system, alluding once again to institutional path dependency.

Marsh and Tant: Thatcherism and the BPT

In developing this analytical approach, Tant and David Marsh address how 'a narrow and elitist concept of representation became institutionalised', sustaining a tradition of strong, decisive government in which: 'The task was to find the national interest and act upon it, even if the policies thus pursued were unpopular with, and opposed by, the particular interests' (Marsh & Tant, 1989: 7–8). The tradition of strong government and an elitist conception of representation persisted throughout the twentieth century. The project of Thatcherism harnessed the BPT for its own ends, further reinforcing institutional stability within the British state. The notion of 'elective dictatorship'[6] attributed to Thatcherism epitomises the essence of the BPT (Bogdanor, 2009). Responsible government means acting as the custodian of the national interest. As such: 'strong, centralised, decisive and independent government is always emphasised' (Marsh & Tant, 1989: 8).

This elitist view of democracy is predicated on a narrow conception of political participation where decision-making and democratic deliberation is carried out by ministers and officials on behalf of individual citizens (Stoker, 2004). British government is regarded by Marsh and Tant as a highly secretive process. The status of civil servants as serving democratically elected ministers ensured that their anonymity was protected, while records of decision-making were safeguarded. The *Official Secrets Act* constrained officials from speaking publicly (Marsh & Tant, 1989; Tant, 1993).

Marsh and Tant aver that 'classical' accounts of British government emphasise *who* should govern on the basis of *what* authority, rather than *how* the nation should be governed and whether government 'has the right to make decisions independently and on behalf of the people' (1989: 10). The dominant strand of the BPT based on a conservative notion of responsibility displaced the liberal concept of representation, reinforcing a narrow and elitist view of British democracy. In contrast, the participatory challenge posed by ethical and guild socialism drew on a legacy of popular struggle and conflict in British political history, from the Tudor revolution in government under Henry VIII to the major upheaval and structural change in the British state culminating in the Great Reform Act of 1832.[7] Even so, the threat was effectively neutralised over the course of the twentieth century.

Marsh and Tant allude to the importance of a dominant political tradition. There are inevitably overlapping and contested traditions in British politics. However, a particular tradition gained ascendency as the political class drew on a narrow, power-hoarding view of British democracy. The resonance of an elitist style of government among actors and institutions is asymmetric. The BPT does not block change; there are always competing and divergent traditions. The dominant tradition 'circumscribes the possibility of radical change', creating a shared culture where 'centralising government knows best' (Marsh & Hall, 2007: 257). This tradition coincides with the interests of ministers and officials; any challenge occurs within the context of the BPT, creating a strategically selective environment in which particular norms and beliefs are privileged (Hall, 2011; Kerr & Kettell, 2006). An 'elitist' approach to statecraft shapes the evolution of institutions within the British state (Evans, 2003). As such, post-1997 constitutional reforms qualified, but did not curtail, executive dominance and the influence of the Westminster model.

Richards and Smith (2004) argue that the BPT and the Westminster model have endured since their core narratives legitimate the position of elite actors and institutions. Ministers attempt to secure their historical 'legacy' by acting in the national interest; officials uphold constitutional 'proprieties', ensuring governments remain legitimate and effective: 'Both sets of actors tend to appeal to these narratives when justifying and legitimising their behaviour' (Richards & Smith, 2004: 798). Indeed, 'from that tradition they have drawn different, but by no means incompatible, narratives' (2004: 781). The Whitehall paradigm is predicated on particular notions of power, sovereignty and governance.

The 'critical wave' literature alludes strongly to path dependency. Marsh and Tant challenge 'classical' accounts which fail to properly explain the legitimacy accorded to the dominant institutions of British politics, in turn examining how participatory models of democracy are neutered by the inhibitive role of the BPT.

Evans: Challenging the BPT

Similarly, Mark Evans (1995) relates the BPT literature to contemporary debates about constitutional and political reform. Pressure groups such as Charter 88 sought to advance an inclusive, participatory conception of democracy. However, they were unable to mount a successful challenge in the context of a political system where the axiom of responsible government was predominant. What is more, Evans (2003) provides a sophisticated conceptual approach to understanding continuity and change, underlining the importance of agency, and the contingencies that arise through unintended consequences (Hall, 2011).

Evans' work has the capacity to explain contemporary developments including New Labour's approach to Whitehall. Intriguingly, Evans affirms that agents have the ability to develop strategies in order to affect change over the political and constitutional system. The priority for Charter 88 was to redefine the 'elitist conceptualisation' of democracy, legitimacy and authority underpinning the institutions and practices of the British polity (Hall, 2011). The group must sustain the radicalism of its demands in order to challenge the dominant paradigm. The effectiveness of Charter 88 and the coherence of the principles underpinning the campaign's strategy have a critical bearing on its ability to overturn the basic precepts of the BPT and the Westminster model.

This alludes to path dependency rather than path determinism where actors have the capacity to reshape the dominant tradition, but face the prospect of sustained opposition to any concerted challenge. This view is reinforced by 'critical' accounts of the BPT. Path dependency acknowledges the iterative and dialectical relationship between structure and agency, and the role of contingency and unintended outcomes in patterns of continuity and change.

Evans emphasises that path dependent analyses of the BPT need not neglect agency. There are several dimensions of the BPT alluding to the role of agents. Firstly, individuals are socialised into shared sets of norms derived from the BPT. Secondly, individuals develop their own interpretation of the core executive and the Whitehall paradigm drawing on the BPT, as actors are immersed within a diverse 'bricolage' of ideas and norms (Gains & Stoker, 2011). The BPT not only constrains agency; it enables elite actors to achieve their goals through a centralising and top-down conceptualisation of British democracy. The dilemma for radical politics has been about whether to work within the existing constitutional parameters, which foreclose far-reaching reforms of economic and social institutions, or whether to mount a sustained challenge to the current orthodoxy. As such in Hay's (2002) terms, the BPT is both 'conduct'- and 'context'-shaping. According to Evans, the historical failure of radical parties such as Labour and the Liberals to successfully challenge the dominant order in the early twentieth century has ensured the continuing survival of the BPT.

Interpretive Accounts of the BPT

In contrast to critical realist accounts of the BPT developed by Marsh, Tant and Evans, Mark Bevir and Rod Rhodes (2003) advance their own interpretive critique of the BPT literature. This amounts to a comprehensive assault on the dominant epistemological assumptions of orthodox political science. They argue that no structures exist beyond the beliefs of agents; traditions are contingent and have no essential characteristics; there are multiple traditions rather than a single, dominant BPT. As such, Bevir and Rhodes have sought to undermine notions of path dependency. At the heart of the disagreement between interpretivists and critical realists is a distinction between pluralist and hegemonic conceptions of political tradition. On the one hand, interpretivists insist traditions in British politics are fluid consisting of numerous interwoven and competing ideas (Bevir & Rhodes, 2003; Gamble, 1990; Kenny, 1999). On the other hand, critical realists contend there is a dominant tradition reflecting an elitist notion of top-down, centralising government (Marsh, 1980; Marsh & Tant, 1991; Tant, 1993).

Bevir and Rhodes offer an interpretivist critique drawing on a 'post-foundational' epistemology: there is no dominant tradition in British politics but a multitude of competing traditions which have to be interrogated and unpacked. Bevir and Rhodes insist that in analysing political institutions, it is essential to grasp the beliefs and meanings ascribed by actors. Ideologies do not exist aside from the beliefs of agents, while traditions are 'inherited beliefs' about the institutions and practices of government. Bevir and Rhodes attest that the aggregate concept of the BPT, shared by the 'classical' and 'critical' wave literature, conflates actors into pre-determined traditions. They insist:

> Tradition must not be reified – tradition is a starting-point, not something that fixes or determines future actions; traditions are contingent and produced by individual actions. The account of traditions must identify a set of connected beliefs and habits.
>
> (Bevir & Rhodes, 2003: 34)

Drawing on Weber's hermeneutic approach emphasising how agents interpret and ascribe meaning to the world, the task is to explore how individuals are socialised into shared traditions (Bevir & Rhodes, 2003). Weber's concern with *gesellschaft* meant exploring 'communities of belief', patterns of tradition that prevail in society (Shils, 2006: 175). Individuals are influenced by their backgrounds, but structures and institutions do not determine their actions. Agents are able to judiciously adapt and modify the traditions they inherit, questioning the path dependency that Bevir and Rhodes ascribe to both 'classical' and 'critical' accounts of the BPT.

Bevir and Rhodes (2003) identify four traditions within British government: Tory, Liberal, Whig and Socialist. They dispute the claim that traditions are a timeless, unchanging essence. By stressing that tradition is contingent and reproduced by agents, Bevir and Rhodes challenge the Whig conception of history where institutions evolve organically and naturally. Bevir and Rhodes' interpretivism and post-foundational approach sought to challenge an absence of sensitivity to meaning, subjectivity and context apparent in the dominant mode of 'modernist empiricism' in political science. This is influenced by the post-structuralist epistemology of Jacques Derrida, Michel Foucault and Paul Ricoeur. Bevir and Rhodes define a typology of governance in which agents are constantly modifying traditions, where institutional change is ubiquitous.

Bevir and Rhodes contend that traditions comprise 'webs of belief' which agents inherit without subsequently shaping their attitudes and actions. By the mid-1970s, the British polity was characterised by conflict and instability, altering subsequent interpretations of the BPT. While British society grew more diverse, it was harder to define core practices and ideas. Political discourse was shaped against the backdrop of 'multiple identities' across the United Kingdom questioning the survival of the dominant *British* political tradition (Ascherson, 1990; Kenny, 1999; Nairn, 1980). According to Bevir and Rhodes, the notion of a hegemonic tradition cannot be justified. The BPT ought to be disaggregated into the constituent elements outlined by Bevir and Rhodes in Table 1.1.

Bevir and Rhodes allude to the interpretation of governmental traditions promulgated by academic authors and political actors. Greenaway (1995) and Chapman (1988) praise the *Tory* tradition anchored in a Platonic, non-partisan public service, protecting established institutions and constitutional procedures. Similarly, *Whig* authors such as Hennessy (1997) advocate gradual evolutionary reform in the civil service which is broadly sympathetic to the BPT. In contrast, *Liberal* exponents such as Fry (1981) and Niskanen (1974) offer a critique of bureaucratic inefficiency, insisting that private sector management techniques are required to overhaul civil service delivery. Finally, the *Socialist* tradition epitomised by Barber (2007) and Mulgan (1996) advocates measures to improve the efficacy of state action, principally 'joined-up' government and 'evidence-based' policy-making. Bevir and Rhodes insist that traditions are always plural and overlapping, an amalgam of ideological and ideational beliefs. There is inevitably contestation; traditions change over time as actors respond to dilemmas.

There is an overlap between Bevir and Rhodes' interpretivism and the 'classical' wave of Beer, Birch and Greenleaf.[8] Bevir and Rhodes emphasise the continuing struggle between traditions which adapt in order to resolve dilemmas. Dilemmas arise where individuals are compelled to accept beliefs which are opposed to current conventions and practices. Tradition does not tell people how to respond to dilemmas, but serves as an intuitive guide; political change

TABLE 1.1   British governmental traditions

Tradition	Tory	Liberal	Whig	Socialist
Defining narratives	Commitment to non-partisan bureaucracy and platonic custodianship celebrating traditional civil service virtues	Restore authority of central state and impose new disciplines through competition and New Public Management. Break up traditional public sector monopolies	Safeguard civil service as balancing mechanism against political and constitutional change protecting virtues of representative government. Reform civil service through gradual and piecemeal reform	Fabian lineage of efficient bureaucratic reform and guild socialist conception of participatory democracy. New Labour rejected both command state of 'Old' Labour and marketisation of New Right emphasising partnership and networks
Key authors and exponents	Greenaway (1995); Chapman (1988)	Fry (1981); Niskanen (1974)	Hennessy (1997)	Barber (2007); Mulgan (1996)

Source: Bevir & Rhodes (2003)

involves 'the pushing and pulling of dilemmas and traditions' (Bevir & Rhodes, 2003: 22).

Bevir and Rhodes' approach provides valuable insights stressing the historical contingency of the BPT. The dispute between interpretivists and critical realists is, in any case, seemingly overstated (Elgie, 2011; Hay, 2011). Both acknowledge that traditions are modified by agents in response to the contingent circumstances they face. Bevir and Rhodes emphasise unintended consequences and the role of ideas. Nonetheless, Bevir and Rhodes' account still has weaknesses. By dismissing the influence of path dependency and insisting that agents are autonomous of their institutional context, Bevir and Rhodes appear to endorse a radical post-structuralist position (Hay, 2011). They dismiss the salience and resonance of the dominant BPT through its constraining effect on agency, rarely acknowledging that agents operate in pre-structured settings. Their view of plural traditions is problematic since the rationale for the particular governing traditions they highlight is never elucidated. As such, Bevir and Rhodes repeatedly emphasise discontinuity referring to 'an ever changing pattern of governance' (2006b: 98). They separate continuity and change treating them as a dualism, rather than considering how continuity and change are iterative and mutually constituted.

Like McAnulla (2007), this study contends that interpretive accounts over-emphasise how far agents have the capacity to alter and shape the context they inherit. Instead, 'the past' is always influencing and moderating 'the present'. Rather than viewing tradition as inherently 'malleable', tradition should be conceived as a set of 'concrete social habits' informing everyday practice (Frohnen cited in McAnulla, 2007: 15). This emphasises the role of a dominant tradition based on a narrow and top-down view of British democracy. McAnulla draws on the work of Edward Shils examining how the past is always exerting a grip over the present. Individuals rarely have the incentive to break with current practices, being reluctant to discard inherited knowledge. It is inevitable that actors should derive meaning from their connections with the past (McAnulla, 2007).

Martin Smith (2008) argues that Bevir and Rhodes implicitly reject the American sociological interpretivism of Erving Goffman, Harold Garfinkel, Peter Berger and Thomas Luckmann. Bevir and Rhodes infer that no 'practice or norm' fixes how people act yet 'classic interpretivists are exactly concerned with how norms do fix the way people act' (Smith, 2008: 145). Social realities are context-shaping, having an existence beyond individual actors. Through power relations and rules of the game, institutional norms have the capacity to constantly reshape human behaviour. Indeed, Bevir and Rhodes infer that the Westminster model is a system of power into which ministers and officials are socialised through the concept of 'situated agency' (2006: 32). However, the notion of 'situated agency' alludes to how individual actions are the product of contingency, rather than determined by institutions and practices. Bevir and Rhodes insist that practices and norms cannot determine how individuals act. How the socialisation process underpinning the Westminster model operates is therefore left unclear.

Critical realists concur that interpretivism underemphasises the resonance of the BPT and Westminster model, portraying the narrow and elitist conception of British democracy as one of several equally influential frameworks of cross-cutting ideas and practices. Bevir and Rhodes rarely consider how 'meanings are inscribed in institutions and processes' (Marsh & Hall, 2007: 216). Under the guise of interpretivism, Smith insists that Bevir and Rhodes denude political science of 'critical edge', implying that, 'all stories are as good as each other' (Stones quoted in Smith, 2008: 153).

In summary, 'classical' BPT accounts emphasise the relationship between institutions and ideas. The 'critical wave' literature draws attention to how the dominant tradition reinforces a 'power-hoarding' view of democracy. Both allude to path dependency, where particular assumptions and norms are hard-wired into governing practices and institutions. As such, the meta-theoretical orientation of the British political system towards majoritarianism, parliamentary sovereignty and the Westminster model is resistant to challenge and cannot be ascribed merely to the interpretations and meanings of actors (Flinders, 2008; Tant, 1993). Above all, Whitehall reform occurs within institutional settings inscribed and underpinned by the BPT. The literature on the BPT closely informs the theoretical approach of this study.

Conclusion

This chapter highlighted key elements of institutional path dependency reinforced by the dominant tradition in British politics. By examining the 'quasi-elitist' meta-constitutional orientation of the British political system, incremental reforms of the Whitehall model and its leading institutions can be placed in the appropriate context. The chapter sought to analyse and understand political traditions in relation to the norms and beliefs which are viewed as legitimate among political elites embodied in the BPT, offering a further perspective on continuity and change in the core executive and the institutions of the contemporary British state:

- The BPT draws on a 'top-down' and 'elitist' conception of democracy shaping the institutional norms and practices of British government, while conditioning the beliefs of ministers and civil servants (Evans, 2003; Marsh, 1980; Marsh & Tant, 1991).
- The approach to Whitehall reform has occurred within an institutional context animated by the BPT. This weakened the impetus towards radical change in the permanent bureaucracy and the core executive.
- As such, the dominant tradition neutered the claims of participatory democracy and governance in British politics.
- The BPT made a shared culture of 'centralising government knows best' integral to the British political system.

The literature on the BPT stressed the essential role of tradition in British politics, while emphasising the importance of stability and path dependence within the institutions of the British state. The scope for Whitehall reform is conditioned by the formative phase in which the institutions of the state were constructed.

The Northcote-Trevelyan model was characterised by a hierarchical mode of Weberian bureaucracy; neutral, permanent and anonymous officials motivated by the public interest; and a willingness to administer policies ultimately determined by ministers. This bequeathed a set of theories, institutions and practices to subsequent generations of administrators in the central state. New Labour's view of the machinery of government adhered to an elitist model of governance upholding key elements of the BPT, reinforced by robust attachment to the 'power-hoarding' Westminster model. That said, the party's approach was characterised by a paradox:

> Notwithstanding New Labour's public policy objectives of greater pluralism, more inclusiveness, and an emphasis on devolved decision-making, the Blair administration quickly acquired a reputation of extending excessive central control.
>
> (Foley, 2000: 24)

Labour has been torn between pursuing modernising reforms on the one hand, and 'playing the game' of maintaining its power through 'elite governing competence' on the other (McAnulla, 2006: 193). New Labour had radical aspirations, but its reforms were constrained by pragmatism, tradition and continuity with the party's past. The approach adopted in this chapter is anchored in critical realism and historical institutionalism, acknowledging the contested role of norms, ideas and traditions in the process of institutional change. The following chapter will examine how the BPT is reflected in the Westminster model, and subsequent accounts of how power and policy-making operate in Whitehall.

CHAPTER 2

The Westminster Model and the Whitehall Paradigm

It would be too optimistic [...] to suggest that the Whitehall model will be replaced by a carefully designed new model of political-bureaucratic relations. Whatever the difficulties, strains and contradictions evident in the model, it may continue. Indeed, the proponents of the Whitehall model can argue that its capacity to survive the Thatcher years is evidence of its adaptability.

Campbell and Wilson (1995: 314)

The central issue in British politics has not been how to curb the elective dictatorship model but how to capture it [...] Regardless of whether it is called a top-down model or an elective dictatorship, the formal concentration of political authority in Britain is remarkable.

Kavanagh (1986: 285)

Introduction

Both the classical and critical accounts of the dominant tradition in British politics analysed in the previous chapter are reflected in the literature on the Westminster model and the Whitehall paradigm. According to Evans (2003: 18), 'The Westminster model forms the basis of the British Political Tradition and in the course of the nineteenth and twentieth centuries became the political orthodoxy of British government.' This chapter will address how a conceptualisation of British politics shaped by the Westminster model influenced conventional understandings of Whitehall and the core executive. The literature examines how the Whitehall model ought to operate, framing interpretations of the role of the civil service, Cabinet government, power relations between departments and the centre, and the relative powers of the prime minister in the British political system.

The Westminster model is a further influential organising perspective in British politics, offering a benchmark for assessing patterns of continuity and change in the machinery of the British state. While BPT accounts examine the ideas underpinning institutions and processes, the Westminster model has mapped key institutional relationships in the British polity. Moreover, the BPT provides a 'legitimating mythology' justifying the extensive power that the Westminster model places in the hands of elites, shaping the beliefs and attitudes of actors, while influencing the culture and 'club rules' prevailing in Whitehall (McAnulla, 2006). This relates to the view that the Westminster model 'tends to operate as a kind of comfort blanket for the core executive. It is very rare for a minister to potentially risk the loss of this comfort blanket by challenging the model while in office' (Richards, 2008a: 200).

There is a wide-ranging literature on the Westminster model which refers to 'the concepts, questions, and historical story used to capture the allegedly essential features of British government that, mainly through sheer longevity, form the present-day, conventional or mainstream view' (Bevir & Rhodes, 2003: 25). The Westminster model is based around a set of mutually reinforcing values, beliefs and norms:

- There is a focus on institutions in relation to the rules, procedures and organisational structures of government.
- Indeed, institutions are seen as an 'expression of human purpose', articulating distinctive choices about how political relationships should be conducted, and emphasising the interaction between institutions and ideas (Gamble, 1990: 409; Johnson, 1989).
- This is coupled with a Whig historiography in which the Westminster model captures 'the practical wisdom of Britain's constitutional arrangements' (Gamble, 1990: 409).
- The model views power implicitly as an object located in particular actors and institutions.

As such, in the Westminster model, Britain is a 'unitary state' (Rhodes et al., 2003) where power is concentrated at the centre:

> The final hallmark of the UK's meta-constitutional orientation was a normative belief in the value of centralisation – both territorially and politically. The Westminster model was therefore a 'power-hoarding' or 'power concentrating' model of democracy.
> (Flinders, 2010: 22–3)

The constitutional tenets of the Westminster model are pithily summarised by Birch:

> This [Liberal] view [...] comprised four distinct but interrelated doctrines. First there was the theory of representation [...] the eventual aims of which were crudely expressed in the popular slogan 'one man, one vote; one vote, one value'. Second there was the doctrine of parliamentary sovereignty, combined with the belief that in any conflict between the two Houses the views of the Commons ought to prevail [...] Third, Liberals insisted that ministers of the Crown were accountable to Parliament

for their actions [...] only in this way [...] could the political system provide for responsible as well as representative government [...] Fourth Liberals attached great value to certain legal principles than came to be known as 'the Rule of Law'.

(Birch cited in Rhodes, 1997: 32)

Historically among the Left in British politics, the Westminster model constituted Britain's parliamentary road to a new socialist commonwealth, in which the United Kingdom stood as a beacon of democracy to the world. Labour's approach 'was contingent on the need to appeal to the traditional discourse of British politics associated with the Westminster model' (Richards, 2008: 197). Meanwhile, for the Conservatives, the stability of Britain's parliamentary institutions contrasted positively with the turmoil and discord on the European continent. All mainstream political parties broadly accepted the logic and precepts of the Westminster system. Of course, in the academic literature, accounts drawing uncritically on the Westminster model inevitably have weaknesses. Bevir and Rhodes (2003: 218) have challenged 'the institutional descriptive legacy' of British political science which, in their view, has been unduly influenced by the Westminster model.

Literature on the Whitehall Paradigm

Within the Westminster model, there is a Whitehall 'paradigm' which shapes the relationship between ministers and officials, defining the institutions of the central state and the core executive, as depicted in Table 2.1 (Campbell & Wilson, 1995).

The literature on Whitehall explores the nature of institutional power and changing forms of governance: in particular whether power is pluralised or concentrated, and how power shapes the structure and processes of policy-making. Nevertheless, these accounts invariably operate with a concept of power that is, at best, implicit. The literature is framed by a series of dichotomies: prime-ministerial *versus* Cabinet government; central executive *versus* departmental policy-making; ministerial *versus* civil service power (Bevir & Rhodes, 2006a; Marsh & Tant, 1989; McAnulla, 2006; Smith, 1999; Tant, 1993).

The literature is inevitably dominated by discussion of the prime minister's role and the incipient 'presidentialisation' of British politics (Foley, 2000). British political studies have drawn heavily from the Whig tradition where 'understanding British politics meant understanding the workings of British parliamentary government' (Gamble, 1990: 407). Johnston notes that invariably in the literature 'politics is narrowly conceptualised as the domain of a political elite competing for power within the central institutions of the state' (1998: 1).

TABLE 2.1   The Westminster-Whitehall model of government

Westminster	Whitehall
Parliamentary sovereignty	Permanence
Governing party with majority in the House of Commons	Anonymity
Cabinet ministers: collective responsibility	Neutrality
Party discipline	Knowledge and expertise
Voters offered choice between 'disciplined parties'	Informal 'village-like' networks
Accountability through free and fair elections	Accountability to ministers
Strong Cabinet government and executive dominance	Defence of the public interest

Source: based on Richards (2008)

The wide-ranging literature on Whitehall offers an analysis of continuity and change in the political and administrative machinery of government (Rhodes, 1995). The section that follows considers the Whitehall literature in terms of an analytical framework based on institutional path dependency, and how this frames discussion of the role of the civil service, the interaction between the centre and departments, ministerial government, and the office of the prime minister.

Continuity in Whitehall

Institutional *continuity* is highlighted by accounts of bureaucratic co-ordination, baronial government and Cabinet government.

Bureaucratic Co-ordination

The literature on bureaucratic co-ordination infers that the structure and processes of policy-making lie outside the control of democratically account-able ministers (Benn, 1981; Miliband, 1972; Rhodes, 1997). Complementary versions of this account are developed: one by radical elements on the Left dissatisfied by the Labour Party's record in power since the Attlee government (Benn, 1981; Crossman, 1975). Another originates with the New Right of the 1970s, where bureaucratic vested interests and 'state overload' were viewed as the primary cause of Britain's relative economic decline (Howell, 1971; Joseph, 1975). These perspectives allude to institutional continuity and path dependency: 'What is interesting about the conspiratorial view is that while politicians who embraced it have tended to come from the more radical wings of their respective parties, the view they offered of the civil service is strikingly similar' (Richards, 2008a: 144).

The Left account focused on how the civil service undermined radical ministers who posed a threat to the established constitutional order. The leading exponents were parliamentarians including Tony Benn, Brian Sedgemore and Stuart Holland, alongside advocates of an Alternative Economic Strategy (AES). It was claimed that departmental officials encouraged Whitehall Cabinet committees to block controversial proposals, warning Number Ten in advance to ensure policies were vetoed (Benn, 1981). Elected politicians might be constitutionally accountable, but parliamentary and ministerial responsibility was a fiction given the structural power of the capitalist state in determining the interests of government (Miliband, 1972). As secretary of state for industry (1974–5) and energy (1975–9), Benn grew increasingly frustrated at the determination of the civil service to veto alternative strategies during the 1970s crisis. Benn insisted:

> Civil servants think that continuity of government works within the department and people come in and stay for a year or two in the bridal suite of the Grand Hotel but they still run it [...] I think they do think that and it's your job not to get angry about that, but just to shift it.
>
> (cited in Richards, 2008a: 150)

A Labour government would inevitably struggle to implement a socialist programme:

> The problem arises from the fact that the civil service sees itself as being above the party battle, with a political position of its own to defend against all-comers, including governments armed with their own philosophy and programme. Whitehall prefers consensus politics [...] they are always trying to steer incoming government back to the policy of the outgoing government, minus the mistakes that the civil service thought the outgoing government made.
>
> (cited in Richards, 2008a: 150–1)

This view is to a large extent confirmed by Sir Anthony Part, permanent secretary at the Department of Industry between 1974 and 1975:

> The civil service always hopes it is influencing ministers towards the common ground [...] it is the civil service trying to have a sense of what can succeed for Britain, and trying to exercise its influence on ministers to try to see that they do capture the common ground with their ideas, from whatever origin they start.
>
> (cited in Ponting, 1986: 7)

The New Right accounts implicitly mirror the Left's assumptions about the role of the civil service. The power of the permanent bureaucracy was used to delay, dilute and weaken radical initiatives to reduce the size and capacities of the state, taking advantage of officials' influence over the flow of information. Ministers were encouraged to disrupt proposals threatening the Whitehall status quo, opting out of controversial initiatives such as financial efficiency programmes designed to reduce departmental expenditure. Only Number Ten and the Treasury were capable of imposing institutional reforms (Joseph, 1975). John Nott, a Thatcherite minister, insisted: 'Whitehall is the ultimate monster to stop governments changing things' (cited in Hennessy, 2000: 184).

This critique viewed the civil service as the custodian of the established postwar Keynesian welfare state consensus. It drew on public choice accounts of bureaucratic behaviour where the public sector was depicted as inefficient and self-interested, insulated from the rigours of market competition (Dunleavy, 1991; Fry, 1981; Niskanen, 1974). The rational choice critique of bureaucracy combined with the notion of an 'overloaded polity' to produce the powerful Thatcherite agenda of rolling back the frontiers of the state (Adonis & Hames, 1994; Gamble, 1994; King, 1975). Nonetheless, the Thatcher governments were unwilling to reform the civil service until their third election victory in 1987. Even then, the senior echelons of Whitehall survived largely unscathed (Dolowitz et al., 1996; Gamble, 1988).

The literature alludes to a theme at the heart of this study, namely why do initiatives that restructure the state prove difficult to implement in practice? The New Right insist that British government exhibited path dependency in relation to the relative size of the state. The proportion of national income distributed through state benefits and services has grown continuously since 1945 (Flinders, 2009; Pierson, 2004; Steinmo, 1996). In addition, the Left decried the capacity of the permanent bureaucracy to water down and undermine politically radical programmes. This literature relates to the role of state structures in defining who has power, what kinds of groups have access to power, and who influences public policy outcomes. The argument is that state actors play a key role in shaping and mobilising political ideas and interests (Steinmo, 1996).

Moreover, the Westminster model and Whitehall paradigm emphasise that officials and ministers operate on the basis of *symbiosis* rather than conflict. The assumption at the heart of the Haldane model[1] is that officials are inseparable from ministers: their interests are indistinguishable. However, the bureaucratic co-ordination literature indicates that the civil service is able to conceal the real nature of its power. The Whitehall model is underpinned by the tradition of elitist, top-down government, upholding stability in central state institutions.

'Baronialism' and Ministerial Government

In contrast, the literature on 'Baronialism' emphasises the structural power of government departments in Whitehall. Departments are not only the principle unit of administrative decision-making; they are autonomous 'fiefdoms' which play a key role throughout the policy process (Marsh et al., 2001). British government is structured around departments as the institutional concentration of 'political and bureaucratic resources': the principle agent of policy-making and implementation (Marsh et al., 2001). The strength of departments is a source of institutional continuity and stability in Whitehall.

Marsh, Richards and Smith (2001) examine the activities of Whitehall departments. They insist that the analysis of departments has been neglected in favour of more prestigious institutions such as Number Ten and the Treasury. Normative assumptions about where power lies reinforce the overriding concern with observable decision-making at the centre of government. The influence of behaviourism and rational choice theory has focused attention on what agents can be observed doing, and how this is measured. In contrast, critical realists address the *unobservable* dimensions of power, particularly how power operates through underlying structures within the central institutions of the state.

There is a diverse literature examining the scope and function of departments. *The New Whitehall Series* looked in detail at the role of departments and departmental cultures, offering descriptive analysis of the policy-making process and a glimpse of life within departments (Johnston, 1965). These accounts emphasise that ministers are inevitably pulled towards departments where they forge their reputations. Ministers' success depends on policy implementation through departments, rather than engaging in the collegiate structures of Cabinet decision-making. Mulgan (2008) attests that during the New Labour years, policy development was undertaken by departments: central units had little formal power and there was a distinctive 'departmental view'. On policy delivery, the prime minister's role is inherently limited: departments and arms-length agencies inevitably control the levers of implementation (Rhodes, 1994). Burch and Holliday (1996: 71) conclude:

> Very few non-governmental agencies – such as pressure groups – are able to deal directly with the Cabinet system. Instead most work through departments. Government departments therefore act as an important gatekeeper into the system. They are usually major sources of information and advice, and also develop policy initiatives of their own accord.

While prime ministers veto policies in exceptional circumstances, they rarely impose initiatives on departments (James, 1995). Expertise and resources are concentrated at the departmental level. Ministers have strategic assets that are denied to the prime minister: specialist staff, legislative capacity, access to expertise and networks, and departmental programme budgets (Heffernan, 2005). Corry (2011: 1) insists 'although the centre is theoretically very powerful, in international terms it is relatively weak in its ability to devise and see through its strategies'.

The prime minister cannot intervene across every aspect of the policy-making arena (Marsh et al., 2003). Indeed, the strength of departments has led to growing concerns about the isolated and fragmented nature of the policy-making process. Labour's programme of 'joined-up' government sought to challenge the 'pathology' of departmentalism. It was claimed that officials operated in policy silos, protecting their territory rather than advancing the government's collective interests (Richards & Kavanagh, 2001).

Departments are structurally powerful, as ministers are responsible for what departments do: ministerial responsibility is the lynchpin of the British constitution (Flinders, 2008; Norton, 1999). Ministers invoke quasi-judicial powers in the Ministerial Code. While Cabinet government co-ordinates the policy process, ministers choose to conceal decisions, protecting the sovereignty of their department. The doctrine of parliamentary accountability underpinning British government plays an important role in sustaining departmentalism (Judge, 1993).

That said, there are significant gaps in the literature on Whitehall departments. The study of central government inevitably focuses on the organisation and management of departments (Rhodes et al., 2003). This also addresses constitutional debates that arise in the context of parliamentary accountability and delegated authority (Flinders, 2008; Kavanagh & Seldon, 2001). However, a substantial lacuna emerged concerning the informal rules of the game governing the role of actors in departments. This void is partially addressed in Heclo and Wildavsky's study, *The Private Government of Public Money* (1981), examining the relationship between the Treasury and departments. Heclo and Wildavsky highlight intimate ties across the 'Whitehall village'. The formal hierarchy of the civil service is augmented by an informal ethos and *esprit de corps* which reinforces mutual dependency between the centre and departments.

The strength of the Baronial government literature lies in highlighting the constraints on the prime minister's role in the policy process. The interaction between the centre and departments is contingent, depending on the type of 'policy role' adopted by ministers (Headey, 1974; James, 1995; Marsh et al., 2001). Four roles are distinguished in the literature (Richards & Smith, 2002).

'Agenda-setters' are ministers who act as agents of change, instigating a permanent shift in the institutionalised policy preferences of departments. 'Initiators' lack strategic vision, but develop policies that are contrary to the department's strategic preferences. 'Selectors' are rarely pro-active, choosing initiatives from a range of options presented by officials. Finally, 'legitimators' merely rubber-stamp existing departmental policies.

This account emphasises that the role of departments varies according to ministerial style, and is addressed by Norton's (1999) work on ministers and the concept of a 'baronial' model in British government. Ministers are analogous to 'medieval barons' with vast policy territories and courtiers, fighting to protect departmental interests. Norton dismisses the claim that ministers are merely objects of the prime minister's rule: the premier will often struggle to dislodge powerful barons. Ministers retain the capacity to shape and implement policy: departments are the key building-blocks of British government (Norton, 1999). As such, the prime minister can achieve little without the co-operation and assistance of departments (Rose, 1971). Departments are a force for institutional stability and organisational inertia in Whitehall.

Cabinet Government

The defenders of collegiate decision-making in British Government view the Cabinet as integral to the British constitution and the UK political system (Johnson, 1989; Norton, 1999). Cabinet government is a further source of institutional continuity in the Whitehall paradigm. Since the 1960s and 1970s, there has been a debate about whether Cabinet government has been displaced by 'prime-ministerial predominance'. The arguments are well rehearsed: Hennessy (1997) suggests that the Cabinet gives focus to a fragmented system, acting as the bolt or 'hinge' pulling together the machinery of government. The Cabinet provides constitutional legitimacy through the system of collective responsibility, bringing together ministers instead of relying on a narrow coterie of advisers. This leads to stronger, more rigorous policy-making with formal checks and balances, avoiding the errors associated with the 'presidential' style of government (Foley, 1993; Foster, 2005; Foster & Plowden, 1998; Savoie, 2008).

Hennessy is sceptical of the 'presidential' model of prime-ministerial leadership arguing that, 'command models sit ill with open societies' (2000: 79). Britain's political culture is 'parliamentary', therefore incompatible with 'presidentialism': Cabinet remains the appropriate body through which to resolve departmental conflicts and maintain collective responsibility. However, Heffernan and Webb (2007) allege Cabinet decision-making has been weakened by the growth of ad hoc committees, with greater reliance on bilateralism and prime-ministerial predominance. Although cautious about 'presidentialism' given the contingent nature of executive power, Heffernan and Webb infer that the lines between prime-ministerial and 'presidential' government have been blurred. The *Power Inquiry* identified the widely held perception that under Blair:

> The Prime Minister makes decisions and brings them to the Cabinet simply for endorsement. Indeed, there is much evidence in the public domain to support this view. The political conventions of British government – that the Prime Minister is the first among equals and that policy is the product of discussion and negotiation within Cabinet – are now seriously eroded.
>
> (*Power Inquiry*, 2004: 134)

However, the prime minister's influence is constrained by the need to sustain the loyalty of Cabinet colleagues. The doctrine of collective Cabinet responsibility still carries weight, while Jones (1985: 216) provides a useful antidote to those professing the end of Cabinet government:

> The Prime Minister is the leading figure in the Cabinet whose voice carries most weight. But he is not the all-powerful individual which many have claimed him to be. His office has great potentialities, but the use made of them depends on many variables, the personality, temperament, and ability of the Prime Minister, what he wants to achieve and the methods he uses [...] A Prime Minister who can carry his colleagues within him can be in a very powerful position, but he is only as strong as they let him be.

James (1995) adopts a similarly measured approach, inferring that the Cabinet has moved from being the sole decision-making body in British government to a 'court of appeal', adjudicating on issues referred up from ministers. The growth in Cabinet committees reflects the purposive expansion of governmental activity over the last 40 years. Jones and Blick recall that 'the precise nature of the British Cabinet has always been subject to vagaries' (2010: 86). Gladstone remarked of the Cabinet in the 1870s:

> It lives and acts simply by understanding, without a single line of written law or constitution to determine its relations to the Monarch, or to the Parliament, or to the nation; or to the relations of its members to each other or its head.
>
> (Blick & Jones, 2010: 86)

In a similar vein, Smith affirms: 'The debate [on Cabinet government] is essentially irresolvable because its participants believe that power can be fixed to the Cabinet or the prime minister, and therefore fails to understand the complexities of core executive relations' (1999: 71). Nonetheless, the focus on Cabinet government offers a further perspective on institutional stasis in Whitehall.

Change in Whitehall

If continuity and change in the central state machine are considered as a duality rather than a dualism, it is necessary to examine accounts emphasising *discontinuity* in British government. Change is highlighted in particular by the literature on prime-ministerial predominance, 'cliques' and the 'end of Whitehall'.

Prime-ministerial Predominance

The literature on 'prime-ministerial predominance' (Heffernan, 2005) draws on influential debates at the heart of British politics about the scope of 'presidentialisation'. This infers that the constitutional principle of Cabinet government and collective responsibility has been eroded (Foley, 1993; Heffernan, 2005; Hennessy, 2000; Kavanagh & Seldon, 2007; Poguntke & Webb, 2007).

In *The British Prime Minister* (1985), King insists that too little attention is paid to the importance of the prime-ministerial office, especially the power to sign treaties and declare war, alongside powers of patronage such as 'hiring and firing' ministers and reorganising departments. Only the premier can determine the size and remit of departments and Cabinet committees, asserting a decisive influence over the machinery of government. Examining the role of the prime minister is not straightforward, however, given there is no formal definition of prime-ministerial powers and responsibilities. Hennessy echoed Asquith's dictum: 'It would be an exaggeration to declare boldly and baldly that the premiership is what the Prime Minister does, but there is an element of truth in that' (2000: 17).

Heffernan insists: 'As with much in the British political system, the prime ministership is shrouded in custom and convention, its true nature only really evidenced in a cumulative variety of reportage, commentary and scholarly analysis' (2005: 605). Ministers and departments are widely viewed as subservient to prime-ministerial power. In the case of Blair and Thatcher, the prime minister's personality is invoked to explain their domineering style of government. Butler and Kavanagh (2001) emphasise Blair's statecraft was shaped by a view of 'strong leadership'; Brown, in contrast, struggled to impose strategic direction over his government (Seldon & Lodge, 2010).

Of course, there is a danger of confusing historical events with structural changes in the nature of the premiership. It is important to distinguish between fundamental change and contingency: transient moments rooted in particular personalities and structural circumstances (Bevir & Rhodes, 2003; James, 1995; Smith, 1999). This suggests a degree of scepticism is necessary in relation to Foley's claim of an emerging British 'presidency':

> The prolific references to 'presidential style', 'presidential supremacy', and 'presidential approach' in relation to the Blair premiership satisfy two discernible requirements in the usage of such a characterisation. First, it is a way of giving dramatic emphasis to what is taken to be the exceptional magnitude of Blair's hegemony. Secondly, by deliberately opting for a term that is conspicuously at variance with the standard rationale of British government, it becomes a way of expressing a qualitative shift in the political process. In other words, the prominent deployment of 'presidential' as an instrument of description is seen as warranted by the idiosyncratic properties of the Blair premiership.
>
> (Foley, 2000: 3)

In contrast, Poguntke and Webb (2005) focus on how 'prime-ministerial' and 'presidential' regimes are constrained in their projection of authority. Blair was portrayed as a presidential figure by his advisers, an image they sought to cultivate. Jonathan Powell, chief of staff in 10 Downing Street (1997–2007), remarked:

> Cabinet died years ago. It hardly works anywhere in the world today. It is now a matter of strong leadership at the centre and creating structures and having people do it. I suppose we want to replace the departmental barons with a Bonapartist system.
>
> (quoted in Kavanagh & Seldon, 2000)

Powell insists Cabinet 'is not a policy-making body, but the political manifestation of a strong and united government' (2010: 58). In the context of an uncodified constitution, the prime minister has the advantage that 'the outer limits of authority are so ill-defined' (King, 1985: 137). At the same time, changes in the nature of the premiership are contingent and evolutionary. The equilibrium of British government has rarely been punctuated since the mid-nineteenth century.

Prime-ministerial Cliques

This variant of the literature on prime-ministerial government relates to the role of 'cliques'. The prime minister's authority and influence are 'collective attributes' of an inner circle of advisers (Donoughue, 1987; Dunleavy & Rhodes, 1990: 23; King, 1985; Rhodes, 1995). Prime ministers require political and bureaucratic support; there has been a considerable growth in strategic and administrative capacity at the centre (Bennister, 2012). This relates to the concept of 'court politics', an analogy explaining how 'courtiers operate ideally to carry out the purposes and wishes of the top man – they are responsible to the man, not to their own careers or to the professionally defined task' (Dexter quoted in Walter, 2010: 18).

Prime-ministerial influence is focused not only on policy-making but policy implementation, monitoring 'front-line' public sector delivery. The literature explains how the prime minister's authority is reinforced by leading figures with the power to exert the centre's will (Hennessy, 1997; Rhodes, 1995). After 1997, enforcers including Peter Mandelson and Jack Cunningham were appointed to strengthen the power of 'the core of the core, the centre of the centre' (Burch & Holliday, 1996: 31).

In the UK, the 'enforcer' role is scattered throughout the core executive, notably among Number Ten, the Cabinet Office and the Treasury. The prime minister's staff are shared between the Private Office made up of six private secretaries, the Political Office consisting of the political secretary and key aides, and the Policy Unit comprising policy experts employed as temporary civil servants and special advisers. Number Ten Downing Street alongside the Cabinet Office is increasingly seen as a *de facto* prime minister's department, 'an executive office in all but name' (Burch & Holliday, 1996: 31). Burnham, Jones and Lee (1998) view the role of advisers as enabling co-ordination between the Cabinet and departments. This includes an 'early warning system' alerting the prime minister to departmental initiatives that may create controversy or political fall-out. What is more, prime ministers require support in chairing Cabinet and negotiating with ministerial colleagues.

The account of 'cliques' became prominent following an expansion in the role of advisers and the growth of policy units at the centre of government (Peters, 2004). Indeed, advice on politics and policy has a powerful position in a system predicated on 'government by conversation' (Pyrce, 1997: 11). While Britain has yet to emulate the 'Cabinet' system of continental Europe, commentators insist politically appointed advisers play a more influential role than ever (Hennessy, 1997; Kavanagh & Seldon, 2001; Riddell, 2006). Critics have attacked these parallel political networks for undermining the civil service, duplicating existing structures, confusing parliamentary accountability, and encouraging the covert politicisation of Whitehall (Chapman, 1988; Foster, 2005; Foster & Plowden, 1998). The intimate relationship between ministers and officials, the central tenet of parliamentary accountability, is allegedly threatened (Flinders, 2008; Greenleaf, 1987; Norton, 1999).

Former Cabinet Secretary Sir Richard Wilson testified in evidence to the Public Administration Select Committee (PASC):

> We do not have a Presidential role for the Prime Minister in this country. We have a system where legal powers and financial resources are vested in the Secretaries of State. The Prime Minister has few executive powers other than administration of the Civil Service. He exercises his power through patronage, appointment and dismissal of ministers, and through the chairmanship of committees, and his or her power varies from time to time according to the extent his Cabinet colleagues permit him to have that power [...] I think the term 'Prime Minister's Department' implies a different role for the Prime Minister and a major constitutional change that I would tell you has not taken place.[2]

Nonetheless, the critique of Number Ten's role and the impact of political advisers highlight the extent of institutional change in the machinery of government, having much in common with the literature on the 'end of Whitehall'.

The 'End of Whitehall' View

These accounts analyse and assess the decline of the Whitehall model since the mid-1970s. The argument is that a post-Whitehall, 'minister-dominated' paradigm has emerged at the heart of the British state (Campbell & Wilson, 1995). Such accounts observe greater centralisation within the British political system, arising not from the leadership personality of the prime minister, but structural and institutional factors (Campbell & Wilson, 1995; Foster, 2005; Foster & Plowden, 1998). The centralisation of decision-making has increased since the Treasury adopted the Medium-Term Financial Strategy (MTFS) and tightened its controls over public expenditure in the early 1980s. Campbell and Wilson (1995: 11) insist:

> The centralisation of power in British government was also strengthened by the governance strategy that centralised power in order to shrink the role of the state; only a strong centre could curtail the apparently inexorable tendency for the government to claim an ever larger share of the national income.

The synergy between political leadership and a non-elected bureaucracy that characterised the Whitehall system has been replaced by 'executive disarray and the subservience of career civil servants to the (often faddish) will of their political masters' (Campbell & Wilson, 1995: 3). According to Campbell and Wilson, the prestige and authority of the permanent bureaucracy has been fundamentally altered. The system commanded respect given its relative efficiency in overseeing Britain's postwar recovery after 1945. Commonwealth countries such as Australia, New Zealand and Canada sought to replicate the British model (Campbell & Wilson, 1995). However, the Thatcher administration allegedly weakened and demoralised the civil service. Officials were increasingly subservient to their political masters, implying the end of the Haldane system (Campbell & Wilson, 1995; Foster, 2005):

- The *monopoly of civil service advice* was diluted as politicians drew on wider sources of expertise, notably thinktanks and task forces. Ministers moved away from their dependence on officials. At the Treasury, the chancellor increasingly drew on economic analysis from independent forecasters and special advisers (Thain, 2009).

- Formal civil service policy advice was undermined by prime-ministerial units challenging the ethos of *non-partisan permanence*. Foster argues: 'The Blair Government are stopping most officials from being policy makers, except for the few who *de facto* become special advisers' (2005: 285).

- The civil service was socialised into norms that were a marked contrast to those of the mid-nineteenth century (Greenaway, 1995). This resulted in growing *politicisation*, and the resolve of officials to 'speak truth to power' was weakened: 'Contemporary civil servants have advanced through a system in which enthusiasm for government policies has been rewarded more than honest criticism' (Campbell & Wilson, 1995: 182).

- The civil service is no longer a privileged and hermetically sealed profession. Whitehall recruits outsiders to senior positions, encouraging late entrants from other disciplines (Burnham & Pyper, 2008). The imposition of *Next Steps* agencies formally separating policy advice from implementation encourages a managerialist orientation (Chapman, 1988).

The 'end of Whitehall' view reinforced the claim that Britain was developing a centralised and politicised system of government. Foster (2005) posed the question of why Britain was now so incompetently governed. The 'crisis' of British government is attributed to the decline of Cabinet decision-making and an absence of effective parliamentary scrutiny, alongside the unchecked power of political advisers. Foster insists that the authority of departmental ministers has weakened, undermining the constitutional authority of the civil service and increasing the fragmentation of the state 'into a mass of bodies with complex but ill-defined relations' (Foster, 2005: 14). This is a system 'which, despite its protestations, is less interested in delivering results than managing news'. More pointedly, former Cabinet Secretary Robin Butler (2004) attacked the denigration of Cabinet government and the damaging 'informality' of the Downing Street machine under Prime Minister Blair.

TABLE 2.2 The mainstream literature on policy-making in central British government

Literature	Agency	Structure	Power
Prime-ministerial power (Foley, 2008; Heffernan, 2005; Butler & Kavanagh, 2000; King, 1985)	PM is able to subordinate ministers and departments to their will, building up the strength of Number Ten. The PM is increasingly 'presidential'	PM operates within a non-codified constitutional settlement, and is largely unconstrained by the external environment	Is an object located in Number Ten
Prime-ministerial cliques (Bennister, 2011; Rhodes, 1995; Donoughue, 1987; Jones, 1985)	PM's advisers are 'all seeing, all knowing'; policy process is conducted through 'sofa government' and the increasing role of prime-ministerial units in steering departments	Strengthening of capacity at the centre reconstitutes the power of the central state, permitting the untrammelled imposition of executive authority	Is an object located in Number Ten and the Cabinet Office
Cabinet government (Norton, 2006; Foster, 2005; Hennessy, 1997)	Cabinet is the 'key decision-making body' and a cornerstone of the British constitution. Government functions through the collective responsibility of ministers	Cabinet government will constrain the discretion of the PM and limit their freedom of manoeuvre	Is an object residing within the Cabinet
Baronial government (Marsh et al., 2001; Burch & Holliday, 1996; Johnston, 1965)	Departments have remained the dominant policy-making institution in Whitehall controlled by ministers through a symbiotic relationship with civil servants	Departments concentrate political and bureaucratic resources	Is an object located within government departments

Literature	Agency	Structure	Power
Bureaucratic co-ordination (Rhodes et al., 2003; Benn, 1981; Joseph, 1975; Howell, 1971)	Whitehall mandarins and the permanent bureaucracy dominate the policy-making arena	The policies of democratically elected ministers are thwarted by the structural interests of the state which continues to shape public policy outcomes	Is held by tightly interconnected groups of officials in Whitehall who comprise the power structure of the British state
End of Whitehall (Foster, 2005; Campbell & Wilson, 1995; Greenaway, 1995)	Politicisation has denuded officials of their traditional role in the policy process, prompting the shift towards a 'minister-dominated paradigm'	The policy-making process in Whitehall is determined by networks of ministers, political appointees, and external bodies such as thinktanks	Is held by ministers and special advisers

The last 30 years have unquestionably witnessed major changes in Whitehall: the growth of private sector contracting, the erosion of the civil service as a 'lifetime career', the expansion of *Next Steps*, outsourcing and market-testing. Greenaway (1995) feared that the public service ethos in Whitehall may have been undermined. The claim was that the machinery of government was politicised more than ever: bureaucratic reforms led to a 'minister-dominated' model (Campbell & Wilson, 1995: 8). These accounts attest that Conservative and Labour governments since 1979 sought to radically overhaul the permanent bureaucracy. They emphasise change and discontinuity rather than stability in the apparatus of the central British state.

The Whitehall Literature: A Critique

The contribution of the literature on Whitehall to theoretical debates about structure, agency, and power in the core executive is summarised in Table 2.2.

More recently, critics have argued that the Whitehall literature operated with an unduly simplistic conception of power (Dunleavy & Rhodes, 1990; Marsh et al., 2001; Smith, 1999). Power is usually framed as a dualism in which particular individuals and institutions gain or lose. In that regard, power is analysed as a zero-sum game rather than dispersed within, and between, institutions implicated in the policy-making process (McAnulla, 2006). The growing body of research influenced by the concept of the 'core executive' was precisely intended to evolve a more sophisticated conception of power in the central state territory (Dunleavy & Rhodes, 1990; Smith, 1999). Accounts of bureaucratic co-ordination rely on a conspiratorial view of power: agents are bearers of structural interests which they articulate on behalf of the capitalist state (Miliband, 1972). This relies on a crude conceptualisation of structure and agency, ignoring the capacity of actors to think and act strategically. Former practitioners such as Foster invoke the metonym of crisis to explain the decline of the Whitehall paradigm, without specifying what they mean by 'crisis' in the context of Britain's political institutions. The notion of crisis is thrown around indiscriminately both in everyday discourse, and in more theoretically informed accounts.

Overall, the literature is criticised for being somewhat antiquated, failing to take account of contemporary developments in Whitehall including the role of interest groups, and the impact of European integration. In contrast, 'critical wave' BPT authors draw attention to the pre-democratic nature of the British state, where Parliament is controlled by the executive and the political elite have access to knowledge and resources enabling them to dominate the policy process. The literature on Whitehall is too often bounded by the precepts of the

Westminster model and the 'classical' BPT, offering an idealised and seemingly anachronistic view of British democracy and the political system.

Conclusion

This chapter has averred that the Westminster model continues to influence orthodox accounts of how power operates in the British core executive, reflected in the voluminous literature on Whitehall. The Westminster model has reinforced the influence of the Whitehall paradigm addressing in particular the role of ministers and civil servants, and the relative powers of the prime minister in British government:

- The accounts of bureaucratic co-ordination, baronial government, and Cabinet government emphasise *continuity* in the core executive. In contrast, the literature on prime-ministerial government, 'cliques', and 'the end of Whitehall' has focused on the dynamics of institutional *change* in the central British state.
- There is, as such, a tendency within accounts of British government and Whitehall to treat continuity and change as a 'dualism', rather than a duality (Marsh, 2010). By a 'duality', we are referring to an understanding of how continuity and change are interconnected and interwoven. There is a strong inclination to overemphasise either stability or discontinuity ignoring how continuity and change can be mutually reinforcing, offering a misleading account of the process of institutional reform in British government.
- Rather than positing generalised claims about continuity and change in Whitehall, it is important to disaggregate changing patterns of governance in the core executive, assessing how far the centre in Number Ten sought to bypass departments in the policy-making process.

The focus of the literature on the Whitehall paradigm is the role of institutions: the processes, procedures and organisational practices of British government. This complements the overarching framework of the Westminster model, where the central state underpinned by a strong executive and the doctrine of parliamentary sovereignty has the capacity to drive through and implement policy. As this chapter has argued, the Westminster model makes implicit assumptions about power which are seen to shape the behaviour and motivation of actors, conceiving power as an object located within particular institutions and agencies in the central state (Rhodes, 1997; Smith, 1999).

The perspective of this study is that while elements of the Whitehall paradigm have adapted over time, key precepts such as the symbiotic relationship between ministers and officials have remained substantially intact. The pattern that emerges is one where New Labour's reforms of the core executive are grafted onto traditional constitutional arrangements, predicated on the unitary state, core executive autonomy, and a 'monogamous' relationship between ministers and the civil service upheld by the major political parties within the British state. As this book focuses on the Blair and Brown administrations between 1997 and 2010, the Labour Party's conception of the state, governance and power will be addressed in the next chapter.

CHAPTER 3

Interpreting Continuity and Change in the Labour Party's Statecraft

We always demand from our civil servants a loyalty to the State, and that they should serve the government of the day, whatever its particular colour. This undertaking is carried out with exemplary loyalty. Any departure from this system would mean the adoption of a spoils system, and that would destroy our Civil Service.

Attlee (1948)

The absence of a written constitution gives British politics a flexibility enjoyed by few nations. No courts can construe the power of the British Parliament. It interprets its own authority, and from it there is no appeal. This gives it a revolutionary quality, and enables us to entertain the hope of bringing about social transformations, without the agony and prolonged crises experienced by less fortunate nations. The British constitution, with its adult suffrage, exposes all rights and privileges, properties and powers, to the popular will.

Bevan (1952: 100)

It is an interesting comment on the nature of the British Labour Party that some of its leading left-wing figures, such as Aneurin Bevan, Michael Foot, and Tony Benn, should be the strongest defenders of parliamentarism and of what is essentially a pre-socialist view of the constitution.

Theakston (1992: 4)

Introduction: Labour and Path Dependency

Chapter 1 addressed the conceptualisation of democracy within the British state, alongside the role of ideas and the British Political Tradition (BPT) in interpreting institutions and practices. Having explicated various debates about the Whitehall model in Chapter 2, this chapter examines Labour's approach to the state and the party's willingness to adhere to a centralised, top-down governing strategy, further evidence of path dependency and institutional continuity in the core executive. Despite the emergence of a Third Way within social democracy committed to institutional reform and a system of partici-patory democracy, New Labour deferred to core precepts of the BPT and the Westminster model. The party's development and constitutionalisation during the twentieth century reinforced path dependency, overriding the pluralist conception of democracy and latterly the critique of Whitehall bureaucracy which gained momentum in the 1960s and 1970s.

This chapter examines how far Labour's approach to the state is characterised by path dependency. A conception of the state ought to play a crucial role in political analysis. However, the role of the state in British politics has remained diffuse and under-theorised (Jessop, 2007; Smith, 2009). According to Jones and Keating (1985), the state normatively prescribes central government's claim to authority and legitimacy. Within the tradition of British political studies, the state rarely features as an organising concept (Kenny, 1999). While Labour has been positioned as the party of the state in British politics, the leadership has traditionally been remarkably reluctant to specify and mark out changes to the machinery of government.

The chapter will assess Labour's changing attitude to the state. Prior to 1997, New Labour sought to make the case for state modernisation, taking account of changes under Thatcherism, alongside contemporary developments such as globalisation. However, an implicit tension arose between 'state-centrism' and the 'retreat of the state' in Labour's governing approach. This chapter assesses the contingency of the party's strategy, and the evolution of its governance agenda between 1997 and 2010. The core paradox of New Labour is that the instinct to devolve and decentralise power is tempered by the willingness to enact reforms through bureaucratic central state control.

Chapters 1 and 2 inferred that actors interpret ideas within an institutional context drawing on precepts and norms from within the BPT. This chapter will examine how Labour sought to define a distinctive conception of the state, reflecting a fundamental tension arising from contested beliefs about the British political system: a 'liberal' view based on power-sharing, openness, inclusivity and accountability; and a 'Whitehall' view focused on power-hoarding, stability, elitism and strong government (Birch, 1964; Flinders, 2010). Within the Labour tradition, the commitment to 'English pluralism' – an impulse towards democratising the administrative machinery of the state – was in reality outweighed by an underlying commitment to the Westminster model. Despite a wide-ranging programme of constitutional reform, Labour was determined to project strong leadership and elite governing competence.

The chapter explores how the party was accommodated within the dominant tradition given its roots in dissenting radicalism: why the potential challenge of participatory democracy was neutered following the Attlee government's seizure of the commanding heights of the state in the 1940s. A key perspective in the literature is that a central operating code was established ensuring the party was assimilated within the established constitutional system (Howell, 1981; Marquand, 2008; Miliband, 1972; Tant, 1993). This meant that Labour absorbed a set of values and norms integral to the Westminster model, epitomised by the quotation at the head of this chapter from the Labour politician Aneurin Bevan. Above all, it is necessary to contextualise the party's strategy for power, highlighting the contingency and unforeseen circumstances shaping its attitude to the state. Labour's 'maturity' as a parliamentary actor cannot be assumed: it must be *explained*.

The Constitutionalisation of Labour

The chapter begins by assessing the process of Labour's 'constitutionalisation' (Tant, 1993). It infers that since the 1920s, the party was increasingly influenced by a particular conception of British socialism, where parliamentary sovereignty and the centralised state were considered essential for achieving 'democratic socialism in one country' (Marquand, 2008).

The concept of constitutionalisation alludes to path dependency in Labour's approach to the state. There are a range of historical accounts which explore how the party was incorporated within the established political order (Fielding, 2003; Howell, 1981; Marquand, 2008; Morgan, 2010; Shaw, 1996). The tendency was to ascribe Labour's rejection of participatory democracy to an inevitable process of maturation, as the party sought legitimacy within the dominant framework of British politics (Tant, 1993). This implies that Labour's acquiescence was *pre-determined*: the parliamentary leadership was committed to political stability and continuity, rather than radicalism. However, such claims fail to account for contingency arising from the changing balance of power between actors and institutions.

The dominance of the parliamentary tradition was challenged by wider forces within the labour movement, notably trade unionism, syndicalism and guild socialism. At the outset, the ascendency of parliamentarianism was far from assured (Howell, 1981). The Labour Party was always a highly ambiguous construct, melding together socialist societies, the trade unions, the Fabian Society, the Independent Labour Party (ILP), and the Social Democratic Federation. Having been created to represent working-class interests in Parliament, however, conflict quickly emerged about whether the Labour Party was even a socialist party (Gamble, 2003; Miliband, 1972). According to Miliband, there was an inherent conflict between Labour's socialist aims, and its status as a legitimate parliamentary force. The leadership prioritised constitutional legality over the pursuit of socialism by extra parliamentary means. As a result, 'Labour is depicted as lacking the capacities, even if it had the strategy, to present an effective challenge to the dominant system of power' (Gamble, 2003: 204).

Nevertheless, the process by which the party constructed a governing strategy compatible with the BPT ought to be carefully analysed (Bevir & Rhodes, 2003; Tant, 1993). Accounts that interpret Labour's acquiescence to the BPT as foreordained have weaknesses (Beer, 1965; Birch, 1964). The literature assumes parties seeking power within the British state are compelled to embrace dominant institutions and practices to attain governing authority (Tant, 1993). In fairness, Beer's position is more subtle, inferring that Labour embraced the postwar consensus as the accepted body of political beliefs permeating British society. Moreover, the BPT offered a set of governing instruments enabling the party to pragmatically pursue a social democratic strategy (Howell, 1981). If there was a constitutional settlement into which Labour was absorbed, however, the extent of the political consensus has to be fully explained.

Tant (1993) insists that Labour was gradually brought within the established orthodoxy, inculcating the dominant discourse of the BPT and the necessity of governing through the Westminster model alongside the established Whitehall institutions. This gave the British political system a substantive defence against inclusive and participatory conceptions of liberal representative democracy. The forces of constitutionalisation ensured the ideological identity of a once radical party was compatible with the values and norms of the BPT. In contrast to 'classical' accounts of the BPT, however, the question addressed by Tant is *how* this process occurred.

As such, Tant relates the process of constitutionalisation to the projection of elite leadership authority within the BPT. The responsibilities of Westminster government weakened the appeal of socialist democracy, entailing an alternative form of representation acknowledging inequalities in the distribution of economic power, and the inherent limitations of civil and political rights (Beer, 1965; Judge, 1993). This vision of democracy immediately aroused suspicion about Labour's objectives within the dominant class, threatening to shift the balance of power decisively towards the working-class and organised labour, while challenging the dominant structures of British capitalism and the state (Coates, 1975; Miliband, 1972 Shaw, 1996).

To secure power within the Westminster system, Tant infers that Labour was compelled to abandon alternative 'syndicalist' conceptions of democratic representation. Rather than directly threatening the labour movement, however, the ruling class absorbed the pressure of working-class radicalism by demonstrating that collectivist programmes could be achieved through the established

political system (Miliband, 1972). In the contest between 'bottom-up' participatory democracy and 'top-down' centralisation, the latter secured a decisive
victory. Labour demonstrated its readiness for office by upholding prevailing constitutional norms: 'From initially representing a threat to the British
Constitution, it has come to be one of its major guarantors' (Tant, 1993: 191).

However, it was not only the hostility of Britain's political culture that shaped
the party's attitude towards the dominant institutions of the state (Fielding,
2003; Shaw, 1996; Tant, 1993). While Labour had been the inheritor of dissenting traditions epitomised by the Levellers, Thomas Paine, the Chartists and
William Cobbett, the process of ideological development within the party
exposed underlying weaknesses in doctrine and strategy. The utopian strand in
Labour's thought led to an apparently naive faith in the power of moral exhorta-
tion, manifested in the lack of an adequate theoretical and analytical model for
the critique of capitalism and programme for its transcendence. The prevailing form of labourism emerging in the early twentieth century was profoundly
conservative, structured to defend the rights and privileges of the organised
working class (Gamble, 2003; Marquand, 1991; Tant, 1993). As the twentieth
century progressed, the party became increasingly attached to the ideal of a
universal welfare state upheld by a strong central state, encapsulated in 'the
finest hour' of Labour's 1945 victory.

It was striking that the intellectual culture on the Left was shaped by
Fabianism and the New Liberalism professing a belief in gradualism, class
co-operation and the neutrality of the state, thereby conveying broad sympathy
with the existing order (Howell, 1981). Most party intellectuals were unlikely to
confront the essentially defensive and cautious mind-set of the parliamentary
leadership (Coates, 1975; Gamble, 2003; Kenny, 1999; Miliband, 1972). Labour
appeared unconcerned about the fundamental structures of power operating in
British society (Marquand, 2008). As Howell (1981: 118) attests:

> The party had always been disposed to work through existing institutions, trusting
> in the rationality and acceptance of consensual values of those with whom it had to
> bargain. Integrationism was a meaningful strategy for politicians who accepted the
> fundamental values enmeshed within a culture shared with their opponents, seeing
> differences as negotiable and honouring the rules of the game. The strategy implied
> that Labour sought to improve the existing social order, not to change it.

Labour's allegiance to 'utopian radicalism' embodied in the ethos of the
Independent Labour Party (ILP) meant the party lacked a distinctive concep-
tion of the state through which to govern and steer society (Cronin, 2005;
Marquand, 1988). According to Howell, 'the ILP was strong on idealism and

emotional appeals, but weak on practical proposals and strategic considerations' (1981: 27). The environment was one in which 'the culture of the party and of the wider labour movement remained much more comfortable with opposition than with government' (Gamble, 2003: 201). Miliband chastised Labour for refusing to acknowledge that the capitalist state was an instrument of the ruling class, depicting an 'aristocratic embrace' where the party leadership and parliamentarians were 'seduced' by the trappings of high office (1972: 95–6).

Nonetheless, despite the case for path dependency in the Labour tradition and the impact of constitutionalisation, the significance of the participatory challenge in the party ought not to be underestimated. G.D.H Cole and Harold Laski insisted that the political system was in danger of undermining the party's reformist aspirations (Marquand, 2008; Morgan, 2010; Stears, 2002). They viewed Whitehall and 'the theory and practice of the centralised, sovereign state' (Evans, 2003: 20) as inherently undemocratic. This reflected ambivalence within the labour movement about the expansion of state activity after World War I, compounded by the traumatic defeat of 1929–31: 'Not only did it terminate its efforts to govern at that moment but also prevented the party from dealing constructively with the question of how it would utilise state power to intervene in the economy and to deal with social problems' (Cronin, 1988: 225).

Other scholars insist: 'The views of the leadership of the party have generally held sway' (Richards, 2008a: 20). Labour's leaders were content to work within the established framework of the Westminster model. Critics, notably Crossman and Benn were marginalised, exercising little influence on the leadership (Blair, 2010; Theakston, 1998). As Theakston (1992: 13) observes:

> The historical record indicates that when Labour is in office, the party leaders pay much more attention to Civil Service advice and to the findings of government-appointed committees of inquiry on the question of reform of the Whitehall machine than to the views and advice coming from party circles or sympathetic intellectuals.

On the other hand, it is important to take account of the emerging critique of the state and centralised bureaucracy within the party. During the opposition years between 1951 and 1964, the Westminster system and the civil service became the focus of growing criticism. This was captured in debates about Britain's relative decline in the 1960s and 1970s (Gamble, 1984; Kenny & English, 2000). A range of powerful contributions emerged, notably Balogh's *The Apotheosis of the Dilettantes* (1959), and the later Fabian report, *The Administrators* (1964). Balogh, an adviser to Harold Wilson, castigated the 'amateurish' style of Whitehall. Both reports were highly critical of the Treasury's role in enforcing economic orthodoxy (Theakston, 1995).

The Wilson government sought to portray itself as engaged in the modernisation of anachronistic British institutions, establishing the Fulton Committee on the future of the civil service. Reporting in 1968, Fulton recommended greater specialisation among civil servants ending 'the cult of the amateur', the creation of the civil service training college, and the establishment of a civil service department in Whitehall. This was not enough to prevent a vigorous debate on the Left about the capabilities of the state bureaucracy. In addition, there was a significant gap between Fulton's coruscating critique of Whitehall together with the failings of the administrative elite, and the seemingly vacuous nature of the committee's proposals (Greenaway, 1995; Hennessy, 2000; Theakston, 1995).

Despite the emergence of an 'English pluralist' view of British democracy and the power structures of Whitehall, Labour never developed an alternative conception of the democratic state resonating across the party, beyond a relatively narrow circle of syndicalist and guild socialist intellectuals such as Laski, Cole, Philip Snowden, A.J. Penty and Edward Carpenter. Cole's model of Guild Socialism insisted that the Fabians were mistaken in attaching British socialism to a defence of the liberal democratic state (Cole, 1920; Judge, 2006). The syndicalist vision of a pluralist state challenged the basic principles of parliamentary democracy, advocating worker's guilds through which power would be radically decentralised. Representation based on the civil and political rights of the individual should be augmented by collective economic representation through industry and the workplace (Wright, 1979).

What is striking is the lack of resonance of Cole and Laski's ideas within the labour movement. Although the leadership's turn towards orthodoxy appears inevitable in retrospect, the outcome was contingent on the strategic choices of actors. Labour eschewed an alternative statecraft, focusing on the nationalisation of key industries, economic planning and the consolidation of the postwar welfare settlement (Howell, 1981; Marquand, 1988; Stedman-Jones, 1983). K.O. Morgan describes the process whereby 'The original themes of Labour's constitutional thinking – Laski's pluralism, Cole's Guild Socialism, workers' programmes such as the Plebs League in South Wales which excited the young Nye Bevan – faded away' (2013: 74).

Although their embrace of the established British state was far from certain, Labour's theorists were concerned with social and economic reform rather than radical constitutional change. As such, Labour's attitude was the product of path dependency rather than path determinism. The narrative in which the party casts aside its early radicalism in order to win elite legitimacy overstates the initial commitment of the labour movement to overhauling Britain's political institutions. Since its foundation, key elements of the Labour Party have exhibited deeply conservative attitudes to the British constitutional state.

As such, Labour's sanitisation as a party of power had a profound effect on the structure of the postwar settlement. Some observers emphasise that collectivist measures were implemented through institutions inscribed by the values of nineteenth-century liberalism, inhospitable to demands for collectivism and state action (Cronin, 1988; Marquand, 1988; Tant, 1993). There was little sustained attempt to construct developmental state capacity: Keynesian economic management and welfare universalism were created without stable institutional underpinnings in a political culture hostile to collectivism. This foreshadowed the process of state retrenchment and the economic crises of the 1970s. The price of Labour's acquiescence was the abandonment of any coherent project to forge avowedly social democratic institutions in Britain (Marquand, 1988; Tant, 1993).

There are, inevitably, alternative explanations of Labour's subservience to the dominant structures of the British state. Subsequent accounts attribute Labour's experience of government during, and after, World War II as 'hard-wiring' ministers' attachment to the norms and values of the Westminster model (Richards, 2008a: 26). The model offered considerable powers to an incumbent administration encapsulated in the Haldane model of minister-civil servant relations (Campbell & Wilson, 1995; Richards & Smith, 2004; Richards et al., 2008). The ability to implement reforms that advanced social justice and the public good had an appeal for generations of Labour's leaders (Marquand, 1996; Richards et al., 2008), feeding the heroic reputation of the Attlee government (Gamble, 2003; Howell, 1981). This is related to Beer's claim that the political system was congenial to collectivism and democratic socialism. The concentration of power and authority enabled governments to carry through far-reaching social reforms:

> Old traditions of strong government, paternalism, and the organic society have made easier the massive reassertion of state power that has taken place in recent decades, often under Conservative auspices. Old ideals of authority have been adapted to the conditions of mass suffrage in a theory of representation which we may call 'Tory Democracy'.
>
> (Beer, 1965: 69)

This account was still problematic, as Beer (1982) subsequently conceded. It over-estimated the extent of the postwar consensus which had always been more fragile and contingent, and was challenged by the 'overload' and governability crisis of the 1970s (Adonis & Hames, 1994; King, 1975). However, it is striking that in scores of ministerial diaries and memoirs, this view of the British state affording untrammelled powers to an incumbent government was readily embraced (Attlee, 1965; Benn, 1981; Blair, 2010; Callaghan, 2006; Crossman, 1975; Darling, 2011; Powell, 2010; Wilson, 1986).

Much of the literature emphasises that the precepts on which ministers and officials have drawn continued to be shaped by the Westminster model (Marsh & Hall, 2007; Marsh et al., 2001; Rhodes, 2012; Richards, 2008a). This framework entrenched a narrow, power-hoarding view of British democracy in which 'government knows best', where the role of citizens is essentially passive and legitimating (Marquand, 2008; Richards, 2008; Tant, 1993). This literature challenges the assumption of radical discontinuity between 'Old' and 'New' Labour (Evans, 2008; Fielding, 2003; Judge, 2003). Both 'Old' and 'New' Labour adhere strongly to the Westminster model and the notion of democracy therein.

This assessment is endorsed by Shaw's (1996) interpretation of Labour's traditionalism. Shaw examines the influence of 'the established and highly traditional national culture', on Labour's status as a governing party (1996: 146). The parallel between Shaw's conception of national culture and the BPT is striking. An attachment to the symbols of British power encouraged the Labour Party to uphold the imperial state, underpinned by a global conception of Empire (Coates & Krieger, 2004; Shaw, 1996; Vickers, 2004). The leadership's outlook was captured in a speech by former Foreign Secretary Ernest Bevin in 1946:

> Her Majesty's Government does not accept the view [...] that we have ceased to be a great Power, or the contention that we have ceased to play that role. We regard ourselves as one of the Powers most vital to the peace of the world, and we still have a historic part to play. The very fact we have fought so hard for liberty, and paid such a price, warrants our retaining that position; and indeed it places a duty upon us to continue to retain it.
>
> (Bevin quoted in Vickers, 2003: 1)

Shaw claimed that imperialism destroyed Labour's efforts to develop a radical social democratic strategy in the aftermath of war. Resources were diverted from the creation of the welfare state and the National Health Service to maintaining the remnants of Empire. Labour's ambition to create a more humane and reformed capitalism was constrained by the party's acquiesce to institutional orthodoxy and the dominant political tradition. Labour was further inhibited by the harsh economic circumstances of the late 1940s, and the sporadic fiscal crises of the postwar era (Marquand, 2008; Shaw, 1996).

The anomaly in this periodisation of the party's development was the turn towards constitutional reform in the late 1980s. In the 1992 election, Labour endorsed a programme of constitutional reform reflecting heightened concerns about the inadequacy of Britain's governing agreements. The Thatcher governments were portrayed as centralising and authoritarian, imposing 'an elective dictatorship' on Britain (Driver & Martell, 2004; Gamble, 1988; Judge, 1993; Marquand, 2004). Bogdanor (1999: 142) attested that Thatcher 'so strained the conventional limits of the British constitution that the constitution itself became part of party politics'. The argument was that the untrammelled executive power afforded to the Thatcher administration ought to be constrained through constitutional modification. This compelled Labour to develop a reform agenda, drawing on the initiative of pressure groups such as Charter 88 (Evans, 2003; 2008).

On the one hand, this proved a short-lived conversion. New Labour's governance code after 1997 went with the grain of the party's historical development, fashioning a governing strategy compatible with the norms of the British political system (Evans, 2003; Gamble, 2003). On the other hand, the British Left had begun to re-engage with pluralist and decentralist elements of the socialist tradition suppressed in the postwar years (Evans, 2003; Judge, 2006; Marquand, 1991). There had been criticism of the party for adopting an excessively statist, centralising orientation (Bevir, 2011; Stears, 2002). Social democracy could no longer rely on traditional assumptions about ideology and class. It searched for an appeal appropriate to late twentieth-century Britain anchored in institutional and political modernisation (Bogdanor, 2009). This illustrates the on-going tensions within the Labour tradition, torn between a participatory view of democracy and adherence to an elitist model of statecraft which were subsequently reflected in New Labour's approach to the reform of Whitehall and the core executive.

Labour's Approach to Governance and the British Political Tradition

This chapter has briefly traced the historical development of Labour's approach to governance and power, entailing faith in the efficacy of the top-down, centralising state drawing on a constitutionally conservative view of political change. This section will examine the fundamental tension at the heart of the New Labour project between the 'state-centric' mode of governance and the 'retreat of the state' view, alongside divergent interpretations of Labour's approach to the state.

There are several influential accounts of New Labour's governing strategy and its overarching conception of state power. One interpretation emphasises continuity between Labour and Thatcherism (Coates, 2005; Hay, 1996; Heffernan, 2000). Others insist New Labour was committed to the radical modernisation of British politics (Darendorf, 2000; Driver & Martell, 2006; Giddens, 1998). Another account claims that New Labour was not really *new* at all: there was substantial continuity with 'Old' Labour (Fielding, 2003; Gamble, 2003; Meredith, 2008).

Both critics and supporters endorse New Labour's novelty as marking a break with the Labour tradition. The 'pessimists' emphasise that the party deviated from any recognisably social democratic path by acquiescing to Thatcherism (Coates, 2005; Hay, 1996; Shaw, 1996). 'Optimists' insist it was necessary to demarcate the party from 'Old' Labour's failings (Cronin, 2005; Gamble, 2003; Kenny & Smith, 2001). However, the stark choice between accommodation and modernisation prevents 'a multidimensional and disaggregated characterisation' of New Labour which acknowledges its inherent complexity as an ideological formation (Kenny & Smith, 2001: 234).

Arguably both supporters and critics have negated the role of *ideas* in the party's development. The distinction between 'Old' and 'New' Labour enforces a false historical categorisation exaggerating the magnitude of difference between past and present Labour governments (Fielding, 2003). Of course, Attlee's programme in the 1940s was markedly different to the Blair and Brown agenda of the 1990s. Three decades of liberal economic policy led to the abandonment of economic planning, nationalisation, public ownership and import controls (Grant, 2003). Labour's 1989 policy review crystallised an explicit endorsement of the market economy (Jones, 1996; Shaw, 1996).

Inevitably, approaches emphasising either accommodation or modernisation neglect underlying continuities between the party of the past and the present. It is necessary to contextualise contemporary political ideologies and to trace their historical roots. Every Labour government relied on a system of managed capitalism, generating resources to fund welfare redistribution and spending on public services (Callaghan, 2000; Gamble, 2010; Howell, 1981). Both 'Old' and 'New' Labour were committed to the Atlantic alliance, maintaining Britain's special relationship with the United States (Shaw, 1996; Vickers, 2004). All Labour governments since the 1920s have been determined to uphold existing constitutional conventions and norms, preserving the unitary status of the British parliamentary state (Evans, 2008; Judge, 2003; Richards, 2008a). These approaches are consistent with a view of democracy where 'centralised government knows best'. This attitude to the state was hard-wired into Labour's conception of governance and power conditioning the party's attitude and approach to Whitehall.

The Third Way and Labour's Whitehall Reforms

So far, this chapter has examined the process of Labour's constitutionalisation, challenging interpretations of the party's strategy that overemphasise discontinuity on the basis of a stark rupture between past and present. Nevertheless, it is misleading to ignore the significance of contemporary challenges to the nature of governance and state authority. New Labour sought to fashion a credible approach following a sustained period in opposition during which the Thatcher and Major governments initiated major changes in the structure and politics of the state.

The Third Way's claim was that state-centric governance was no longer feasible in the wake of Thatcherism and globalisation (Giddens, 1998). The Thatcher administration insisted that the British state was inefficient and overloaded: public officials were self-interested, utility-maximising bureaucrats committed to high-spending collectivist government (Adonis & Hames, 1994; Gamble, 1994; Hay, 1996). The Conservative Party's determination to reduce the size of government went hand in hand with enhancing the authority of the central state (Gamble, 1988).

The 1979–97 governments initiated radical changes in the structure of the British state by in particular imposing New Public Management (NPM) reforms. NPM is a disparate set of ideas alluding to the application of private sector techniques and market competition to the delivery of public services. *Next Steps* was the definitive NPM reform, delegating operational responsibility from departments to 'arms-length' agencies (Dunleavy, 1995; Hood, 1996). The notion of separating policy from implementation while breaking up the public sector into 'discrete management units' was the decisive reform of the Thatcher era, nonetheless echoing the Northcote-Trevelyan reforms initiated 150 years previously (Wrisque-Cline, 2008).

In due course, the New Labour government faced a dilemma as to whether such changes were reversible (Richards, 2008; Richards & Smith, 2004). Managing the Thatcherite inheritance posed a conundrum: ministers inherited a system of government from a party which had fundamentally reshaped the institutional and policy context of British politics. The longevity of the Thatcher governments inevitably curtailed their successor's room for manoeuvre (Gamble, 2003). Kenny and Smith provide a synopsis of the Conservative's reforms (2001: 247):

- Roughly 20 per cent of the national economy was directly controlled by government in 1979 through nationalisation and public ownership. By the mid-1990s, only the Post Office remained in the public sector.
- The institutions that enabled governments to intervene in the economy and regulate employer/labour relations – the National Enterprise Board (NEB), the National Economic Development Council (NEDC), and the Manpower Services Commission (MSC) – had been abolished.
- The Department of Trade and Industry's (DTI) interventionist role had been curtailed, and its budget dramatically reduced.
- The civil service workforce shrank from 505,815 civil servants in 1979 to 431,400 in 1997: three-quarters of officials were now employed in agencies rather than departments. This relative decline in the civil service workforce is captured in Figure 3.1.

The Labour governments inherited a central state formation in which regulatory and interventionist powers had been dismantled. The demise of the Wilson/Callaghan governments was associated with the collapse of corporatism, reflecting a shift of elite opinion away from state activism (Coates, 2005; Hay, 1996; Kenny & Smith, 2001; Thompson, 1996). New Labour was aware that previous governments adopted a form of radical rhetoric in opposition which they were forced to abandon when confronted by the harsh realities of

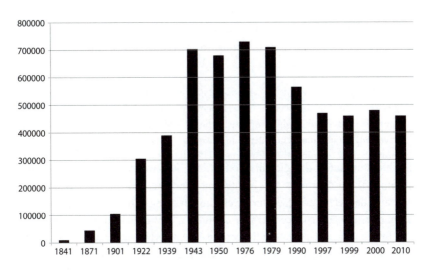

Source: Theakston (1995)

FIGURE 3.1   The size of the British civil service 1841–2010

power (Blair, 2010; Giddens, 1998; Gould, 1996). The leadership was compelled to embrace a 'new realism', acknowledging that the modern state had finite capacities and resources (Smith, 2002). As a consequence, NPM reforms were advanced steadily further in public services (Giddens, 1998; Smith, 2008). There was an expansion in audit bodies and inspectorates after 1997, inaugurating a period of 'hyper innovation' and institutional renovation in the British state (Moran, 2003).

Having accepted that the party could not revert to the corporatist strategies prevailing under postwar governments (Barber, 2007; Blair, 2010; Powell, 2010; Riddell, 2006), Labour sought to tackle the pathologies of governance that had emerged since the 1970s. This concerned in particular the growing inability of central government to co-ordinate and control the policy process (Richards & Smith, 2004). The policy-making machinery was fragmented across networks, institutions and actors (Bevir & Rhodes, 2006b). The incoming government was compelled to search for alternative models of policy delivery and implementation (Mulgan, 2008).

Despite the lack of ideational substance in the Third Way and the absence of a coherent governing programme, the Third Way narrative was highly influential in New Labour circles (Driver & Martell, 2006; Fielding, 2003; Gamble, 2003; Shaw, 2007). The Third Way constituted a break with the past, eschewing Labour's traditional approach to statecraft. The leadership absorbed the implications of NPM, influenced by David Osbourne and Ted Gaebler's work on *Reinventing Government* (1990), and Mulgan's account of *Connexity* (1996).[1] Both stressed the intricacy of governing through the state in a more fragmented, pluralised political environment. As Flinders (2002: 55) contends:

> The word governance is deeply embedded in the Labour Government's rhetoric [...] It is clear that at the heart of the Government's modernisation agenda lies the acceptance of the need to modify both institutional and cultural aspects of the current governing arrangements in order to increase the centre's governing capacity.

The literature infers that globalisation and markets weaken the authority of the 'command-and-control' state. Identifying new mechanisms of implementation and delivery was necessary given the changing nature of society and the economy: 'The governance narrative counters a view of British government that sees Britain as a unitary state with a strong executive' (Bevir & Rhodes, 2003: 60). The Third Way sought to transcend the command state of 'Old' Labour and the minimal state of the New Right (Bevir & Rhodes, 2006a; Giddens, 1998; Gray, 1996). Globalisation had eroded established bases of power and authority (Driver & Martell, 2006; Etzioni, 1995; Giddens, 1998). The challenge of globalisation and modernity meant the centre-left had to identify new mechanisms to deliver its goals, entailing a combination of bureaucracy, markets and networks. This meant reconstituting the 'steering capacities' of the centre while forging partnerships beyond central government, accompanied by an element of decentralisation and democratisation (Flinders, 2002; Giddens, 1998; Judge, 2006).

New Labour and State Transformation

New Labour's conception of governance, power and the state is captured by the implicit tension in the literature concerning state transformation and globalisation. Some accounts emphasise that a fundamental shift has taken place from 'government', where Whitehall made policy and was the dominant actor, to 'governance' where a disparate array of agents and networks were implicated in the governing process: pressures such as globalisation altered the environment in which the state operated (Richards & Smith, 2002). This is the distinction in the literature between the 'retreat of the state' and 'state-centric' governance (Albrow, 1996; Bell & Hindmoor, 2009; Giddens, 1998; Hay, 1998; Held, 2005; Hirst & Thompson, 1996; Sorenson, 2004; Strange, 1998). The disjuncture between 'governance' and 'government' captures the dialectic of institutional continuity *and* change in New Labour's statecraft: both narratives successively shaped the party's approach.

On one side, the nature of governance shifted from a 'directive' state to a more 'fragmented' state, representing a fundamental challenge to the BPT and the Westminster model (Bevir & Rhodes, 2008; Peters, 2004). This analysis was replicated in the work of leading thinktanks, notably Demos and the Institute for Public Policy Research (IPPR) providing 'a conveyor belt that relays ideas and concerns back and forth', to the party leadership (Bevir, 2005: 30; Miliband, 1994; Mulgan, 1996; 6, 1998). New Labour's statecraft acknowledged that traditional conceptions of state power were ebbing away. According to Giddens (1998: 69):

> Reform of the state and government should be a basic orientating principle of third way politics – a process of the deepening and widening of democracy. Government can act in partnership with agencies in civil society to foster community renewal and development.

Yet this 'retreat of the state' view was only one element in New Labour's armoury of ideas. On the other side, 'state-centric' accounts insisted that central government remained dominant, retaining significant executive and legislative authority. For example, Jessop (2007: 6) draws on the work of Poulantzas emphasising 'each national state has its own distinctive, path-dependent, national balance of class forces, its own institutional and organisational specifities'. The nation-state maintained its distinctive identity as the result of *national* class struggle. Poulantzas was unsympathetic to claims that national governments were declining in the face of globalisation and world markets, although his writings pre-date the 'globalisation debate' (Sorenson, 2004). Nation-states were not in retreat, but had maintained sovereignty and power (Hirst & Thompson, 1996). Other authors allude to the persistence of the BPT within the British political system as symptomatic of the sovereign state's indivisible authority and power (Marsh et al., 2001).

Indeed, despite the salience of change the New Labour leadership absorbed many state-centric assumptions compatible with the BPT. Their model for reconstructing British society and the polity was modernist and state-orientated. The state would reshape civil society and the public sector in the name of national efficiency, ensuring Britain remained competitive in the global economy (Moran, 2003; Richards & Smith, 2004; Scott, 1998; Smith, 2009). As Evans (2003: 3) astutely observes:

> New Labour's competition state project focuses on the transformation of the state from within with regard to the reform of political institutions, functions and processes in an attempt to adapt state action to cope more effectively with what they defined as 'global realities'. State intervention was aimed not only at adjusting to, but also sustaining, promoting and expanding an open global economy in order to capture its perceived benefits.

Smith (2009) insists that New Labour's ideas marked a shift from an interventionist Keynesian welfare state towards programmes that were intended to transform the lifestyles and behaviour of citizens. Fifty years on, New Labour was heavily influenced by the modernism and rationalism of the post-1945 state. The party sought to identify governing instruments that had the potential to 'reconstitute individual identities' (Smith, 2009: 178). The state's focus shifted from controlling economies to reshaping the social and moral behaviour of citizens. The aim was to persuade individuals to embrace dominant values and norms, integrating the excluded through 'Foucauldian conceptions of power' (Smith, 2009: 178). This required a centralised bureaucracy powerful enough to enact its intentions on the citizen (Moran, 2003; Scott, 1998; Smith, 2009).

A further manifestation of Labour's attachment to 'state-centric' governance was the Blair administration's scepticism about multilateralism and global cosmopolitanism (Gamble, 2003; Held, 2005). Ministers fought to defend the notion of 'indivisible sovereignty' in negotiating the European constitutional treaty. The Labour government renounced the United Nations' role in the Middle East, and was complicit in removing Saddam Hussein's regime in Iraq (Coates & Krieger, 2004). The British political elite historically drew from hard notions of 'Westphalian sovereignty' based on a unitary state (Richards & Smith, 2010). Labour was resistant to ceding control as the dominant actor within the territorial domain of the United Kingdom (Evans, 2004; Flinders, 2010). The party was determined to preserve the autonomy and authority of the state, reinforcing its dominance over the policy-making arena alongside the prevailing norms and practices of the BPT (Evans, 2008; Marsh & Hall, 2007; Marsh & Tant, 1991).

Analysing the Nature and Contingency of New Labour's Reforms

Having explored the ideational constructs informing Labour's conception of governance and the state, this chapter maps the impact of institutional continuity and change through the party's approach to Whitehall reform and the core executive. At one level, Labour adapted pragmatically to the realities of power seeking to avoid the division and dissent that engulfed previous governments (Barber, 2007; Blair, 2010; Gamble, 2003). In the year of Labour's election, Blair declared: 'People have to know that we will run from the centre and govern from the centre' (cited in Richards, 2008: 37). The leadership was determined to restore the efficacy of the state in affecting change over the economy and society: ministers were committed to an executive-dominated approach encapsulated in the Westminster model (Barber, 2007; Driver & Martell, 2006; Riddell, 2006).

This made the imperatives of reform distinct from the Thatcher period. New Labour sought to utilise state power to modernise social and economic institutions without returning to the corporatist legacy of the postwar settlement. It is striking, nevertheless, that the post-1997 Labour governments are characterised by underlying ambivalence about institutional reform, adhering to basic precepts of the Westminster model. This acts as a powerful force for stability in the institutions of the central state machine.

Preparing for Office: 1994–7

There was a widely held perception among commentators that New Labour lacked an adequate understanding of the machinery of government and the policy-making process before assuming office (Rawnsley, 2006; Riddell,

2006; Seldon, 2006). The party had been tactically astute in avoiding costly and undeliverable commitments in opposition. Shadow ministers attended a series of workshops at Templeton College, Oxford on how to manage government departments.[2] While the notion of a Third Way between the new right and social democracy framed the party's ideational approach to the state and Whitehall reform, New Labour nonetheless lacked a coherent governing strategy confronting:

> The structural problems facing Britain [...] we didn't really figure out how to rebalance the economy, to avoid over-exposure to financial services, and it didn't catch up with us for a few years. We didn't really re-theorise the role of the state, of government. And we didn't figure out [...] the 'steering versus rowing' thing. We didn't really change the civil service or have much to say about it.[3]

The challenge Labour faced was that 'it was still in this Gerald Kaufman mode where I go in with a bright adviser, we pull the levers and the Rolls Royce machine works'.[4] As Driver and Martell (2006: 56–7) remark: 'Labour, like its predecessors, remains a party of traditional loyalty to the Westminster model.' The most effective policies 'started to be thought about under the previous government [...] [New Labour] tended to overestimate area effects at the expense of family dynamics'.[5] In opposition, Labour had done 'almost no underpinning thinking about the causes of social exclusion', and was heavily reliant on civil service policy-making capacity. The new government was vulnerable to policy amnesia and an absence of clear strategic purpose.[6] For example, Labour reversed the Conservative government's internal market reforms in the NHS immediately after the 1997 election. By 2001, however, it sought to recreate a system of 'quasi-market' competition in public services (Blair, 2010; Riddell, 2006).

In relation to the machinery of government, New Labour's aim was to strengthen the prime-ministerial centre. In their infamous book, *The Blair Revolution* (1996), Peter Mandelson and Roger Liddle drew on the advice of Sir Terry Burns, then permanent secretary at the Treasury.[7] Ironically, a senior Treasury mandarin urged a more heavyweight Number Ten operation, a Prime Minister's Department 'in all but name' drawing on the combined resources of the Cabinet Office and 10 Downing Street (Barber, 2007; Hennessy, 2000). Critics including former Cabinet Secretary Sir Robin Butler argued that the incoming administration failed to distinguish between the role of Number Ten, and the constitutional function of the Cabinet Office. Mandelson himself conceded: 'We probably understated the role of the Cabinet Office in bringing together the government as a whole.'[8] Nonetheless, a set of ideas emerged about how to reorganise the centre that were taken up by the new Labour administration.[9]

Labour's Reform Programme Mark I: 'Wiring up' the British State and Modernising Government?

Initially, the Blair administration emphasised 'joining-up' government to improve policy co-ordination combined with initiatives to modernise the civil service. Labour's programme sought to overcome debilitating Whitehall turf wars leading to disputes between departments over territory, resources and power. The *Next Steps* reforms and the principle of concentrating delivery around operational agencies were consolidated by the new government. However, *Next Steps* had not been intended to address the weakness of policy co-ordination. The case for 'joining-up' government was articulated by one of Blair's advisers, Geoff Mulgan (2001: 21):

> The 'tubes' or 'silos' down which money flows from government to people and localities have come to be seen as part of the reason why government is bad at solving problems. Many issues have fitted imperfectly if at all into departmental slots. Vertical organisation by its nature skews government efforts away from certain activities, such as prevention – since the benefits of preventive action often come to another department. It tends to make government less sensitive to particular client groups whose needs cut across departmental lines. It incentivises departments to dump problems on each other – like schools dumping unruly children onto the streets to become a headache for the police [...] Over time it reinforces the tendency common to all bureaucracies of devoting more energy to the protection of turf rather than serving the public.

As a result, the *Modernising Government* White Paper (Cabinet Office, 1999) committed the civil service to major changes: New Labour was concerned not only with improving efficiency, but redefining the role of Whitehall as a delivery agent. The capacity of departments to work collectively was limited by the doctrine of ministerial responsibility, however, which reinforced the institutional separation of departments (Flinders, 2010). Moreover, New Labour was, on the whole, mistrustful of the civil service. This was not overtly ideological, driven by the fear that Whitehall mandarins had a hidden agenda. The concern was that civil servants lacked the means to develop and implement policy: New Labour increasingly sought policy advice from a range of external actors. A plethora of tsars, task forces and ad hoc bodies were established curtailing officials' monopoly of advice, alongside the appointment of unprecedented numbers of special advisers (Jones & Blick, 2010; Richards, 2010; Seldon, 2006).

Social scientists were increasingly drawn into the process through an emphasis on 'evidence-based' policy-making (Newman, 2005; Richards & Smith, 2004).

The granting of executive powers to Jonathan Powell (Number Ten chief of staff) and Alistair Campbell (Number Ten director of communications) to instruct civil servants, alongside the creation of the Strategic Communications Unit (SCU) in Number Ten, was an attempt to consolidate the centre's grip over the machinery of state. One senior minister in the New Labour years argued vociferously: 'It was an inspired decision [...] creating a chief of staff who would act within Number Ten as a pivotal point between the civil service, the political advisers, the communications staff, and government relations.'[10] As Blair remarked in an interview for this study, 'I was conscious of the fact that if you didn't have a strong centre, you weren't going to be able to enforce the culture of New Labour throughout the system.'[11]

As time progressed, there was frustration at the inertia of the state bureaucracy, an acknowledgement that the centre needed to push harder for change. Tellingly, in 1998–9 the NHS experienced one of the worst 'winter flu crises' for half a century, focusing attention on Labour's apparent failure to deliver sustained improvements in public sector performance (Barber, 2007; Riddell, 2006). This made a 'command bureaucracy' increasingly attractive to frustrated, seemingly impotent, politicians operating the 'rubber levers' of the traditional Whitehall machine. The levers were pulled with ever greater conviction after 1997. However, there was a dawning realisation that too often they were not connected to anything.[12]

Labour's Reform Programme Mark II: State-centric Core Executive 'Command and Control'?

Consequently, New Labour's second term entailed further changes in the political and administrative machinery of the state. The Number Ten Policy Unit more than doubled in size, re-established as the Prime Minister's Policy Directorate (PMPD) after the 2001 election. The PMPD's role was not only to provide policy advice to the prime minister, but to oversee departments through a network of ministers and special advisers. Within the Cabinet Office, an array of prime-ministerial units was created, including the Prime Minister's Delivery Unit (PMDU) and the Prime Minister's Strategy Unit (PMSU). The Delivery Unit co-ordinated bi-monthly 'stock-takes' between the prime minister and the secretary of state, agreeing the indicators by which success should be measured through Public Service Agreements (PSAs) alongside the Treasury (HMT). This created a line of accountability directly to the centre in 10 Downing Street.

The aim of the reforms was initially to shift the balance of power towards the centre, institutionalising departmental dependency on Number Ten over politics and policy. This was combined with an approach to public sector restructuring aimed at improving productivity and outcomes through centralised control, including sanctions and targets (Newman, 2005). This mind-set which led to the centralisation of core executive capacity during the New Labour years is captured by one of Blair's most senior ministerial allies:

> Blair thought the Cabinet and large swathes of the civil service would have blocked what he was trying to do. And therefore what you had to do was step around them […] operate a sort of *force majeure* that didn't give them the chance to fight back.[13]

Number Ten enhanced its role in implementation by establishing relationships directly with front-line providers and local agencies, launching delivery initiatives from street crime to school truancy bypassing departments (Barber, 2007; Blair, 2010). In relation to education, the City Academies initiative was conceived in 10 Downing Street, while Number Ten advisers continued to directly manage and oversee the delivery programme alongside departmental officials (Adonis, 2012; Blair, 2010). There was little confidence that the Department for Education and Skills (DfES) had the capacity to deliver the reform agenda.

In relation to delivery, the post-1997 Labour government argued that the traditional public sector model did not always ensure the efficient delivery of public goods: it was rigid and driven by a culture of 'one-size fits all'; the system was cumbersome and unresponsive; services were focused more on the producer than the consumer. Moreover, the supply of public services was controlled by a narrow monopoly of public sector providers. According to Le Grand (2005), public servants were 'knaves as well as knights', motivated by self-interest as much as altruism: choice was a way of redistributing power to the 'citizen-consumer'.

Rather than transferring power to markets, New Labour opted to control the producers of public services by widening choice, aligned with robust oversight by the core executive. For example, it increased central controlling capacity, using targets and the PMDU as a mechanism for ensuring providers fulfilled the government's objectives. Labour sought greater pluralism in the delivery of public services, but within a highly controlled context. This *hybrid* of marketised neo-liberal management and the retention of a hierarchical state led to a process of institutional 'layering' (Streeck & Thelen, 2005). The governing party imposed a pluralised notion of delivery onto the traditional institutions of the

Westminster model, reconstituting the core executive's capacities by strengthening the centre through 'unit-building' (Richards & Smith, 2004).

Labour's Reform Programme Mark III: Pluralising Delivery in the Central State Machine?

Nonetheless, by 2003–4 the limitations of the centralised approach were increasingly apparent. There was growing interest in the role of quasi-markets, managed competition and operational autonomy for front-line managers (Stoker, 2006). Additionally, Number Ten contracted in size: there were fewer political advisers by the end of the second term. The responsibility for driving the reform agenda was increasingly dependent on departments. Blair was confident that, at last, he had an experienced and ideologically sympathetic team of ministers in place (Blair, 2010). In 2002–3, the Prime Minister had to restrain his secretary of state for health, Alan Milburn, from going further in advancing market-centred NHS reforms which gave new freedoms to Foundation Trust hospitals, a major cause of friction with the Treasury (Rawnsley, 2006; Seldon, 2006).

The general principles informing this 'Mark III' reform strategy are enunciated by Michael Barber in relation to schools:

> Between 2001 and 2005 what Blair increasingly hankered after was a way of improving the education system that didn't need to be constantly driven by government. He wanted to develop self-sustaining, self-improving systems, and that led him to look into how to change not just the standards and quality of teaching, but the structures and incentives. Essentially, it's about creating different forms of quasi-market in public services, exploiting the power of choice, competition, transparency and incentives.
>
> (cited in Rhodes, 2012: 8)

There was an increased emphasis on long-term planning and strategy, focusing on the preparation of five-year plans in delivery departments.[14] Although dialogue with the centre continued, policy-making was led by departmental ministers. A further wave of institutional innovation was underway: for example, the Social Exclusion Task Force (SETF) replaced the Social Exclusion Unit (SEU), which was judged to have lived beyond its usefulness and was no longer generating 'hard-edged' reforms. The PMDU had been transferred from the Cabinet Office into the Treasury in January 2003, ensuring greater coordination between the monitoring of delivery targets and the allocation of public expenditure through the spending review process.

Labour's Reform Programme Mark IV: 'Crisis Management' following Financial Meltdown?

After Blair's departure in 2007, there was further scaling back of Number Ten. Managerial powers for special advisers in Whitehall were revoked by the incoming Prime Minister. There was evidence of Cabinet government re-imposing itself through longer and more frequent meetings, as executive powers in the Ministerial Code were amended (Seldon & Lodge, 2010). However, ambitious proposals in the 2007 *Governance of Britain* Green Paper, including the review of prerogative powers and reform of the House of Lords, never materialised. Brown's Number Ten developed a reputation for 'micro-management', interfering in the business of departments but failing to give a clear steer about policy decisions (Corry, 2011; Darling, 2011; Seldon & Lodge, 2010).

In the aftermath of the post-2008 crash, economic policy became of paramount importance. This led to further changes at the centre and the creation of the National Economic Council in October 2008. The role of the NEC was to bring together Whitehall departments ensuring more effective co-ordination to offset the impact of the crisis. The NEC was a Cabinet committee chaired by the Prime Minister which met in the Cabinet Office Briefing Room A (COBRA) 'crisis response' area in the Cabinet Office. The NEC had a wide membership of ministers (Corry, 2011; Rutter, 2011). The committee had an active secretariat supporting meetings of departmental permanent secretaries, special advisers chaired by the Prime Minister's senior economic adviser, Dan Corry, and a commissioning process which brought together the officials staffing the NEC, the Number Ten permanent secretary, and the Prime Minister's Policy Unit (PMPU).

Over thirteen years, the cumulative impact of New Labour's reforms on the nature of the state and the UK core executive has been all too apparent:

- Critical accounts such as the *Better Government Initiative* (2010) and Foster (2005) emphasise that Labour was intent on centralising and politicising Whitehall, marking a wholesale transformation in the governance of Britain. Previous governments strengthened the capacities and resources available to the prime minister. Under Blair and Brown, there was a fundamental change in the size and influence of the centre (Heffernan, 2003; Marquand, 2004; McAnulla, 2006; Richards, 2008).
- There were major alterations in the nature of the policy-making process, which became increasingly empirical and guided by performance data (Barber, 2007; Richards, 2008). Performance indicators within Public Service

Agreements meant that departments were increasingly held to account by the centre.

- The structure of dependency inevitably shifted: Number Ten had direct contact with front-line providers at 'street-level' (Marinetto, 2003; Richards, 2008). The role of the centre went beyond co-ordination, intervening directly in the process of implementation (Barber, 2007; Marquand, 2004; Richards, 2008).

The conception of institutional continuity and change in the literature is too often analytically imprecise. Furthermore, the impact of the reforms was more partial and contingent than numerous accounts have implied. At the same time, New Labour's institutional changes are too rarely situated in their historical context. There is a tendency to exaggerate the scale and impact of change in the light of a powerful critique of the reforms.[15] This has entrenched the 'end of Whitehall' view as the dominant interpretation of New Labour's approach to institutional modernisation, inferring that a critical juncture had been reached. This study argues that such accounts understate the importance of ad hoc adaptation, incrementalism, evolutionary reform, and institutional inertia. Moreover, like the Thatcher governments, the Blair and Brown administrations were unwilling to reappraise the fundamental tenets of the Westminster model, qualifying their reform credentials.

The force of institutional conservatism is intriguing in the case of the Labour governments, since they were ostensibly committed to a programme of constitutional reform entailing devolution to Scotland, Wales and Northern Ireland, freedom of information, the Human Rights Act and reform of the House of Lords. What is striking is the determination of ministers to preserve and uphold the ethos of strong government, elitist political rule and executive dominance (Flinders, 2009; Judge, 2006; Marsh & Hall, 2007). This weakened Labour's attempt to reform the institutional machinery of the state.

As a result, the much-debated changes to the central government machinery were often relatively insubstantive, even cosmetic. For example, the creation of the PMSU was an important development in strengthening core executive capability. The PMSU employed 60 officials at its peak, however, and was vastly outnumbered in capacity by the large delivery departments. There was no attempt to create a Prime Minister's Department, or a system of ministerial *cabinet*. While there was a reconfiguration of the centre, arguably most policy-making and implementation still occurred in departments, a claim that will be substantiated in subsequent chapters.

The evidence is that Labour consolidated changes which occurred under the Thatcher administration, strengthening the contractual nature of the 'public service bargain' between ministers and civil servants (van Dorpe & Horton, 2011). However, at no point after 1997 did ministers seek to fundamentally challenge the central assumptions of the Haldane model premised on a symbiotic relationship between politicians and civil servants. The regime based on 'serial monogamy' remained intact. With this in mind, it is necessary to consider how far the Westminster model acted as a constraint which blunted the impact of structural and institutional change in Whitehall.

The Labour Party and the British Parliamentary State

This chapter sought to characterise Labour's view of the political and administrative machinery of government, locating the party's historical approach to the state within the contours of the BPT. The penultimate section of the chapter summarises Labour's ambiguous attitude to the state and the party's willingness to adhere to an elitist model of governance.

Path Dependency and the Labour Tradition

Labour historically embraced a view of the Westminster model as impartial and unbiased, combining an acceptance of the constitutional status quo with limitless optimism about the state's capacity to reform the capitalist system. The leadership's aim was 'to establish Labour as a legitimate and responsible party of government through flexible and adaptive British institutions' (Richards et al., 2008: 9). Labour consolidated its position as a mainstream party in British politics through the Beveridge report, the National Health Service and a major extension of public ownership. Early twentieth-century Labour governments remained cautious about constitutional reform: 'They sought to capture the state, not to transform it' (Bogdanor, 2009: 40). Jones and Keating aver that Labour's conservatism was symptomatic of attitudes to the state within the British labour movement: 'Rooted in persistent and pervasive native traditions, political radicals in Britain exhibited a cautious conservatism in their dealings with the state, rarely confronting it and seeking incremental reform of its institutions' (1985: 10).

The Fabian tradition meant focusing pragmatically on the tasks the state should perform. Britain's institutions had stood the test of war and rapid societal change (Crosland, 1956; Crossman, 1972; Durbin, 1948; Wright, 1979). In *The Unprincipled Society*, Marquand (1988: 9) laments the party leadership's 'naive' approach to the state: 'The point of social democratic politics was to get back in the engine room and search for the levers.' Evans insists

Labour's approach 'rested on a centralist tradition in which strong executive government was viewed to be the key instrument of statecraft for achieving and promoting greater social equality' (2008: 3). Indeed, New Labour's strategy cannot be separated from long-standing scepticism about constitutional reform: 'Labour and Conservative governments have conspired in a High Tory approach to the constitution in praise of existing constitutional arrangements' (Evans, 2008: 3).

The Westminster Model: The Benefits of Incumbency

Consequently, Labour ministers were cautious about any fundamental challenge to the dominant institutions of the British state, holding out the prospect of substantial executive authority to the incumbent government. The party's election after 18 years in opposition reinforced the desire to gain control of the levers of power, reorganising the central machinery of the state: an 'accretive' process of strengthening the centre (Burch & Holliday, 2000). The Haldane model governing the relationship between ministers and civil servants legitimised the concentration of power at the centre. Ministers believed that the untrammelled control afforded by the Westminster model would bolster the government's ability to drive through and implement strategic reforms (Barber, 2007; Flinders, 2008; Lee, 2009; Riddell, 2006). The power residing with the incumbent administration should not be ceded to other actors in the policy process.

Preserving Elite and Top-down Government

Likewise, New Labour was determined to ensure that constitutional reform would not threaten the controlling capacities of the state (Evans, 2003). Labour's modernisation programme entailed devolution, freedom of information, the Human Rights Act, pluralist electoral systems, new mechanisms of representation in local government, and directly elected mayors (Flinders, 2010). In that regard, the BPT and the Westminster model provide the frame of reference conditioning the beliefs of actors. They functioned as 'the stem-cell of modern UK government' (Judge, 2006: 17). Flinders and Curry attest that Labour's approach did not shift the nature of British democracy but instead 'sought to apply different models at the periphery and the core: *bi-constitutionality*' (2008: 99). The dominant system remained 'executive hegemony', accompanied by limited autonomy and democratisation through reforms at the periphery. Bogdanor (2009) insists that Labour's reforms merely redistributed power *within* the political elite, prohibiting the development of a popular constitutional settlement. Cairney (2011) observes that the devolved Scottish administration has not developed a more participatory view of governance and democracy. Similarly, Mitchell (2009) argues that the Westminster model has remained pivotal in shaping the administrative machinery of Scottish government even after devolution.

The 'Comfort-blanket' of the Westminster Model

Above all, New Labour acknowledged that rejecting the BPT and the Westminster model was potentially dangerous for a party with only erratic experience of office. Labour had been in power since World War II for brief intervals: 1945–51, 1964–70, and 1974–9. The Conservatives dominated the political landscape as the natural party of government. Labour was under continuous pressure to affirm its credentials as a responsible governing party. The leadership was reluctant to invest resources in overhauling the established political system, where the Westminster model apparently suited its immediate need to deliver Labour's electoral promises. A neutral and technically competent civil service experienced in the Whitehall game provided a genial 'comfort-blanket' for newly appointed ministers (Richards, 2008: 53). The claim that Whitehall had been politicised over the previous 18 years was explicitly rejected (Powell, 2010).

The Triumph of Expertise

Finally, New Labour's approach emphasising the importance of bureaucratic expertise and 'evidence-based' policy-making was consistent with the elitist element of the BPT. The Fabian tradition of enlightened, technocratic proficiency reached its apotheosis during the 1964–70 Wilson government and re-emerged under New Labour (Moran, 2003). The rise of the expert reflected a shift in the progressive ideal, espousing a conviction that the nation's problems could be solved without the need for class struggle. It was, as Benedict Anderson describes, 'a vocabulary of bourgeois rationality calculated to appeal to both expert and egalitarian impulses' (cited in Moran, 2003: 86). A cadre of experts would take politics out of the policy process, creating a more efficient, ordered and harmonious society. The rise of neutral, value-free expertise allowed politicians to draw on specialised knowledge in an increasingly complex, technologically orientated society (Bevir, 2007; Moran, 2003). The claim to offer neutral advice 'uncontaminated' by ideological distortion was 'strongly associated with the rise of functionalist, elitist, and institutionalist theories of democracy in the early part of the twentieth century' (Bevir, 2007: 21). This was echoed in New Labour's commitment to elite governance, delegation and depoliticisation (Burnham, 2002; Flinders, 2008).

Conclusion: New Labour, Governance and Whitehall Reform

This chapter sought to historicise New Labour's conception of the state and the machinery of government within the context of the BPT, once again drawing attention to the relationship between institutions and ideas. The literature offers rich analytical insight into the changing nature and form of the British state, alongside Labour's role in shaping the machinery of government:

- The post-1997 constitutional reforms introduced important changes including devolution to power centres outside England and freedom of information, but they did not fundamentally threaten the Westminster model.
- New Labour's instinct was to work within the parameters of the BPT and the British parliamentary state. The party characteristically acted as a tenacious defender of the Westminster model, while safeguarding its asymmetric status within the policy-making system (Richards et al., 2008).
- This is testimony to the enduring role of the power-hoarding tradition within the BPT, shaping governmental institutions and processes. Such narratives enabled ministers and officials to justify their position, legitimating the concentration of power in the central state.
- This 'government down (to the people)' view was nonetheless under challenge: Labour's approach sought to address the needs of a rapidly changing society, while retaining control as the dominant actor at the apex of the central state. The paradox of the party's tradition is that New Labour sought to modernise Britain's institutions through central fiat, accompanied by a conditional willingness to devolve power. The party's reforms after 1997 pointed in varying directions implying 'both democracy and managerialism, the doctrine of individual rights and dirigisme, asymmetrical devolution and centralism' (Morgan, 2013: 76).
- Although the party leadership's embrace of orthodoxy appears inevitable in retrospect, the outcome was contingent on the strategic choices of actors. Labour's view of the state was neither unavoidable nor pre-determined, while an attitude of pessimism and ambivalence about the state was never entirely expunged from the party's DNA.

This volume is concerned with how Labour altered the political and administrative machinery of the state. New Labour's attitude to the state is shaped by competing values based on 'power-sharing' and 'power-hoarding', anchored in the dominant political tradition. The Labour Party's disparate, heterogenous tradition consists of competing elements: an 'English pluralist' view premised on 'liberal' values, outweighed by a commitment to the Westminster model and the centralised, unitary state. Moreover, successive attempts at institutional reform have entailed a dynamic conception of the role and transformative capacities of central government, combined with an implicit desire to maintain the traditional power-hoarding structures of the British state.

Chapters 1, 2 and 3 have been concerned with path dependency in the central institutions of the state. This illuminates an understanding of the dialectical and iterative relationship between continuity and change, structure and agency, and institutions and ideas. As such, Chapter 4 will consider a diverse literature which has sought to theorise change alongside continuity in Whitehall, drawing on a more sophisticated conception of structure and agency. The governance literature is associated with a path-breaking view of change in the central state machinery and the core executive. Such accounts emphasise the importance of structural change in the governing process, acknowledging that political leaders have sought to strengthen central steering capacity while rebuilding governance capability within the state (Peters, 2004). The literature addresses the multiplicity of institutions, power relations, policy networks and strategic actors implicated in the processes of contemporary governance.

CHAPTER 4

The Core Executive, Governance and Power

Looking at British government in terms of who has 'the' power or 'too much' power is productive only if more for one side means less for the other...we find that the primary fact of life is reciprocity. Virtually every point of potential conflict is also a point of unavoidable mutual dependence.

Heclo & Wildavsky (1981: 373)

This history of the core executive shows that features regarded as constituting and typifying the new phase of governance, as opposed to government, are not unique to the present or to the past twenty years. In fact, they have been a feature of the government machine for some time.

Marinetto (2003: 605)

There has been a longstanding tension in Britain between centralisation and fragmentation, or between the rival concepts of 'government' and 'governance'.

Lowe and Rollings (2000: 100)

Introduction

This chapter considers a voluminous literature theorising structural change alongside continuity in the political and administrative machinery of Whitehall and the core executive. The literature can be organised around a number of contrasting approaches. The Anglo-Governance School and Differentiated Polity Model emphasise structural *change*, focusing on the role of institutions and actors outside the central state in undermining the unitary nature and cohesiveness of the Westminster model. In contrast, core executive accounts and the Asymmetric Power Model underline the importance of structural *continuity*: the differentiated polity exaggerates the extent of decentralisation and the 'hollowing-out' of the state. The core executive retains central steering capacity; structural inequalities of power in the British state remain pre-eminent. Nonetheless, both the DPM and APM acknowledge that stability and change in the British polity are iterative, interactive and dialectical. More recent literature on strategic relational and meta-governance approaches has augmented these generic models of British politics.

The Anglo-governance school provides a substantive critique of the Westminster model and the BPT, depicting segmentation and fragmentation in the structures of the state (Bevir & Rhodes, 2006b; Marinetto, 2003). The claim that power is located within formal institutions at the interface between the prime minister and Cabinet is interrogated and unpacked. Governance theory[1] sought to reconceptualise the dominant approach of the Westminster model. The focus is how states respond to pressures associated with globalisation and modernity, enhancing their capacity to govern (Bell & Hindmoor, 2009). According to Lodge (2013: 5), 'Governance, in many ways, was supposed to have come to the rescue of the 1970s state in crisis.' This chapter examines contrasting approaches associated with the work of Bevir and Rhodes (2003, 2006a); Pierre and Peters (2004; 2000); Richards and Smith (2004); Burch and Holliday (2004); Jessop (2007); and Saward (1997).

Understanding continuity and change entails an analytically robust understanding of power, drawing on approaches conceptualising the diverse institutions and practices of British politics. The chapter considers the 'first wave' governance and hollowing-out literature highlighting discontinuity in the structures of the state. This is further advanced by the notion of a differentiated polity. Through a sympathetic critique of the DPM, the APM highlights continuity in the institutions of British governance. The asymmetric polity analyses the iterative and dialectical relationship between continuity and change, institutions and ideas, and structure and agency.

Having assessed the nature of governance and power, the chapter considers the interpretive critique of path dependency associated with Bevir and Rhodes. Strategic relational and meta-governance approaches offer an additional perspective on the dynamics of continuity and change in the central state. Finally, core executive accounts provide a cogent analysis of agency, structure and power, theorising continuity and change as interwoven and mutually reinforcing. The core executive approach sustains and underpins the subsequent analysis of Whitehall and the core executive undertaken in Chapters 5, 6 and 7.

Governance Narratives

The wide-ranging literature on governance attempts to explain the complex interrelationship between the changing nature of the state and society. The term 'governance' was coined by Sidney Low in 1904 having its origins in the Greek term for 'steering'. However, the concept of governance remains elusive and contested (Bell & Hindmoor, 2009; Flinders, 2002). American research in the 1950s and 1960s on the role of pressure groups and networks has been a key influence (Beer, 1965; Dahl, 1976; Finer, 1958). Governance concepts were further refined as markets became increasingly prevalent in the public sector: complexity and fragmentation meant that governments relied on other actors to achieve their goals (Bevir & Rhodes, 2003; Pierre & Peters, 2000; Rhodes, 1997). 'First wave' governance accounts emphasise discontinuity, questioning key precepts of the Westminster model. An increasingly disaggregated policy-making arena had transformed the nature of the governing process; there was no longer a unitary state characterised by a strong executive and parliamentary sovereignty. Indeed, several key themes recur across contrasting accounts of governance (Flinders, 2002):

- The concerns of the governance literature go beyond structures and institutional design, addressing the interaction between institutions and citizens.
- Governance relates to the *horizontal* distribution of power within the nation-state, as well as the *vertical* distribution of power across tiers of government.
- Governance offers a wider approach to understanding the policy-making process than the traditional focus on the core executive.
- While certain accounts stress that the state has remained the dominant actor, others insist that governments are in decline as the result of hollowing-out.

The Anglo-Governance school focuses on the hybrid combination of public, private and third sector agencies (Bevir, 2011; Marinetto, 2003; Rhodes, 1997). 'Actor-centred institutionalists' address the decision rules that structure the policy networks in which agents operate (Bevir, 2011; Kenis & Schneider, 1991). The hollowing-out and centre-less state literature emphasises the extent to which the state's powers have worn away, diminishing the core executive's role in the policy process (Jessop, 2007; Peters & Pierre, 2000; Rhodes, 1995; Richards, 2008). Alternative accounts examine governance in terms of the reconstituted state: while national governments confront complex, multidimensional challenges, nation-states enhance their capacity to govern and steer society. Central government deliberately fashions instruments of intervention that widen and extend its dominance, a key driver of the 'modernising government' agenda (Holliday, 2002; Marsh et al., 2001; Moran, 2003; Richards, 2008; Smith, 1999).

The Centre-less State Approach

It is important not to conflate the wide-ranging governance literature with empirical claims about the hollowing-out of the state. Rhodes as the progenitor

of the centre-less state claims that outsourcing, privatisation and agencification weaken the capacities of the central state: 'current trends erode the centre's
capacity to steer the system – its capacity for governance' (1994: 46). The
Westminster model which formed the centrepiece of British political science
was being comprehensively undermined and eroded. Since entering the EU,
power shifted 'upwards' to the supranational level, as well as 'sideways' and
'downwards' from central government to subsidiary bodies at the periphery.
The centralised, unitary state was ebbing away.

Rhodes contends that the attrition of the core executive and the unitary state
meant a segmented executive governing through disparate policy networks.
Governance theory seeks to understand the role of networks which have relative
autonomy from the state, incorporating a range of actors in the policy-making
process. Central government operates from 'a shrinking policy intervention
base' (Marinetto, 2003: 5), with diverse power centres allocating resources
through bargaining games outside the direct authority of the core executive.
The Westminster model is replaced by the managerial state as 'the informal
authority of networks supplants the formal authority of government' (Rhodes,
1997: 3).

This literature illuminates key challenges confronting contemporary states.
Governance narratives depict the struggle to deliver policy goals in an environment shaped by disorder and 'fragmentation' (Smith, 1998). The long-standing
debate about the 'presidentialisation' of British politics and 'prime-ministerial
predominance' is revealed as anachronistic (Heffernan, 2005; Smith, 1998).
The government no longer manages industries and enterprises: policy-making
is characterised by constant bargaining and negotiation between Whitehall
and non-governmental actors beyond the state (Hill, 2005; Lipsky, 1980).
Meanwhile, governments cease to take responsibility for directly providing public services. Commissioning and contracts specify the outcomes that
providers should achieve: an ethos of 'steering rather than rowing' (Osbourne
& Gaebler, 1990; Stoker, 2004).

The centre-less state has, nevertheless, endured criticism for overstating
institutional discontinuity. One group of critics affirm that central government remains the dominant actor (Holliday, 1997, 2000; Smith, 2009). The core
executive has significant power resources at its disposal, and there are more
personnel in strategic functions intervening to impose control over the policy
process. The centre in Number Ten and the Cabinet Office remains a prolific
actor. The 'first wave' governance literature emphasising the role of networks
(Bevir & Rhodes, 2003; Marinetto, 2003; Rhodes, 1994; 2005) concealed the
on-going effect of bureaucratic centralisation, augmented by New Labour's

imposition of a command-orientated operating code. There is no one-dimensional, unilinear shift denuding central government of control. The argument is that privatisation and NPM-led agencification made central government less overloaded and bureaucratic, creating a window of opportunity to enhance the central state's capacity and authority over the policy process.

The BPT and the Westminster model traditionally emphasised the importance of limited decentralisation to the periphery (Bulpitt, 1986; Greenleaf, 1983a; Judge, 1993). Rhodes exaggerates the extent of state fragmentation, giving insufficient attention to the historical evolution of the British state. Critics of hollowing-out question whether EU membership led to an inexorable drift of power from the nation-state (Gamble, 2003; Marsh et al., 2003). European integration enables Whitehall to consolidate its grip over the policy-making machinery: the Cabinet Office negotiates policy positions on draft directives in advance of negotiations with member-states (Bache & Flinders, 2004; Richards & Smith, 2002). This does not amount to a fundamental erosion of central executive authority.

The concept of a centre-less state relates to key themes in the literature, especially the impact of globalisation on the nation-state. This alludes to 'depoliticisation', where governments create 'arms-length' mechanisms to oversee economic and social institutions, protecting political actors from the consequences of unpopular decisions (Burnham, 2002; Flinders, 2002; Hay, 2002). However, empirical research questions whether the capacity of the state has eroded, entailing a shift from government to governance (Bell & Hindmoor, 2009; Fawcett, 2010). As such, the centre-less state addresses the changing balance of relationships within the state. The 'first wave' governance literature infers a single, pre-determined logic of modernisation: it is harder to discern the role of actors and institutions. The neglect of agency means little credence is given to the relationship between institutions and ideas. The ideas which inform and underpin governance practices are downplayed.

The Reconstituted State Approach

In responding to debates about hollowing-out, Peters (2004) insists that the restructuring of central governments had come 'full circle'. There is a growing emphasis among political leaders on rebuilding and enhancing governance capacity, illustrating how change reinforces underlying continuities. Political actors are anxious to demonstrate their capacity to exert authority, reasserting control without recreating Weberian hierarchy and centralisation. The claim of a centre-less state is undermined by the notion of a reconstituted state:

Although power has shifted from the parliamentary arena, the executive arena still retains significant and important resources. There is a continuing role for national leadership. Leadership may be more concerned with managing networks than simply directing, but leaders often have the legitimacy, and the electoral and parliamentary support, to take authoritative decisions and therefore to orient the policy direction of networks.

(Smith, 1999: 243)

Martin Smith argues that nation-states have faced constraints throughout their history. The evidence of fragmentation emerged in the 1940s and 1950s, and was hardly unique to Britain (Cronin, 1991; Lowe & Rollings, 2000; Marinetto, 2003). Governments in the 1950s and 1960s struggled to impose their own macro-economic policy regime in the face of increased exposure to the international political economy. The state has been 'reconstituted' rather than hollowed-out: Smith (2009) focuses on how states have sought to evolve new mechanisms of power. This entailed a shift from collective aggregates based on classes and interests, to overseeing and regulating individual behaviour. Similarly, Moran (2003) and Saward (2001) attest that actors respond to the threat of weakened state capacity by fashioning new governing instruments. The core executive makes strategic decisions about how to sustain its rule. Public management reforms strengthen the power of the centre by amassing administrative control; central government maintains authority over public sector agencies and resources.

Jessop (2007) provides an account of the reconstituted state based on structure, agency and power. Jessop observes that although the contemporary state is less centralising and dirigiste, it determines the rules of the game: controlling regulation and shaping the structures in which markets, networks and bureaucracies operate. Contemporary states retain the capacity to distribute authority and resources. While pluralists and Marxists view the state as a fixed institutional entity with its own bureaucratic purposes and interests, neo-Marxists conceive the state as determined by 'wider social relations': a strategic-relational conception of power. While the state has become 'less hierarchical, less centralised and less *dirigiste*', this does not 'exclude a continuing and central political role for national states' (Jessop, 2004: 66).

In assessing state power in the British polity, two further theoretical approaches contribute analytical substance to an understanding of continuity and change in Whitehall and the core executive, namely the Differentiated Polity Model and the Asymmetric Power Model (Gamble, 1990; Judge, 1993; Richards, 2008; Smith, 2008).

The Differentiated Polity Model

The concept of the differentiated polity draws on the notion of the centre-less state previously discussed, privileging change over stability and continuity. As Rhodes (1995) emphasises, the DPM has six distinguishing characteristics which underline the pluralistic and diverse nature of the British polity along-side the extent of institutional change (McAnulla, 2006: 35):

- *Intergovernmental relations*: an emphasis on governance rather than govern-ment in which the unitary state has withered away. There are a multiplicity of networked relationships involving public sector bodies, local and central government organisations, and private and voluntary sector actors.
- *Policy networks*: the policy process is predominantly structured around networks rather than markets or hierarchies. Networks link the core execu-tive with a host of external institutions and actors.
- *Governance rather than government*: actors outside the core executive perform a vital role in implementing policy. The process of decision-making involves exchanges between actors.
- *A hollowed-out state*: the state lost power 'upwards' through globalisation and the development of the European Union, and 'downwards' to agencies, the private sector and public sector agencies.
- *Power dependence*: policy actors depend on each other. The core execu-tive is characterised by exchange relations rather than compliance and subordination.
- *A segmented executive*: the prime minister and Number Ten have limited control over departments, ensuring the policy-making process is fluid and segmented.

The concept of a differentiated polity challenges the British Political Tradition and the Westminster model as an organising perspective, predicated on a unified, hierarchical state and an 'indivisible' notion of sovereignty. Rhodes' work on the differentiated polity in *Beyond Whitehall and Westminster* (1988) and *Decentralising the Civil Service* (Rhodes et al., 2003) examines changing patterns of governance. The latter addresses the lacuna in empirical studies of Whitehall emphasising 'a decentred approach (which) does not seek a general model of power in the core executive or the power of the prime minister. It offers narratives of the contingent relationships in the core executive' (Bevir and Rhodes, 2008: 733).

The DPM emphasises the fragmented nature of the contemporary polity, undermining the narrow precepts of the Westminster model. In so doing, the DPM draws on a neo-pluralist conception of power: British government is viewed as an oligarchic arena in which interest groups compete; power is scattered throughout. Rhodes adopts the pluralist position of scholars such as Lindblom (1984) and Middlemas (1979), acknowledging the importance of corporate power in influencing the policy process. The postwar state in Britain sought hands-on controls; this was no longer tenable in an era of globalisation creating a more segmented, fragmented policy-making arena. An operating code was required offering an alternative to habitual intervention by the centre (Rhodes, 1997).

A Critique of the Differentiated Polity Model

The DPM highlights the inadequacies of the top-down, Weberian model of the contemporary state. Indeed, Bevir and Rhodes have brought questions of state theory back into debates about the changing nature of contemporary governance by challenging the concept of social structures that irrevocably shape the actions and beliefs of individual agents. In contrast, critical realists have argued that the differentiated polity is anchored in pluralism and post-structuralism, ignoring the impact of hierarchy, inequality and asymmetries of power (Marsh et al., 2003). The DPM underpins the alleged pluralism of the British political system, reinforcing its tendency to neglect inequalities in the distribution of power. In foreseeing an exchange of resources and bargaining games between mutually dependent agents, the DPM's neo-pluralist perspective ignores the asymmetrical nature of power. Like earlier pluralists such as Birch and Beer, the differentiated polity fails to address the elitist and top-down nature of British democracy (Marsh & Hall, 2007; McAnulla, 2006).

Rhodes (1997) (later Bevir & Rhodes, 2003, 2006b) insists that aggregate concepts should be decentred, exploring the beliefs and practices that shape actors' behaviour. Individual attitudes and preferences are not pre-determined and unchanging, but develop against the background of tradition in reaction to dilemmas (Bevir & Rhodes, 2003, 2006; Rhodes, 2007). The approach of Bevir and Rhodes yields valuable insights, and the attempt to deconstruct the traditions on which agents draw is innovative (Elgie, 2011; Hay, 2011). Bevir and Rhodes (2010: 26) attest:

> Policy cultures are sites of struggles not just between strategic elites, but between all kinds of actors with different views and ideals reached against the background of different traditions. Subordinate actors can resist the intentions and policies of elites by consuming them in ways that draw on their local traditions and their local reasoning.

In addition, Annesley and Gains (2010) have drawn attention to the preponderance of unequal power relationships in the core executive: policy-making involves a closed hierarchy rather than diverse networks of actors. Governments are influenced by social and economic forces conditioning the dynamics of power within the state. For instance, the balance between the parliamentary and industrial wings of the Labour Party is shaped by the performance of the economy. In the context of full employment and rising living standards, the trade unions assert their bargaining power, forcing the parliamentary leadership to address their demands (Tant, 1993). The balance of power is distinct from one of crisis and retrenchment where the bargaining position of the working class is markedly weakened. This emphasises that while power is positional, it is also context-dependent. The notion of 'situated agency' underpins a 'decentred theory of governance': institutions and practices cannot determine how individuals act. Instead, action is always based on contingency, uncertainty and choice (Bevir & Rhodes, 2003). The DPM obscures the structural context of the parliamentary state, however, particularly the relationship between capital, labour and the political economy.

At the core of the differentiated polity is an empirical claim that the BPT and the Westminster model are anachronistic. As an organising perspective, the Westminster model has obvious limitations, promoting misleading assumptions about the British political system such as the view that power is hermetically sealed within the central state. However, the normative precepts of the Westminster model continue to influence how actors think and behave (Flinders, 2010; Marsh et al., 2001; Richards, 2008). The DPM understates how power relations reinforce the elitist dimensions of the BPT. There is little consideration of institutional continuity and path dependency. Chapter 3 highlighted that Labour was determined to defend the Westminster model, based on the notion of strong, decisive government and majoritarian democracy (Flinders, 2010; Marquand, 2008; McAnulla, 2006; Richards, 2008). The DPM exaggerates how far the British state has been fragmented and hollowed-out. As McAnulla (2006: 42) remarks:

> The DPM fails to account for on-going processes of centralisation, rather than fragmentation. It is argued that successive governments have actually enhanced the scope and range of central government power over the policy process [...] the notion of 'governing without government' displays a 'fatal conceit'.

The task of governing has undoubtedly grown more complex over the last fifty years (Gamble, 2006; Hay, 1996; Sorenson, 2004). Even so, it is premature to claim the death of the unitary state and the normative conception of power implicit in the BPT and Westminster model.

The Asymmetric Power Model

The APM arises out of the DPM literature, positing an alternative set of assumptions about the British political system, while emphasising the importance of continuity alongside change. In *Changing Patterns of Governance* (2001), Marsh, Richards and Smith examine the interaction between ministers and civil servants within departments, revealing that the traditional Whitehall paradigm has remained cohesive and substantially intact.

The APM emphasises the narrow, elitist and centralising nature of British democracy. As a model of asymmetrical power relations, politicians and officials operate within narratives of the BPT inscribed into the Whitehall culture and rules of the game (Judge, 1993; Marsh & Tant, 1991; Marsh et al., 2001). There is a dominant tradition in which institutions and ideas reflect, and reinforce, an elitist and top-down system of government. Any conception of British politics drawing wholly on the traditional Westminster model is unsatisfactory. The view of the state as neutral between competing interests is challenged by Marxism and post-structuralism (Miliband, 1972). The focus on Westminster and Parliament disregards other aspects of the state system, notably the security and intelligence services, the armed forces and the media (Middlemas, 1979).

The APM seeks to go beyond the Westminster model, identifying five core characteristics of the British polity. These encompass material and ideational components, alluding to underlying continuities in political institutions (Marsh et al., 2003; McAnulla, 2006: 43):

- *Structural inequality*: British politics does not operate on a 'level playing field' among a plurality of agents and interests. The institutional practices of British government are conditioned by broader patterns of inequality in British society, determining who controls the policy agenda.
- *The British Political Tradition*: emphasising strong and decisive government, the BPT stresses a top-down view of British democracy characterised by a belief that 'central government knows best'.
- *Asymmetries of power*: the balance of power between government and other actors is 'asymmetrical'. The state has access to authority, bureaucracy and resources unavailable to other participants in the policy-making process.

- *A limited pattern of external constraint*: the British state has significant autonomy and freedom of manoeuvre, despite the constraints imposed by global interdependence.
- *A strong, segmented executive*: there is no unified executive, but power is inevitably concentrated in the central institutions of the state. Departments remain structurally powerful, relatively autonomous from the centre in Whitehall.

The APM draws attention to the state's capacities and the emergence of a reconstituted state (Bevir & Rhodes, 2003; Peters, 2004; Pierre, 2000). In so doing, the model does not privilege continuity over change, but emphasises the essentially dialectical relationship between stability and discontinuity. The British state has adapted and responded to a range of domestic and external forces, enhancing its capacities to govern contemporary society (Holliday, 2000; Richards & Smith, 2002; Saward, 1997). While the state has shifted from provider to commissioner, it has performed an increasingly activist role following the post-2008 crisis (Flinders, 2010; Gamble, 2009; Lodge, 2013; Osbourne & Gaebler, 1990; Stoker, 2004; Thompson, 2010). Central government develops 'new forms of intervention to sustain its position as the dominant actor in the policy making arena' (Richards, 2008: 98). The elitist governing code epitomised by the BPT is entrenched: the British polity is characterised and shaped by structural inequality. The APM is important in challenging the implicitly pluralist assumptions of the differentiated polity, where power is merely dispersed among a range of institutions and actors.

A Critique of the Asymmetric Power Model

While the APM provides valuable insights, it is not above criticism. The APM emphasises asymmetries of power and the continuing strength of dominant actors within the British polity (Heffernan, 2006; Marsh & Hall, 2007). There is a danger, however, that highlighting the structural power of actors merely reimposes the anachronistic dualisms that informed the earlier literature such as the 'prime-ministerial' versus 'Cabinet' government debate. The APM exposes weaknesses in differentiated polity accounts, highlighting the significance of the BPT as a conception of British democracy widely shared among agents. Nevertheless, the APM literature does not give sufficient attention to the 'structurally selective' environment in which agents operate. While policy agendas compete to win influence within the state, particular ideas are able to attain structural dominance (Hay, 2002; Jessop, 1996). For example, the interests of financial capital have long predominated over manufacturing industry in the conduct of British economic policy. According to Jessop (1999: 12), the structurally selective nature of policy-making necessitates:

> Examining how a given structure may privilege some actors, some identities, some strategies, some spatial and temporal horizons, some actions over others; and the ways, if any, in which actors (individual and/or collective) take account of this differential privileging through 'strategic-context' analysis when choosing a course of action.

While the APM highlights asymmetries of power, it lacks an understanding of what creates and reproduces inequality in the political system. Like the mainstream literature on Whitehall, there is no encompassing theoretical account of the state. It is important to examine the range of mechanisms by which states wield power such as legislation, regulation, resources and surveillance, as well as ideological power (Miliband, 1972; Smith, 2009). The empirical background to the APM is the Thatcher and Major governments, and the early years of the Blair administration. The model should be updated in the light of subsequent developments: the expansion of the regulatory state and the profusion of auditing and inspection bodies, altering how power is organised within the UK political system (Flinders, 2008; McAnulla, 2006; Moran, 2003). The APM presents a static view of the state giving too little attention to evolution and adaptation, where elements of Whitehall reform are bolted onto the traditional constitutional model in an ad hoc, piecemeal, and arbitrary fashion.

The Literature on the Strategic Relational Approach

The DPM and the APM provide important insights defining the strategic context in which actors and institutions operate; however, core assumptions about continuity and change are still under-developed. British central government is an environment where power is hierarchical and resources are distributed asymmetrically, but outcomes are contingent and actors make choices about the tactics and strategies they follow (Smith, 1999).

Drawing on the DPM and APM, strategic relational and meta-governance accounts offer a complementary approach to analysing continuity and change in the core executive. The literature addresses the structural environment in which actors operate: particularly the institutions, ideas and processes that shape central state power (Fawcett, 2011; Hay, 2002; Heffernan, 2003). The focus of strategic relational approaches is how agents negotiate structures in order to achieve outcomes (Hay, 1996). This acknowledges the role of asymmetries of power without conceiving outcomes as pre-determined. According to Hay, 'the state constitutes an uneven playing field privileging some forces and interests while proving less accessible to others' (1996: 7). This makes the process and *modus operandi* of the state amenable to distinctive strategies and mechanisms of power.

Jessop characterises 'the trends and counter-trends in state restructuring', where destatisation is countered by an emphasis on the enhanced capacity of the state to operate through 'meta-governance': 'the governing of governance' (Fawcett, 2011; Jessop, 1999: 210). Those tendencies in the policy-making process which relocate power to institutions and actors outside the central state are countered by the centralising force of the core executive. This analytical framework underlines the importance of particular modes of governing, principally hierarchies, markets and networks. Policy making and implementation involve an intricate combination of markets, networks and hierarchies which are adopted in the light of governance challenges, overseen by the central state (Fawcett, 2011; Jessop, 2007). Meta-governance emphasises the extent to which government remains stratified and hierarchical, as power resources are rarely distributed evenly among key actors (Heffernan & Webb, 2005; Jessop, 1999).

As such, action occurs within a context where the interests of certain institutions and actors are privileged. The structured context of the British state and the core executive is 'an unevenly contoured terrain' (Hay, 2002: 128). This does not pre-determine political outcomes: it means particular strategies have a greater likelihood of success; agents have the capacity to alleviate structural constraints, drawing on strategic knowledge of their situation. For example, the likelihood of industrial action against the government succeeding will depend on the condition of the economy, the legislative framework determining strike action, the governing party's electoral popularity, the current supply of raw materials and so on. As such, outcomes in politics are always contingent and uncertain. This highlights 'the complex interplay of intentions and constraints' in the British polity, transcending the dualism of structure and agency (Johnson, 1998: 11; Hay, 1996). The notion of structured context and the strategic relational approach captures the interactive and mutually dependent relationship between structure and agency.

This account of 'strategic selectivity' is augmented by Giddens' notion of structuration in which structures are posited as both enabling and constraining agents (Hay, 2002; Giddens, 1984; Johnston, 1998). Structures restrain action: at the same time, structures provide resources through which outcomes are achieved. Jessop (1999) and Hay (1996) insist that agents consider their position strategically and adopt a set of tactics to achieve their goals. In Jessop's writings, 'structure' and 'agency' are treated as purely analytical concepts which are, in practice, inseparable. Reflexive actors reproduce structures 'in a constant interplay of rule-following and rule-creating' (Tucker, 1998: 81). Peterson (1983) avers: 'There is no social action without structures, but also no structures without social action, because only the routine, day-to-day enactment of the latter constantly reproduces the structures.' He continues:

> Analysing the structuration of social systems means studying the modes in which such systems, grounded in the knowledgeable activities of situated actors who draw upon rules and resources in the diversity of action contexts, are produced and reproduced in interaction.
>
> (Peterson, 1983)

Agents are neither entirely free to pursue their goals, nor are actions structurally pre-determined. There is an affinity between structuration theory and historical institutionalism, emphasising how 'structures conflict so as to privilege some interests while demobilising others' (Hall and Taylor, 2001: 937). Hall and Taylor explore how institutions, 'distribute power unevenly giving some groups or interests disproportionate power through access to the decision-making process' (2001: 941). While structuration theory may be regarded as a sociological truism, the literature examines how the BPT modifies the choices and actions of agents, shaping patterns of continuity and change in the British state (Giddens, 1984; Hay, 1996; Smith, 1999).

The point to emphasise is that actors and ideas do not operate on a level playing field. Instead, the resonance of ideas among actors is asymmetrical and shaped by material constraints. The BPT is hard-wired into the institutions and practices of UK central government (Hay, 2002; Marsh, 2008). Of course, outcomes are never pre-ordained, nor do structures persist indefinitely. Heffernan (2003: 1), for example, emphasises the fluidity of power:

> The more resources, the more powerful and predominant the prime minister is; the fewer resources, the less powerful and predominant they are. Such resources are necessarily transient, being accumulated and inevitably dispersed, acquired and lost, and are never permanent. When possessed, they can grant the prime minister considerable, if never overwhelming, intra-executive authority and influence, and the opportunity to be a stronger, but not the only element within the core executive.

Jessop (2005) emphasises that it is not the state that has the capacity to act, but ministers and officials operating within a structured context. The issue is what governance regimes and instruments are used in particular strategic circumstances. The structured context approach underlines that resources do not confer institutional and ideological power in and of themselves. Power is dependent on how skilfully and effectively actors deploy resources. This point is highlighted by Jessop (2004: 52) who argues government and governance exist in 'dialectical tension', emphasising various facets of state authority:

> The forms of intervention associated with the state and statecraft are not confined to imperative co-ordination, that is, centralised planning or top-down intervention. Paraphrasing Gramsci who analysed the state apparatus in its inclusive sense as 'political society + civil society' and saw state power as involving 'hegemony armoured by coercion', we could also describe the state apparatus as based on 'government + governance' and as exercising 'governance in the shadow of hierarchy'.

This relates to the complexity of the state as an institutional and ideological formation, alongside the extensive and varied literature on state theory (Hay, 1996; Jessop, 2007; Lister & Marsh, 2006; Skinner, 1978; Tilly, 1975). As Moran (2003) attests, the state is comprised of a series of regulating bodies and agencies operating within a hybrid public sector. The state is 'an assemblage of more-or-less centrally co-ordinated apparatuses, institutions and practices' (Hay, 1996: 11).

A Critique of the Structured Context Literature

The strategic relational and structured context approach alludes to the co-existence of government and governance 'in a dynamic and iterative relationship with one another' (Fawcett, 2011: 8). The literature on strategy and structured context alters the terms of debate about the nature of the state: the focus is how particular strategies which take into account the nature of the political environment and the interests within it are more likely to be rewarded than others; however, outcomes are neither pre-structured nor foreordained. As the next chapter will demonstrate, the Department of Trade and Industry has always been amenable to market-orientated, liberal free trade policies. This does not infer that protectionist policies towards British industry will never be adopted. Nonetheless, the manufacturing sector has traditionally faced an uphill struggle in securing its interests within the British state (Grant, 2003).

It may be the case that strategic relational and structured context approaches 'are less innovative' than they initially appear (Elgie, 2011: 72). The inference of the literature on structured context is that change is ubiquitous. For example, Jessop and Hay imply that the institutional context of British government is ever changing: actors use strategic knowledge and resources to modify their environment. However, strategic relational approaches fail to address whether actors have the capacity to internalise constraints: rather than altering their structural context, agents may respond by transforming their own identity and interests to conform to the structural environment in which they operate (Johnson, 1998).

For example, Chapter 3 demonstrated that the post-1918 Labour Party viewed the British state as broadly enabling. However, the British constitution meant the party was compelled to operate on terrain which it found less advantageous than its opponents. Labour ministers absorbed the structural context of the state redefining their role as actors, rather than using an alternative body of ideas – such as syndicalism and Guild Socialism – to reconstitute the state. McAnulla insists that an agent's 'reflection of particular conditions will crucially depend on their understanding, construction and interpretation of a given context' (1998: 11). Actors achieve their aims within pre-determined institutional settings (Johnson, 1998).

Despite these limitations, the APM and structured context approach enrich our understanding of Whitehall, governance and power, offering a coherent conceptualisation of structure and agency. While the APM anchored structural change within the BPT, structured context accounts offer a nuanced conceptualisation of the British political system, highlighting continuity alongside change (Hall & Taylor, 2001; Hay, 2002; McAnulla, 2006; Richards & Smith, 2002; Weir & Skocpol, 1985). The 'strategic relational' view of power is especially adept at interpreting the interaction between the centre and departments, alongside ministers, civil servants and political aides which will be explored in subsequent chapters. Power, as ever, is fluid, diffuse, amorphous and multi-faceted.

The Core Executive Literature

In analysing the nature of continuity and change in the administrative machinery of government and the core executive, it is necessary to develop a coherent conception of structure, agency and power. Having examined the broader context of governance and power within the differentiated and asymmetric polity, the chapter turns to the core executive literature, providing a systematic framework for analysing the central state (Dunleavy & Rhodes, 1990; Smith, 1999).

The origins of core executive analysis are found in Benson's 'resource dependency' approach and Dunleavy's model of 'bureau-shaping'. Benson (1975) alongside Yutchtman and Seashore (1967) emphasised that actors in the policy-making arena were unable to achieve their goals without assistance and resources from other institutions and agents. The policy-making process is characterised by resource dependencies and bargaining games between various institutions and actors. Madgwick (1991) defined the concept of the 'central executive territory', denoting changing relationships, structures, contexts and policy actors within the central state.

The power dependency model exposes the limitations of zero-sum conceptions of power, where a single actor is able to subordinate others. Each actor has access to resources which they exchange, but no agent or institution has the monopoly over authority and control (Benson, 1975; Burch & Holliday, 1996; Smith, 1999; Yutchman & Seashore, 1967). There is not a straightforward dichotomy where actors in Whitehall either gain resources or are defeated by other institutions and agents: success is always dependent on the choice of tactics and strategies (Rhodes, 1995; Smith, 1999).

In the core executive, power is both positional and contingent having multiple origins and affects. In contrast to the Westminster model, power is everywhere rather than concealed and fixed within one particular institution in the central state. This draws on Foucault's post-foundational conception of power and knowledge. Foucault insists that knowledge and discourse are of central importance in constituting the state. The nexus of 'power/knowledge' defines the parameters between state and civil society, as well as the nature of political institutions. As such, 'power is not conceived as a stable and fixed entity that could be stored at particular institutional sites but signifies the result of a mobile and flexible interactional and associational network' (Lemke, 2007: 13). Prime ministers, the Cabinet and officials are immersed in structures of mutual dependency shaped by the formal and informal rules of the Whitehall game.

The most distinctive variant of the core executive literature is 'public choice' accounts, offering a particular view of how power operates within the public bureaucracy. The 'bureau-shaping' model goes beyond the mainstream literature on Whitehall explored in Chapter 1 (Dunleavy, 1991; Dunleavy & Rhodes, 1990; Rhodes, 1995). In *Democracy, Bureaucracy and Public Choice* (1991), Dunleavy examines the architecture of the state, concluding that self-interested bureaucrats restructure their departments as staff agencies, preserving their proximity to power and protecting their functions from Treasury-imposed austerity.

Disarmingly, Dunleavy concludes that rationally motivated civil servants are not primarily interested in the size of programme budgets, as public choice theorists had claimed (Becker, 1992; Buchanan, 1986; Niskanen, 1971). The priority is maximising utility from the routine tasks of public administration. Officials prefer to operate in slimmed-down 'elite agencies', rather than large-scale bureaucratic organisations where the burden of routine management is disproportionately high. Dunleavy insists that the task of submitting policy advice is highly valued by civil servants: 'It involves innovation and often entails working in small staff units in close proximity to political power sources' (1991: 202). Officials prioritise agencification, 'off-loading' burdensome management tasks to public bodies outside the central state. Dunleavy (1991: 203–4) attests:

> Collective bureau-shaping strategies are likely to be pursued to shape organisations by a variety of means including major internal reorganisations to promote policy work over routine activities, transformations of internal work practices, redefinition of relations with external partners to enhance policy contacts, competition with other bureaux to protect the scope of interesting work, load shedding, hiving off and contracting out functions which are seen as undesirable.

This is an agency-centred analysis where civil servants behave according to models of bureau maximisation enhancing their status and power. Dunleavy's account helps to rectify omissions in the literature informed by a zero-sum view of power, challenging public choice theorists such as Niskanen (1971) who depict public servants as motivated by a rational choice ontology. The focus is the fluidity of power and how resources are shared among actors and institutions (Dunleavy & Rhodes, 1990; Smith, 1999). James (2003) draws on bureau-shaping models, demonstrating that officials prefer policy work over routine management, 'hiving off' mundane activities to non-departmental public bodies.

Nonetheless, the politicised context of Whitehall is absent from Dunleavy's analysis; as a result, his account has received some criticism (Bevir & Rhodes, 2006b; Marsh et al., 2003). The bureau-shaping model pays insufficient attention to the strategic context in which officials operate. Their ability to alter management and policy-making routines is inevitably constrained, not least by ministers. Rational choice theorists criticise Dunleavy for ignoring the role of political actors. The claim that civil servants prefer policy advice to operational management has not been sustained by subsequent research (Dowding and James, 2004). Dunleavy's analysis assumes particular intentions and preferences, rather than providing a systematic account of change. What is more, the concept of power is under-theorised.

The core executive literature demonstrates that agents are influenced by the structural environment in which they operate, retaining the capacity to influence and modify structures: the core premise of structuration theory (Giddens, 1984). In analysing the core executive, Smith (1999) draws on distinct conceptions of agency, structure and power. Actors within the core executive confront structures which are reproduced through human agency and are constantly modified. Structures condition agency, defining the range of plausible strategies that can be adopted. Agents are strategically calculating actors whose approach is shaped by their structural context. Power operates through resource exchange; the focus is not 'who dominates who, but the nature of the interaction between ministers and civil servants based on the roles and resources of each' (Smith, 1999: 187). This goes beyond zero-sum conceptions of power, enabling continuity and change in the central state to be elaborated. Table 4.1 illustrates contrasting interpretations in the literature on the contemporary state and core executive.

TABLE 4.1   Contrasting narratives of governance

	Governance Narrative I	Governance Narrative II
Literature	'Differentiated state' (Bevir & Rhodes, 2006b; Rhodes, 1994)	'Reconstituted state' (Burch & Holliday, 2004; Marsh et al., 2001)
Policy making arena	Multiple actors operating across policy terrains	Multiple actors operating across policy terrains
Conception of state power	Neo-pluralist based on oligopoly in the political marketplace	Concentrated and elitist conception of British democracy
Core executive	Power of the core executive fundamentally eroded	Core executive strengthened as actors respond strategically to process of state transformation

Source: Richards (2008: 87)

Conclusion

The chapters so far have enumerated the theoretical framework on which this book is premised. Chapter 1 developed an explanation for institutional path dependency building on the BPT literature, making the argument that there is a dominant tradition in British politics. Within the BPT, power is exercised through norms and beliefs that are held to be legitimate by ministers and officials, sustaining the core precepts of the Westminster Model and the Whitehall paradigm. The asymmetry of power reinforces the tendency towards stability and inertia in Whitehall and the core executive examined in Chapter 2. Chapter 3 expanded this approach in the context of the Labour Party's development, examining the party's absorption within the BPT. In the 1990s, a novel approach to governance was enunciated through the conception of modernised social democracy and the Third Way. It is clear that New Labour continued to operate within the parameters of the dominant political tradition, however, remaining firmly attached to the Whitehall model.

Chapter 4 addressed the governance literature alluding to path-breaking change in the structure and processes of the state, alongside subsequent accounts of the core executive which sought to capture the dialectical relationship between continuity and change. While particular elements of the Whitehall paradigm have adapted and evolved, other institutional precepts appear relatively fixed across time. This alludes to the core paradox of New Labour: key institutions in the British state, notably the constitution, the civil service and the core executive have been reformed, but without surrendering the central levers afforded by the traditional 'power-hoarding' model. As such, the chapter contends:

- The lack of attention to the complexity of continuity and change leads to impoverished assumptions about the structure of the central state machine. Empirical research needs to treat continuity and change as a duality, as iterative and dialectical, rather than a dualism (Hall, 2011).
- Governance accounts emphasise the fragmentation of the contemporary state and the anachronistic claims of the Westminster model, underpinned by a dynamic, path-breaking conception of change. Even so, political actors have sought to reconstitute their capacity to govern from the centre.
- The DPM and APM have offered conceptual insight. However, there are few empirical studies of the interaction between central units and departments which have informed the theoretical analysis of the contemporary British state.
- The core executive approach depicts 'resource-rich' agents influenced by the institutional settings in which they operate, but retaining their capacity to shape and modify structures.
- The rationale for institution-building in Number Ten has rarely been addressed. The analysis of structural change has more often focused on Blair's first term. The later period is neglected, including the extent of continuity between the Blair and Brown administrations.

To analyse and assess these claims, subsequent chapters address key research questions arising from the core executive framework. These accounts examine how institutions and actors within the central state are bound together by structures of dependency and resource exchange. The study addresses the interaction between institutions and ideas, alongside competing doctrines within the British polity: the 'liberal' view of 'representation' and the conception of strong, 'responsible' government comprising the BPT outlined in Chapter 1.

This provides an organising perspective addressing the changing political and administrative machinery of the state, a theoretical approach which assesses the dynamics of continuity and change. The focus is the nature and contingency of New Labour's statecraft and its approach to the central executive territory of the state.

As such, it is necessary to examine the structural relationships which shape the attitudes and actions of agents. As Bulpitt (1983) reflects, governance is a latent structure whose content should be interpreted through the ideas, language and behaviour of actors engaged in the context of political action and power. Chapter 5 will outline the case studies of policy-making in academy schools, Family-Nurse Partnerships and the National Economic Council, while Chapter 6 addresses the 'hidden wiring' of the core executive and examines the changing role of the centre and departments in Whitehall. Chapter 7, in turn, analyses key developments within the British state during the New Labour years, notably the pluralisation and politicisation of the policy process. In so doing, this study draws together a body of theory on governing Britain with how politics and policy-making operate in practice.

Part II
The Practice of Governing Britain

CHAPTER 5

Mapping the Case Studies of the 'Primeval Policy Soup'

There are some people in government who do not think we are very good, who think we are an obstacle […] One of the things which I don't think ministers understand sufficiently clearly is that [the civil service] is a fantastically loyal institution. I always compare it to a rather stupid dog that wants to do whatever its master wants and, above all, wants to be loved for doing it. I don't think ministers understand that.

Mottram (cited in Watt, 2002)

While many ideas float around in this policy primeval soup, the ones that last, as in a natural selection system, meet some criteria. Some ideas survive and prosper; some proposals are taken more seriously than others.

Kingdon (1984: 60)

Introduction

This book examines the changing nature of power, governance and the state by addressing core empirical themes relating to Whitehall reform and the core executive: how far did the centre displace departments in the policy-making process? What was the extent of continuity and change in relation to key trends such as politicisation and pluralisation? To what degree are contemporary governance practices shaped by the British Political Tradition (BPT)? The theoretical and methodological approach is underpinned by a wide-ranging literature based on 'classical' and 'critical' interpretations of the BPT, alongside core executive accounts underpinned by a critical realist epistemology addressing the nature of power, and the dialectical relationship between structure and agency. The purpose is to examine the role of actors and the ideas underpinning governing institutions and practices in the Whitehall model.

The chapter will outline the strategic context of the case studies which inform this analysis, and the assessment of continuity and change in Whitehall and the core executive. The starting point is not a descriptive analysis of the centre and departments, but how ministers and officials understand, interpret and implement policy. The chapter will consider the extent to which ideas matter in the policy-making process, and how actors at the centre of the state sought to regain control over the governance of public policy. The case studies of Academy Schools, Family-Nurse Partnerships (FNPs), and the National Economic Council (NEC) reveal a 'primeval policy soup' in which numerous issues and agendas float around the policy process: policy-making is haphazard and cannot be easily controlled. This depiction of the case studies will contextualise the subsequent analysis of power relations between the centre and departments undertaken in Chapters 6 and 7.

Mapping the Case Studies: Structural Context

The case studies address key New Labour reforms, namely academy schools, FNPs and the NEC. The cases are atypical given that each has been subject to a high level of intervention from Number Ten; most policy is decided in departments about which the centre is, more often than not, unaware. The case studies demonstrate that even where the centre does intervene, however, departments retain their relative autonomy in the policy process. In the following section, the structural and institutional background to the case studies is examined. New Labour's statecraft rested on its claim to modernise and transform the public sector and public services, enhancing the capacity and authority of the central state (Bell & Hindmoor, 2009; Blair, 2010; Powell, 2010; Riddell, 2006). Labour under Blair and Brown sought to adapt and reshape the centre of the state, reforming the British model of political economy for an age of global competitiveness (Moran, 2003). The party had a state-led programme to modernise British society and the polity: a common thread running throughout the case studies.

As such, academy schools were totemic of New Labour's public service reform agenda, in which Blair particularly invested enormous political capital. FNPs never had significant political profile, but were a vivid demonstration of New Labour's commitment to technocratic policy programmes addressing the challenge of entrenched inter-generational disadvantage. The NEC was an institutional innovation designed to achieve stronger co-ordination across departments in Whitehall, pulling the levers of the state and enabling the United Kingdom to overcome the economic consequences of the post-2008 financial crisis.

Academy Schools (2000–7)

Academies were the fulcrum of Labour's reform strategy after 1997. The party's approach acknowledged that expectations of state services had risen exponentially since World War II; more had to be done to satisfy the electorate's aspirations (Barber, 1997; Glennerster, 2006; Le Grand, 2005). Under the Conservatives between 1979 and 1997, education spending had been frozen, declining over time as a proportion of GDP. In the first two years under Labour, education spending rose by 2 per cent in real terms, higher than the 1979–97 average of 1.5 per cent: throughout the first term, spending increased by 3.6 per cent. After 2001, it rose by 5.6 per cent per annum, appearing generous relative to the Conservative legacy (Chowdry et al., 2010; McCaig, 2001).

New Labour outlined its commitment to achieving a step-change in performance in the 1997 manifesto:

> With Labour, the Department for Education and Employment will become a leading office of state. It will give a strong and consistent lead to help raise standards in every school. Standards, more than structures, are the key to success.
>
> (Labour Party, 1997)

The New Labour government argued that additional spending should be accompanied by strategies for school improvement, consistent with the aim of transforming the educational landscape and bringing pedagogy under political control (Barber, 2007; Blair, 2010; Rawnsley, 2006; Seldon, 2005). After 1997, Education Action Zones (EAZs) were created replacing 'failing' school managers and local authorities, encouraging private sector engagement in state education (Labour Party, 1997; Smithers, 2001). However, there were concerns that secondary schools were not improving fast enough: additional resources had not led to improvements in outcomes. According to the Institute for Fiscal Studies:

> National school test results have improved under Labour across all age groups. However, these improvements have not been as fast as the government hoped, with numerous national targets being set and subsequently missed.
>
> (Chowdry et al., 2010)

Institutional reform was initially rejected in favour of the 'standards agenda' including interventions such as the literacy and numeracy strategy, but Labour eventually turned its attention to school structures. The aim was to reinvent the comprehensive system (Adonis, 2012; Barber, 2007; Blair, 2010; Riddell, 2006). The Prime Minister was increasingly held accountable for performance as a mark of leadership competence, realising that institutional reforms had to go much further than was envisaged before 1997. By 2000, the City Academy model in secondary education had been developed as a manifestation of the reform imperative (Adonis, 2012; Barber, 2007; Powell, 2010; Rawnsley, 2006; Seldon, 2005).

Labour's intention was that academies should transform secondary school performance, especially in disadvantaged areas (Adonis, 2012; Barber, 2007). Academies would be nominally independent of local administrative control, while remaining within the state system. Schools required sponsorship in which private and third sector bodies contributed £2 million, alongside £27 million from central government (Ball, 2009). Anastasia De Waal from the thinktank Civitas attests: 'The academies programme under New Labour was about inner-city children and improving life-chances in inner-city areas.'[1] The first academy opened in 2002: provider chains were then established, including the United Learning Trust and Harris, managing up to a dozen schools.[2] By May 2010, 203 academies had opened with a target of 400 by 2015 (Blair, 2010; Chowdry et al., 2010; Labour Party, 2010).

Academy schools were formally created in the Learning and Skills Act (2000); their freedoms were subsequently extended in the Education Act (2002). Nonetheless, there was significant opposition to academies within the teaching profession, local authorities, the parliamentary party and among Blair's ministers, notably the deputy prime minister, John Prescott (Seldon, 2006). New Labour was battling to reconcile structural forces shaping the electorate's increasingly individualist aspirations with the collectivist instincts of social democracy (Prabhakar, 2004). The party remained committed to an ethos of social equality enshrined in postwar comprehensive education (Leonard, 1997). However, Labour was forced to acknowledge the growing importance of parental aspirations (Alexander, 1997; Gould, 1996; McCaig, 2001). Blair's government was convinced that education standards were now a 'valance issue' in the minds of voters. Moreover, human capital acquisition was positioned as the key to global competitiveness within New Labour's ideological lexicon.

Academies were viewed suspiciously by many in the party, since they explicitly drew on the experience of the previous Conservative administration (Adonis, 2012). Nonetheless, the structure and organisation of institutions are often shaped by the strategic choices of their predecessors (Hall, 1985). Historically, the Department for Education (DfE) had rarely been involved in policy implementation and delivery. The DfE's role was confined to issuing circulars to LEAs, while direct contact with schools was infrequent (Smithers, 2001). A former DfES permanent secretary observed: 'Education policy barely existed [...] the Secretary of State for Education had always been a relatively junior appointment.'[3]

Similarly, few prime ministers had taken great interest in schools policy. This began to change following Callaghan's Ruskin College speech in 1976: 'a watershed in policy discourse' (Perry et al., 2010: 7). Callaghan exposed the drastically under-performing school system in which power was monopolised by professional elites (Callaghan, 1987; Moran, 2003). The approach was taken up by Conservative and Labour administrations after 1979, reflecting the salience of education policy and the scope for prime-ministerial activism. This paved the way for ground-breaking reforms such as the National Curriculum and City Technology Colleges (CTCs), followed by academy schools after 1997 (Alexander, 1997; Willets, 1988). A senior official remarked: 'The idea that you might set down from the centre of government the things that pupils in English schools had to learn was an extraordinary change.'[4] Appendix II (A) depicts the policy governance process for academy schools.

Family-Nurse Partnerships (2005–10)

Family-Nurse Partnerships originated in New Labour's social exclusion agenda. The term 'social exclusion' arose in the 1980s given ministers' reluctance to acknowledge relative poverty, symbolising a shift from the narrow focus on paid work and material resources (Burchardt et al., 2001; Levitas, 1998). The concept emphasised that existing welfare structures were struggling to guarantee inclusion for all citizens, breaking the cycle of multiple disadvantage (Annesley, 2001). Programmes initially addressed the geographic and area-based effects of deprivation (Power, 2001). In Whitehall, the focus was streamlining delivery, creating the Social Exclusion Unit described by Blair as 'the most important change in government machinery since Labour came to power' (cited in Hills & Stewart, 2005: 12).

However, there was concern that too little progress had been made in reducing the proportion of multiply deprived 'problem families' (Blair, 2010; Halpern, 2010). The *Strategic Audit* exercise undertaken by the Prime Minister's Strategy Unit in 2003 notes: 'Despite opportunities presented by educational, economic and social change, family origins continue to exert a strong influence on adult outcomes' (Cabinet Office, 2003). A subsequent Cabinet Office review concluded:

> Around 2% of families – or 140,000 families across Britain – experience multiple and complex problems. If we are to reach out to families at risk we need to identify and exploit opportunities to build the capacity of systems and services to 'think family'.
> (Cabinet Office, 2008)

Every government must co-ordinate the complex flotilla of agencies engaged in social policy (Levitas, 1998; Oppenheim, 1998). Attention focused on the impact of policy networks and the role of actors beyond the core executive

(Marsh & Rhodes, 1992; Peterson, 2003; Rhodes, 1997). The SEU was created to address an absence of departmental co-ordination. Multi-dimensional 'wicked issues' had rarely been confronted in the administration of social policy (Rittel & Webber, 1973). The SEU's purpose was to break the cycle of inter-generational disadvantage, 'improving understanding of the key characteristics of social exclusion and the impact of government policies' in England (Levitas, 1998: 148).

The SEU's aim was to 'join-up' institutions and actors in different spheres of governance, initially focused on school truancy, drugs, rough sleepers and the worst estates.[5] According to Annesley (2001), however, critics saw the SEU's role as signalling more cosmetic approaches to poverty. The underlying drivers of inequality in the labour market and the structures of economic disadvantage in an increasingly globalised economy were scarcely addressed (Coates, 2005; Dodds, 2009; Hills & Stewart, 2005; Levitas, 1998).

The idea of Family-Nurse Partnerships emerged after the 2005 election. Hilary Armstrong had been appointed as the Cabinet-level minister for social exclusion in May 2006. The SEU was located in the Department for Communities and Local Government (DCLG) following its transfer from the Cabinet Office in 2002. It was subsequently reorganised as the Social Exclusion Task Force, and merged into the Prime Minister's Strategy Unit (PMSU). The SETF/SU adopted an informal policy-making style focused on fulfilling the goals of the centre.

According to Armstrong's advisers, civil servants 'became used to dealing with Hilary in an incredibly open way'.[6] They met three to four times a week with open access to the minister: 'It was at times like a very good team of Master's students who were sat round an academic that they really admired.' The presentations covered 'how you map social exclusion, policy initiatives, charities and what they were doing that was innovative'.[7] Armstrong recalls: 'For me it was great because they weren't traditional civil servants. They were just buzzing with ideas.'[8] FNPs symbolised New Labour's commitment to tackling the crisis of intergenerational disadvantage and family breakdown through new institutions and governance structures (Blair, 2010; Halpern, 2008).

FNPs consist of programmes of visits by nurses to 'low-income, first-time mothers' while they are pregnant and for two years after the baby is born (Dodds, 2009: 501). The partnership aims to improve parental capabilities, encouraging women into education, structured training and the employment market. Although FNPs differ from previous approaches, the programme is consistent with New Labour's social exclusion agenda (Dodds, 2009). The aim of public policy is to pinpoint the most 'at-risk' groups so that interventions can be suitably targeted: 'while FNPs are intended to perform these acts of intervention' (Dodds, 2009: 500), there is still uncertainty about the relationship between risk factors and vulnerability to social exclusion.

The FNP programme employs nursing professionals rather than social workers, on the assumption that nurses are more likely to be trusted by clients.[9] FNPs are health-led initiatives built around Sure Start and Children's Centres. Armstrong attests that health-driven models were particularly valued and accessible for those 'who had a negative experience of the state' (cited in Dodds, 2009: 502). FNPs were voluntary since mothers had to opt in; 'no financial incentives to induce compliance are offered' (cited in Dodds, 2009: 502). This distinguished the programme from compulsory schemes in the United States such as 'workfare' (Annesley, 2001). Appendix II (B) depicts the policy governance process for FNPs.

The National Economic Council (2008–10)

The NEC was Whitehall's response to the post-2008 crisis. This began as a collapse of bank solvency arising from high-risk practices of financial intermediation, spreading to the real economy as businesses and households became indebted and risk-averse (Gamble, 2009; Krugman, 2009). Output and growth in the United Kingdom contracted sharply while unemployment began to rise following a decade of relatively strong performance with historically low inflation and unemployment matched by rising *per capita* GDP (Faucher-King & Le Gales, 2010).

Between 1995 and 2008, a form of statecraft was adopted in the UK based on 'depoliticisation', with the goal of maintaining the confidence of the financial markets (Burnham, 2002; Hay, 1996). New Labour sought to discard the party's 'tax and spend' reputation, attempting to persuade voters, industry and capital that the party could be trusted to manage the economy and to safeguard stability. The creation of the NEC and the government's 'activist' response to the financial crisis signalled the 'repoliticisation' of economic policy and the weakening of the previously dominant neo-liberal regime (Crouch, 2010; Gamble, 2009; Thain, 2009). The impact of the crisis had major implications for public administration, and the historical dominance of the Treasury over British economic policy.

Treasury control had been central to Britain's political economy since World War I (Cronin, 1988 ; Grant, 2003). New Labour redefined the Treasury as an agent of economic modernisation, achieving macro-economic stability while increasing the long-term growth potential of the economy (Seldon,

2006). This contrasted sharply with the Wilson government's creation of the Department of Economic Affairs (DEA) as a separate institutional power base, intended to represent the interests of the national economy by rationalising British industry and enabling industrial enterprises to compete in world markets (Donoughue, 1987; Gamble, 1994). In 1997, the Treasury ceded operational control over interest rates to an independent Monetary Policy Committee (MPC). Responsibility for regulating financial markets and the supervisory functions of the Bank of England (BoE) was transferred to the Financial Services Authority (FSA) (Westrup, 2005). The Treasury's focus adapted but it still controlled Whitehall's 'purse-strings', seeking to shape core departmental agendas on welfare reform, employment and public services (Thain, 2004).

By 2008–9, the British economy entered a vulnerable phase, buffeted by unprecedented instability in the aftermath of the crisis (Darling, 2011). While the immediate response focused on saving the banking system from collapse[10] following 'major discontinuities' in the global and domestic economy (Macpherson, 2009), policy was of paramount importance: 'New machinery was needed at the heart of government to reflect these new and urgent priorities' (Corry, 2011: 4). The impetus for the NEC came from the Prime Minister. Brown believed that cross-departmental co-ordination would help galvanise Whitehall, 'turbo-charging' the government machine and removing 'the usual departmental blockages'.[11]

The NEC was a Cabinet committee overseen by the Economic and Domestic Secretariat (EDS) in the Cabinet Office. This restoration of Cabinet government challenged the Treasury's hegemony over the conduct of economic policy. Historically, the Treasury had been a co-ordinating department (Deakin & Parry, 2000). The formation of the NEC in October 2008 signalled that ministers had concerns about the Treasury's approach to post-crisis management. Brown himself believed that the Treasury was ideologically committed to financial orthodoxy, reducing the budget deficit through cuts in public expenditure rather than using Keynesian reflation to restore stability and growth.[12] The perception was that the Treasury had been captured by the financial sector, and was incapable of reforming the City of London.[13] One Downing Street adviser remarked:

> Brown's support for the NEC revealed his basic attitude to the Treasury when he was Chancellor. He and [Ed] Balls saw themselves as working against, not with the Treasury as an institution because of its institutionally embedded ideology, which is why so many senior Treasury officials packed their bags and left. [Brown's] critique of [Alistair] Darling was that he allowed the institution to dominate him.

Hence Gordon Brown as Prime Minister supported the NEC as an attempt to provide countervailing fire.[14]

Moreover, the Treasury was instinctively hostile to government intervention: protecting vulnerable sectors meant wasting public subsidies on 'picking winners'.[15] This echoed longstanding criticisms of 'the Treasury view' given its preference for balanced budgets, and the Treasury's aversion to state activism (Clarke, 1989; Cronin, 1988; Gamble, 1988). The Number Ten position was that the Treasury saw its purpose as controlling the public finances and protecting Britain's reputation in the international markets (Corry, 2011). This was necessary, but insufficient. The Whitehall machine had to be overhauled in the face of an impending economic catastrophe.[16]

The Council met twice weekly in the COBRA room: the intention was to create a culture of action and urgency in Whitehall.[17] The NEC was described by the *Daily Telegraph* as 'an economic war cabinet' (cited in Seldon & Lodge, 2010). Ministers from the major departments attended, while the secretariat was supported by the Prime Minister's Policy Unit (PMPU) and the Prime Minister's Delivery Unit. There was a high-level committee of permanent secretaries who met weekly to co-ordinate follow up (NEC (O)), alongside an NEC co-ordinating group consisting of special advisers from key departments.[18]

The NEC was envisaged as 'a real policy making body', providing 'a co-ordination function to the Cabinet Office over the rest of Whitehall which outside a Budget or Spending Review doesn't really exist on economic policy'.[19] The Prime Minister was not convinced that the Treasury machine was delivering compelling policy ideas, and sought to impose his own strategic view on departments.[20] The NEC forced the Treasury 'to think more laterally and quickly',[21] insisting that departments work together, a recurrent challenge in Whitehall. This entailed 'exceptional, active measures to limit the impact [of the crisis] and contain the damage to our economy' (BERR, 2009). The PMDU worked alongside the NEC to monitor implementation across departments.

The financial crisis led to profound changes in the structure and politics of the core executive. The approach to decision-making centred on an informal and *personalised* style under Blair and Brown (as chancellor) was replaced by *collective accountability* incorporating a range of institutions and actors (Savoie, 2010; Thain, 2009). The civil service regained a measure of authority and influence over the policy process, symbolised by Jeremy Heywood's appointment as chief of staff in Number Ten. The NEC indicated the strengthening of Cabinet government, a marked contrast to the 'dual premiership' of the Blair/Brown years (Rawnsley, 2005). Of course, key figures insisted

Brown's inclination towards power-hoarding was as strong as ever (Rawnsley, 2010; Seldon & Lodge, 2010). Appendix II (C) depicts the policy governance process for the NEC.

Policy-making in Whitehall: A Primeval Policy Soup?

The case studies highlight New Labour's objective of modernising the policy-making institutions of British governance, underlining the increasing confidence of political elites as the central state has developed new mechanisms of power for intervening in society. So far, the chapter has explored the structural and institutional background to the case studies, but it is important to define the nature of the policy-making process in Whitehall. There is no simple, linear pathway in which 'policy aims are identified in terms of the values of the policy-maker; the organisation identifies systematically all the means to achieve those aims and then selects the best' (Cairney, 2012: 232). There is a 'primeval policy soup' and 'garbage can' of problems and solutions from which policy ideas emerge (Kingdon, 1984; Stoker & Gains, 2011; Weiss, 1979). This relates to the capacity of central government to influence the formulation and implementation of policy, as multiple actors from front-line agencies to non-governmental thinktanks and pressure groups influence and shape the policy process.

In addition, it is necessary to consider the extent to which ideas matter in the politics and structure of policy-making. The case studies highlight that the policy process draws on particular ideas from the social sciences, notably new institutionalism,[22] policy networks,[23] communitarianism,[24] and Keynesian neo-endogenous growth theory (Bevir, 2011).[25] The social sciences not only offer empirical insight into a changing society and polity. They develop forms of expertise that enable actors to govern society through the state (Bevir & Gains, 2011; Newman, 2001). New Labour's 'high modernism' encourages the search for levers through which the power of the central state might be imposed on civil society (Moran, 2003; Smith, 2009).

The 'Primeval Policy Soup'

Nonetheless, the concept of a 'primeval policy soup' underlines the 'haphazard' connection between ideas and policy change, alongside the absence of a rigid boundary between the centre and departments. There is a constant flow of ideas, operating concepts and programmes 'back and forth' (Gains & Stoker, 2011) between ministers, civil servants, advisers and front-line managers:

Generating alternatives and proposals in this community resembles a process of biological natural selection. Much as molecules floated around in what biologists call the 'primeval soup' before life came into being, so ideas float around in these communities. Many ideas are possible, much as many molecules would be possible. Ideas become prominent and then fade. There is a long process of 'softening up': ideas are floated, bills introduced, speeches made; proposals are drafted, then amended in response to reaction and floated again. Ideas confront one another (much as molecules bumped into one another) and combine with one another in various ways. The 'soup' changes not only through the appearance of wholly new elements, but even more by the recombination of previously existing elements.

(Kingdon, 1984: 60)

New Labour interpreted policy-making as: 'The process by which governments translate their political vision into programmes and actions to deliver 'outcomes' – desired change in the real world' (Cabinet Office, 1999: 6). More recent literature exploring the transfusion of ideas from the social sciences into public policy emphasises that the process is rarely linear or straightforward (Bevir & Gains, 2011; Gains & Stoker, 2011). Policy making involves complex patterns of interdependency between actors at the centre and departments (Kingdon, 1984; Weiss, 1979). The analysis of Family-Nurse Partnerships illustrates how ideas move through 'a disorderly set of interconnections' (Weiss, 1979: 31) between social scientists and practitioners.

The process of policy transfer and lesson drawing is an important aspect of contemporary policy-making (Dolowitz et al., 1999; Rose, 1985). In developing ideas, Australia and the Scandinavian countries are highlighted as an important influence on New Labour.[26] According to David Miliband, the theoretical stimulus came from Michael Walzer's critique of communitarianism, John Rawls' writings on the nature of justice and 'the rigorous critique of Marxism Today and the sociological analysis of Anthony Giddens'.[27] This guiding philosophy was reflected in the final report of the Commission on Social Justice (IPPR, 1995), subsequently influencing Labour's approach to the welfare state and public services (Driver & Martell, 2006).[28] The following section illuminates the variety of policy ideas in the case studies and the richness of the policy soup, contextualising the relationship between the centre and departments in the policy-making process.

Academy Schools

The influence of ideas on the development of academy schools was multi-faceted. The drive towards school autonomy, competition, contestability and choice has been attributed to an ideational shift over the last 30 years culminating in the hegemony of neo-liberal policy (Ball, 2009; Smithers, 2001). The Thatcher administration had been influenced by New Right thinktanks including the Centre for Policy Studies (CPS) and the Institute of Economic Affairs (IEA) (Denham & Garnett, 1998). They developed a powerful free market philosophy. Nonetheless, it is misleading to infer that New Labour was merely the continuation of Thatcherism (Hay, 1996; Meredith, 2008; Smithers, 2001). Indeed, the post-1979 agenda had been influenced by the Callaghan government's focus on standards and parental choice in the late 1970s (Donoughue, 1987; Fielding, 2003; Smithers, 2001).

Breaking with the New Right?

New Labour was influenced by ideas anchored in communitarianism and institutionalism, entailing delivery through networks, collaboration between public service providers, and new forms of public–private partnership (Ball, 2009; Bevir, 2005). In contrast, New Public Management (NPM) was an approach to reform which sought to curtail resistance to change, taking on budget-maximising, self-interested bureaucrats (Cockett, 1995; Niskanen, 1971). The neo-liberal view affirmed strong faith in the power of markets, tackling the bureaucratic inefficiency of corporatist institutions and postwar collectivism (Gamble, 1994). Traditional public sector organisations were broken up, separating purchasers and providers while emphasising the role of quasi-markets and competition within the public sector (Le Grand, 1982). As was the case elsewhere in Western Europe, however, NPM remained strongly contested within the central state (Moran, 2003; Newman, 2005).

The degree of continuity between Conservative and Labour administrations was striking. New Labour continued their predecessor's aim of scaling back the role of Local Education Authorities (LEAs), adopting centralised mechanisms to embed the National Curriculum, prescribing pedagogical interventions such as the literacy and numeracy strategy, and managing academy schools from Whitehall (Barber, 2007).[29] The schools inspectorate, Ofsted, heralded an insistence on higher standards in the cause of economic efficiency. There was the adoption of rhetoric about parental choice; additional scope for selection by aptitude; greater accountability for expenditure through performance tables; devolution through local management of schools; and traditional pedagogical standards were emphasised as the progenitor of academy schools (McCaig, 2001; Smithers, 2001). That said, the motivation for policy innovation was more complex than ideological acquiesce to Thatcherism (Kenny & Smith, 2001).

New Labour's account of structural changes in the economy, the labour market and employment was crucial. Ministers had to confront the managerial challenge of increasing investment without relying on central government expenditure, given the decision to maintain the spending limits agreed by their predecessors for the first two years after 1997 (McCaig, 2001). Their approach was avowedly flexible, pragmatic and non-ideological (Peck & 6, 2006). As McCaig (2001) notes, since public satisfaction with the education system began to be measured in opinion surveys from the early 1980s, greater attention was paid to educational performance leading to the politicisation of standards (Alexander, 1997). Labour sought to address the divide between state schools and the independent sector which had reinforced class-based inequalities for much of the twentieth-century. Rather than dismantling private schools, they would be assimilated into the state system (Adonis & Pollard, 1996). An adviser in Number Ten confirms that during the New Labour government:

> The internal market was liberalised through a whole set of changes [...] allowing successful schools to expand, money following the pupil, successful schools having an incentive to recruit more, local management of schools, and changes to faith admissions criteria. What academies did was that they strengthened the internal market in that they actually provided more successful schools that parents wanted to send their children to.[30]

Labour's modernisation strategy is summarised by Ball (2009: 100):

> Academies are indicative of and contribute to a set of more general and highly significant experimental and evolutionary policy 'moves' which involve the reinvention of public sector institutions and a reformation of the overall institutional architecture of the state.

New Labour linked improvements in performance to diversity and competition among schools (Le Grand, 2005; McCaig, 2001). Such ideas reflect:

> A strong international trend towards greater diversity of provision within and between secondary schools [...] Scandinavia and the Netherlands are pioneering choice and diversity in the supply of secondary schools, something their social democratic parties regard as essential to sustaining quality and public satisfaction in universal state education. Secondary level reform has become a key issue in the US, including the creation of independently managed charter schools.
>
> (Labour Party, 2003: 43)

Labour sought to demonstrate that the ideas informing academy schools sat within the mainstream of international best practice on education reform (Adonis, 2012; Barber, 2007).

An Enabling State

Drawing on the doctrine of the Third Way and modernised social democracy, academies emphasise flexible forms of delivery through partnership between the state and a variety of private and voluntary sector actors (Blair, 1996a; Driver & Martell, 2006; Giddens, 1998). New Labour's approach meant greater institutional diversity and parental choice (Driver & Martell, 2006). Even so, the Treasury was hostile to greater competition and quasi-markets, envisaging reform as a process in which extra resources are made accountable through targets defined by central government (Rawnsley, 2006; Richards, 2008a). Treasury officials were concerned that non-state providers entailed risk for the public sector, and the state would be forced to deal with irregularities, bail-out failing institutions (Kaletsky, 2010; Richards, 2010). As chancellor, Brown was attuned to the limits of markets and competition in the delivery of public services: quasi-markets apparently posed a threat to the public sector ethos.[31]

In contrast, the Prime Minister's advisers developed a 'personalisation' strategy emphasising choice and competition between providers, with contestability and a 'right of exit' for 'consumers' of public services (Labour Party, 2005; Le Grand, 2007). Academies sought to strengthen the internal market; the comprehensive model was allegedly subject to 'gaming' by the middle class justifying the break-up of traditional public sector monopolies (Barber, 2007; Blair, 2010; Le Grand, 2007; Seldon, 2006).[32] As one interviewee remarked, 'academies were specifically for areas that needed extra dynamism, bringing in the private sector'.[33] Only quasi-markets and competition empowered both affluent and disadvantaged households. Modernisation meant greater use of market mechanisms and public sector competition, accelerating the implementation of the academy programme (Giddens, 2007; Le Grand, 2005).

Reforming Public Services: The Free Economy and the Strong State?

The academy model encapsulated what Gamble (1988) terms 'the free economy and the strong state' according to one Number Ten adviser:

> The strong state was needed to establish the academies in the first place [...] but it was a social market policy designed to create a wholly new relationship between

the private sector, the voluntary sector, and the state in public services. You had to have a strong state in order to bring about the establishment of institutions which were intended to be and have proved to be self-governing. It was never the intention […] that this strong state was somehow taking over the management of secondary schools. The fundamental analysis of the policy was that local bureaucracies and central bureaucracies of all kinds are not good at managing schools.[34]

The development of academies acknowledged that Labour's early flagship reform designed to improve standards – Education Action Zones – had failed to have much impact (Chowdry et al., 2010; McCaig, 2001). It was hoped that EAZs would promote change, drawing on the resources of the private and voluntary sectors. EAZs placed substantial powers in the hands of the centre. Indeed, the 1998 Education Act creating EAZs gave the secretary of state more than 100 additional powers (Rafferty, 1998). Zones were a spatial mechanism for targeting resources towards the least advantaged (Peck & 6, 2006). However, EAZs struggled to deliver New Labour's transformation in educational standards.[35] There was increasing scepticism about the efficacy of area-based strategies throughout central government. The very fact of being targeted led to stigmatisation, while interest in Health Action Zones (HAZs) rapidly faded as ministers grappled with reorganising the core of the NHS (Peck & 6, 2006).

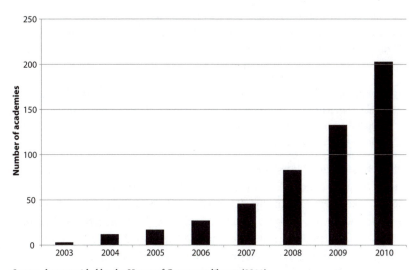

Source: data provided by the House of Commons library (2011)

FIGURE 5.1   Growth in the academy programme since 2002

The comparative dimension of academy schools is also significant. As has been noted, academies shared many features of City Technology Colleges. There were further similarities with the model of Charter Schools in the United States and Free Schools in Sweden (Wiborg, 2010). It was the example of CTCs on which Andrew Adonis, Tony Blair's education adviser (1998–2005), drew in developing the academy model: 'People like Andrew Adonis saw these things as good ideas at root; much more autonomous schools, better led, reducing LEA influence [...] the long-term way of developing the system and raising standards.'[36] Figure 5.1 depicts the growth of the programme after 2002.

By 2010, there were 203 academies in the English school system: inevitably, it had taken time for momentum to build.

Institutional Reform: A New Territorial Code?

Academies illustrate how policy innovation is preceded by a shift in the climate of ideas (Barber, 2007; Hall & Taylor, 2001; Mulgan, 1996). Likewise, policy change is dependent on structural reform, emphasising the relationship between institutions and ideas. Local government was generally hostile to academies, which were perceived as threatening the public service ethos and the commitment to universal public services free at the point of use. This meant the expansion of the academy programme was ever more dependent on strong, centralising government (Stoker, 2004). New Labour's territorial operating code was concerned with raising standards, addressing parental aspirations through centralised intervention (Bulpitt, 1983; John, 2011). Academies were directly funded through Whitehall, as Adonis confirmed:

> Though we used the term 'independent state school', we never intended that they should be independent in the sense of non-regulated. What we meant was essentially independent of local bureaucracy. The funding agreements in terms of academies made clear these were state regulated institutions.[37]

What was apparent was that the centre did not trust weak performers at the periphery, either LEAs or poorly performing schools, to invest additional resources judiciously (Goodwin, 2011). Promising money with modernisation, New Labour sought to enhance the managerial and administrative efficiency of the state (Newman, 2005; Shaw, 2007). As a result, New Labour's centralising tendencies were reinforced (Goodwin, 2011; Lee, 2009; Marquand, 2004; Peck & 6, 2004). Labour's approach relied on new institutional strategies, but remained fundamentally anchored in the British Political Tradition and a 'power-hoarding' model. On the one hand, notions of networked and polycentric governance emerged which emphasised that power is inherently fluid, never permanently fixed to one institution or actor (Ball, 2009). On the other hand, traditional Weberian hierarchies and top-down government were emphasised. This alludes to the dialectical and iterative relationship between institutions and ideas informing New Labour's governing strategy (Fawcett, 2011).

Family-Nurse Partnerships

Similarly, the ideas influencing FNPs had a distinctive comparative dimension, having been in the firmament of social policy debate since the late 1970s. This includes controversies about the underclass and an attack on the 'dependency culture' originating in the United States (Driver & Martell, 2006; Murray, 1985). Such ideas reflected anxiety in the political class about the growth of single parenthood, implying that the state had replaced the family as the dominant provider of social welfare. This allegedly fuelled a crisis of permissiveness and moral irresponsibility (Glennerster, 2006). As a consequence, the Department of Social Security (DSS) began to chart new approaches to family deprivation taken up by Labour in the late 1990s.[38] This included the tacit recognition that statist approaches struggled to meet the needs of excluded populations within a complex and heterogeneous society (Annesley, 2001).

Understanding Social Exclusion

The thinktank Demos had contributed extensively to debates about social exclusion in New Labour circles during the early 1990s (Levitas, 1998; Mulgan, 2008; Oppenheim, 1998). One researcher noted that Demos 'in many ways was trying to get away from analysis of traditional political structures and debates'.[39] The history of British social policy was characterised by institutional continuity; the welfare state was still recognisably that of the 1940s, despite the emergence of entrenched social problems (Glennerster, 2007). Demos became an advocate of holistic, 'joined-up' governance, urging the creation of the Social Exclusion Unit (SEU) and underlining the influence of thinktanks in opposition, if not in government (Mulgan, 1996; Peck & 6, 2006). After 1997, the SEU strove to ensure that public expenditure on social policy was effectively targeted through the spending review process. The Unit's purpose was:

> To improve understanding of the key characteristics of social exclusion, and the impact on it of government policies [...] promoting solutions, encouraging

co-operation, disseminating best practice and, where necessary, making recommendations for changes in best practice machinery or delivery mechanisms.[40]

However, there was frustration at the SEU's lack of impact during the government's first term (Blair, 2010). Number Ten believed that the Unit was too orientated towards empirical analysis rather than focused on policy delivery and improving outcomes.[41] The evidence informing the SEU's work stressed that exclusion was spatial and area-based, apparently ignoring the emphasis on the inter-generational transmission of disadvantage (Barber, 2007; Blair, 2010).

Prompted by the secretary of state, Peter Lilley, the permanent secretary at the then Department of Social Security (DSS) convened an away-day in the early 1990s focused on 'problem families' receiving multiple and costly interventions from the state (Halpern, 2008). Nonetheless, little substantive policy emerged until the end of Labour's second term. New Labour's approach can be separated from the New Right, addressing structural circumstances as well as personal responsibility (Driver & Martell, 2006). The Labour administration acknowledged that government had a duty 'to intervene in issues of social inequality and believes that welfare states are still a mechanism for tackling social disadvantage. Helping those who are not in a position to help themselves is the mark of a civilised society'.[42]

Tackling Multiple Disadvantage within Families

By the end of the second term in 2004–5, the Prime Minister was still concerned that Labour had made insufficient progress with families suffering the most intractable exclusion (Blair, 2010). This was estimated to comprise the bottom 2.5 per cent of the adult population, measured on indices of social deprivation.[43] The Number Ten adviser Paul Corrigan used the phrase 'marching through the deciles' to characterise the Labour government's approach.[44] The provision of welfare benefits and services led to the gradual erosion of poverty after 1945. But despite progress, certain groups were still exposed to intractable, long-term disadvantage. This cohort required proactive intervention 'to drag them into the mainstream'.[45] It was acknowledged that many excluded groups had a negative experience of state services: 'health-based models' led by professional nurses improved levels of trust (Dodds, 2009).[46]

The *Social Exclusion Action Plan* (2006: 8) insisted: 'The persistent and deep-seated exclusion of a small minority stands out ever more starkly.' This alluded to a 'cycle of disadvantage' in which 'deprivation in one generation is likely to pass down to the next' (2006: 9). The long-term impact of inter-generational deprivation was 'very costly'.[47] Traditionally, Whitehall struggled to produce coherent policies across departments, in particular linking the tax and benefits system with employment and the labour market (Bogdanor, 2001). The SEU had been created to tackle the pathology of departmentalism (Mulgan, 2001; Peck & 6, 2006).

American Welfare Policy: A Hidden Influence?

The process of policy change and welfare reform was shaped by a set of cross-cutting ideas. The United States has been widely regarded as a key influence on British social policy since the 1970s (Annesley, 2001; Prideaux, 2005). An official in the Prime Minister's Strategy Unit argued that UK policy-makers:

> Have a bias towards English-speaking countries [...] the US is full of interesting things to replicate but with Germany and the Scandinavian countries it is much more difficult. There was a running joke that in Scandinavia you obviously have things that are better but we can't have the level of taxes that we have here and get Scandinavian public services.[48]

American ideas infused the rhetoric and practice of UK welfare policy, reflecting both communitarian and New Right ideologies (Annesley, 2001; Dolowitz et al., 1999). FNPs emerged from evidence-based programmes in Colorado and New York, 'as early years policy was becoming fashionable on both sides of the Atlantic'.[49] The programme was developed through randomised research trials, yielding a culture of experimentation in welfare policy (John, 2011). Studies of families engaged in FNPs found lower levels of child abuse and neglect, and sharp reductions in disruptive behaviour (Dodds, 2009). The focus on early intervention was encouraged by James Heckman, one of America's leading social scientists: 'Like it or not, the most important mental and behavioural patterns, once established, are difficult to change once children enter school' (2005: 17).

The FNP programme symbolised an approach predicated on the management of risk within socially excluded populations (Dodds, 2009; Moran, 2003; Smith, 2009). The role of social policy was to identify 'the most at risk households, individuals and children so that interventions can be targeted more effectively' (Cabinet Office, 2006b). This contrasted with a previous generation of social scientists, notably 'underclass' theorists such as Charles Murray, who insisted that benefit claimants were dependent on the welfare state since it was in their rational self-interest. FNPs acknowledged that disadvantage is primarily *structural*, perpetuating poverty and state dependency (Prideaux, 2005).

Risk Management and Early Intervention

The literature on the early years anchored in social science and clinical practice led to greater interest in pre-school intervention, building on the legacy of Michael Rutter in child psychiatry. Rutter attests: 'The circumstances of early childhood can cast a long shadow' (1998: 16). Halpern recalls:

> We spent a lot of time analysing the longitudinal data to work out where experiences and family interconnections were predicting a host of outcomes. Good modelling, as good as you will find [...] it illustrates that just throwing a huge amount of evidence at a problem wasn't enough to do it.[50]

Another PMSU official noted, 'a lot of econometric work was done [...] we were trying to decide what is cost effective'.[51] This entailed a shift towards evidence-based approaches and the modernisation of the policy process (Levitt & Solesbury, 2005). The *Modernising Government* White Paper (Cabinet Office, 1999) sought to 'help people make well informed decisions about policies, programmes and projects by putting the best available evidence at the heart of policy development and implementation' (Davies & Nutley, 2002: 11).

The Prime Minister's objective was 'more support for very young children born into vulnerable circumstances' (Cabinet Office, 2006a). Health-led home visits improved outcomes for 'at risk' families (Dodds, 2009). Analysis of health visiting practices revealed an 'inverse care law': higher income groups were more likely to get support from state services (Le Grand, 2006). FNPs aimed to channel resources into areas of greatest need (Cabinet Office, 2006a). Seven million pounds was invested in ten pilot areas, adapting the scheme for implementation in England and Wales.[52]

UK Public Policy and Social Science

The focus on best practice was encouraged by 'a remarkably successful relationship between social science and policy in the UK, almost unique worldwide'.[53] This involved a process of research utilisation where 'social science and policy interacts influencing each other and being influenced by the larger fashions of thought' (Weiss quoted in Gains & Stoker, 2011: 486). Ministers were receptive to the evidence emerging from social science:

> If they are broadly in the zone like on early years, people are much more open to the evidence. There was a point when Margaret [Hodge] tore out this page with the Feinstein graph and literally stuck it in front of the Prime Minister and said 'what are we going to do about this?' It did crystallise out that people were willing to do something.[54]

Feinstein's work comparing the outcomes of a 'smart but poor' two-year-old to a 'dim but rich' child (Feinstein, 2011) had a decisive impact on Labour ministers, underlining the lack of progress on social mobility in Britain.[55] The evidence concerning early intervention and cognitive development confirms that achievement in tests at age 22 months and 42 months tends to predict later outcomes: notable differences in life-chances are evident well before pupils enter the formal school system. This is illustrated in Figure 5.2 below.

However, empirical evidence was not sufficient to persuade political actors to adopt FNPs. The FNP programme was implemented since ultimately, ideas matter in the policy process. According to one adviser:

> There was a battle of ideas and if you got a team that could come up with superior policy that is implementable, effective and swift, you are going to be able to make the weather in government [...] you have to ensure the people you are embedding are genuinely good thinkers, otherwise it diminishes the centre and they get patronised.[56]

The roll-out of FNPs was more rapid in England than had been the case in the United States, covering more than a third of local authorities by 2010.[57] American states are highly innovative with considerable autonomy; however,

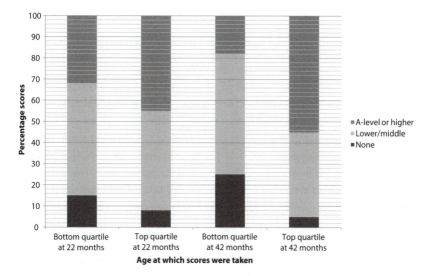

Source: Feinstein (2003)

FIGURE 5.2 'Inequality in early cognitive development' – highest educational qualification at age 26 years by test performance at 22 and 42 months[58]

few programmes are expanded nationally (Olds et al., 2004). Britain's tradition of strong, centralising government predicated on the concentration of power allowed the post-1945 welfare state to develop rapidly.[59] The centralised system of UK governance encourages the rapid diffusion of ideas and best practice, in contrast to more federal polities (Dolowitz et al., 1999). Furthermore, FNPs illustrate the diversity of ideas shaping the policy process, and the constant flow 'back and forth' between practitioners and policy-makers.

National Economic Council

This section considers the policy-making process in the core executive and the role of ideas in the formation of the National Economic Council. It examines how ideas have informed crisis management in economic policy, and the institutions of British economic governance (Balls et al., 2004; Grant, 2003). Through this framework, New Labour established discretionary rules in macro-economic policy (Gamble, 2009; Gamble & Kelly, 2001; Grant, 2003). Governments operated according to principles of depoliticisation and constrained discretion. A long-term approach was developed sustaining credibility with economic agents, as well as the trust of the British electorate (Balls et al., 2004).

Taking Politics out of the Economy: Depoliticisation?

New Labour's conception of macro-economic policy underlined the shift towards rules-based approaches, alluding to Burnham's 'depoliticisation' thesis (2002). Ministers sought to curtail the *political* nature of decision-making, 'offloading' responsibility to arms-length agencies. The Treasury moved to exert authority over economic policy after the breakdown of the Keynesian consensus in the 1970s, 'doing less, but doing it better' (Grant, 2003: 128). The logic of this approach meant policy-making was increasingly in the hands of technical experts and non-elected officials. There were some Keynesian economists who argued that policy discretion in the hands of ministers had, if anything, amplified the economic cycle making the problem of instability in the British economy more acute.[60]

The 1976 IMF crisis signalled the abandonment of Keynesianism within the nation-state (Gamble, 2009; Hay, 2010). New Labour was apparently enthusiastic in its adoption of the neo-liberal policy regime established between 1979 and 1997 representing 'the final triumph of monetarism and the defeat of Keynesian economic policies' (Arestis & Sawyer, 1998: 41). The Blair and Brown governments were apparently the agents of a dominant, neo-liberal regime (Gamble & Kelly, 2001). Abandoning the class compromise between capital and labour epitomised by the postwar Keynesian consensus, New Labour's enabling state sought to forge public–private partnerships, while investing in human capital and public infrastructure (Driver & Martell, 2006). This highlighted the role of 'neo-Keynesianism', combining a stable macro-economic framework with supply-side intervention (Balls et al., 2004), described by Ed Balls, chief economic adviser to the then Shadow Chancellor, as 'neo-endogenous growth theory'.[61] The secretary of state for trade in the Clinton administration (1992–6), Robert Reich, stressed that government activism was necessary to ensure globalisation was inclusive and that 'a rising tide would lift all boats' (Reich, 2002). Critics alleged that New Labour had discarded the party's commitment to a social democratic interventionist state (Coates, 2005; Hay, 1996).

Labour's strategy emphasised the need to raise the economy's long-term productive potential. However, New Labour rejected the pro-manufacturing bias characterising party policy in the 1960s and 1970s (Thompson, 1996). The priority in the Department of Trade and Industry's 1998 White Paper was the hi-tech 'knowledge economy' sector (DTI, 1998: Gamble & Kelly, 2001; Mandelson, 2010). According to one interviewee, 'the New Labour story of Blair and Brown in the 1990s was one of reassurance, and that meant lack of confidence about intervening in markets'.[62]

The Influence of Neo-liberalism

On the other hand, to insist that the ideas informing New Labour's approach were wholly 'neo-liberal' is misleading (Kenny & Smith, 2001). Marketisation and financialisation were key influences, but there were other important elements in the policy approach (Bevir, 2005). Margaret Beckett, as secretary of state at the DTI (1997–9), established a Company Law Review, examining the legal framework of companies and the link between corporate governance, investment and productivity.[63] The science budget increased sharply, alongside a number of research partnerships between universities and industry. A review of how banks ought to support small businesses was initiated (Corry, 2011). However, many critics feared that Labour was avoiding the institutional reforms necessary to break out of the low-skill, low productivity, low wage equilibrium in the British model of political economy (Gamble & Kelly, 2001; Hutton, 1995). Such concerns significantly predated the financial crisis.

The 2008 Financial Crisis: Making the Case for Industrial Activism?

Moreover, the 'rules-based' policy framework was gravely weakened by the financial crisis. This revealed that many long-term structural weaknesses – inadequate human capital, weak productivity, a low rate of investment in plant and machinery, highly leveraged bank and household debt – were never adequately addressed during New Labour's term of office (Corry, 2011; Faucher-King & Le Gales, 2010). The financial crash drew attention to instability in markets, alongside the failings of a 'light touch' regulatory regime (Akerlof & Shiller, 2009). It underlined the absence of an industrial strategy leading to overdependence on the financial sector and neglect of manufacturing industry (Gamble, 2009).

The NEC was intended to remedy this lacuna given the Treasury's deflationary orthodoxy, and the barriers to institutional co-ordination among departments. As has been noted, this had been a perennial concern in Whitehall since the 1940s. The Department of Economic Affairs (DEA) was created in 1964 partly to overcome the Treasury's hostility to state intervention (Grant, 2003; Thain, 2009).[64] The crisis underlined the importance of neo-Keynesian activism (Gamble, 2009). While ministers initially believed the crisis was short-term and the UK economy was fundamentally resilient and stable (Darling,

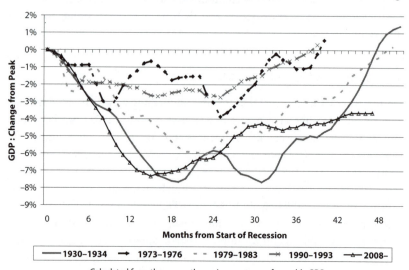

Calculated from three-month moving averages of monthly GDP

Source: NISER (2012)

FIGURE 5.3   The profile of the economic downturn in the UK

2011; Gamble, 2009),[65] Figure 5.3 illustrates the severity of the recession in the UK post-2008.

It is striking that Whitehall officials were sceptical about the strategic purpose and efficacy of state intervention in the economy. Civil servants accepted the case for 'horizontal' activism through investment in training and skills, productivity and human capital. The development of strategies for particular sectors, however, was 'an ideological line that could not be crossed':[66]

> Government was about setting the right frameworks rather than getting into what was basically government deciding on what businesses were doing in the national interest; making judgements that would affect particular businesses [...] The whole idea of pro-active government had been ideologically discredited because of the social contract in the 1970s.

This meant 'there was no obvious model of success', through which innovative approaches to government activism might be developed.[67] In the Treasury and the DTI, 'there had been a big change in the civil service'.[68] Both the City and regulatory agencies such as the Financial Services Authority (FSA) attracted 'the most talented civil servants', according to one former minister, further denuding departments of intellectual capacity.[69]

New Labour's dilemma was that sustained growth in the previous decade meant 'the left of centre had vacated serious thinking about the economy'.[70] The party avoided the task of forging 'an intellectual alternative to neo-liberalism and monetarism', although it underwent a hesitant, post-crisis 'rediscovery of Keynes'.[71] The DTI had experienced 'an intellectual lobotomy'. Most regulators 'were influenced by the authors of Institute of Economic Affairs tracts'.[72] In 1979, the leading Thatcherite ideologue, Sir Keith Joseph, had famously drawn up a reading list for senior officials at the DTI to acquaint them with the core tenets of new right ideology, including works by Adam Smith, Milton Friedman and Lionel Robbins (*The Economist*, 2010). Twenty years on, economic liberalism had become deeply embedded and entrenched within the department. There was consequently a lack of confidence about intervening in markets, reinforced by the Treasury's scepticism towards subjecting market forces to state control.[73] Government's purpose was to promote markets,[74] as Balls, Grice and O'Donnell (2004: 6) attest:

> The government's role is not only to support but positively enhance markets in the public interest. Policy is therefore directed to ensuring dynamic, properly functioning markets with fair and accurate information possessed by consumers; fair competition between many suppliers, with low barriers to entry and free mobility of capital and labour.

Similarly, despite being one of the authors of the 'New Industry, New Jobs' White Paper on industrial activism published in 2009, the Department for Business, Innovation and Skills (BIS) chief economist, Vicky Pryce, remained sceptical about the argument for government intervention in the economy.[75] Pryce believed the historical track record of British governments in achieving a higher rate of growth through indicative planning and discretionary macro-economic policy was unimpressive; her officials were cautious about industrial activism, recalling the 'bureaucratic co-ordination' literature examined in Chapter 2. Over time, ministers grew increasingly frustrated at civil service inertia, insisting that departments lacked the 'commitment and energy' to deliver results.[76] The NEC brought together macro-economic management with industrial and supply-side policy,[77] aiming to galvanise Whitehall departments (Mandelson, 2010; Rawnsley, 2010; Seldon & Lodge, 2010).[78]

Crisis and the British State

The creation of the NEC was an admission that the crisis had exposed fundamental weaknesses in the policy-making architecture of the British state (Thain, 2009). After initial hesitancy, the government responded to the turmoil following Northern Rock's collapse in the autumn of 2007 and subsequent instability in the banking sector (Gamble, 2009). However, it became apparent that the central state lacked mechanisms that might bring about long-term structural change in the British economy (Grant, 2003). The personalisation of the policy-making process created tight-knit teams of ministers and advisers operating on the basis of 'court politics'. Arguably, this perpetuated a culture of narrow, myopic decision-making which led to the mismanagement of the financial services sector, adding to the severity of the UK recession (Savoie, 2008; Thain, 2009). The financial crisis emphasised the perils of 'group-think', leading to over-reliance on conventional forecasting models and financial instruments. There was a refusal to foresee the impending storm created by 'light touch' regulation and inadequate risk management (Krugman, 2009). A narrow clique of ministers, advisers and officials dominated the policy debate, failing to consider counter-evidence and warnings that the long boom in financialised and service-orientated British capitalism would not last. What was required, critics argued, was a more rules-based, transparent system of public administration, challenging vested interests and financial orthodoxy (Foster, 2005; Thain, 2009).

Conclusion

This chapter sought to map the structural context of the case studies of academy schools, Family-Nurse Partnerships and the National Economic Council, illuminating the breadth of ideas that arise in policy-making, and the 'thickness' of the Whitehall policy soup:

- The case studies are atypical since they are characterised by a high degree of involvement from the centre, and do not relate to routine departmental policy-making.
- However, even where the centre does intervene, departments retain their relative autonomy and Number Ten is still dependent on departments.
- The analysis of power relations between the centre in Number Ten and departments should take account of the complexity and non-linear nature of the policy process. There is no straightforward 'conveyor belt' in which ideas become policy, then a green paper, then a white paper, then legislation, and are then finally implemented on the ground.
- The literature which emphasises that there is a 'primeval soup' of policy problems, policy agendas and policy solutions offers a powerful analytical approach to mapping the policy-making process in the central state.

Overall, the claim that British central government has lost governing capacity and control over policy appears somewhat overstated. The case studies reveal attempts by political actors to create an integrated approach to the task of governing, improving the capability to work across the diverse institutions of British governance (Peters, 2004). The chapter has sought to conceptualise the policy process in Whitehall and the core executive in order to assess how far the centre displaced departments, a subject more fully addressed in Chapter 6.

CHAPTER 6

The Centre and Departments in the Policy-making Process

Whitehall did not actually undergo a revolution. Rather, we see that the actual practice of the administration and management of the state has finally begun to enshrine the ideal model developed by Northcote and Trevelyan.

Wrisque-Cline (2008: 158)

The centre appears powerful because it makes announcements, but it then gets very frustrated because they are not turned into delivery.

Senior official[1]

Introduction

This chapter relates to how far the centre in Number Ten after 1997 sought to undermine departmental fiefdoms, strengthening the influence and reach of the core executive. The determination to expand the centre of government through new strategic policy units was intended to widen the reach of state power, rebuilding governing capacity. While political reform and devolution are emphasised, the centralising tendencies of New Public Management permit 'the remarkable comeback of state elites' (Le Gales, 2012: 151). The relationship between continuity and change is mediated through the British Political Tradition and the Westminster model.

The chapter examines the resources and capacities of the core executive, addressing the accusation that the centre under New Labour deliberately marginalised departments in the policy-making arena. In reality, departmental autonomy is the result of Whitehall's devolved and federated structure: most of the time, the centre is able to achieve little without the co-operation of departments. The argument of the chapter is that the interaction between Number Ten and departments is characterised by *mutual dependency*: 'Dependency being a state in which the probability that the action will be undertaken and the chance of its success change in relation to what other actors are, or do, or may do' (Bauman, 1991: 7).

The chapter outlines the growth of centralised capacity and the expansion of bureaucratic and political resources around Number Ten. This includes an assessment of how central units are perceived by actors in departments, a 'bottom-up' approach which is rarely undertaken in the literature. While it is not credible for the strategic centre of government to take over or displace departments, opposition to Number Ten emerged through criticism of the 'hyperactive' centre, alongside Blair's apparent inclination towards 'sofa' government.

The commentary on Whitehall is often characterised by generalisations about structural change in the core executive: the process of change is too rarely disaggregated and the role of actors in policy-making is seldom explored. It ought to be remembered that the centre and departments consist primarily of reflexive *agents*. Whitehall operates through 'political administrators': ministers and officials moving seamlessly between the bureaucratic and political worlds. Actors are integral to policy-making, operating as administrators, advisers, managers and policy entrepreneurs. Informal practices shape outcomes alongside more formal rules of the game, making it essential to consider the *politics* of the policy-making process. Finally, the case studies are analysed through the prism of the power dependency model, addressing the fluid and relational nature of power in the core executive, and the iterative and dialectical relationship between continuity and change in the Whitehall system.

The Growth of Capacity at the Centre

In assessing change in the core executive, it is necessary to consider the institutional expansion of bureaucratic and political power resources around Number Ten. A number of accounts emphasise the increase in central steering capability after 1997, strengthening the administrative capacity of the centre while replacing the Whitehall paradigm with 'prime-ministerial predominance' (Foster, 2005; Heffernan, 2006; Blick & Jones, 2010; Kavanagh & Richards, 2001). Moreover, New Labour had an explicit goal of augmenting the policy and implementation capabilities of the core executive, modernising the policy-making institutions of the state (Judge, 2006; Smith, 2011). For much of the postwar period, the centre has been the object of continuous reorganisation, creating the impression of rapid and momentous change. One Cabinet Office official observed:

> The centre is structurally but not intellectually bolted down. It can move much faster. There is a structural and institutional inertia in a department of 10,000 people that is not true in a highly changeable centre with less than twenty key players. That gives it the ability to move much faster in a way that is annoying to departments.[2]

Too often, the literature fails to delineate between the various resources and powers available to the prime minister. The centre is strong formally with the weight afforded by prime-ministerial influence. The prime minister is 'resource-rich', having the power to reorganise departments, appoint and dismiss ministers and determine the membership of Cabinet committees, while vetoing policies which clash with the government's political priorities (King, 1985). However, even where the prime minister has enhanced policy-making capability, Number Ten is invariably weak relative to departments, having fewer institutional and bureaucratic instruments at its disposal; prime-ministerial power is more often provisional and contingent. The core executive in most of the industrialised countries operates on a larger scale than in the UK, while Number Ten is dependent on departments for delivery (Parker et al., 2010). The weak centre has perpetuated a fragmented response to 'wicked' policy issues (Mulgan, 2008). Lord Birt averred: 'You need a strong and capable centre because the centre has got to develop, talk to all the people, understand the challenges, and get the master plan.'[3]

After 2001, the PMPU was re-designated as the Policy Directorate. The Unit's staff more than doubled in comparison to the Major years (Hennessy, 2000; Riddell, 2006). The intention was that policy activism would no longer rely on prime-ministerial personalism. Number Ten sought to intervene directly in the Whitehall machinery. This was augmented by the PMSU, invented along

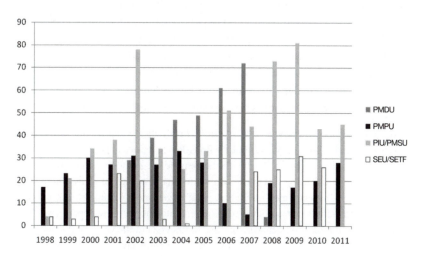

Source: based on data provided by the House of Commons library[5]

FIGURE 6.1   Personnel in central Whitehall units 1998–2011

similar lines to the Central Policy Review Staff (CPRS) in the 1970s. Although formally working alongside departments, the PMSU had the discretion to bypass traditional Whitehall processes. It was not accountable to any Cabinet committee, and strategy reviews were commissioned directly by the prime minister and his officials. Similarly, the Prime Minister's Delivery Unit involved the centre in policy implementation to an extent that had not occurred previously, developing tools to assess whether, and how effectively, policy was being delivered on the ground.

As the result of greater capacity at the centre, the role of civil servants in providing policy advice was allegedly weakened (Foster, 2005; Foster & Plowden, 1998). Referring to Number Ten's influence during the New Labour years, former Cabinet Secretary Gus O'Donnell, stated: 'There has been a greater involvement in the initiation and delivery of policy since 1997. This has resulted from the centre being stronger and more influential.'[4] The growth of capacity in the core executive is illustrated in Figure 6.1 above.

The Pathologies of the Whitehall System?

While underlying structural continuities make the claim of transformation in the core executive and the Whitehall paradigm questionable, there were undoubtedly important institutional changes. This raises the question of why the strategic centre of government was relentlessly expanded during the New Labour years. The institutionalisation of policy-making machinery in Number Ten arose partly as a consequence of impatience with civil service capability. The deputy prime minister, John Prescott, insisted early in the second term: 'The reality is we know that departments do not deliver.'[6] Labour's anxiety is captured in Peter Hyman's memoir about life in Number Ten. Hyman was a member of the Prime Minister's senior team between 1997 and 2003:

> The civil service as a whole [...] was stuck firmly in the approaches of the past. What we discovered in 1997 was not the Rolls-Royce service of popular myth but an organisation ill-equipped to deal with the demands of a fast changing world. Civil servants were still being recruited with far too narrow a set of skills. There were few project managers which meant that many government IT projects ran into the ground and wasted vast amounts of taxpayers' money [...] Few departments had modern communication departments able to understand the views of the public or communicate adequately with frontline staff [...] Most civil servants moved jobs so frequently within departments they were never held accountable for delivering anything. Success was measured by any criteria other than the one that mattered: delivery. There was huge resistance to outsiders coming into the civil service, yet

some of our best successes proved to be when outsiders and existing civil servants worked together in teams.

(Hyman, 2004: 73–4)

Philip Collins, one of Blair's speechwriters, was typically disparaging of Whitehall's performance:

The civil service isn't nearly as good as it needs to be. The fabled independence of the civil service is a self-justifying myth. The Whitehall culture is one in which caution is rewarded and risk-taking is frowned upon. The pliant progress up the ranks more reliably than the mavericks […] The anachronism of ministerial responsibility, which shields officials, should be abolished.

(Collins, 2011)

Similarly, Lord Birt, strategy adviser in Number Ten between 2001 and 2006, voiced criticism about the paucity of strategic policy-making capacity in Whitehall:

There is too much invested – and this is a general truth in a lot of public policy – in the status quo. Do not under-estimate the extraordinary inertia within the departments and within the Civil Service itself on many questions. It is honest and it is well intentioned but it is inertia and it is the enemy of change.[7]

Nonetheless, the most critical account is narrated by Andrew Adonis:

The notion that Britain has a 'permanent' and 'expert' civil service is largely a misnomer. Most career civil servants change job every year or two, unrelated to the needs of the state. They mostly possess superficial subject specific knowledge and front-line experience and few skills beyond those acquired at school and university […] Project management skills were in especially short supply, not least among those possessing the title.

(Adonis, 2012: 73)

Of course, it might be argued that Number Ten political advisers have a direct interest in denigrating the official machine. The sense of acute frustration with civil service conservatism and weak departmental capability is not confined to the New Labour years, however, as Nigel Lawson's commentary on education reform in the Thatcher era underlines:

The process would start by Margaret [Thatcher] putting forward various ideas – she had the Number Ten Policy Group heavily involved in the subject, and its then head, Brian Griffiths, was engaged in little else at this time – and there would then be a general discussion, to which I would contribute my four pennyworth. At the end of it, Margaret would sum up and give Kenneth [Baker] his marching orders. He would then return to the next meeting with a worked out proposal which bore little resemblance to what everyone else recalled as having been agreed at the previous meeting, and owed rather more to his officials at DES [Department of Education and Science]. After receiving a metaphorical hand-bagging for his pains, he would then come back with something that corresponded more closely to her ideas, but as often as not without any attempt by his Department to work them out properly.

(Lawson, 1992: 609–10)

Rather than blaming the Whitehall machinery, senior officials insist there was a pattern of mutual misunderstanding between New Labour and the civil service:

The civil service has been very reactive and often fails to get ahead of the game. They do very little scenario-planning or analysis, and are often ill-prepared. I wasn't aware of the civil service doing any serious work around where Blair wanted to go on key issues […] trying to work out scenarios and options. Ministers used to get really frustrated because they wanted the civil service to come up with lots of ideas, but just couldn't provide them. To be fair, there was also a lack of clarity coming from the top. I remember talking to a senior civil servant in the 1980s. He said he always knew in any situation where Thatcher was coming from. They were about 'making markets'. Even before the government had proposed privatisation, the Treasury was doing serious work on how to privatise services like water and gas. The civil servants always knew that the policy was about market-making. There was not the same clarity with New Labour […] the approach to public service reform emerged only slowly.[8]

The argument is that while the civil service during the Thatcher years had been used to dealing with ministers who had a strong ideological agenda, relatively few Labour ministers after 1997 had a clear view of what they wanted to achieve in their departments.[9] This state of mutual incomprehension is attributed by a former Cabinet secretary to Blair's credentials as prime minister:

My view of [Tony] Blair is he is composed of four quadrangles: Fettes School; St John's College, Oxford; The Inns of Court; and Parliament. He was […] a small organisation person who believed that you got things done through your own efforts working with a very small number of people. And that's how barristers work, it's how MPs work, it's how academics work. But it is not how an organisation of five million people works. Civil servants, on the other hand, are large organisation people. They believe in systems, and authorities, and mandates. You give people targets and you motivate them […] Blair had this idea that if something was wrong, you fixed it. If street crime was wrong, I will call a meeting of Chief Constables, as opposed to getting this built into police strategies. The natural thing is you would keep very small the number of people that you dealt with, and issue a series of personal instructions.[10]

That said, it was not only the perceived gap in civil service capability that motivated the expansion of the centre. Blair had never previously been a minister, nor had he managed a government department. After 1997, the new Prime Minister felt isolated and unable to challenge the Treasury machine, as one interviewee remarked:

> He learnt after a period that Gordon Brown had the Treasury and a thousand officials working for him. He felt he was up against this Treasury machine and would say, 'where are my men?' It was about getting a more even playing field. He saw that as time went on, in public services he wanted radical ideas for reform and wasn't getting them, from the Treasury or anywhere else.[11]

Despite augmenting the institutional power resources of the centre, the nature of the British political system ensured that departments remained structurally powerful, and ministerial government continued. This study will demonstrate that Number Ten continued to depend on departments, just as the prime minister is ultimately dependent on his or her ministers.

Departments and the Centre

The section below examines how far the centre displaced departments in the policy-making process between 1997 and 2010. Drawing on the core executive literature, power in British government is conceptualised as a series of exchange relationships rather than a zero-sum game (Bell & Hindmoor, 2009; Smith, 1999). The issue is not whether the prime minister is able to dominate and command departments. Departments have constitutional and operational autonomy, while departmental officials have an accumulation of expertise, resources and direct contact with the front-line. Where Number Ten exerts influence, the relationship between the centre and departments is usually characterised by *interdependence*, rather than subservience. The 'end of Whitehall' view privileges change over continuity, ignoring how underlying continuities persist over time.

Moreover, Number Ten and departments consist of actors seeking to shape and influence policy-making. The role of agents is crucial: it is vital to assess the purposive role of actors in the diverse institutions of British governance (Giddens, 1984; Hay, 2002). This section of the chapter examines how agents understand and navigate the policy process, framing issues by linking agendas of problem identification, policy formulation and implementation: 'Policy entrepreneurs act as catalysts for moving issues onto the policy agenda of government' (Gains & Stoker, 2011; Gamble, 2002: 294). The case studies of Academy Schools, Family-Nurse Partnerships (FNPs) and the National Economic Council (NEC) illuminate how agents influence the policy process, operating on structured terrain shaped by the centre and departments.

Academy Schools

Academies epitomise New Labour's objective of imposing control over policy formulation and delivery from the centre. The process of centralisation had been underway for two decades through the Department of Education and Science (DES) (Exley, 2012; Smithers, 2001). The creation of the National Curriculum emphasised the role of the DES as 'leading change within the system'.[12] However, this approach was contentious:

> There were a lot of political discussions even at that time about what it was appropriate for the department to be doing. Obviously the department was really stretching the boundaries and exceeding its competence in both senses of the word.[13]

According to one former permanent secretary, 'when 1997 came along, almost literally from day one, the department gave out a signal that it was going to be much more activist and in a leadership role'.[14] He continued:

> I think you saw in the form of a vehicle like the Standards and Effectiveness Unit something that intended to provide professional leadership to drive change in the education system, rather than maintaining administrative oversight of the system. I think that was a profound change and probably that view of professional leadership of the system survived all the way through to 2010 [...] We were moving from pure policy, not to delivery but something in between which was implementation.[15]

The emergence of discrete categories of state school, including academies alongside grammar schools, City Technology Colleges, foundation (Grant Maintained) schools, specialist state schools, voluntary aided (church) schools and secondary moderns in areas where the 'eleven-plus' was retained, increased central government's capacity to define and monitor their policy goals (Ball, 2009). What this hybrid institutional 'mix' had in common was that the flow of authority and resources went more directly to the centre.

Although academy providers gained the freedom to 'hire and fire' staff and pursue subject specialisms, their performance was overseen by the centre (Riddell, 2006). Interviewees based in DfES suggested central government 'sought to fill the void created by the absence of LEAs'.[16] The declining influence of veto players such as local government and the trade unions permitted the imposition of strong, centralising government (Marsh, 2008). Within Whitehall, the focus of decision-making shifted towards the PMPD[17] (Exley, 2012; Perry et al., 2010).[18] According to key players, DfES became more responsive to Number Ten, alluding to the centre's accretion of power. This marked an important change in Whitehall policy-making. While Number Ten had in the past intervened to resolve disputes, it rarely developed initiatives short-circuiting the policy-making role of departments (Campbell & Wilson, 1995; Donoughue, 1987; Foster, 2005).

One of Ruth Kelly's advisers at DfES (2005–6) remarked: 'The direction of travel undoubtedly came from the centre.'[19] Another official observed of academies: 'It was an idea largely developed in Downing Street.'[20] They continued: 'This was a period in which so much was set and driven from the centre [...] lots of programmes locally delivered but under a very tight grip.' Another civil servant confirmed, 'everyone was ultra-conscious of the breath of Number Ten on our necks'.[21] When Estelle Morris intended to reduce the capital budget for academies in 2002, she was overruled.[22] Number Ten summoned a DfES civil servant, Bruce Liddington, to negotiate an expansion of the programme. Rather than fighting the department's corner, the official 'regarded himself as doing the Prime Minister's personal work'.[23]

Number Ten's reluctance to 'let go' resulted from the Conservative government's failure to implement its flagship reforms in the 1990s. The development of City Technology Colleges was hampered by a shortage of sponsors, alongside ferocious opposition from LEAs. Only fifteen CTCs had been launched by the mid-1990s, despite being a key Thatcherite reform (Riddell, 2006). The department's capacity to oversee and implement policy remained questionable: 'The skill set required to make academies happen was completely beyond the civil service [...] it needed a particular form of public–private partnership in terms of engagement with sponsors and new school providers.'[24] If the academy programme was to flourish, the prime minister's patronage and imprimatur[25] were essential.[26] This meant 'both the policy and the implementation came very directly from Number Ten'.[27] Furthermore, Adonis 'wasn't just the adviser'. He was 'managing the programme which meant finding the sponsors and doing the deals that were necessary'.[28] Adonis conceded: 'Academies were very unusual. Both the ideas and the drive for delivery essentially came from Number Ten. I can't think of another example across government where this was the case.'[29]

The pressure for DfES to become more 'hands-on' grew as the role of local authorities diminished. Ministers were increasingly held accountable for pedagogical performance.[30] One permanent secretary insisted this was hardly surprising given the influence of the PMDU and Number Ten:

> At times as a senior official and I suspect as a minister you felt in a rather awkward position sitting at a delivery session, say with the Prime Minister, having to explain the performance of eleven-year-olds in Barnsley. And just occasionally you would think, 'am I the head teacher of the nation where I have to explain everything?' [...] Quite what were we saying about where responsibility lay within the system?[31]

In one instance in 1999, the schools minister, Estelle Morris, appeared on *BBC Newsnight* justifying homework policy for seven-year-olds:

> We'd launched a policy on homework. We'd said that infants had to do 10 minutes of homework a night [...] and I thought what the hell am I doing! Even at the time I thought this was going too far. And yet I think it was for the best of motives.[32]

Number Ten had considerable influence over the policy and implementation process for academy schools. This was a contingent response to the failings of previous initiatives, alongside centralised intervention in the school system in the light of the declining role of LEAs. One official inferred that DfES broadly welcomed Number Ten's focus on education: 'It was great to have the Prime Minister's interest. There is just no alternative to having sponsorship from the top [...] because we knew we had it, it suddenly made things possible.'[33] A former permanent secretary agreed:

> One of the stories that people could tell about 1997 onwards was that the Education Department became a really interesting place to be [...] it was the focal point of a huge amount of attention of prime ministers and chancellors. I think that is nothing other than a positive. I think that Labour really changed the mood music about the importance of the Department of Education, and therefore education as a policy priority for government.[34]

Of course, academies are atypical; their genesis was scarcely indicative of the entire Whitehall policy-making process after 1997. Nonetheless, the department was still able to frustrate the centre's goals:

> It is fair to say that the department was often able to see off the radical options that Number Ten really wanted. The department had the monopoly over information; when it came to understanding the impact of governance changes, the department just knew more than Number Ten did. Underpinning the actions of the department was the need to manage Number Ten.[35]

The adviser added: 'Number Ten is at a huge disadvantage because the time and attention needed to follow up the implementation of a White Paper is immense. The ability of Number Ten to do this is actually very weak.'[36] Will Paxton, policy adviser at DfES (2005–6), observed: 'The centre appears powerful because it makes announcements, but it then gets very frustrated because they are not turned into delivery.'[37] One PMPD adviser conceded that although the role of local authorities weakened:

> Most officials were close to LEAs. Don't get me wrong, they were always thoroughly professional. But the whole culture of DfES was about a very close partnership with LEAs. What City Academies brought about was the concept of independent state

schools [...] this was a cultural revolution in the department because they were outside the direct control of LEAs.[38]

This meant opposition within the department towards academies grew:

> The officials only accepted it because they saw it as a marginal experiment that would gradually fizzle out. They weren't wildly obstructive but they certainly didn't help to facilitate the policy [...] Most senior officials saw academies as toxic, partly because LEAs didn't like them and many officials ended up going back to be the Director of an LEA.[39]

A Number Ten official acknowledged that neither the centre nor the department fully controlled the implementation process:

> Not a single academy was in fact set up without the LEA ultimately agreeing. So they always had a veto and the veto was for real [...] there were still no-go areas for academies where one way or another, local authorities had been able to stop them.[40]

There is continuity over who influences the policy process, since local government continues to operate as a veto player despite the dilution of LEA powers through the introduction of legislation such as Local Management of Schools (LMS) in the late 1980s. Similarly, interviewees concede the impact of Whitehall reforms has been overstated.[41] The aim of NPM was to impose market disciplines on the public sector. Nonetheless:

> The culture of reform created by NPM completely bypassed government departments. It never affected the culture of the civil service and the motivation and incentives to which civil servants are subject. NPM only really affected the front-line. There are no league tables for civil servants or equivalent measures of success.[42]

While Number Ten rarely controls the departmental agenda, the centre selectively imposes strategic initiatives on departments. It is important to emphasise the fluid and dynamic nature of power, alongside the limited reach of prime-ministerial influence. Much policy is essentially routine and of no immediate concern to the centre. Moreover, Number Ten lacks the political and bureaucratic resources to sustain a command-and-control regime across Whitehall.

The Role of Actors and Institutions in Academy Schools Policy

This point is emphasised by considering the role of actors in the policy process. Policy making involves not only ministers and civil servants, but political appointees, thinktanks and special advisers. Gains and Stoker reveal advisers 'play a key but under-researched role in transmitting policy ideas in government' (2011: 485). Academies highlight the importance of advisers translating ideas into policy. Adonis in particular ensured the centre maintained oversight of the reform process (Barber, 2007; Blair, 2010; Blick, 2004). The centre curtailed its dependence on DfES, identifying potential academies and negotiating sponsorship arrangements using Number Ten as a resource to shape the market of providers.[43] A trade union official recalled a meeting in which Adonis outlined plans for the reorganisation of secondary schools in a small market town, demonstrating a detailed grasp of the English school system and highlighting the shift towards micro-management of policy change from the centre.[44]

An unorthodox actor, Adonis served as a policy entrepreneur in Whitehall (Weissert, 1991). This went beyond 'gate-keeping' and synthesising policy advice, advocating ideas while undertaking 'coupling' and 'brokerage' activities to maintain the momentum of reform (Gains & Stoker, 2011; Kingdon, 1995). In creating 'windows of opportunity', actors such as Adonis appeal to sympathetic politicians with the authority to act, skilfully 'coupling' the policy problem – inner-city educational underachievement – with the policy solution – a quasi-market of independent state schools (Annesley et al., 2010; Gains & Stoker, 2011; Kingdon, 1984; Richards & Smith, 2010).

What is more, actors assimilate influences and ideas that challenge the bureaucratic interests of departments (Rhodes, 2011). According to one close Blair adviser:

> The array of advisers who sit around in government are in part specialists in translating information, judgement, access to those very different species of knowledge. So it is definitely helpful to have advisers who are fairly confident about what is going on in social science around the world. Equally, it is really important that they have a feel for the implementation context, whether it is the party, or parliament, or a school.[45]

While neo-liberalism influenced New Labour's education strategy (McCaig, 2001; Smithers, 2001) the transmission process is complex, and the agenda was shaped by a variety of ideological influences (Gains & Stoker, 2011). Assuming that agents are indelibly imprinted by neo-liberal ideology is wide of the mark. Actors take inspiration from a plurality of ideological paradigms, beliefs and traditions (Gamble, 2002). The role of agents in proselytising ideas in government emphasises the duality of structure and agency.

The orthodox core executive literature has emphasised formal rules of the game in Whitehall policy-making (Barberis, 1997; Dunleavy & Rhodes, 1990; Smith, 1999). On the other hand, interviewees highlight the importance of informal relationships and the ecology of power politics. A former departmental adviser remarked: 'There was an extraordinary difference between Ruth Kelly and Ed Balls in terms of their relationships with Number Ten [...]

it felt weaker under Brown in relation to departments in terms of influence and power.[46] Another insisted: 'Number Ten regarded Estelle [Morris] as more of a pushover than a heavy weight.'[47] He continued:

> [Blunkett] was generally a pretty hyper-active minister [...] although Andrew Adonis was doing education at Number Ten at that time, there wasn't a big space for Andrew to operate. When Estelle [Morris] came in she was a quieter Secretary of State, which created more space for Number Ten to push much harder.

Blunkett argued in dealing with the centre 'you're having to demonstrate you're not going to be pushed about [...] in the department and across Whitehall'.[48] Many officials and ministers allude to the importance of personalism: 'It was a constantly fluid system in which power moves according to individuals and relationships [...] it's all part of an ecology, it's not a rigid system.'[49] Core executive accounts emphasise the limitations of ministerial personality as a causal variable, underlining that actors operate on structured terrain in the central executive territory (Dunleavy & Rhodes, 1990; Madgwick, 1991; Smith, 1999). Nonetheless, agency and personality inevitably impact on the nature of policy-making across departments and the centre.

Family-Nurse Partnerships

Unusually, FNPs were initiated outside the departmental policy framework; however, this meant the FNP initiative was vulnerable from an early stage since it had no guaranteed programme budget. The policy was conceived by the PMSU, the SETF in the Cabinet Office and the PMPU in 2005–6.[50] This epitomised the role of the centre in challenging the departmental status quo, as one senior PMSU official remarked:

> People who have worked in an area for ten or twenty years sometimes find it very difficult to step back and say, 'why do we do things like that at all, why can't we do things in a radically different way'? We wanted people with intellectual skills to apply to a range of policy problems, without the hang-ups of accumulated intellectual baggage. Now obviously the danger is they will lack the specific knowledge to be sensible. My rejoinder to that was if we were working as far as possible with departments, that's where you got the specific knowledge from. People with generic skills have much more open minds and are able to respond to ministers with fresh ideas.[51]

This emphasises that the relationship between Number Ten and departments is characterised by mutual dependency. There is a widespread view that SETF/PMSU was stymied by the absence of departmental resources, despite being located at the centre: 'We had no infrastructure behind us, we were this Unit in the Cabinet Office [...] the SEU had no budget. We only had the leverage of the Prime Minister's support.'[52] The proposal for FNPs was contested since departments were anxious to maintain their control over social policy. According to one adviser, 'It was a very tense period.'[53] The Department for Children, Schools and Families (DCSF) saw itself overseeing family policy, deterring interference from the centre. The Department of Health (DoH) was anxious for FNPs to be regarded as a public health intervention:

> DfES obviously had a very strong stake in teenage pregnancy policy and 'looked after kids' policies. They were worried that we would just cut across their priorities [...] I haven't been on a single Strategy Unit project where there hasn't been pushback. It's like, 'why the hell are you doing this'? It's a common reflex for departments.[54]

The DCSF focused attention on reducing teenage pregnancy rates and was unenthused by family intervention programmes.[55] Identifying resources to fund FNP pilots announced in the 2006 *Social Exclusion Action Plan* required Armstrong's special advisers 'to scrabble around desperately trying to secure the money [...] relationships with civil servants were not functioning.'[56] At a Cabinet committee chaired by the Prime Minister in September 2006, only £15 million was forthcoming despite the request from Number Ten for £60 million.[57] Blair appealed to David Miliband, secretary of state at the Department for Communities and Local Government (DCLG) in 2005–6, which had under-spent on its 'decent homes' programme.[58]

However, no further resources were forthcoming from DCLG. Most departments were unwilling to support the FNP programme. The centre relied on departments to make resources available through allocated budgets, but FNPs contributed little to departments' delivery priorities and PSA objectives. Having created a performance management system based on PSAs where departments are encouraged to behave not in a collegiate fashion, but as rational, self-calculating actors, it was unsurprising that officials had little sympathy with Number Ten's plea for additional resources.

The FNP programme sought to create more effective 'joining-up' on the ground through multi-agency co-ordination.[59] One of Hilary Armstrong's advisers explained:

> Without these specific grants for multi-agency working you can't drive the change at the front-line that you need to bring different agencies together [...] it was about having the right individuals and a programme that worked led by local government and PCTs.[60]

FNPs were initiated through local authorities and Primary Care Trusts (PCTs) (Cabinet Office, 2006a) rather than imposed from the centre. Local partnerships applied for funding, demonstrating their ability to implement policy according to clinical guidelines and locally driven demand.[61] The programme was prescriptive, allowing providers little scope for flexibility and discretion: 'That was a success factor because people had to stick to it.'[62] This form of central intervention involved 'changing the way that local services worked around individuals. If you want to take waste out of public services, you need agencies to work with one person, sit down with them and go through their needs, tidy up the wiring behind the scenes'.[63]

FNPs confront a perennial dilemma in the policy-making institutions of the central state. On the one hand, FNPs had no programme budget on which to draw, so the policy risked falling between the cracks that separate Whitehall departments. As a former Cabinet Office social exclusion minister remarked:

> If you don't have the money to go with what is in theory your responsibility, it is really hard to achieve things. For us to achieve on the social exclusion agenda meant that we had to have the goodwill of departments that had the programme budgets. We introduced Family-Nurse Partnerships by [...] exhorting departments to sign up where you were in the lead, but they would pay for it [...] that's a very difficult thing to do in Whitehall.[64]

On the other hand, no department would champion programmes that did not promote their strategic interests. The funding of ten pilots costing £15 million, a tiny sum in relation to total central government expenditure, depended on the personalism of prime-ministerial patronage and the political will of Armstrong's Cabinet Office team. One of Armstrong's advisers attests:

> We wanted some pilots as part of the spending review and getting the money was so difficult. I am not sure Special Advisers can really do this, but I had to personally ring round officials in the departments, the Home Office, Health, Local Government and Communities, to get £15 million for the pilots. As a Special Adviser it wasn't really my role, but as I say relationships with officials were not functioning, and the Home Office was particularly obstructive. I had to ring Moira Wallace, who was a Deputy Director, who I knew from my time there previously, and basically managed to lever the money out of them.[65]

This emphasises that the centre struggles to develop policy without the tacit support of departments. Even where policy is initiated from Number Ten, the segmentation of the core executive and the institutional strength of departments impose hurdles at each stage of the policy process.

The Role of Actors and Institutions in Family-Nurse Partnerships

The role of actors is crucial, since 'policy entrepreneurs' articulate the salience and relevance of policy agendas throughout the core executive (Gains & Stoker, 2011). Their involvement was vital in the gestation of FNPs, translating ideas into practice[66] and drawing on research undertaken by social scientists and clinicians. The PMSU adviser David Halpern coupled problem identification, policy formulation and implementation. Halpern had 'a unique style'; he generated background evidence and data-gathering, while redesigning FNPs for delivery in the UK.[67] Halpern subsequently followed up programme implementation with pilot sites. In emphasising the importance of social science, inspiration for the programme came from an American academic, Professor David Olds.[68]

The case of FNPs further emphasises the importance of personalism and primeministerial leadership. Tony Blair had reached the final phase of his premiership in the spring of 2006, appointing a close ally,[69] Hilary Armstrong, to pursue the agenda as part of his prime-ministerial legacy (Riddell, 2006). The imminence of Blair's departure was used to accelerate the pace of policy change. Prime ministers have personal and structural power, but are rarely predominant (Heffernan, 2006; Smith, 1999). Leaders operate in a structured context shaped by wider political, economic and ideological forces (Jessop, 2007). This ensures that the prime minister's powers are contingent: Blair's position weakened as the result of a sharply reduced parliamentary majority in 2005, and wars in Iraq and Afghanistan. Growing discord with his Chancellor made it harder to get things done (Blair, 2010; Mandelson, 2010; Powell, 2010; Rawnsley, 2006). Giving testimony before a select committee, Michael Barber recalls:

> I remember in 2003 that one of the things Tony Blair was considering was ring-fenced funding for schools [...] but he chose not to take it to the Cabinet because he was exhausted. It was immediately after the Iraq war and he did not think he had the political capital to take it through [...] A year later there was exactly the same issue, exactly the same principles; he felt powerful enough to take it through, so you get an ebb and flow in prime ministerial power.
>
> (House of Lords Constitution Committee report, 2009: 32)

Similarly, commenting on the power of the Treasury, Deakin and Parry (2000: 2) contend:

> When the curtain is lifted, events taking place on the stage and behind the scenes show that power is exercised conditionally, not absolutely and by negotiation, not fiat [...] the abiding lesson is that, whatever its apparent strength, Treasury power is less than absolute.

Like the Treasury, Number Ten's power is contingent, often relying on co-operation and agreement from departments. Departmental autonomy constrains Number Ten. The centre and departments are locked in a contingent relationship based on mutual dependency. Number Ten and the Cabinet Office relied on the Department of Communities and Local Government (DCLG) and the Department of Health to contribute towards FNPs. Armstrong succeeded because 'I had allies in the major spending departments.' The SETF drew on departmental expertise, determining how FNPs should be delivered through a health-led service model.[70] Nonetheless, Naomi Eisenstadt, who led the SETF, argues that being located at the centre was constraining:

> In terms of making things happen, it was really difficult. You have no budget, you know, you have no authority, you are not the Treasury, you are not Number Ten. So in terms of the triumvirate you are the least powerful […] I feel that my career has been about my ability to charm, to bring people together. I was quite effective in that but it is a real struggle.[71]

Despite the contingency of prime-ministerial power, however, departments struggled to resist the centre where Number Ten was determined to impose its will.[72] One civil servant noted 'the examples where Secretaries of State with Number Ten backing push things through. Academies, foundation trusts […] clearly things have been done.'[73] Similarly, Number Ten imposed the National Offender Management Scheme (NOMS) on the Home Office:

> Institutionally, the Home Office gave up the fight. A lot of the senior people had been sacked, Blunkett had done a big purge. They were inundated with policy on asylum and policing from Blair, and trying to see off the Birt report on drugs. And they just said, 'we'll do it'. And it was a complete disaster because no one had ever really thought through how to implement it.[74]

What is required is a nuanced perspective acknowledging that power in Whitehall is context-dependent. This relates not just to resources and strategic influence, but the ability of experts and policy specialists to pursue ideas. The role of policy entrepreneurs is highlighted repeatedly,[75] reworking ideas for policy change while overcoming traditional bureaucratic obstacles and constraints (Kingdon, 1984). This emphasises the role of ideas alongside institutions: 'Assumptions and organising concepts play an important part in how agendas and issues are constructed and defined' (Gamble, 2002: 305). Ministers were attracted to public service reform proposals which enabled them to establish hegemony in political debate against their opponents (Blair, 2010; Bulpitt, 1986; Driver & Martell, 2004; Powell, 2010). Furthermore, ideas enable agents to overcome structural impediments within the permanent bureaucracy, emphasising the dynamic relationship between structure and agency, institutions and ideas, and departments and the centre in the core executive.

National Economic Council

The aim of the NEC was to place the machinery of Whitehall on a 'war-footing' after the financial crisis, giving the Prime Minister 'a line of sight' into economic management.[76] As a result, the Treasury viewed the NEC as a threat to its authority over macro-economic policy.[77] One former adviser to the Chancellor remarks: 'It was seen as another way of interfering in the Treasury's business. Senior people in the Treasury did not like it and refused to engage with it.'[78] A Number Ten official recalls: 'Relations were difficult enough without us putting a new institution in place.'[79] While the NEC was intended to improve co-ordination in Whitehall, it proved impossible to resolve substantive policy disagreements through a committee structure: meetings descended into thinly veiled disputes between departments.[80]

The NEC did relatively little to improve the centre's capacity for enforcing decisions with departments, despite the financial crisis. One former BIS minister averred:

> If you've got no control over the departmental budgets, the capacity to influence departmental behaviour and spending priorities is quite limited [...] If you don't have the money to go with what is in theory your responsibility, it is really hard to achieve things in Whitehall.[81]

An adviser from Lord Mandelson's department insisted that despite a succession of initiatives, from job guarantee schemes for the unemployed to VAT and National Insurance deferral for smaller businesses, 'the NEC wasn't giving us extra leverage given that some of our own officials were against those policies'.[82] Mandelson recalls the struggle to establish an active industrial policy in Whitehall:

> The department until it was expanded in 2009 had less capability than I had remembered when I was at the DTI. There just seemed to be fewer people, fewer senior policy officials, fewer people to turn to, to do the spadework. Secondly, the prejudice against industrial policy was still alive and well, first in my department and across Whitehall. I basically persuaded the Prime Minister to come with me using political rather than policy arguments. I said whatever doubts you have about the policy, surely you can't question the need for us to show politically that we are pulling every lever and pressing every button in order to save the economy and give ourselves an economic future? So even if you think the policy is not going to work, you can't

question my political instinct that we need to show the country we are doing everything possible to create jobs.[83]

As the Prime Minister's senior economic adviser, Dan Corry, noted:

Departments on the whole were not used to going at such a fast pace, and were institutionally reluctant to disrupt their other work or reallocate key staff. It was more about delivery, we wanted to do lots of stuff and we wanted it to happen quickly. The civil service isn't always good at that, it is very tribal, the departments don't work together.[84]

This meant implementation emerged as a crucial challenge for the NEC: 'Many of the schemes and initiatives involved working with other non-governmental stakeholders [...] they were complex and difficult to push along fast' (Corry, 2011: 9). Indeed, bank lending emerged as a critical issue: 'Unless government actually takes over these lending decisions and becomes a bank, which it doesn't want to do, then you can encourage and exhort as much as you like, but nothing will happen.'[85]

The institutional mechanism of the NEC was atypical in the context of Whitehall, and a specific consequence of the post-2008 crisis. What the NEC emphasised was the pushing and pulling of conflicting pressures towards state-centric 'government' and devolved 'governance' at the centre of the state. The central state machine assumed greater responsibility for the delivery of public services, while government was forced to intervene rescuing the ailing financial sector following the crash (Gamble, 2009). This entailed *governing from the centre*. However, it was clear that numerous agencies were beyond the control of the central state. The impact of globalisation, marketisation, NPM and public sector reform had led to the shift from a 'directive' state to a 'centre-less' state (Dunleavy & Rhodes, 1990; Smith, 1998). Even the banks subject to government 'bail-outs' were largely immune from Treasury control (Corry, 2011). New Labour was forced to develop strategies for *governing beyond the centre*, acknowledging the limits of state authority.

The NEC emphasised New Labour's struggle to overcome departmentalism in Whitehall, as it sought to 'join-up' central government: 'It didn't fundamentally change the way that Whitehall worked.'[86] The government experimented with strategies to improve policy co-ordination: PMSU project teams, non-departmental 'sponsor' ministers, working groups and 'COBRA-style' emergency meetings. However, it was hardly 'any more joined up on the difficult issues that cross departmental boundaries than it had been in 1997'.[87] According to the business minister (2007–10), Pat McFadden:

New Labour found it difficult to get cross-departmental working right because of the way departments are structured. We moved from a one year budgetary cycle to a three year budgetary cycle, and the money went to individual departments [...] the programme expenditure is where the power is, where the real power of decision making lies.[88]

The NEC sought to address these concerns implying a shift of bureaucratic resources towards the centre, at the same time weakening the Treasury's power.[89] Nick Pearce, head of policy in Number Ten (2007–10), commented:

It gave the Cabinet Office a real locus on economic policy making which remained important [...] you had a set of permanent officials working on economic policy in the Cabinet Office which became a support function for Number Ten. It was a means of preparing thinking and working with departments on policy.[90]

The NEC highlights the perennial tensions and ambiguities in the UK core executive. To exert influence over economic policy during crisis episodes, the Prime Minister created an institution at the centre of government. The NEC had political influence and permission to drive policy initiatives through Whitehall. This challenged the asymmetric status of the Treasury in economic policy, enhancing the role of the Business Department. Civil servants in BIS welcomed the change: 'The fact that your paper has been given to the NEC gives you a bit of visibility and certainly gives you more attention at the ministerial and permanent secretary level.'[91] The NEC was not a central unit, however, but a Cabinet committee comprised of ministers and officials. This reinforced the collegiate and departmental style of policy-making in Whitehall.

Departments remained powerful and influential within the core executive, while Number Ten's interventions were selective and did not confer dominance over the policy process. The Treasury's role evolved and adapted over time. After Alistair Darling's appointment as chancellor in 2007, there had been an important power-shift within the Treasury.[92] Special advisers, particularly Ed Balls, had been 'all-powerful' during Brown's tenure but 'the officials decided to take revenge. The advisers would get shafted quite a lot; we wouldn't be able to see papers [...] not pleasant at all.'[93] This indicates that the civil service, led by the new permanent secretary, Nicholas MacPherson, sought to regain control over the policy process from political appointees. Nonetheless, within months of the financial crisis, the Prime Minister was concerned that the Treasury was losing its political grip, struggling to establish a convincing plan for stability and recovery.[94]

The Role of Actors and Institutions in the National Economic Council

The NEC's creation strengthened institutional co-ordination, seeking to improve the flow of ideas into government. Agents were, again, crucial in the process of reshaping the core executive. The Prime Minister's chief of staff, Jeremy Heywood, a former Treasury official, acted as interlocutor between Whitehall, the Bank of England, regulatory agencies and the financial sector. Heywood's influence signalled that the civil service retained a powerful role following a decade in which policy advice had allegedly been politicised and pluralised among thinktanks and special advisers, an issue addressed in Chapter 7. As Number Ten chief of staff, Heywood was a permanent official whereas Jonathan Powell had been a political appointee, symbolising the strengthened influence of officials in Whitehall.

The NEC was created as 'a new model for driving from the centre [...] an interesting approach to how Cabinet government could be done differently' (Rutter, 2011: 3). A further unintended consequence was to enhance the position of the Business Department, which historically had a 'second-rate' reputation in Whitehall.[95] Mandelson's appointment as secretary of state was pivotal:

> [He] punched above the department's weight in Whitehall. If you talk to officials in the Department of Business, they would probably say that in the last 20–25 years, Michael Heseltine and Peter Mandelson as Secretaries of State were regarded most highly because both were big beasts. They overcame this fear of intervening in markets [...] that's what energised BIS [Department of Business, Innovation & Science], not so much machinery of government changes.[96]

Mandelson initiated 'a long-term strategy for industrial activism', drawing on his experience as European trade commissioner, and his familiarity with 'stakeholder' models of capitalism in Northern Europe.[97] The decision to appoint one of Labour's senior figures, together with institutional changes in the machinery of government, had a decisive impact. This underlines the importance of personalism in Whitehall: a minister's influence relies on the ability to persuade and build support among colleagues. As such, ministers operate on structured terrain while personal authority is necessarily contingent.

The turbulent relationship between Blair and his chancellor, Gordon Brown, is chronicled in a series of ministerial diaries and memoirs (Blair, 2010; Darling, 2011; Gamble, 2012; Mandelson, 2010; Naughtie, 2005; Rawnsley, 2006). Despite this, the relationship between the prime minister and chancellor is still based on mutual dependency (Smith, 1999). The prime minister relies on the chancellor to safeguard the government's reputation for economic competence, while the prime minister's authority may be required to impose limits on public expenditure, enforcing financial discipline on ministers and departments.

During Blair's premiership, rival centres of advice emerged: the competition between Number Ten and the Treasury was intense (Bevir & Rhodes, 2006b; Seldon, 2006). According to Rawnsley: 'Brown conceived of the new government as a dual monarchy, each with its own court' (2001: 20). However, it is striking that the post-2008 crisis curtailed the chancellor's room for manoeuvre (Donoughue, 1987). Managing the fall-out required the collective involvement of the Cabinet, rather than a dual premiership. According to one adviser: 'The Prime Minister wanted to use the weight of other ministers to push Alistair in directions he didn't want to go [...] I think there was a collegiate spirit in the face of adversity, given the crisis.'[98]

This chapter highlights the enduring importance of departmentalism, alongside contingency in the relationship between the centre and departments. Departments have remained the decisive agent within the core executive. While the centre retains the capacity to intervene, Number Ten rarely challenges the policy-making autonomy of departments. The chapter has sought to emphasise that any generalised claim about patterns of intervention from the centre ought to be treated cautiously. This study is designed to disaggregate macro-explanations of structural change in the core executive. The policy process within the central institutions of the state, and the relationship between Number Ten and departments, has to be understood through reference to actors. This requires an analytically robust conception of the interaction between structure and agency.

The rational and public choice literature defines actors as self-interested utility-maximising agents.[99] These accounts promote an 'agency-centred' view which ignores how actors are socialised into the traditions and beliefs underpinning the institutions and practices of British governance. This study reveals that the centre and departments are comprised of actors operating on institutional terrain, negotiating bureaucratic and political constraints while remaining closely intertwined and mutually dependent on one another. As ever, the relationship between structure and agency is iterative, dialectical and constantly changing.

The Federal Structure of Whitehall

The analysis in this book indicates that Whitehall is characterised by exchange relationships between actors in the centre and departments, rather than strict compliance with the centre's goals. Richards and Smith observe: 'Government departments provide the organisational terrain within which the majority of policy is formulated, developed and operationalised' (2002: 195). The policy-making machinery in the core executive is organised around departments. Andrew Graham, special adviser in Harold Wilson's Policy Unit (1974–6), remarked: 'If the Whitehall machine is heading firmly in one direction, it is very hard to stop' (Seldon, 1995: 117). This remains so 30 years on: the majority of policy decisions are still taken within departments.

The structural power of departments reflects Whitehall's devolved and federated nature. The Institute for Government (IfG) has revealed that although departments failing to hit performance targets faced the prospect of central intervention, the likelihood of weakly performing programmes being cut or adverse career consequences for officials was not very great (Parker et al., 2010). According to comparative surveys, Whitehall remained a 'light touch' regime despite New Labour's reforms. While British government is relatively centralised, the structure of Whitehall itself is devolved and focused around departmental fiefdoms. Ministers have the highest levels of 'budgetary discretion' among the industrialised countries (Parker et al., 2010). This is a reflection of the constitutional convention that ministers are accountable to the 'Crown in Parliament'. The doctrine of parliamentary accountability is a cornerstone of the British constitution: a core element of the British Political Tradition (Flinders, 2008; Hall, 2011). Geoff Mulgan, Director of the PMSU (1999–2004), noted: 'We have a very small centre. Most of the work of government is done in departments, it has to be done in departments, and can only be done in departments.'[100] Mulgan attests:

> A Secretary of State running a large department with budgets of many billions, sometimes hundreds of thousands of staff working for them – these are very powerful people. We only succeed to the extent that we can persuade those individuals that we are adding something to their work.[101]

Richard Wilson, the former Cabinet secretary, agrees:

> We have a system where legal powers and financial resources are vested in the Secretaries of State. The Prime Minister has few executive powers other than the administration of the Civil Service. I think the term 'Prime Minister's Department' implies a different role for the Prime Minister and a major constitutional change that I would tell you has not taken place.[102]

At the end of New Labour's tenure, the IfG concluded:

> The office of the British Prime Minister holds a concentration of formal power greater than that of almost any other country in the developed world. In contrast, the fragmentation and lack of coordination at the centre of the civil service – the Treasury,

Number Ten and the Cabinet Office – leads to an administrative centre that is relatively weak. This curious situation has created a strategic gap at the heart of British government, which inhibits the ability to set overall government priorities and translate them into action.

(Parker et al., 2010: 8)

The symbolic power of Number Ten underlined by claims of 'presidentialism' (Foley, 2008) and 'prime-ministerial predominance' (Heffernan, 2006) should not be confused with the capacity to affect change in the structure and processes of policy-making in the core executive. There is, as ever, a disjuncture between the 'image' of the centre as omnipotent and all powerful underlined by the Westminster model, and the reality of contingency and constraint on Number Ten's capacity to affect policy change.

The Culture of Departments

The case studies emphasise the pre-eminence of departments despite various initiatives to bring policy-making under central control. Indeed, departments have distinctive cultures, interests and relationships leading to entrenched policy preferences. There is a departmental 'viewpoint', the repository of embedded knowledge about policies from the past (Rhodes, 2011). Moreover, there are deeply entrenched ideological and institutional biases operating in departments. Departments overseeing delivery have strong ties to producer interest groups (Newman, 2005). The departmental agenda is shaped by power relations structuring the policy process (Marsh et al., 2001; Miliband, 1972). The institutionalisation of structural bias makes it harder for Number Ten to significantly alter the policy agenda of departments (Gamble, 2002).

This section of the chapter examines the culture shaping the actions and attitudes of departmental actors. Departments are not neutral bureaucratic institutions, but complex organisations shaped by historically constructed ideologies, values and beliefs. The departments relating to the case studies are Education (DfES/DCSF), Health (DoH), Business (DTI/BIS), the Home Office, and the Treasury.

Intra-departmental Divisions

The evidence is that ideological beliefs and interests vary as much *within* departments as between them. Departmental cultures consist of philosophical viewpoints and positions setting the framework in which ministers and officials operationalise policy (Marsh et al., 2001). The culture of departments is never monolithic, fixed or immune from change. For instance, the DfES balances a wide array of professional interests, from the teaching unions to local government. The department's relationships were transformed by the shift towards choice, competition and Local Management of Schools (LMS) in the late 1980s. The culture of DfES was altered further by the allocation of family and children's policy to the department in 2004–5, according to a Grade 5 ministerial policy adviser in DfES:

> There was a clear distinction between the Schools Directorate and the directorate that dealt with children and family policy. Schools were seen as the serious bit of the department if you were a civil servant. The cultures were very different. In the Schools Directorate you got some heavy-weight generalist civil servants who had been around Whitehall. The Children and Families Directorate was much more NGO-like. They had a bit of DFID [Department for International Development] about them.[103]

Similarly, the Department of Trade and Industry was characterised by disagreement between advocates of market liberalisation and officials with close links to sectors and interests seeking the protection of the state.[104] These philosophical traditions reflect divergent historical views of trade and industry policy (Marsh et al., 2001). As the former Conservative minister Lord Young described: 'There was a great difference in philosophy between the Trade people and the old Industry people' (Young, 1990: 244). During the 1980s, the department made the transition from the corporatist state towards the promotion of deregulation and free enterprise (Gamble, 1988; Marsh et al., 2001). However, the DTI still confronted the Treasury's dominance over productivity and industrial policy (Crafts, 2007).

The diversity of departmental cultures is acknowledged by numerous actors. One of the teaching union representatives who dealt with DfES remarked: 'The junior and middle-ranking people […] were trapped in this horrendously bureaucratic culture.'[105] A permanent secretary involved in the merger of Education and Employment added:

> The cultural difference between the Employment Department which traditionally had lots of operations and managed things, and the Education Department, which was essentially a policy-forming department, was enormous. Chris Woodhead [the former Ofsted Chief Inspector] was so impatient with the slightly cerebral, hands-off approach of the department in the late 1980s and early 1990s […] in the early 1990s, it was still you got change by sending out a circular.[106]

The department struggled since: 'DfES just handed out money to LEAs before the 1990s. It had no legacy of challenging failure.'[107]

Charles Clarke, home secretary between 2004 and 2006, remarked: 'The Home Office culture was far stronger and more resistant to change.'[108] The Home Office was regarded as one of the 'great departments of state' with a prominent position in the Whitehall hierarchy, maintaining a judicious balance between civil liberties and state authority. The department's role overseeing the criminal justice system led to 'a culture of fear about a terrorist attack or a massive prison breakout'.[109] The Home Office saw itself 'as a quasi-constitutional body that aimed to reach compromises between the police who wanted to lock everybody up, the judiciary who just wanted to follow procedure, and lots of pressure groups'.[110] A Number Ten official continued: 'The idea that they were there to deliver on crime was counter-cultural.' Blair railed against the department's fatalism and weak delivery culture:

> A Home Office team came to make a Power Point presentation to the Prime Minister in the Cabinet Room on crime, complete with multi-coloured graphs showing that the crime rate would rise inexorably. When Tony asked why crime would rise, the officials replied that it was because the economy was growing and that put temptations in the way of criminals. We scratched our heads. I asked the team what would happen if the economy were to go into recession. Without missing a beat, the officials replied that crime would rise because people would be deprived and more of them would have to resort to robbery to survive.
>
> (Powell, 2010: 72)

Towards the end of his premiership, Blair infamously labelled the Home Office 'not fit for purpose', echoing David Blunkett and John Reid's pronouncements as home secretary (Barber, 2007; Blair, 2010).

In contrast, the ethos of the Department of Health was shaped by its ideological commitment to the NHS. As one minister observed, this encouraged the tendency towards management through centralising dictat: 'A top-down directive tendency, the idea that people want to tell people how to run things.'[111] DoH was able 'to pull the levers and get instructions right down the system, right out to the grassroots immediately'.[112] One official advising on health policy in Number Ten found the department deeply resistant to reform:

> The thing that surprised me the most was the extent to which the Department of Health had been captured by the NHS. And that's not by the doctors or nurses, which you might expect to be the chief obstacle to the reforms that Tony Blair and I wanted to push through. Somebody did a survey of the top mandarins at the department of health and discovered that out of thirty top people in the department, the senior civil service, twenty-nine of them had come from within the NHS. There was only one who eventually became the Permanent Secretary, Hugh Taylor, who was a traditional 'Sir Humphrey' type civil servant who has come through the ranks. This

was a rather different animal so to speak to deal with than the one I thought I was going to deal with, which was about dealing with the Sir Humphreys of the world. What I and Tony Blair were dealing with, and ministers and their special advisers were dealing with, was a group of people who had grown up through the NHS, whose careers were strongly identified with a bureaucratic, monolithic Soviet-style NHS. And not only their own careers but those of all their friends. And if you're pushing through market-type reforms, choice and competition reforms of the kind we were pushing through and I had been taken on by Blair to try to push through because that's where my intellectual credentials came from; if you tried to push that through, you are implicitly criticising personally their careers, and their friends. So it is a tough call in some ways. And rather different than if you'd been dealing with the doctors or with traditional civil servants.[113]

There had been 'a period of confusion about whether the people at the top of the department were mandarins accountable for the department in Whitehall and to the Cabinet secretary; or were they truly hands-on NHS people?'[114] This highlighted a perennial tension between civil servants as managers overseeing delivery, and their role in steering the policy process on behalf of ministers (Page, 2010). Officials cannot operate within a Whitehall enclave, since departments depend on front-line agencies to deliver services and implement policy change.

The notion of organisational culture is central to the analysis of structural change in Whitehall. While the expansion of managerialism and the growing autonomy of ministers have served to question whether departmentalism will continue in its current form, traditional structures and processes remain intact. Fawcett and Rhodes (2007: 86) insist: 'It is hard to escape the conclusion that here was a government intent on centralising policy making.' Nevertheless, if New Labour intended to centralise the policy process within the core executive, it did not wholly succeed. Departments have entrenched cultures, as well as expertise, knowledge and bureaucratic resources, enabling them to frustrate interventions from the centre. Tellingly, Andrew Adonis concedes: 'Inadequate leadership, drive and support for academies within the Whitehall machine was to dog the academies programme throughout its life' (Adonis, 2012: 72). The capacity of Number Ten to displace departments in the policy-making and implementation process was inevitably partial and highly contingent.

The Treasury's Role in Whitehall

Each department in Whitehall is affected by the Treasury: literature overlooking the role and status of the Treasury offers an inherently partial account of the core executive (Deakin & Parry, 2000; Thain, 2009; Thain & Wright, 1995). Most departments rely on public expenditure allocated by the Treasury. As such, the Treasury impacts directly on departmental policy-making. Heclo and Wildavsky (1981) emphasise that Treasury dominance is maintained through relationships of trust and mutual dependency. Treasury officials are relatively few in number which means gaining 'the co-operation of operating departments is essential' (1981: 7). Moreover, the claim to financial expertise underlies the Treasury's authority and power: 'That it indeed does so is an important part of the Treasury's culture' (1981: 42).

Spending departments are particularly suspicious of the Treasury, since its function was to maintain control and oversight of public expenditure. This entails monitoring public spending to ensure it is consistent with the government's priorities: resources must be used as Parliament intended (Campbell & Wilson, 1995; Richards, 2008). This has created 'a historical relationship with deep suspicion and deep mistrust on both sides. I observed people behaving very oddly'.[115] There was always conflict beneath the surface. Departments were determined 'to put the Treasury back in its box'.[116]

Alistair Darling, chancellor of the Exchequer between 2007 and 2010, reflected that during the financial crisis not a single official had been at the Treasury during Britain's exit from the Exchange Rate Mechanism (ERM) in 1992 (Darling, 2011). The culture of HMT was shaped by 'very young, very smart officials [...] who were much more brutal and dispassionate about policy decisions than departmental officials were'.[117] This fed a 'machismo culture' in which civil servants were praised for 'slapping down spending departments'.[118] HMT's custodianship of the national finances meant saying 'no'.[119] The Treasury was the guardian of taxpayer's money and 'Gladstonian fiscal rectitude' (Thain, 2002: 124). Officials performed a 'bad cop' role: 'It was a bit like the Millwall chant: "everybody hates us but we don't care"'.[120]

Of course, the Treasury's role under Brown went beyond the focus on managing delegated public expenditure. The Chancellor outlined his vision of the Treasury shortly after coming to power: 'A Labour-run Treasury would need to be not just a Ministry of Finance, but also a Ministry working with other departments to deliver long-term economic and social renewal' (Brown, 1999). The Treasury influenced the minutiae of policy in health, education, social security and the labour market, going beyond the financial framework (Deakin & Parry, 2000; Thain, 2002). According to one official:

> The Chancellor was running his own policy machine in a way I had never experienced. This wasn't what Chancellors did up until this point. The Sure Start programme

[…] was largely developed at the Treasury and taken forward by us with a huge slug of money. On higher education, there was a complete stand-off; we were caught in between the Prime Minister and the Chancellor. The Treasury remains the most powerful influence on government if it wants to be.[121]

Thain noted the paradox that 'An administration committed in some policy areas to decentralisation and devolution has presided over a growth of Treasury power and influence quite unprecedented in the postwar era' (2002: 219). Treasury control over departmental expenditure has grown markedly since the early 1990s. Nevertheless, Treasury influence is usually confined to target-setting and performance management, particularly through the Comprehensive Spending Review (CSR) and Public Service Agreements.[122] The Treasury's relationships vary considerably among departments.

Departmental Perceptions of the Centre

In understanding the iterative and dialectical relationship between continuity and change in the Whitehall paradigm and the core executive, this study provides a 'bottom-up' perspective assessing how departmental actors viewed the centre and Number Ten. This is rarely considered in the literature on the core executive which tended to focus on the observable dimensions of power at the centre of government, implicitly neglecting the role of departments. Former Cabinet Secretary Richard Wilson described the expanded Downing Street operation as '*Yes, Minister* meets the *West Wing*.'[123] However, there was a marked contrast of view between ministers, officials and advisers. Those who experienced the Whitehall machine in the 1960s and 1970s, including Harold Wilson's special adviser, Bernard Donoughue, struggled to comprehend New Labour's determination to operate through Number Ten.[124]

Ministers grew frustrated at the centre's attempts to impose its agenda on departments, insisting that the Prime Minister's advisers had an inherently limited understanding of the practicalities of reform.[125] An official in the Home Office stated: 'the general view towards the small, central units is that they are ephemeral and not to be taken too seriously' (cited in Flinders, 2002: 67). In addition, few civil servants were prepared to criticise the centre during the Blair and Brown years, emphasising the passive and deferential culture of Whitehall. Much of the conflict between Number Ten and departments was *ministerial,* alluding to the *political* nature of policy-making. This section of the chapter assesses how Number Ten units were perceived by actors in departments.

The Prime Minister's Policy Unit

The justification for creating the PMPU was to ensure that original and innovative ideas flowed up to the centre, bringing evidence together with the values underpinning the government's agenda and promoting long-term thinking on policy.[126] According to Donoughue, the Policy Unit 'made a major contribution to the growth in the Prime Minister's power and his capacity to intervene effectively' (quoted in Seldon, 1995: 119). Similarly, John Hoskyns (Unit Head between 1979–82) conceived the PMPU as 'a counter-cultural change agent' (quoted in Seldon, 1995: 121).

This remained the rationale for the PMPU after 1997 although under Labour, the centre's role went beyond co-ordination to developing policy within departments. Kavanagh and Seldon (2000: 266) argue the PMPU combines 'the roles of being a think-tank (working up policy and seeking ideas from outside policy specialists) and a French-style *cabinet* reinforcing the political direction of the Prime Minister'. Hyman (2004: 174) noted 'the impotence that every Prime Minister feels when the departments over which he has some, but not much control, do their own thing'. One Number Ten special adviser remarked: 'In those circumstances where the department has been captured by the providers, the only hope is to have a really radical centre. The centre is probably the only one that can do the job properly of driving radical reform.'[127]

As a result, accusations about New Labour's politicisation of Whitehall and the hyperactive centre were never far away (Rawnsley, 2010; Richards & Smith, 2002; Seldon & Lodge, 2010). The Number Ten Policy Directorate attracted particular hostility. A leading educationalist contested 'the notion that a parallel universe should be set up in Number Ten with greater power'. He continued:

> If you've got a Department for Education, you don't need education policy as well being made in a different place. It seemed a very odd way to run a government. In the end, Number Ten won because Number Ten always wins, just like the Treasury. But Blair did make the job of one of his major public service delivery departments very difficult.[128]

A Number Ten official remarked that the PMPU was perceived by departments as:

> Highly directive, highly managerial, very micro. They would have seen ministers as essentially pawns of Number Ten [...] The Private Office actually arranged for me to see every submission to ministers in the Department of Health. The civil service

would say that effectually, sometimes more ineffectually, they were overseen by Number Ten.[129]

Another minister observed: 'If there is not a shared agenda then there's bound to be a very destructive clash which is in nobody's interests.'[130] The tension between departments and the PMPU grew as ministers 'didn't feel they [Number Ten] lived in the real world'.[131] The minister insisted:

> Essentially you can cut it in two: Downing Street and the real world [...] I'm not an admirer of Number Ten advisers. The outside world were even closer to the delivery bit than you were. The thing they brought in was practical ideas and a more nuanced view of what you were doing. They could speak the language of people.

A Cabinet Office official averred that the PMPU's approach led to the centralisation of policy-making with profound consequences: 'One is it left departments and departmental civil servants feeling pushed more towards being the implementers of policy. And secondly, it changed the balance between the power of the Prime Minister and departmental secretaries of state.'[132] Some ministers rebuked the PMPU as 'Tony's narks in Whitehall' (Kavanagh and Seldon, 2000: 22). For instance, Adonis regularly intervened to influence education policy within the department. One official opined: 'If anyone knew Andrew was behind a policy, it automatically made people suspicious' (cited in Fawcett & Rhodes, 2007: 82). Adonis recalls:

> A good part of my job was to act as persuader-in-chief. Much of the leadership of the education department [...] expected that this latest Blairite fad would either wither and die, or be kept small and on the margins like the City Technology Colleges. I had to persuade them otherwise.
>
> (Adonis, 2012: 74)

Another DfES special adviser underlined the propensity for tension between the centre and departments to escalate based on Ruth Kelly's tenure as secretary of state (2004–6):

> On the Schools White Paper, it got quite fierce. I remember going to Chequers, and Tony [Blair] had got John Hutton [Cabinet Office minister] along. We didn't know he was going [...] he started arguing that private schools should take over secondary schools. His special adviser and the Policy Unit advisers were also there. There was obviously something being contrived. Every school should be run for profit. Ruth was just like, 'I've been beamed into planet mad!'[133]

Similar criticisms relating to the role of the Policy Directorate were applied to the Prime Minister's Delivery Unit in Whitehall.

The Prime Minister's Delivery Unit

The creation of the PMDU represented an important shift during the Blair era, giving the centre capacity to influence the implementation process 'using data in a new way'.[134] This revealed the extent to which streamlined co-ordination between 1997 and 2001 failed to deliver effective oversight from the centre (Richards & Smith, 2006). The drive towards 'joining-up' had not broken down departmental silos (Ling, 1998). This led Number Ten to amass further resources over implementation, as well as policy development (Barber, 2007; Smith, 2011). The PMDU sought to galvanise departments, wielding the threat of prime-ministerial intervention.[135] An official conceded:

> It is good that there was some kind of centre of government scrutiny of what departments are doing [...] I never felt the department was being micro-managed, and if any department might have thought it was being micro-managed, it would have been education.[136]

Michael Barber insists the purpose of the PMDU was to bring order to the policy delivery process:

> I would have people like Andrew Adonis and Peter Hyman coming to see me in the department to ask if I had any new ideas. I would say well, yes, of course I've got lots, but actually we haven't properly implemented the old ones yet. The centre tended to hop around a lot from thing to another. We needed to inject rigour and routine into the governing process. It wasn't just about monitoring performance data [...] bringing a sense of routine to government was key. Otherwise, you just get government by crisis.[137]

Jonathan Powell claimed the PMDU 'adopted a collaborative approach with departments rather than being perceived by them as threatening' (2010: 75). An official acknowledged that the PMDU 'was certainly regarded by the departments as very demanding. It made the departments feel under pressure and hectic'.[138] Nevertheless:

> We had a very high quality staff in the PMDU. They were really effective and non-bureaucratic, and departments recognised and welcomed that [...] We were one of the only central units to conduct a regular survey to find out what departments thought of us, both ministers and officials.[139]

However, the PMDU invariably provoked territorial disputes in Whitehall. As one minister remarked:

> The relationship that schools had with Ofsted was replicated in the relationship departments had with PMDU [...] The minute Michael [Barber] came to us and said

they were going to grade us competitively, it changed the relationship. They had stars and all the rest of it. They were rating departments against each other. The minute they started doing that, we stopped telling them certain things. It did change the relationship. He [Michael Barber] wasn't our critical friend.[140]

These disagreements arose from New Labour's refusal to clarify whether the centre's role was about working alongside departments, or installing a command-and-control regime from Number Ten.[141] One secretary of state complained: 'Tony believed that Cabinet ministers were basically outposts of the central operation and I think that was a terribly mistaken view.'[142] The Prime Minister misconceived the nature of the delivery challenge: 'He thought that determination through Number Ten, his own speeches, his own arguments, his own weight of personality, his own advisers could carry it. Actually, the story was they couldn't.'[143]

This resulted from confusion in New Labour circles about the strategic role and purpose of central government (Riddell, 2006). Although targets had been created under the Thatcher and Major governments, the Labour administration went further, expanding the number of targets and applying league tables across the public sector (Barber, 2007; Blair, 2010; Riddell, 2006). This encouraged ministers to intervene more frequently, given they saw themselves as politically accountable for performance. Smith concurs: 'The accountability imperative – reinforced by electoral and media pressures – often forces ministers into taking back control of problems even after they have been formally contracted out to external agencies' (2011: 169). The delivery pressures are captured in a series of memoranda by Blair's election strategist, Philip Gould. In one memo half way through the first term, Gould warned: 'TB promised a New Britain, a transformed NHS and public services; all we have got is more of the same. Too little change, not too much.'[144]

As a consequence, Riddell observes: 'The central state was taking responsibility for more outcomes on the ground without having the means to achieve them' (2006: 56). There is a disjuncture between intensions in Whitehall and the front-line: an implementation gap (Lipsky, 1980; Marsh & Rhodes, 1992). Reform initiatives sought to redefine the role of the civil service as a delivery agent; however, observers questioned whether central government had the capacity to implement change at 'street-level' (Le Grand, 2006; Mulgan, 2008; Riddell, 2006). According to one senior official:

The Labour experiment has failed. Policy in areas like health and education is out of sync with what organisations on the ground can deliver. Often when decisions are taken there is no-one in the room who knows about the subject or about how the policy can be delivered – so the policy's crap and the delivery is unattainable. A great deal of money has been wasted.

(cited in Cameron, 2009: 7)

The public service agenda epitomised the new-found confidence of political elites in modernising and steering the central British state. Nonetheless, the New Labour administration assumed responsibility for the performance of local agencies and institutions over which they had little formal control believing they had received an unequivocal 'instruction to deliver' from the electorate.

The Prime Minister's Strategy Unit

Similarly, the PMSU prompted a series of Whitehall turf wars. The PMSU originated in separate units: the Performance and Innovation Unit (PIU) launched in 1998, and the Forward Strategy Unit (FSU) created in 2000. While the PIU was generally open and informal in style under the leadership of Suma Chakrabarti (1998–2001), the FSU in contrast acquired a closed and secretive reputation (Halpern, 2010).

The Prime Minister's adviser in the FSU, Lord Birt, insisted that policy reviews of the criminal justice system and drugs policy were conducted privately.[145] This was justified since 'there are certain issues where you need to give ministers space to explore options and consider ideas'.[146] The PIU's work programme was agreed in conjunction with departments. In contrast, the FSU's projects were initiated by the Prime Minister's office. The PIU focused on cross-cutting issues which fell outside departmental priorities. The FSU addressed core departmental agendas such as crime, health, transport and education (Halpern, 2010). The FSU reflected the Prime Minister's frustration that too few rigorous ideas originated in departments (Barber, 2007; Blair, 2010; Powell, 2010).

Both approaches were brought together in the PMSU after the 2001 election. The PMSU's methodology was to initiate evidence-based reviews, as one senior official explained:

PMSU's approach to strategy was very simple. We used to say that we were concerned with the important rather than the urgent. We were concerned with bringing clarity to what government was trying to achieve. What were the things you needed to do in the short, medium and long term to try to get there? It was really a very simple conception of strategy. In terms of methods we were utterly eclectic. We used whatever analytical and other methods help us to do our job.[147]

Stephen Aldridge, Director of the PMSU (2005–9), insisted the approach was collegiate: 'There is a whole series of ways in which, through working with departments, we are able to support them as well as to advance the wider strategic objectives that government has.'[148] Mulgan insists:

> I set the goal that half of our commissions should come from departments, not from the centre which we roughly achieved within a couple of years. For every project we would try to get at least a minister and often a permanent secretary with some tie-in.[149]

This is confirmed by a PMSU official:

> We were there to support the Prime Minister and he would not have tolerated anything else. But you should try and work with departments, try and influence them, bring them along. That might mean you make some compromises to the purity of your strategy, but a lot of the prize was more effective implementation and delivery. Now in an ideal world you wouldn't stray off the purity of your strategy. Public administration and politics being what it is, maybe sometimes you need to accept the good rather than the best [...] The PMSU could not deliver a damn thing on its own, could it? Fifty people might come up with some good analysis and some good ideas, but we couldn't actually deliver anything.[150]

The PMSU was 'essentially a consultancy at the heart of government',[151] respected in Whitehall for its analytical rigour, the empirical insight it brought to the policy-making process, and the emphasis on building interpersonal relationships with departments:

> We were able to build up influence with departments because we put such a high premium on good quality, rigorous analysis. The PMSU was respected for the quality of its people, thought to be rigorous and evidence-based, as well as [...] thinking about how you use your interpersonal skills and guile to achieve influence. There is a regiment of the British army whose motto is 'it's not my force but my guile'. I think that is a good motto for civil servants and central units if they want to be successful.[152]

Nonetheless, it is apparent that departments were generally disengaged from the PMSU's work. According to ministers, departments struggled to understand the logic behind PMSU reports.[153] The PMSU's approach was influenced by private sector management consultancy.[154] New Labour's strategy was concerned with modernising policy-making capability, drawing on sources of advice beyond the civil service. A wide-ranging review of education policy undertaken by Lord Birt and the McKinsey consultant, Nick Lovegrove, in 2002 proposed an extension of the internal market in schools through greater private sector involvement.[155] The report 'enraged' the DfES permanent secretary,

David Normington. An official observed from a meeting where the findings were discussed:

> Normington was just going more and more red, and angrier and angrier, until finally he couldn't contain himself any longer. He said, 'not only do we not agree with any of this stuff, if this report ever comes into the public domain we will publically say we disagreed with it completely'.[156]

The PMSU was accused of excessive secrecy and lack of transparency in its use of evidence. For example, the chair of the PASC, Tony Wright MP, complained that analysis undertaken on the impact of parental choice was never published.[157] The data influenced the government's decision to extend quasi-markets and competition between schools (Barber, 2007; Le Grand, 2005). Similarly, a single copy of the FSU's review of the criminal justice system was allowed into the Home Office: it was promptly locked in the Permanent Secretary's safe and never discussed among officials.[158] This friction replicates accusations made against the Central Policy Review Staff, cutting across departments and antagonising ministers (Blackstone & Plowden, 1988; Donoughue, 1987; Mulgan, 1996).

What is more, no clear mechanism existed by which PMSU policy recommendations might be translated into change on the ground:

> The PMSU's understanding of how you got things done across government was always very naive and under-developed. I didn't think Blair really realised the importance of getting hearts and minds from the officials either [...] if you don't bring on board officials it can destroy an idea at an early stage. You've got to have an understanding of how these systems work.[159]

Many departments employed tactics to avoid implementing the PMSU's reports as far as possible.[160] This meant ignoring recommendations on the basis that the Prime Minister would lose interest, or appearing to assimilate policy proposals while diluting the findings.[161] A senior PMSU official acknowledged:

> Clearly some officials felt threatened. These people felt the PMSU was usurping their role. Sometimes I felt the senior civil service was not entirely bought into it. They felt this was weakening their role, increasing the power of the centre versus departments.[162]

Nevertheless, by the time of Blair's departure, departments were creating their own strategy units. According to Halpern: 'This created a new network of relationships across Whitehall of people who share a common history and, more importantly, an empirically rigorous, long-term and politically attuned approach to policy making' (2010: 275). It is important to note that even under New Labour, strategic policy-making was anchored within departments rather than enforced through the centre: an enduring feature of the Whitehall paradigm.

The 'Hyperactive Centre' – A Critique

Whatever the contingencies shaping the centre's influence over departments, a critique of New Labour's reforms was developed in which a small 'cabal' of unaccountable advisers came to dominate policy-making. Actors were prone to 'group-think', lacked practical understanding of public sector management, and sought to undermine traditional accountability structures (Hennessy, 2005; Kilfoyle, 2000; Marquand, 2004; Savoie, 2008; Short, 2008). It was argued that an irreversible shift occurred in the policy-making process during the New Labour years from departments to the centre. One senior Cabinet Office mandarin saw the growth of central units:

> As a gesture of contempt towards departments; saying I need all this advice, I don't consider the Secretary of State for Health to be the principle adviser to me on health. I'll bring in someone to advise me on health in the Policy Unit. I think that is an unhealthy development.[163]

Indeed, this position is endorsed by a minister with close links to Blair:

> What the civil service could not foresee was that the Prime Minister and his staff were beginning to operate as if there was no other part of the government apart from the Prime Minister and Number Ten. I mean their disdain for the rest of government, the working of Cabinet, the principle of collective responsibility, was palpable.[164]

Sir Robin Mountfield (former permanent secretary at the Cabinet Office from 1995 to 1999) warned that special advisers behaved as 'unaccountable junior ministers' (House of Lords Constitution Committee report, 2009: Chap. 2). A minister remarked: 'I said no one from my department must talk to Number Ten. I resisted people coming from Number Ten and trying to talk to staff.'[165] For some, Blair and Brown's lack of governmental experience is telling, reinforcing a limited understanding at the centre of how to ensure policy was effectively delivered on the ground:

> The point that a reform goes from being a campaign speech to another speech to a Green Paper to a White Paper with the Bill then being amended in the Commons, amended in the Lords, and then the implementation strategy […] that's a long process and nothing goes through that process without being changed dramatically at a whole set of different stages.[166]

As Mottram confirmed:

> One of the big problems in government is there is no understanding at the top, and this can include officials as well as ministers, of what life is like for the people who are doing the delivery and no understanding of their capacity to absorb frequent changes of message.[167]

Kate Jenkins, an Efficiency Unit adviser in the 1980s, noted that ministers rarely grasped the complexity of the delivery machinery in the central state:

> Working with a large number of extremely well-intentioned ministers [...] I have seen over and over again this deep frustration about why the machine does not respond as they want it to respond, which is based on what I could only describe as a naive innocence of the complexity of running these very big functions.[168]

That said, a DoH official insisted there was an inevitable tension within the implementation process: 'Civil servants are very good at managing up, their job is to manage upwards. They're acutely aware that my success is what I do upwards. In the NHS, your success depends on what you do downwards.'[169] There are contrasting cultures and incentives in departments and the public sector. The Public Service Bargain[170] (PSB) in Whitehall departments is overwhelmingly concerned with officials serving ministers through vertical lines of accountability. In the public sector, PSBs rely on managers operating through horizontal as well as vertical structures, incentivising staff and motivating performance at the front-line (Hood & Lodge, 2006). Inevitably, Whitehall departments struggle to develop credible strategies for reforming policy and delivery in 'street-level' agencies where the incentive structures and cultures are markedly different to central government.

In Labour's first term, Number Ten was considered 'entirely ineffective in understanding how to get things done across government'.[171] The centre frequently underestimated the commitment to cultural change within departments. In DfES, both Michael Bichard and David Normington 'certainly changed the culture as Permanent Secretary'.[172] There was scepticism that imposing centralised initiatives on departments would produce the intended outcomes. Heavyweight intervention is required which may prove counter-productive:

> The Prime Minister couldn't attend every meeting. He couldn't fight every battle. Therefore you had to be much cannier in creating alliances and coalitions. Certainly CPRS [the Central Policy Review Staff] made this mistake; most of its projects just annoyed departments and didn't lead to results. In the British system, the presidential model doesn't really work; or it works when the Prime Minister has lots of political capital and lots of time. If he then goes off to fight a war or his opinion poll ratings go down, then you are left high and dry.[173]

A Number Ten special adviser alluded to the instability and confusion engendered by frequent changes of personnel at the centre:

> I think it was all a bit odd. Tony's strategy when he saw a problem was to bring in somebody else. You had John Birt, you had Geoff Mulgan, you had Matthew Taylor, all these big beasts essentially circling the court [...] I think it was a problem.[174]

As New Labour sought to improve co-ordination augmenting the institutional power resources available to the prime minister, further confusion arose about where power lies at the centre. Insiders allude to how various bodies around Number Ten became locked in a struggle for ascendency, creating confusion within departments about who speaks for the Prime Minister, undermining the delivery of departmental goals. The creation of new institutions at the centre further fragmented the central state, despite the quest for 'joined-up government'. Prime-ministerial units struggled to have an impact across most political systems according to a key Number Ten strategist: 'We studied a lot of central units around the world, and so many of them produced interesting things which didn't actually have traction with the machine.' A memorandum to the Prime Minister from one of his senior policy advisers in June 2003 referred to:

> A problem at the centre. No.10's ability to synthesise politics, strategy and tactics is much weaker than a few years ago. The political inputs to decisions are now even more dominated by short-term communications or political management considerations than before; meanwhile, the people working on policy generally have far less political experience than was the case five years ago. As a result, oddly for a mid-term, the mood is highly short-termist.[175]

Despite New Labour's instinct to govern from the centre, the capacity to shape policy still rested with departments, as one former PMSU adviser noted:

> In Number Ten you've got advisers and you've got a few in support, but there is obviously a capacity issue. They [departments] would know more about how to draw up regulations and how policy works with existing legislation. The department knew who to talk to in terms of all the different funding streams.[176]

Officials are the custodians of inherited knowledge about past policy initiatives, institutional legacies, legislative history and policy implementation. The fluidity of power and the requirement of actors in the core executive to exchange resources through bargaining games points towards the contingency of outcomes, rather than an unambiguous shift towards a top-down command structure. This is underlined by the limits to central state authority, and the risk of overemphasising central government's capacity to impose reforms on civil society.

The Limits of Central Control

Within the New Labour leadership, the futility of imposing reforms through central dictat was widely acknowledged as the government's period of office progressed.[177] The delivery model was evolving from command-and-control to devolution, decentralisation and empowerment (Barber, 2007; Mulgan, 2008).[178] Lord Birt characterised this as 'a model of a lean, mean centre and the maximum of devolution of delivery'.[179] In Labour's 2005 manifesto, Blair argued there was 'no going back to one-size-fits-all monolithic services'; the goal was 'driving innovation through diversity of provision and power in the hands of the patient, the parent and the citizen'.

However, one observer acknowledged: 'It is difficult to set up a system designed around central control and then to try and step back.'[180] There is too little capacity due to over-prescription. In the teaching profession, 'there was literally an opening the cage mentality and people not wanting to step out'.[181] Hyman (2004: 360) acknowledges: 'Government policy is too prescriptive [...] head teachers seem too scared to be very imaginative.' The dilemma is posed by Blunkett in an interview conducted for this study:

> The challenge for us [...] was to make sure you have levers to pull but you know when to let go of them. That was the real difficulty. What happened post-2002 reinforced in my mind that we were right to drive from the centre. Once the foot came off the accelerator, the results just plateaued again [...] But we didn't necessarily have an exit strategy from the centralised approach.[182]

Another adviser conceded: 'We were really bad at driving bottom-up change.'[183] This alludes to the nature of policy-making at the centre of government. Analysing the policy process within the core executive obscures fundamental relationships between the state, public policy and civil society:

> The model of change which still distorts a lot of policy making assumes that pulling a lever at the top through a law or a programme actually has a series of effects. Most of the time it doesn't, actually, particularly if you're concerned with policing or schools or hospitals. The default for governments and a lot of social scientists is wanting to believe that interventions can make all the difference as opposed to family, environment, and all sorts of things that are less amenable to intervention.[184]

Matthew Taylor, an adviser at Number Ten between 2003 and 2006, concurred:

> One of the things that Labour did not really get – and this goes back to the institutional memory point – was that you could pull a lot of levers at the centre, not having a great deal of impact. It is a caricature, but ministers spent time in their

offices pulling levers and it was not for a couple of years before anybody bothered to tell them that those levers were not necessarily connected to anything outside.[185]

Taylor's argument is that focusing on Whitehall obscures the challenge of translating policy goals into delivery at 'street-level'. The commentator Peter Riddell concludes:

> What was so often underestimated was the time it actually took to achieve change on the ground. The Blairites did begin to understand how long it takes to transform schools and academies – that achieving change on the ground is very difficult. It is to do with the time it takes to affect change in institutions. At times, the approach to achieving change was oversimplified.[186]

There is a tendency in Whitehall to treat public policy as a process of linear transmission from central government to local agencies and actors. However, the relationship between Whitehall and front-line delivery is complex, mediated by exchange relations and the bargaining process where policy goals are constantly redefined and interpreted by agents. Policy making and delivery rely on a myriad of institutions and actors outside the direct authority of the central state. Having emphasised the complexity of the governance arena, this chapter has addressed the nature of power and the politics of the policy-making process in the institutions of the British state.

Conclusion: The Power Dependency Model

Those accounts portraying the relationship between departments and the centre as a zero-sum game (Foster, 2005; Foster & Plowden, 1998; Hennessy, 2005; Kavanagh & Seldon, 2001) do not address the inherent fluidity of power within the core executive. They erroneously privilege change, under-playing how the interaction between departments and the centre has always been characterised by exchange relations, bargaining games and mutual dependency between a plurality of actors. The power to affect change exists throughout central government: the influence of particular actors and institutions is shaped by contingency and unintended consequences.

Table 6.1 summarises the case studies of policy-making in Whitehall. The aim is to assess continuity and change within the central state, addressing power asymmetries and institutional relationships. This is underpinned by the relational and contingent notion of *power dependency* examined in Chapter 4: no actor has the monopoly over resources. Rather than conceptualising power as a zero-sum game, actors in the core executive rely on other agents and institutions in order to develop and implement policy (Dunleavy & Rhodes, 1990;

TABLE 6.1 Modelling power dependency in British governance

	Academy schools	Family-Nurse Partnerships	National Economic Council
Structural context	Investment and reform of public services based on accountability regime of choice and contestability	Social exclusion dealing with inter-generational transmission of multiple disadvantage within 'problem families'	Impact of financial crisis and subsequent downturn in 2008–9
Role of ideas	Both New Right and New Institutionalism encouraged break with traditional models of public sector delivery	Literature on early years emphasised risk of reproducing multiple deprivation within families	Response to aftermath of crisis based on 'New Keynesianism' emphasising role of government activism
Institutional terrain	Prime Minister's Policy Unit was predominant agency driving academy programme, but DfES thwarted its momentum	SETF/Cabinet Office lacked resources, especially programme budgets without clear departmental lead	NEC challenged Treasury dominance over economic policy, bringing other key departments (e.g. BIS) into prominence
Agency	Role of policy entrepreneurs in driving agenda in central government and locally, although departmental actors remained important	FNPs part of prime-ministerial quest for a legacy, hence entailed considerable personalism	Desire for prime-ministerial control over economic policy pursued through framework of 'Cabinet government'
Continuity and change	Number Ten exerted authority over academies, but influence in most areas of education policy more constrained and discretion lay with departments	Highly prescriptive, 'evidence-based' approach widened influence of social science in government policy-making, but did not threaten departmentalism reinforcing centralising tendencies of strong state	Treasury influence ebbed and flowed since 1940s – continuous cycles of influence and decline while crises have contingent effect on relative standing of Treasury and chancellor

Rhodes, 1997; Smith, 1999). Through the prism of the power dependency model, empirical insights emerge about the relationship between departments and the centre during New Labour's 13 years in power:

- Academy schools are the product of a distinctive approach to reform emphasising contestability, choice and diversity. This constituted a break with traditional models of public sector delivery. Such ideas emerged from within the Prime Minister's Policy Unit, where special advisers acted as 'policy entrepreneurs'. Nonetheless, actors in departments had autonomy, and were able to thwart the centre's intentions: there was little that could be achieved if departments withheld support. In sustaining the academy programme, Number Ten conceded that schools' policy would largely be determined in the department. The claim that DfES was taken over by Number Ten is misleading.
- Family-Nurse Partnerships were designed to address the inter-generational transmission of disadvantage within families at the behest of the Prime Minister. The Social Exclusion Task Force lacked bureaucratic resources and access to departmental budgets. It was highly dependent on departments, despite being located in the Cabinet Office. Getting FNPs off the ground required the support of the Prime Minister and his ministerial allies. The programme was prescriptive affording limited autonomy to providers, consistent with the strong, centralising state tradition in British government.
- The National Economic Council underlined the urgency of government activism in the wake of the crisis. The dominance of the Treasury over economic policy was curtailed, bringing other actors and institutions into the decision-making process. The NEC acted as a Cabinet committee, consistent with departmentalism and a more 'collegiate' style of government. The mutual dependency between the prime minister and chancellor remained. The standing of the Treasury has always ebbed and flowed with the passage of events. Even so, the Treasury retains structural power in Whitehall, continuing to oversee public expenditure in departments and intervening across the domestic policy agenda.

This chapter examined how far the centre in Number Ten sought to bypass departments in the policy-making process. It is not merely concerned with whether the prime minister is able to dominate departments, a pervasive theme in the literature (Hennessy, 2000; Kavanagh, 2002; King, 1985). The focus is the capacity of Number Ten, and its leverage over political and bureaucratic resources. The interaction between departments and the centre is dynamic, and cannot be understood as a static relationship based on a command-and-control model. There is a continuous exchange of resources between actors. As one official remarked, 'Power is not a zero-sum game. It is about the whole system and the pattern of relationships.'[187] The size of the operation in Number Ten should not be confused with the centre's capacity to enforce its will. There is a gap between intervention and control: actors can interfere from the centre, but their impact on outcomes may be contingent or even negligible.

Departments are autonomous and difficult to steer, although their sovereignty is 'context-dependent'. Officials have time and expertise, inevitably dominating the process of formulating and implementing policy. Even where Number Ten sought to directly influence policy, the relationship between the centre and departments is characterised by mutual dependency. Rather than positing the 'end of Whitehall', the literature must address both stability and discontinuity in the structures of British government. The pace of change is more often incremental and evolutionary: reform of Whitehall and the core executive has been contained within the existing constitutional framework of the British state. This study's findings are somewhat divergent from mainstream accounts:

- Under New Labour, the policy-making capability and resources of Number Ten was enhanced, but the centre still depended on departments.
- Although exchange relations are based on interdependence rather than compliance and acquiescence, there are disagreements between departments and Number Ten. Ministers in departments often have a negative view of the centre.
- Departments retain their distinctive policy-making role within the core executive of British politics, and ministerial government endures.
- Where changes occurred in the structure and processes of policy-making, the impact of change varies between departments and the policy sector in question. This makes disaggregating the process of change within the core executive essential.
- The study highlighted the importance of stability alongside change in Whitehall and the machinery of government. It is important to emphasise actors have autonomy and resources: outcomes cannot be read-off from the structural and strategic context in which agents operate.

Having analysed the extent to which the centre was able to override departments in the policy-making process, Chapter 7 will focus on the evidence for continuity and change in the Whitehall paradigm. The chapter considers the process of institutional change in the core executive, notably the politicisation and pluralisation of policy-making during the New Labour years. This occurred amid accusations of executive disarray and official subservience to ministerial predominance, leading to growing tensions at the heart of central government.

Government and Governance: Patterns of Continuity and Change in the Whitehall Paradigm

The single most important thing to understand about the civil service is that you are taught in Labour 'lore' that it is a conspiracy [...] a right-wing conspiracy. This is completely wrong. If it is a conspiracy of anything, it is a conspiracy of inertia. And the truth of *Yes, Minister* and *Yes, Prime Minister* is that they are close to being documentaries.

Senior Labour Minister (2012)[1]

The view of the Prime Minister was that trying to be the leader for a government based on a very small private office and a tiny policy unit was not going to produce first of all the degree of radicalism in policy thinking he was after, and the delivery capability [...] When you are in a hurry you want to set standards and you want to get things moving, you direct them strongly from the top, principally with a set of objectives and targets. There is a recognition that takes you so far.

Turnbull (2004)[2]

Britain's senior civil servants are themselves at a fateful crossroads. Behind them, wrecked beyond repair, is the old model of impartial mandarins speaking truth unto power. Ahead, if they choose the wrong path now, lies the real prospect of losing any significant role in policy making [...] Power has been draining out of Whitehall for years. Top civil servants have seen themselves usurped by spin doctors, political advisers, quangos, management consultants, and unelected so-called experts. All too often officials have been cowed into becoming mere courtiers telling ministers what ministers want to hear.

Cameron (2009: 7)

Introduction

The material discussed in Chapters 5 and 6 undermines the claim that the centre in Number Ten unilaterally displaced departments, permanently altering the nature of Whitehall and the core executive. This chapter will examine structural change in the machinery of the state, particularly the politicisation and pluralisation of the policy-making process under New Labour. The chapter will analyse continuity and change in the Whitehall paradigm, consisting of key elements within the Westminster model (Campbell & Wilson, 1995; Flinders, 2002; Page, 2010):

- a permanent bureaucracy of politically neutral officials;
- non-generalist civil servants;
- Whitehall as a 'career for life';
- officials as the 'monopoly provider' of ministerial policy advice.

In their seminal work on 'the end of Whitehall', Campbell and Wilson refer to 'the world of the politician, and the world of bureaucrat, and the interaction between the two. Each world [...] is guided by certain principles and expectations that together constitute the Whitehall model' (1995: 9). This chapter develops a typology of continuity and change, underlining the case for institutional path dependency in the machinery of the central state. The 'critical junctures' in which the equilibrium of the state bureaucracy is punctuated are rare, inferring that change is more often piecemeal and evolutionary. The impact of change is relatively modest since the creation of the civil service necessitated strategic choices about the neutrality and generalist skill-set of the permanent bureaucracy which foreclosed alternative institutional pathways, encapsulated by Northcote-Trevelyan (1854) and the Haldane report (1918) on the machinery of government. Moreover, the system of government creates vested interests reluctant to forego their authority and power, creating a bias towards institutional inertia in Whitehall. This is reinforced by the tendency to graft change apparently seamlessly onto the existing constitutional settlement.

The chapter delineates an analytical framework through which institutional continuity and change is assessed. Practitioner commentary infers that change under New Labour has been ubiquitous: such interpretations have been influential within the academic literature (Fawcett & Rhodes, 2007; Foster, 2005; Foster & Plowden, 1998). Alternative accounts emphasise institutional continuity, questioning how far a dramatic transformation in the Whitehall paradigm has occurred (Burnham & Pyper, 2008; Marsh et al., 2001). While there have been structural changes, key elements of the Whitehall model have persisted: as such, it is premature to posit the end of the Whitehall paradigm.

The chapter's assessment of continuity and change examines key developments, notably the trend towards politicisation through special advisers, alongside the pluralisation of policy-making through thinktanks and nongovernmental lobby groups. The key argument is that while the civil service is no longer the monopoly provider of ministerial advice, officials retain their dominant role within the policy process. Although governments contemplate initiatives to overhaul Whitehall and the civil service, key reforms are more often diluted. According to the logic of path dependency, change is costly and there is an emphasis on maintaining the institutional status quo. Moreover, there are powerful veto points in the reform process (Tsebelis, 2002). The strategic gain from reforming the Westminster model and Whitehall paradigm is limited for any party of power in British politics. The British political class has avoided reform of the Westminster model, threatening the integrity and legitimacy of the existing state (Marquand, 1988).

The final section of the chapter draws together the analysis of continuity and change, building on the Asymmetric Power Model and the Differentiated Polity Model. The chapter relates the dynamics of continuity and change to the question of where power lies within central government, emphasising path dependency alongside structural discontinuity in the Whitehall paradigm.

Continuity and Change in Whitehall

This study focuses on how far New Labour altered the nature of the Whitehall paradigm and the core executive, restructuring the central state machinery after 1997. Chapter 4 addressed the literature on governance and the core executive, and suggested that when the structure and processes of policy-making are disaggregated, there are fluid and contingent relationships in the central state. There are numerous accounts which infer that the Whitehall model has been dismantled over the last 30 years, together with an assault on the status and prestige of the UK civil service (Butler, 2004; Campbell & Wilson, 1995; Foster, 2005; Hennessy, 2000). To proclaim the end of the Whitehall paradigm, however, appears hasty and somewhat overstated.

The evidence for the co-existence of continuity alongside change is rarely considered: while elements of the Whitehall model have been eroded, other characteristics persist over time. The previous chapter highlighted that the 'policy paradigms' informing government programmes tend to change infrequently (Marsh et al., 2003; Rose, 1985). Departments have entrenched structural biases and ideological interests. The argument about the changing nature of governance rests on how far the Whitehall machinery has altered, and whether it has remained stable over time. However, there is a prior question about *where* change happens: whether change occurs at the institutional or the ideational level, and how one reinforces the other. It is important to develop an analytically rigorous conceptualisation of continuity and change, moving away from, and rejecting, implicit binary categorisations.

The case study approach addresses institutional and policy developments in Whitehall during the New Labour years. The purpose is to analyse the relationship between the centre in Number Ten and departments in the core executive, highlighting points of continuity alongside change, while identifying elements of structural discontinuity within the Whitehall paradigm. The process of institutional development exhibits certain patterns and regularities alluding to path dependency in the Whitehall model (Pollitt & Bouckaert, 2009). Table 7.1, drawing on Pollitt and Bouckaert, identifies varieties of institutional change in the machinery of government:

TABLE 7.1   Patterns of institutional change

	Within path/incremental	*Radical/transformation*
Gradual	A. Classical incrementalism	B. Gradual but eventually fundamental change
	(*Tortoise*)	(*Stalactite*)
Abrupt	C. Radical conservatism – rapid return to previous ways	D. Sudden, radical change
	(*Boomerang*)	(*Earthquake*)

Source: Pollitt & Bouckaert, 2009

Analysing Institutional Continuity and Change

According to Pollitt and Bouckaert's typology of institutional reform:

- '*Classical incrementalism*' refers to small-scale but frequent changes, leading to minor alterations in the nature of institutions. This form of incremental change is relatively predictable: there are few radical and sudden shifts of direction (Lindblom, 1979).
- The '*stalactite model*' is broadly stable, but the process of change is cumulative and leads to more fundamental change creating new institutional arrangements over time (Steinmo, 1996).
- '*Radical conservatism*' refers to scenarios where path-breaking decisions are taken as a response to exogenous shocks, but the institutional framework reverts to the status quo: business as usual (Gamble, 2009).
- Finally, the '*earthquake model*' alludes to dramatic and far-reaching institutional change: 'a great leap forward'. The existing trajectory is punctuated and a new phase inaugurated: actors seize windows of opportunity created by exogenous shocks (Cortell & Peterson, 2004; Kingdon, 1995; Pierson, 2004).

This typology is hardly exhaustive: for example, other literature refers to institutional and policy cycles where change proceeds through a series of stages (Howlett & Ramesh, 1995). Pollitt and Bouckaert's framework is, nevertheless, important in assessing and contextualising change. There is a voluminous literature highlighting dramatic change in the shape of the British state and core executive, consistent with the 'earthquake' model of institutional transformation. This emphasises the 'presidentialisation' of British politics, the centralisation of power through Number Ten, the erosion of the public service ethos, and the demise of the Whitehall model (Campbell & Wilson, 1995; Foley, 2003; Foster, 2005; Kavanagh, 2000; Marquand, 2004). The view is that the Whitehall paradigm premised on the indivisibility of ministerial–civil service relations has broken down as the result of the Thatcher administration and, latterly, the reforms introduced by the Blair governments. Gray (2000: 298) concludes the reforms have:

> Led towards the creation of […] a managerial state where new sets of relationships between state and citizen, public and private, providers and recipients, and management and politics are being created. In this respect, control […] has been relocated to new arenas of power.

Similarly, Bevir and Rhodes (2003) insist that significant changes occurred, undermining the centralised nature of the British polity and curtailing Whitehall's control over the policy process. On the other hand, alternative accounts emphasise institutional stability and continuity in Whitehall. Models of British politics such as the APM acknowledge that the contemporary policy-making process is increasingly pluralised and fragmented. However, they point towards the pervasive British tradition of strong, centralising government (Hall, 2011; Marsh, 2008; Richards, 2008; Smith, 2009). Research influenced by the APM highlights institutional stability alongside change: core elements of the Whitehall model persist, notably the continuing role of departments in the policy-making arena. The model of an asymmetric polity alludes to 'incremental' as well as 'gradual but eventually more fundamental' change: institutions evolve over time, although the potential still exists for radical upheaval in the structures and institutions of the state.

Institutional Change in the Whitehall Paradigm

The relationship between continuity and change mirrors the juxtaposition in the literature between narratives of 'government' and 'governance' (Fawcett, 2011; Smith, 2009). The perspective offered by this study is that continuity and change not only co-exist, they maintain an interactive and dialectical relationship to one another. As Fawcett (2011: 1) contends:

> A unidirectional shift from government to governance is too simplistic and an explicit recognition needs to be given to the different ways in which government and governance co-exist. This can be understood as a series of trends and counter-trends in state restructuring.

While the central state is subject to the process of hollowing-out and 'destatisation' (Jessop, 2005; Rhodes, 1994), the core executive's capacities to act are reconstituted. States are ever more intrusive overseeing the launch of new bureaucracies, targets and forms of surveillance: neo-liberalism itself entails programmes of state intervention designed to free markets and unleash the forces of enterprise (Gamble, 1994; Le Gales, 2012). In addition, there are conceptions of change that acknowledge the impact of critical junctures ('Type D' in Pollitt & Bouckaert's typology). These are moments of upheaval which permanently alter the institutional boundaries of the state (Pierson, 2004; Richards & Smith, 1997). The emphasis on continuity may conceal important institutional changes and tipping-points: the 'stalactite model'.

During the period in which there was a transfer of power from Blair to Brown, the role of the core executive was reappraised. From the outset, Brown struggled to impose his authority on departments which 'didn't feel that Number Ten had credible ideas about public sector reform'.[3] A Cabinet Office official remarked: 'Brown's approach was very centralising, but it didn't actually help them to develop their agenda.' The Prime Minister appeared 'heavy-handed', as he struggled to project a coherent strategic purpose either in Whitehall or to the country. Another Cabinet minister referred to 'the dysfunctionality of the centre in the dying days of the government'.[4] As a result: 'Gordon quickly lost authority in Whitehall.'[5] According to a close Brown adviser:

> Number Ten was structurally weaker in Whitehall terms during Brown's period in office for reasons that aren't to be found in the nature of Number Ten, such as what was happening in the economy, GB's [Gordon Brown's] own position, and the political capital he had to deploy at the end of three terms of Labour government.[6]

This highlights the fluid and contingent nature of power at the centre. Beyond the hand-over between Blair and Brown, Heffernan (2006: 21) argues that Whitehall reforms have 'gone a considerable way to help establish an authoritative, prime-ministerial-led centre with Downing Street and the Cabinet Office revamped into a *de facto* Prime Minister's department'. The Conservative minister Kenneth Clarke mirrored this analysis of far-reaching change in the Whitehall paradigm:

> The relationship between politicians and the civil servants has changed very badly. We have taken to a simplistic length the idea that the politicians lay down policy and the civil servants deliver. I think the civil service has lost its policy role. They will administer things better if they play the key role they used to in the formulation of policy. Frank and fearless advice and actual involvement all the way through in the formulation of policy can spare the ministers an awful lot of chaos and anguish.[7]

Similarly Nick Raynsford, a former DCLG minister (1999–2001), averred:

> There is a real danger of excessive central control. Once it gets into micro-management and once it undermines the confidence of departmental officials to really express their views about what is right [...] then you are seriously eroding the principles of good government.[8]

Both Clarke and Raynsford insist that the role of the civil service and Whitehall's capacity to govern effectively dramatically declined during the New Labour years. Since the 1970s, Britain has been portrayed as a *State Under Stress* (Foster & Plowden, 1998).

Institutional Stability in the Whitehall Paradigm

Nonetheless, Clarke and Raynsford appear to overstate their argument; the case studies in this volume of academy schools, Family-Nurse Partnerships (FNPs) and the National Economic Council (NEC) highlight the importance of structural continuity alongside change. For instance, the core premise of the Northcote-Trevelyan reforms, the separation of policy-making from operational implementation, has been strengthened through the creation of *Next Steps*, the growth of the regulatory state, and the promulgation of NPM (Moran, 2003; Wrisque-Cline, 2008). While some characteristics of the Whitehall paradigm have been worn away and eroded, core elements remain firmly in place; indeed, the process of reform may actually entrench the traditional model encapsulated by Northcote-Trevelyan. This point is elaborated by Talbot:

> We still have in professional skills for government a system of apartheid with, on the one hand, people who are good at policy and, on the other, people who are supposedly good at operations and management [...] 'those that can do policy and those that cannot run agencies'. That is the general attitude still among far too many senior civil servants.[9]

Similarly, Kingdom attests: 'The nineteenth-century model of the manderinate has survived two world wars and the Keynesian revolution [...] despite bold words from reformers it is not time to write its obituary' (2013: 64). The division between operational management and policy-making in Whitehall has been reinforced by the contemporary reform process. Moreover, departments have upheld existing programmes and operating procedures, imposing institutional constraints in the policy process. Not surprisingly, Hogwood (1987) concludes that longevity in office is essential for policy change. The most radical phase of legislation occurred during Thatcher's third term after the 1987 election: three consecutive victories were required before the Conservative governments were able to challenge and overturn the institutional biases of departments (Gamble, 1994).

The Duality of Continuity and Change in Whitehall

The view of change as sudden and rapid is evident in accounts emphasising structural instability. These arguments are important, inevitably attracting attention from Whitehall commentators; however, they ought to be carefully dissected and considered. The evidence points towards a subtle fusion of continuity and change: it is important to disaggregate the institutional structures and processes through which policy is made. Historical institutionalism emphasises that gradual and incremental change creates 'tipping points' for more far-reaching change (Streek & Thelen, 2005). Even in atypical cases such as academy schools and Family-Nurse Partnerships, Whitehall departments have resisted instructions from the centre. Departmental interests are entrenched: since the Haldane report after World War I, the Whitehall system has been built around departments (Burch & Holliday, 2000; Hennessy, 2000). Similarly, Talbot disputes whether the reciprocal relationship between ministers and civil servants has altered dramatically in recent decades:

> We have such a close symbiotic relationship between a professional senior civil service, not a politically appointed one, and the government of the day, which I have said to this committee before is serial monogamy. In any other parts of public service, they do not have the same relationship with the executive as they have here.[10]

There are structural continuities in how Whitehall is managed, as Hood (1996: 73) reiterates:

> The traditional picture of a village world regulated in a relatively informal way through largely unwritten rules, a compliance culture and low relational distance between regulator and regulated still appeared to capture much of the style of regulation within Whitehall a quarter of a century after Heclo and Wildavsky's study.

In a similar vein, the view presented by Theakston (1987: 106) continues to resonate:

> Life in Whitehall is not lived in a state of permanent conflict between ministers and civil servants. Analyses of policy making which focus on adversarial confrontations between ministers and the civil service oversimplify and distort. Relations are complex and fluid, and the lines of division are more often than not to be found not *between* the political and bureaucratic elements in government but *within* them as alliances of ministers and officials compete with each other to advance particular goals or defend common interests.

As Rhodes (2012: 12) testifies: 'At the top of government departments we find a class of political-administrators, not politicians or administrators. They live in a shared world.' Aside from empirical observations drawn from a wider literature, continuity and change in Whitehall and the core executive can be analysed through the accounts of 'government' and 'governance' elaborated in Chapter 4.

The Governance Debate

As the recent literature testifies, 'government' and 'governance' are mutually constitutive, existing in dynamic tension with one another (Fawcett, 2011; Jessop, 1996; Lowe & Rollings, 2000). At the core of 'first wave' governance accounts is the view that the changing nature of the policy process has denuded the centre of control (Rhodes, 1997). The plurality of actors, the blurring of the public–private divide and the incorporation of new managerial processes accorded with the perspective which emphasises the hollowing-out of the state (Dunleavy & Rhodes, 1990; Rhodes, 1994).

The case studies informing this research emphasise that policy networks based on resource dependency exist alongside, and reinforce, asymmetrical power relations. The paradox is that power-hoarding tendencies reinforced by the British Political Tradition have had to accommodate the shift towards 'negotiated governance' within a multi-level polity. New Labour's commitment to participation, empowerment and partnership is contradicted by the centralising thrust of its initiatives, a determination to strengthen service delivery by driving policy from the centre (McAnulla, 2006; Newman, 2001). While influence over policy-making is confined to a narrow group of actors in central government, there has been greater emphasis on user participation in policy design (Stoker, 2002). As Mulgan described:

> The language of user-centred design and user-centred policy [...] was way ahead of its time. Bringing in the user voice right at the start to shape policy, whether it was

teenagers at risk of becoming pregnant or 14-year-olds on housing estates. Often it gave you very different insights to what was really going on and what was really experienced, and tended to be very energising for services once they were deeply engaged with user experience.[11]

Nevertheless, case studies indicate that actors rarely deliver objectives and programmes that have not been explicitly authorised by the centre. They have usually been mandated to deliver services according to pre-determined priorities.[12] The core executive is concerned with informal incentives, alongside formal bureaucratic procedures including targets, performance league tables, ring-fenced funding streams and payment by results (Barber, 2007). This emphasises that power has remained hermetically sealed within the central state, as New Labour sought to reconstitute the Westminster model (Marsh et al., 2001).

The extent of institutional change associated with the governance narrative needs to be qualified: the focus of elites is maintaining the status quo to protect their resources and power, implying a strong element of path dependency and institutional continuity (Pierson, 2004; Richards & Smith, 2002). Departmental cultures are deeply entrenched: initiatives to reform the civil service have more often foundered. According to the case studies of the policy process reviewed in Chapter 5, DfES officials were reluctant to undermine the power of local authorities due to complementary bureaucratic interests.[13] DoH officials did not wish to lose control of FNPs which they categorised as a public health intervention.[14] The Treasury fought to prevent the NEC from asserting too much control over economic policy.[15] There are structural constraints in the Whitehall paradigm: critical junctures unfold at rare intervals where endogenous and exogenous forces coincide, stimulating fundamental changes in the structure of the central state.

The continuity observed in the machinery of government emphasises that the centre has limited control over policy-making and implementation. There are few levers translating the core executive's objectives seamlessly into change on the ground (Barber, 2007; Lipsky, 1979). Moreover, reforms to centralise the policy process have produced unintended consequences (Bevir & Rhodes, 2006b). The New Labour administration focused on a range of instruments.[16] According to Jeremy Heywood, initially Tony Blair's principal private secretary (PPS) (1999–2003), there had been a shift of emphasis during the second term. After 1997, the focus was command-and-control: top-down targets, Public Service Agreements, workforce reform and earned autonomy (Barber, 2007). However, a change of direction occurred during the second term emphasising quasi-markets, contestability and choice augmented by 'front-line freedom and flexibility'.[17] During the Brown era, there was a return to centrally driven targets known as 'citizen guarantees and entitlements' (Seldon & Lodge, 2010; Wright, 2004).

'Government' and 'governance' entail a series of 'trends and counter-trends' that have no pre-determined outcome such as the hollowing-out of the state. Academy schools involve a hybrid of targets, inspections, funding agreements and relationships with providers.[18] FNPs required partnership agreements between central government, PCTs and local authorities.[19] The NEC sought to influence the behaviour of banks and financial institutions, tackling the squeeze on credit in the aftermath of the crash.[20] This alludes to strategies of 'meta-governance' fusing together statism, hierarchy and command where the central state seeks to oversee and control the processes unleashed by 'desta-tisation', re-embedding the traditional power-hoarding model (Fawcett, 2011; Marinetto, 2003).

Critical Junctures, Windows of Opportunity and Punctuated Equilibrium in the Whitehall Model

This view of underlying institutional stability ought not to imply that the Whitehall model is entirely immune from structural change. The equilibrium of the permanent bureaucracy can still be punctuated. The 'punctuated equilibrium model' indicates that change is wholesale at moments of critical juncture or crisis (Hay, 2002). That view is in part a reaction against the dominant conception of continuity and change in British politics, centred on gradual adaptation and an evolutionary approach to change which characterises the Whig conception of history (Kerr & Kettell, 2006). This chapter will argue that the punctuated equilibrium model is scarcely appropriate for analysing changing patterns of governance in Whitehall and the core executive, however. Since change occurs within the dominant political tradition, it often appears hesitant and sporadic without a fixed purpose or end-point. For instance, the financial crisis in 2008 was a major shock, but it did not fundamentally overhaul the structures of the British state and is still a long way from any decisive resolution.

The following section of the chapter addresses how accounts of institutional change are applied to the policy process. There are major events such as the '9/11' attacks and the nationalisation of retail banks after the post-2008 crisis which portray a seismic shift in the structure and processes of the state. Hay's model (see Figure 7.1) refers to 'a discontinuous conception of political time in which periods of comparatively modest institutional change are interrupted by more rapid and intense moments of transformation' (2002: 161). This explains

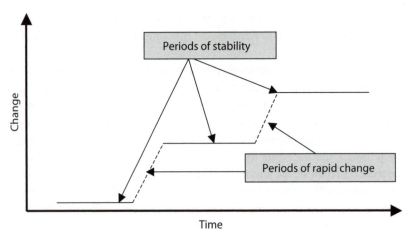

Source: Hay (2002)

FIGURE 7.1   The punctuated equilibrium model

how phases of relative stability combine with moments of periodic crisis. The pace of change significantly accelerates leading to the replacement of the existing paradigm.

That said, an emphasis on structural *crisis* is in danger of confusing how, and where, change occurs. The 'critical wave' literature on the BPT in Chapter 1 indicated that reforms emerge within the context of institutions and practices informed by the traditional paradigm ('incremental change') (Marsh & Hall, 2007). This notion of institutional stability indicates that Hay's model has weaknesses (Marsh, 2010). Hay is criticised for ignoring the material and institutional dimensions of continuity and change focusing on 'the crucial mediating role of ideas' (2002: 166). This infers that the scope and intensity of change has been overstated in the punctuated equilibrium model. In Hay's account, Thatcherism decisively broke the 30-year consensus in British politics, destroying the post-1945 settlement. In contrast, Marsh and Tant (1989) allude to underlying continuities, insisting that the Thatcher governments drew from the British Political Tradition. They pursued neo-liberal reforms through a top-down, centralising mode of statecraft concentrating power at the centre of the state. Hay's analysis overstates the impact of ideas while neglecting the role of institutions. Marsh and Tant reflect on the interaction between the material and the ideational in determining how, and where, change occurs.

In the contemporary era, the financial crisis was a moment of upheaval with implications for the structure and legitimacy of the state. This created a window of opportunity, analogous to the period in which the Winter of Discontent and the International Monetary Fund 'bail-out' allowed the Thatcher governments to narrate contradictions inherent in the state (Annesley et al., 2010; Gamble, 2009; Kingdon, 1984; Richards & Smith, 2002). However, while the creation of the NEC had major consequences it meant 'a return to a more collegiate style of government which on the whole the civil service welcomed'.[21] A BIS official noted the underlying continuity of the NEC with ministerial government: 'I think it was helpful. It worked as a Cabinet committee because that is how civil servants treated it.'[22] Again, what appears on the surface to be fundamental change may, in fact, merely reinforce traditional constitutional procedures and practices.

The literature on windows of opportunity and critical junctures originates in theoretical approaches underpinned by historical institutionalism. Within the punctuated equilibrium model, policy change proceeds through stasis broken by moments of crisis (Hall, 1993; Hay, 2002; Krasner, 1982). Cortell and Peterson (2004) reject this approach, proposing an alternative 'three-stage' model: external pressure creates an opportunity for institutional reform; the potential for change depends on the interests and motivation of actors; in turn, the ability of agents to capitalise on exogenous shocks relates to their status and resources. Windows of opportunity are overlooked or disregarded if they fail to accord with the strategic interests of actors. Additionally, the institutional capacity to implement reforms must exist among the relevant actors within the machinery of the state.

Cortell and Peterson's approach is consistent with the 'critical wave' literature on the BPT. Reforms that threaten the axiom of strong and decisive government have rarely succeeded. In part, this is because the recasting of the Whitehall paradigm rarely accords with the material interests of agents. More often, the asymmetric resonance of ideas and interests ensures that radical reform proposals are dismissed as eccentric and unworkable. This relates to the American sociologist Albert Hirschman's 'jeopardy' thesis: reactionary narratives maintain that the price of a proposed change is too great, threatening to reverse and endanger previous institutional accomplishments (1991: 7). The risk of change is considered too high, thwarting all other attempts at institutional restructuring.

The jeopardy thesis is invoked by the British political class in seeking to protect and uphold the Westminster model – fundamental constitutional reform might threaten the stability of liberal parliamentary government, leading to potentially damaging unforeseen consequences (Birch, 1964; Evans, 1993; Marsh & Hall, 2007; Tant, 1993). The 'three-stage' model and literature on the BPT emphasise the extent of continuity and change in the Whitehall paradigm analysed through structural reforms, notably the politicisation and pluralisation of the policy process.

The Politicisation of Whitehall?

Having reviewed various theoretical approaches to institutional path dependency in the Whitehall model and the British state, the analysis of continuity and change emphasising stability in the Whitehall paradigm can be applied to the *politicisation* of the policy process, notably the growth of special advisers after 1997. A central claim of this study is that the civil service is no longer the monopoly source of ministerial policy advice. Even so, officials have remained predominant in dispensing advice to ministers, while overseeing the policy-making process. The notion that the machinery of government was increasingly concentrated around the centre in Number Ten relies on an exaggerated conception of change, akin to the punctuated equilibrium model.

The concept of 'politicisation' alludes to changes in the ethos and style of public service from a neutral, permanent bureaucracy to the dominance of partisan decision-making, re-establishing the role of politics in shaping state policies (Marquand, 2004). There is evidence from a range of countries in Western Europe and the United States which indicates that the incidence of political appointments in public administration has significantly increased in recent decades (Peters, 2004). This claim of politicisation is epitomised by commentary on Whitehall in the New Labour years:

> The rot may have started under the Tories – remember Margaret Thatcher's strictures about being 'one of us' – but most civil servants agree it has worsened under Labour. Number Ten and the Treasury, both heavily populated by political advisers, have become over-powerful.
>
> (Cameron, 2009: 7)

Of course, special advisers are not the only manifestation of politicisation. Another dimension is the increase in junior ministerial appointments: from 32 in the Attlee government to 77 under Gordon Brown.[23] However, it is New Labour's reliance on political advisers that has been a source of perennial fascination to Whitehall observers, arguably distracting from other more significant developments in the core executive (Hennessy, 2000; Powell, 2010). This chapter examines the dynamic unleashed by the growing number of special advisers in the policy-making process; the politicisation of the Whitehall machinery has been considered elsewhere (Foster, 2005; Kavanagh, 2002; Richards, 2008;

Seldon, 2005). The role and influence of political advisers has been a cause of controversy, giving rise to conflicting judgements. Advisers apparently threaten the integrity of the Haldane model in which there are only two actors in the central state: officials who advise and ministers who take decisions (Foster, 2005; Rhodes, 2011). That said, the debate often misunderstands, and indeed misrepresents, the role of special advisers within the British political system.

Many actors are sceptical that a sudden, wholesale shift has occurred in the Whitehall paradigm, not least because politically appointed advisers were influential during the Wilson and Thatcher governments, and have played a role in British government as far back as Lloyd George's 'Garden Suburb' during World War I.[24] As prime minister, Lloyd George was accused of being presidential and authoritarian, as were Thatcher and Blair. Indeed, one (Grade 2) civil servant insisted: 'I think you can always overstate it and personally I would always defend a lot of what happened [...] it is through a fusion of political leadership and strong civil service support and advice that you get the best policies.'[25] A civil service fast streamer in BIS added:

> Special advisers are an absolutely essential part of the policy making process. I mean the presentation of policy and how things are put through the machinery of government at a senior level. I think special advisers are essential to that because it is a very helpful way to prevent civil servants crossing a line [...] providing a buffer to ministers where they might otherwise be pressing civil servants to cross that line of policy versus politics. It is always a dotted line and it is fascinating to work around it.[26]

Likewise, a former minister and permanent secretary testify to the importance of the political team:

> All the senior civil servants to whom we spoke saw a good political team around the secretary of state as an asset, rather than a hindrance. Good special advisers oil the wheels of the department, helping to translate the political rhetoric into Mandarin speak, and vice versa. The excellent ones also add real value to policy-making and communication.
>
> (Purnell & Lewis, 2012: 15)

The growth in special adviser appointments at the centre and in departments is shown in Figure 7.2.

The number of special advisers in Whitehall doubled between the mid-1990s and 2010. Political appointees at the centre in Number Ten more than doubled: Blair had 27 'spads' on average, while Brown had 23, compared to 12 under Thatcher and 10 under Major (Riddell, 2006). It is the expansion in the role of political advisers at the centre rather than departments that has arguably been

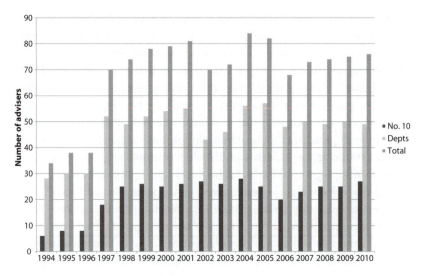

Source: data provided by the House of Commons library (2012)

FIGURE 7.2   Special advisers 1994–5 to 2009–10[28]

most momentous. As one former Cabinet secretary remarked, 'the significance of the number of special advisers is in my mind more in the expansion of the centre than it is the expansion of special advisers'.[27]

Research by the Constitution Unit indicates that a shift has occurred in the type of adviser skills valued by ministers. There is less emphasis on technocratic expertise; political dexterity is more strongly emphasised (Hazell & Jong, 2012). There are a number of explanations for the growth of political staff in British government. More sympathetic accounts emphasise the extent of ministerial overload due to complexity in the policy-making arena, the negotiation of directives relating to Britain's membership of the European Union, and the pressures imposed by the '24/7' media. It is argued that special advisers strengthen ministers' capacity to govern competently and take decisions, coping with a political environment increasingly characterised by fragmentation and disorder. Hyman (2004) goes further, insisting that parties of the Left should want to appoint special advisers as they help to fulfil the democratic mandate of the electorate in government.

Another related explanation for increasing numbers of political advisers relates to the growing appetite for responsive policy-making. Ministers felt this was lacking from the civil service, and sought to strengthen the quality and range of policy advice (Barber, 2007; Blair, 2010; Powell, 2010).[29] Special advisers are integral to overhauling and updating the policy process: 'The array of advisers who sit around in government are specialists in translating information, judgement, and access to very different species of knowledge.'[30] Advisers enhance the efficacy of policy-making, especially in departments which face increasingly complex and wide-ranging governing challenges. There is considered to be a healthy 'tension' between the political drive of ministers and their special advisers, and the institutional risk aversion of the civil service: rigorous questioning, debate and testing leads to better policy.

Those who defend the role of special advisers within the core executive question whether 80 political appointees are likely to overwhelm the power and resources of the permanent bureaucracy: the modest scale and transience of the political machinery is rarely acknowledged. Indeed, the tenure of special advisers is usually short: half of all advisers in the New Labour governments served for three years or less; two-thirds worked for only one minister (Constitution Unit, 2012). Many of the central units around Number Ten were staffed by civil servants or non-political secondments from private sector management consultancy. For example, one interviewee remarked of the PMSU: 'This was not a political unit and could have worked in any administration. There were no politics in this. It was a purely intellectual process.'[31]

Nonetheless, criticism of the role of political advisers ought to be seriously addressed: concerns about political advisers have been aired not just in Britain, but Westminster-based democracies such as New Zealand, Canada, and Australia (Savoie, 2008). This reflects the view that political appointees exercise improper influence, marginalising the permanent civil service while lacking formal accountability (Butler, 2004; Foster, 2005; Foster & Plowden, 1998). Of course, it is argued that those opposed to the growth of political appointees underestimate the role of special advisers in preventing civil servants from crossing the line between policy-making and politicisation. A departmental official in DfES averred:

A note of caution perhaps related to the politicisation point. I found of all my time in central government, Labour ministers were very, very respectful of the line between the 'political' and the 'official'. Some people are surprised when I say this of Ed Balls [...] Ed was really, really clear about the line between the official and the political; he didn't want it to come back and haunt him![32]

Moreover, Page concurred: 'The relationship between special advisers and civil servants appears remarkably non-conflictual' (2010: 7). Unsurprisingly, political appointees and permanent officials find they have a shared agenda, ensuring the efficient management of the department and ministerial private office

(Page, 2010). Advisers are regarded as influential by civil servants in so far as they carry out their minister's wishes. One BIS official remarked: 'I think the point about having people who can give you a bit of intelligence in advance of a decision being made is absolutely critical.'[33] Another acknowledged that advisers' influence is rooted in their proximity to ministers:

> As an adviser you like to think your power comes from your deep intellectual ability, but in fact is about being able to say 'the PM really does care about this' [...] and of course, they can undermine you, because sometimes you get it wrong. And if you go off in one direction but at the next meeting that's not what the [minister] wants, people say 'what are you talking about?' Officials are very quick to work out when you don't know.[34]

In addressing the role and status of political advisers, the civil service in Whitehall emphasises stability over conflict and upheaval. Many officials rationalise the growing influence of political appointees within a Whig narrative focused on an evolutionary conception of change which does not threaten the core tenets of the Whitehall model (Bevir & Rhodes, 2003; Burnham & Pyper, 2008). The emphasis on gradualism is reinforced in the literature, notably Riddell's account of the Blair years:

> The political was intermingled with the official from the start with a big increase in the number of special advisers in Number Ten and the Treasury. In practice, it is doubtful if these two special dispensations made much difference since Number Ten is an inherently political and partisan place. Permanent civil servants in the private office have in the past routinely acted in a political way in advancing and protecting the interests of the Prime Minister.
>
> (Riddell, 2006: 43)

The claim that the civil service has been marginalised from ministerial policy-making was treated sceptically by interviewees. One official remarked:

> I find it hard to square with what I read in the history books, or with what people who were around years and years ago say. There has never been a period where the civil service had a monopoly of policy in Britain, absolutely never. Even in the highpoint of very assertive Cabinet Secretaries and a central civil service, you had an endless stream of many academics going in and out of government. You had strong research departments in the party, you had whole networks and sources flowing into policy from think-tanks, and inspiration from other countries.[35]

Nick Pearce, head of Policy in Number Ten (2007–10), commented:

> In terms of the long view of history I'm not sure you can make a particularly credible argument that the centre has accreted lots more power compared to the nineteenth

or even the eighteenth century. In the long sweep of history, it doesn't make sense to say there is a march towards a more presidential system [...] they are crucially related to contingent factors that are about the external environment and the power of the Prime Minister themselves.[36]

This relates to a powerful counter-trend in the modern British state, namely 'depoliticisation' as a tool of governance justifying the delegation of responsibility to arms-length non-departmental public bodies from monetary policy to food safety (Burnham, 2002; Flinders, 2008). Hyman (2004: 72) remarks that during the Blair governments, contrary to popular myth, ministers and advisers were often depoliticised, acting as administrators and managers rather than 'political advocates'. Instead of redistributing power from civil servants to ministers and special advisers, the realm of political control has contracted in favour of autonomous groups of specialist policy-makers and experts. This provides an entirely different perspective on Whitehall's nominal politicisation.

Michael Trend of the PASC insisted: 'There is a sea change going on slowly but surely in the way in which we are governed.'[37] The Thatcher administration altered the organisational structure and ethos of Whitehall: 'An obsession for them was completely bypassing civil service policy-making capacity.'[38] This was allegedly furthered during the New Labour era:

> What changed structurally to give the centre more capacity, more clout and more intelligence [...] was the creation of the Delivery Unit and the Strategy Unit. Those two worked and they gave Number Ten a brain and a delivery reach into departments [...] those two innovations did mean that the centre was more powerful than it had been in other periods.[39]

Nevertheless, civil servants are cautious about positing a radical break in the Whitehall paradigm. Many saw little tangible difference in the centre's relationship with departments and in the relationship between ministers and officials.[40] This view is not universally shared: one adviser working in the Callaghan government reflected that by the late 1990s, 'the civil service no longer saw itself as in the position of advising ministers in a considered way on policy'.[41] Previously, white papers were prepared by departmental civil servants having little contact with Number Ten. There was 'a very open discussion between ministers and civil servants around what should be happening'. However: 'When I came back in to Whitehall in 1997, that had all gone [...] the view was that ministers ought to have policy ideas based on ideology.'[42]

Similarly, Bernard Donoughue returned to Whitehall after the 1997 election having served in Wilson and Callaghan's Policy Unit (1974–9). Donoughue took the view that there was 'less interest in the quality of policy [...] the quality of Whitehall had diminished.'[43] One official remarked that the composition of white papers: 'seemed to be entirely driven from the centre [...] obviously that is not really the way to do it, you should start from the bottom up.'[44] The Blair administration created 'a new network of ministers who related to Number Ten through their special advisers, alongside the Number Ten special advisers, in a way that British government hadn't really seen before.'[45] Another official remarked: 'Special advisers made a huge difference by challenging the monopoly over policy analysis, and acting as policy entrepreneurs within government.'[46] The fashionable 'end of Whitehall' view may be overstated; nonetheless, it resonates with actors and remains a compelling interpretation of change in the machinery of government during the New Labour years.

The case studies provide cogent examples of the reach and influence of the political network of advisers. On academies, an official insisted: 'The policy is formed by lots of people debating. They need something to break the mould of failing schools [...] But it wouldn't have happened without Andrew [Adonis]. Andrew was developing his own network.'[47] In providing funding for Family-Nurse Partnerships, Hilary Armstrong's advisers were forced to negotiate directly with officials since 'relationships with civil servants were not functioning and the Home Office was particularly obstructive.'[48] The National Economic Council was created where previously:

> The Treasury had been completely dominated by Gordon Brown and his advisers, particularly Ed Balls [...] when Alistair [Darling] came in, he wanted his special advisers to operate as they had done previously, and he also wanted the Treasury to be more hands off with departments.[49]

Former Cabinet Secretary Andrew Turnbull insisted the civil service 'no longer claims a monopoly over policy advice.'[50] Riddell warned: 'Blair and his advisers [...] were insensitive to questions of what were and what were not the right boundaries between politicians and advisers on the one hand, and civil servants on the other' (2006: 54).

However, civil servants are wary of overstating conflict with their political counterparts in Whitehall. Turnbull remarked: 'We welcome the fact that we are much more open to ideas from think-tanks, consultancies, governments abroad, special advisers, and frontline practitioners' (quoted in Heffernan, 2006: 20). An alternative view is that while the politicisation of Whitehall has not occurred so as to threaten the neutral, non-partisan status of officials, civil servants had been compelled to operate within policy-making structures that are increasingly politicised. According to one senior Cabinet Office official, 'there was not a shred of evidence'[51] that civil service appointments were subject to political interference, or that officials became uncomfortably close to ministers. Nonetheless:

> That isn't the problem. The problem is that the work of the civil service was moved into more politically controlled channels. Policy work, things which would come through departmental officials, were given more to special advisers. When a minister wanted to talk to another minister, instead of asking the departmental officials of two private offices, you get the two special advisers to talk. The accusation is marginalisation [...] they allowed the civil service to be marginalised. To my generation of permanent secretaries, we were not as close to our secretaries of state as a previous generation. It is almost the opposite. We retained our purity, but at the cost of being a bit more distant. If you read the account by Douglas Wass of the financial crisis of 1974–8, he was much closer to Denis Healey than any of us ever got close to Gordon Brown. Now there were special advisers around [...] [Nicholas] Kaldor, some of them quite eminent: [Wyn] Godley, Robert Neild, but Healey [...] the first person he would turn to was his Permanent Secretary.[52]

This reflects a widely shared view that the symbiotic relationship between civil servants and ministers encapsulated by the Haldane model atrophied, as the structure and processes of policy-making were subject to pluralisation through an infusion of external policy-making agents. Civil servants advanced their careers by telling ministers what they wanted to hear, rather than 'speaking truth to power'. It was alleged that official's monopoly over policy advice had been broken.

The Pluralisation of Policy Advice

The argument for greater pluralisation in the policy-making structures of the central state and the core executive is that New Labour drew to an unprecedented extent on a network of research institutions, pressure groups and thinktanks, challenging the stagnation and inertia of Whitehall and an oligarchic system of 'club rule' (Heffernan, 2005; Moran, 2003; Rhodes, 1995). A number of task forces and ad hoc policy reviews were created after 1997, covering themes from youth justice and school standards to the future of sport. According to Burch and Holliday (2000: 72), 227 advisory groups were established within Labour's first year of office. Platt (1998) calculates that 192 policy reviews and task forces were set up during the first term. According to Daniel (1997: 27):

> Unlike the Royal Commissions and reviews of previous governments, the task-forces are not intended to sweep issues under the carpet. They are emblems of New Labour's desire to be seen to be implementing manifesto pledges briskly and in a spirit of trust.

The advisory bodies were not merely comprised of ministers and civil servants, but drew on an array of actors from across the public and private sectors, trade unions, charities and civil society bodies. This inevitably altered the nature of dependency between ministers and civil servants (Richards & Smith, 2002). Why then were so many task forces created in the early years of the New Labour government? In 1997, there had been concerns about the neutrality of the civil service, as one minister close to Blair confirms:

> There was a lazy suspicion among Shadow Cabinet members about the civil service. In a sense, it was if you see a civil service that supported a Conservative Administration of one sort or another over eighteen years, you're bound to be a little suspicious. I don't think they really understood that the civil service was absolutely gasping for a change of government, was desperate for it, looking forward to it, and I think in most cases would have done anything to make it happen. You've just got to remember, the Conservative Administration was so hopeless and unpopular and visibly falling apart, for the civil service there was a yearning for a change in administration. They were all natural 'New Labourites' [...] not to a man or a woman, but the sentiment was clear. It was clear every time you met a civil servant how desperate they were to be rid of the Tories.[53]

Over time, this gave way to frustration among ministers about the capacity of departmental officials to execute policy competently and generate innovative policy ideas, as Chapter 5 emphasised. One PMSU official working at the centre concurred:

> People who have worked in an area for ten or twenty years sometimes find it very difficult to step back and say, 'why do we do things like that at all'? We wanted people with intellectual skills to apply to a range of policy problems, without the hang ups of accumulated intellectual baggage. People with generic skills have much more open minds and are able to respond to ministers with fresh ideas.[54]

Another averred: 'There was a problem which is that a lot of the policy advice which was being provided by the civil service was often very anaemic. It just didn't add much value.'[55] According to Lord Birt:

> Frankly, Whitehall was profoundly non-analytical. Everybody thinks this is what the civil service is really good at and it wasn't at all. It is brilliant at understanding sectional interests and pressure groups, political forces and realities, good at telling ministers if you want 'x', these are the consequences in the present environment with the doctors, with the police [...] But it really isn't good at the sort of analysis building up in the private sector and the business schools over the last forty or fifty years [...] There was a huge amount of scholarship going on but it was not strategic. There was absolutely no capacity to bring it altogether, make it coherent, and understand what mattered.[56]

Another minister remarked:

> I would say very few ideas as such came from the officials. They are not very creative [...] there are lots of very intelligent people there, but in fact they were much more about helping you do what you said you wanted to do, than they were about what you should be wanting to do.[57]

The minister continued: 'They saw the big ideas that we came up with as acts of God that came from the politicians which had been put upon them at any given point.' A Downing Street adviser insisted: 'Whitehall is a great servant, but it needs to be told to think in a strategic way.'[58] However, officials have contradicted these accounts by insisting it was increasingly difficult for the civil service to grasp the strategic rationale behind New Labour's reform plans, exacerbated by conflict between Number Ten and the Treasury given the realities of the 'dual premiership' between Blair and Brown:

> Just as the civil service were getting to grips with the top-down, target-driven Michael Barber 'flog the system' approach [...] Tony Blair was moving off that to something else which was the contestability and choice agenda, much less central 'command-and-control'.[59]

One senior figure commented: 'Blair confuses the civil servants around him [...] On the civil service he doesn't know what he wants. They say, in effect, "tell me what you want and we'll do it"' (Fawcett & Rhodes, 2007: 103).

While civil servants felt increasingly marginalised from their policy role, officials placed a premium on their *political* skills, advising ministers of constraints and pitfalls presented by a proposed reform or policy initiative.[60] Given the conventions and practices of the parliamentary state, civil servants have traditionally played a 'political' role in Whitehall (Theakston, 1995). Their authority derives from the capacity of officials to navigate the Westminster system, using expertise and well-trained antennae alongside an ability to synthesise advice and make authoritative judgements. As such, special advisers, political appointees and interest groups appear to threaten the serial monogamy of civil servants' relationship with ministers. The evidence for pluralisation is eloquently marshalled by Cameron (2009: 7):

> High profile people from think-tanks, lobby groups and communications companies continue to crowd into the policy space once occupied by Whitehall mandarins. As we have seen under Labour, all too often their ill-considered policy prescriptions have led to what former Cabinet Secretary Lord Butler describes as 'bad government'. Having been elbowed out of the policy-making process, it is civil servants who are then charged with making the unworkable work and who are then blamed when, inevitably, they fail.

This is endorsed by a retired Cabinet secretary:

> There was a big expansion of the centre and a demotion in the policy role of departments. Officials are, you could say, relegated to the role of delivering policies they have had less effect in devising [...] policies and initiatives tended to come from one of two sources. One was the Prime Minister saying, 'I want something looked at'; so John Birt would do something through the Strategy Unit. Or Gordon Brown would say I have asked Kate Barker to look at planning, or Rod Eddington to look at Transport, or Sir Derek Higgs to look at corporate governance. What I call 'celebrity reviews'. This was very much resisted by secretaries of state [...] this sense that their homework was being marked. I think it was an unhelpful development.[61]

On one level, the tendency towards pluralisation is unsurprising given that pressure groups and NGOs played a key role in the modernisation process leading to the creation of New Labour in the 1990s (Driver & Martell, 2006; Shaw, 2008). Nevertheless, evidence for the pluralisation of policy-making is partial and equivocal. For instance, although a burgeoning literature has emerged on the role of thinktanks (Ball, 2009; Cockett, 1996; Denham, 1996), relatively few of New Labour's ideas emerged from institutions outside the central state. Many advisers and officials expressed frustration at the depth and quality of thinking beyond the formal structures of government. One adviser at the DfES remarked:

> I couldn't remember anyone in the academic world or think-tanks who had any real purchase. Generally, there was a huge gap between government and the academic world. Academia is left-leaning and traditionalist and they never really got the point of reform. The think-tanks were just never really in the game.[62]

Another minister insisted: 'Of all the reforms we did, can you find anything in any of the White Papers that comments on the role that research can play?'[63] Where DfES did draw on academic research, 'it was much less ideas-based, much more about execution and orchestrating what the department was trying to do'.[64] On thinktanks, Charles Clarke insisted:

> The problem about the think-tank world is it is very short-term, by definition. The think-tanks exist [...] because of the total failure of the academic world to be able to engage with the political process. They weren't on our wavelength. The educational research community were essentially contesting everything we were doing.[65]

Like the academy, thinktanks struggled to match the capability of central government departments. One adviser highlighted lack of time for engagement with thinktanks: 'The reality is when you're a special adviser you're bogged down in day-to-day departmental work.'[66] Another official noted that most civil servants dislike the equivocal nature of academic evidence:

> A lot of civil servants don't like academic research because it is not clear enough. You know, it is always couched in terms of 'possibly, we think that, on the best evidence so far', blah, blah. I think policy should be as much about gut instinct and values as other things. We shouldn't put policy above politics. At the end of the day, I don't think evidence can be the only criteria in policy-making.[67]

Despite the appearance of pluralisation, both academy schools and Family-Nurse Partnerships originated in analytical research undertaken by departments.[68] Academies succeeded City Technology Colleges, while FNPs reflected ideas about family poverty developed at the Department of Social Security in the 1990s.[69] The reliance on governmental capacity highlights the on-going importance of the Whitehall model, alongside the premise at the heart of the BPT that 'central government knows best' (Hall, 2011; Marsh & Hall, 2007).

According to this study, the inference that traditional models of Whitehall policy-making have fundamentally altered over the last 30 years is problematic. Like the 1945–51 Attlee Government, the Blair and Brown administrations relied heavily on the policy-making establishment and the civil service to develop feasible and credible plans for governing (Addison, 1976). Although evidence exists that the policy process was increasingly pluralised under Labour, the Whitehall model has not been replaced by a 'minister-dominated' paradigm. The civil service retains an influential and powerful role. As one official remarked: 'the relatively subtle changes which have taken place in the [civil service] reform agenda between 1999 and now don't seem worthy of close analysis from our end of the telescope' (Bovaird & Russell, 2007: 325).

Reforming Whitehall: Old Wine in New Bottles?

Understanding the relationship between continuity and change in political institutions inevitably entails a distinction between the rhetoric of political actors, and the reforms they implement in practice. During the first Thatcher government, the Cabinet Office efficiency adviser, Sir John Hoskyns, advocated making central government more efficient by dismantling the traditional civil service machinery (Campbell & Wilson, 1995; Theakston, 1999; Wrisque-Cline, 2008). However, only after the 1987 election was the civil service exposed to major structural changes, as *Next Steps* challenged the traditional Whitehall paradigm by creating a range of agencies with accountable chief executives operating like businesses in the private sector: 'The reforms of Whitehall during the 1980s have to be viewed in the context of an evolution, not a revolution, a reaction to and consolidation of past *ad hoc* attempts at change' (Dolowitz et al., 1996: 458). The reform process was structurally constrained by an on-going attachment to the constitutional status quo.

Towards the end of the Labour government's first term, Jeremy Heywood instructed Martin Donnelly, a senior official in the Cabinet Office, to develop proposals for a major restructuring of the central civil service.[70] According to a Cabinet Office memorandum to the Prime Minister, departments displayed 'insufficient focus on delivery priorities', conveyed a 'slow speed of response' and had 'poor innovative capacity'. The paper opined that although 'government is seen as highly centralised [around Number Ten] [...] the reality is very different'. The proposals envisaged a 'matrix' structure where officials would be line managed by the Cabinet Office rather than departments. Civil servants would be deployed according to strategic priorities across government.[71] As one Number Ten insider remarked:

> What you needed to put in place was a type of senior civil service manager for whom there was a corporate personnel policy developed in the Cabinet Office [...] and the placement of these people around Whitehall would reflect the corporate priorities of the permanent secretary [...] much more flexibility for the centre to put its best people in quickly and deploy them on what it saw as the main policy problem, switching them to other areas that required attention.[72]

Blair was attracted to the reform proposals, but backed away fearing accusations of centralisation and 'control freakery' (Mandelson, 2010; Rawnsley, 2005).[73] Lord Birt's team developed a plan for restructuring the centre in 2004–5, separating the economic management and public finance roles of the Treasury.[74] The Prime Minister was unwilling to risk a destructive battle with his Chancellor, however, and the proposals were again dropped (Powell, 2010). The transformative character of structural reform is often exaggerated: it is rarely as radical when implemented as initially proposed.

Central government emphasises its interventionist and transformative powers, implicitly maintaining the traditional power-hoarding structures of the British state. Moreover, governance is a process by which institutions and actors refashion society and the state without dismantling centralising government. Governance does not *replace* government, but enhances the power and capacity of the central state (Bell & Hindmoor, 2009; Fawcett, 2011; Peters, 2004). This reinforces the importance of an analytically coherent account of continuity and change in the diverse institutions of British governance.

Competing Theoretical Approaches to Whitehall and the Core Executive: the Differentiated Polity Model and the Asymmetric Power Model

This chapter has assessed the extent of continuity and change in the Whitehall paradigm relating to the politicisation and pluralisation of policy-making in the core executive. The approach adopted aims to move away from the binary analysis of the challenges to, and reforms of, the British central state. The final section of the chapter will examine how far continuity and change in the Whitehall paradigm can be accommodated within formal models of British politics which offer a more sophisticated perspective than that afforded by the Westminster model, namely the Differentiated Polity Model (DPM) and the Asymmetric Power Model (APM). The core assumptions of the DPM and the APM were assessed in Chapter 4 and are summarised in Table 7.2.

The APM was devised by Marsh, Richards and Smith (2001) to examine changing patterns of governance in the core executive. The model of the APM provides a sympathetic critique of the 'first wave' governance literature and hollowing-out (Rhodes, 1994). The asymmetric polity acknowledges the concentration and centralisation of power in the British political system. The APM alludes to the enduring importance of the 'strong government' tradition,

TABLE 7.2 A comparison of the DPM and the APM

Differentiated Polity Model	*Asymmetric Power Model*
Governance, rather than government	Governance, rather than government
Power dependence, involving exchange relations	Power dependence, involving asymmetric exchange relations
Mixed modes of governance with policy networks as main mode	Mixed modes of governance, with hierarchy as main mode
Contested political traditions	Dominant political tradition, with increasing contestation
A segmented executive	A strong, if segmented executive
A hollowed-out state	Strong government, although increasingly challenged
Pluralism	Asymmetries of power and structural inequalities

Source: based on Marsh (2012: 4)

while emphasising the paradoxical nature of contemporary governance (Birch, 1964; Evans, 1993; Hall, 2011; Marsh & Hall, 2007; Tant, 1993). On the one hand, strong centralising government has continued as the central state has legitimacy and resources, as well as legislative and tax-raising powers. On the other hand, multi-tiered governance and new forms of managerialism and participatory democracy lead to the fragmentation of the state. Flinders (2010: 73) highlights the tension through the work of Birch:

> The 'liberal' view incorporated power-sharing related values such as openness, participation, accountability, and inclusion whereas the 'Whitehall' view promoted a set of values – strong government, insulation, control, stability – that were facets of a more power-hoarding model of democracy.

According to Marsh, Richards and Smith (2001), the fusion of contested ideas and traditions leads to a 'hybrid' neo-liberal welfare state characterised by structural contradictions and governing pathologies. For example, pluralistic methods of delivery involving a diverse range of providers are combined with an enhanced role for the centre in defining the policy goals of public service agencies leading to confusion about the overall trajectory of reform (Richards & Smith, 2010). Nonetheless, empirical insights from the case studies underline that the differentiated and asymmetric polity models ought to be revisited in order to take account of institutional developments during the post-1997 New Labour governments:

'Government Knows Best'

The DPM emphasises that policy is shaped by disparate networks outside the core executive. Actors depend on one another: no single group is able to dominate the policy process. However, the DPM risks understating how far actors in the central state are committed to an operating code focused on centralisation and top-down government. The political class believes its role is to initiate reforms in the national interest, rather than engaging citizens in the process of responsive decision-making. The ethos was: 'If you want change, you have to drive it from the top or the centre.'[75] Meanwhile: 'There are structural features of the British state which are more centralist than in comparable advanced economies.'[76] Central government's determination to impose prescribed performance standards inevitably reduces the role of other agencies and actors in the policy-making process. Number Ten 'was more powerful than it had been in previous periods.'[77] Indeed, power remained overwhelmingly hierarchical and concentrated at the centre. As a senior DfES official remarked:

It was a period of centralisation both in terms of central departments, and in terms of government working with communities. The civil servants loved it you know! What was the point of being in government if you couldn't get your hands on things?[78]

As the reform process unfolded, there was some interest in how to devolve power away from the centre, 'but it never really happened'.[79] The emphasis on 'central government knows best' meant there was little concerted attempt to experiment with participatory and negotiated governance: deliberative forums, citizen's panels and user involvement in policy design (McAnulla, 2006; Newman, 2001; Stoker, 2002). The enthusiasm for involving citizens abated as the central state absorbed responsibility for public sector performance, driving delivery through the 'power-hoarding' model. The Blair and Brown governments centralised and reformed the state, securing autonomy for the core executive while subjecting public sector bureaucracies to marketisation and rigid controls. As a result, state elites developed strategies which they believed restored their capacity to govern British society and the economy (Le Gales, 2012).

Asymmetrical Power Relations

Despite the rhetoric of partnership and devolved 'area-based' approaches, Whitehall continued to shape the interaction between providers and actors beyond central government. The relationship between government and other networks was still 'asymmetrical'. The state has an unrivalled set of power resources, notably tax-raising and legislative powers, as well as democratic legitimacy. In addition, governments are able to control the structure of policy networks, while ministerial and civil service actors retain privileged access to the policy-making process. One former Treasury official notes:

It [The Treasury] ended up being very favourably disposed towards the financial services industry, almost by default. The Treasury was undoubtedly very pro-city. The Treasury is the key liaison department with the financial services industry. There are lots of professional relationships and interests. Constitutionally, it is the Treasury's role to regulate and engage with the financial sector. This makes the ties and connections really very close.[80]

Meanwhile, targets, inspection and scrutiny have reduced the scope for local autonomy (Smith et al., 2011). This reflects 'the dominance of a particular view of reforming public services which was most defined and aggressively delivered in Britain'.[81] Policy outcomes continue to reflect the priorities of the core executive, despite the accent on pluralism as the centrepiece of the DPM. In relation to FNPs: 'Although it wasn't driven by the centre, we were very clear what we wanted. It was a highly prescriptive programme.'[82] Local government remained politically weak; the absence of power centres beyond the centre meant reform was able 'to carry all before it', only stopping at the devolved administrations.[83] One adviser conceded: 'In a way, these are ideas that should be coming from local government, and probably would be if we spent some time listening to them.'[84]

Whitehall departments curtailed the freedom of intermediate bodies, while the core executive sought to enhance its control over the policy process. Reflecting on the New Labour period, Rhodes, the progenitor of the DPM, conceded: 'Zones are owned by the centre and local agendas are recognised in so far as they help the centre' (2001: 70). Nonetheless, it is clear that local actors are recalcitrant, able to thwart the intentions of the central state.[85] The core executive struggled to translate its objectives into change on the ground, hence the growth of the implementation gap between the centre and the front-line. The centre articulated policy goals without fully controlling the implementation process. Ministers were increasingly reliant on diffuse mechanisms of indirect management, abandoning traditional 'command and control' directives and operating 'rubber levers' within a segmented policy process (Richards et al., 2008; Rhodes, 2011).

Continuing Strength of the Core Executive

Both the DPM and the APM emphasise the segmentation of the core executive. While there has been centralisation in Number Ten and the Cabinet Office, the DPM emphasises the fragmentation of the policy-making arena. Rhodes insisted: 'Indisputably the British centre intervenes often but its interventions do not have the intended effects and so it cannot be considered control' (2001: 69). A retired former Cabinet secretary remarked: 'The problem was unwieldiness rather than size, and there wasn't a clear enough management or co-ordination structure for the centre.'[86]

The centre still repeatedly intervened and sought to exert control. This study indicates that Britain has a strong executive, while most decisions are taken at the departmental level. On one side, the 'modernising government' agenda enhanced the core executive's oversight of the policy process. On the other, departments have resisted the centre and the imposition of policies favoured by Number Ten. Departments remain the 'focal point' of power and decision-making within the British system of government.

One Number Ten official was sanguine: 'The question you have to keep coming back to is, if the centre was so powerful during this period, why did New Labour not achieve more in government? It is partly because the centre is not actually so powerful.'[87] According to another interviewee, 'my reading of past attempts by the centre was that if they only concentrated central power and imposed it on departments, they would be beaten.'[88] On FNPs: 'The departments never bought it, which made the centre increasingly frustrated.'[89] As Rhodes acknowledges, 'the practice of British government remains familiar. Ministers, the barons at the heart of British government, continue to defend their fiefdoms' (2001: 70).

Many 'joined-up' initiatives are absorbed within departments, while the creation of the NEC emphasised the limitations of Treasury control in Whitehall. The imposition of constraints on the core executive relates to the impact of judicial powers and human rights legislation in the British state: 'This becomes a factor in the consideration of which policy you pursue before you even get to the statute book.'[90] The APM did not address the growing impact of legal and judicial interventions in Whitehall. As one Home Office adviser recalled:

> When I went to the Home Office, the biggest part of my life was spent thinking about court judgements. We were forever being judicially reviewed, and that hugely frustrated David Blunkett. There is a danger of concentrating on Whitehall and Westminster without proper reference to judicial reviews and human rights law.[91]

The courts and the judiciary are increasingly important in the policy-making and governance arena.[92] The Human Rights Act (HRA), for example, represents an explicit challenge to the doctrine of parliamentary sovereignty. Opponents insist the demands of democratically elected governments are being thwarted by judges, threatening to undermine the Westminster model. However, supporters of the HRA argue that the convention helped to protect the vulnerable against the misuse of power by the state (McAnulla, 2006).

New Control Mechanisms

There is little especially *new* in the development of the regulatory state, although there has been a growth of audit and inspection since the late 1990s (McAnulla, 2006; Moran, 2003). This led to the emphasis on public sector self-regulation. The expansion of the regulatory state is intended to ensure the priorities and objectives of central government are properly implemented at the local level (Peck & 6, 2006). While the DPM alluded to the impotence of the centre, Whitehall exerts control over agencies and institutions through policy design, resource allocation and central monitoring. The aim was 'to provide professional leadership to drive change in the education system, rather than providing administrative oversight'.[93]

For example, the PMDU was not only charged with collating data relating to the performance of the public sector. The unit enables the centre to maintain relationships with providers at 'street level', bypassing departments altogether if it so chooses. One interviewee remarked: 'There were convulsions in this department when Michael Barber and others walked through the door. Some of the archetypal civil servants didn't last long because profound change was coming'.[94] The core executive exerted new forms of control over actors in Whitehall and beyond the centre. There were a series of initiatives designed to reassert central government authority over policy and delivery.

In education, for example, the emphasis on standards meant increased central state control, while academy schools involve direct intervention by the centre, bypassing LEAs. Marsh, Richards and Smith (2001: 249) describe 'joined-up' government as an attempt 'to re-impose central executive control' on the various institutions of British governance. In the case of FNPs, joint working at the front-line between local authorities and NHS Primary Care Trusts is concerned with service integration: 'If you want to take waste out of public services, you need agencies to work with one person, sit down with them and go through their needs. That's what will save money.' However, it is still 'a prescriptive, top-down approach', originating in Whitehall.[95]

External Constraint

The 'first wave' governance literature and the DPM emphasise the hollowing-out of the British state. The increasing limits on state sovereignty have rarely been accurately portrayed in the political science literature, however, creating a misleading impression about the changing role of the nation-state. The contingent processes by which states have been subject to external constraint given the internationalisation of the advanced economies is underemphasised (Thompson, 2008). In addition, the hollowing-out literature does not take account of how states respond to such pressures, creating new capacities and tools of governance. New Labour, for example, addressed the perceived decline of standards in public services by cultivating new forms of 'partnership' between the public, private and third sectors with the aim of improving delivery. In responding to the financial crisis, Whitehall developed 'a government-led strategy on the future of the economy'.[96] The aim of industrial policy was to understand Britain's position 'in global terms: what's our future competitive advantage in the world, and what combination of public and private policy do we need to get to it?'[97] It was recognised that the state could act strategically where markets would often fail, while markets are structurally dependent on democratically elected governments. The state remains central to capitalist accumulation in the form of neo-liberal economic policies (Jessop, 2006). This was underlined by the financial crisis in which the Treasury:

> Helped to save the global banking system. The plans they produced for recapitalising the global banking system were emulated all over the world [..] It was an amazing achievement, the recapitalisation of the entire banking system.[98]

New Labour's strategy was to reconstitute the capacities of the central state, reforming governance to enhance the power of political elites.

In summary, the DPM offers a cogent conceptualisation of continuity and change in British politics. Nonetheless, the differentiated polity overstates how far the British state and core executive have been depleted of governing capacity, obscuring asymmetries of power in the British political system and the preservation of the constitutional status quo. The APM sought to challenge the emphasis on pluralism in the DPM: while power is generally fluid and diffuse, actors rarely operate on a level playing field. This study concurs with the APM that agents interact on structured terrain where the distribution of power is broadly asymmetric.

The differentiated polity sought to contest the misleading image of the British political system provided by the Westminster model. It remains the case that the 'image' of the centre around Number Ten as omnipotent and all powerful is inaccurate. However, the notion of the centre-less state in the DPM is less than convincing. According to this study, the British central state retains operational autonomy and governing authority. The APM points towards the influence of the BPT, emphasising a power-hoarding and centralised system of government which continued to inform New Labour's statecraft. Of course, the context in which governments operate is increasingly complex and variegated, underlined by the importance of the HRA and judicial review. Overall, the APM presents a static account of the Whitehall machinery which appears to lack theoretical nuance, despite promulgating a more convincing conception of how power operates in the central state than the differentiated polity view.

Conclusion

This chapter considered a series of claims about the extent of continuity and change in the Whitehall paradigm, relating to the politicisation and pluralisation of the policy-making process. The analysis reflected the pre-eminent theme of earlier chapters, namely how far power has been redistributed within the policy process from departments to the centre of the state. The chapter has examined how far New Labour altered the nature of the central state machinery between 1997 and 2010. The core findings of Chapter 7 are as follows:

- The APM offers analytical insight, providing an organising perspective which addresses the nature of statecraft and power dependency in the New Labour years. This challenges the 'new orthodoxy' of the differentiated polity and the 'first wave' governance literature.
- The study provides evidence for key precepts of the APM, including the notion of asymmetric power relations and the dominance of the core executive in the British system of government. There has been an institutionalisation of central capacity, while departments have retained relative autonomy in the policy process.
- Nonetheless, the extent of pluralisation is exaggerated, while the civil service maintained a distinctive role in providing policy advice to ministers emphasising the *politics* of the policy-making arena.
- The symbiotic relationship between civil servants and ministers endured: the interaction between officials, ministers and political advisers is generally non-conflictual, despite concerns about incipient politicisation.
- Those who insist the Whitehall model has been replaced by a minister-dominated paradigm overstate their case. The departmental view of the centre's role is variable: accounts of change within Whitehall relying purely on the centre's perspective are inevitably biased and partial.
- The literature emphasising discontinuity has tended to operate at the ideational level, underplaying the role of structures, alongside the interaction between institutions and ideas. Changes in ideas about governing are evident in the management and reform of Whitehall institutions.

Campbell and Wilson (1995) define four tests of systemic change in Whitehall: does the civil service still provide a 'neutrally competent' service to the government of the day; has the integrity of officials been protected preventing politicisation; has the civil service continued its 'monopoly' over the provision of policy advice; and are there clear lines of accountability in which ministers take responsibility for decisions and civil servants act on the basis of ministers' views? Only in relation to ministerial accountability is there genuine ambiguity as to the on-going resonance of the Whitehall paradigm in the everyday life of British government (Flinders, 2008; Judge, 2006).

This chapter highlighted the importance of a robust conceptualisation of stability and change underpinned by a coherent theory of the state. The literature on the British Political Tradition (BPT) alludes to path dependency leading to continuity over time, addressing how actors negotiate change within structured terrain. Chapter 8 assesses the impact and influence of the BPT, an alternative account of continuity and change in the Whitehall paradigm. The chapter examines how tradition conditions the beliefs of ministers and civil servants, analysing how attitudes and norms are hard-wired into the governing institutions and processes. Analysing the BPT in relation to institutions and ideas demonstrates 'the change in continuity and the continuity in change' (Sztompka, 1993: 59). The aim is to address the influence of ideas, traditions and institutional norms, modifying the actions and attitudes of actors within the machinery of the British state at the centre.

CHAPTER 8

The Role of Tradition and Path Dependency: New Labour in Power

The Socialist State, far from being a centralised and coercive bureaucracy, presents itself to us as a highly diversified and extremely numerous set of social groupings in which, as we ourselves see it, governmental coercion, as distinguished from National and Municipal Housekeeping, is destined to play an ever dwindling part.

Beatrice & Sidney Webb (1913)

[Tradition] is in practice the most evident expression of the dominant and hegemonic pressures and limits.

Williams (1977: 115)

The politicians and commentators who dominate the national conversation are the products of a restless, febrile age, when the past is apt to be dismissed as unnecessary baggage, and public debate focuses on surface novelties rather than on the deeper currents of long-term change [...] the diverse narratives that make up the British Political Tradition are far richer and more fertile than the constricting common sense of our time admits.

Marquand (2008: 6)

Introduction

This chapter analyses the role of the dominant political tradition in shaping the practices of contemporary governance and the attempt to restore governing capacity at the centre of the state. The chapter examines how far the British Political Tradition (BPT), and the multi-faceted Labour tradition, have influenced the attitudes and actions of ministers and civil servants, structuring broader patterns of continuity and change in the British state. The chapter demonstrates that political actors draw on a variety of traditions and ideological doctrines in responding to governing challenges, but more often continue to operate within the framework of representative and responsible government enshrined in Birch's 'classical' account of the BPT.

Chapters 5, 6 and 7 considered the extent to which the centre constrained departments in the policy-making process, and how far the Whitehall paradigm was altered between 1997 and 2010. The chapters reveal that while much has changed in the machinery of government, long-standing institutions and practices have remained intact given the force of incrementalism and inertia. While key elements of the Whitehall model are being gradually worn away, other pillars remain in place: positing the end of the Whitehall paradigm is overly hasty and, arguably, premature. To understand stability and path dependency, it is necessary to analyse the beliefs and interpretations of actors relating to the literature on the BPT outlined in Chapter 1.

As such, the chapter will enumerate the argument for a dominant tradition in British politics, instead of multiple, competing traditions with equal weighting and importance among political actors. Bevir and Rhodes (2003) insist that the British polity is comprised of a plurality of traditions: political traditions are fluid and mutate over time. Similarly, Marquand alludes to the 'diverse narratives' of the BPT (2008: 6). Bevir and Rhodes' epistemological approach emphasises the contested and dynamic nature of traditions. However, this chapter examines how far there is a prevailing BPT, a dominant and hegemonic force within British politics and the British state. Accordingly, the British political landscape is uneven and political traditions have an asymmetric resonance (Hall, 2011). Power is exercised within a strategic context shaped by structural inequalities and the traditional 'power-hoarding' model. While the BPT is modified over time, it comprises the core values and beliefs of politicians and civil servants. The BPT is focused on a conception of majoritarian democracy: a top-down and elitist system of government from which the Westminster model and Whitehall paradigm are derived (Lijphart, 1999).

The chapter revisits the evidence of power inequalities in the central state machine given the social composition of the civil service, while examining the case for a dominant tradition by exploring the beliefs and interpretations of actors drawing on key elements of the BPT. The BPT is reflected in the values and beliefs of agents, creating the disposition towards path dependency and institutional stability. This argument for path dependency, rather than path determinism, recognises that agents have the capacity to adapt and modify both ideas and institutional settings. While the Whitehall paradigm is characterised by underlying continuities, change is rarely absent from the political and administrative machinery of the state. The relationship between continuity and change is, as ever, fluid, dynamic and interactive.

The chapter then examines the dialectical relationship between continuity and change by *disaggregating* the BPT. New Labour actors developed a particular interpretation of the BPT based on the Labour Party's attitude to the state, and its views of bureaucracy and expertise outlined in Chapter 3. This reflects a core paradox at the heart of the Labour tradition, namely the contest between the dominant mind-set of Fabian socialism and the subordinate decentralising ethic of 'English pluralism'. As a consequence, reforms have more often been grafted onto the prevailing constitutional settlement. Modernising practices such as 'evidence-based' policy and 'joined-up' government emerge from within a dominant tradition committed to a power-hoarding model of statecraft premised on the view that 'central government knows best'.

Such an interpretation addresses the simultaneous but often conflicting role of ideas, traditions and institutional norms. This has, in turn, perpetuated a series of institutional pathologies within the Westminster model and Whitehall paradigm arising from confusion about parliamentary accountability, the structure of 'arms-length' agencies, and the impact of managerialism on the occupational status and prestige of the civil service, each of which are examined in the concluding chapter.

Institutional Inequalities in British Government

The literature on the core executive all too often assumed that the terrain on which agents operated was broadly even, neglecting structural inequalities in the British polity (Dunleavy, 1991; Hennessy, 2000; King, 1985; Marsh et al., 2001). Nevertheless, the analysis of change in the Whitehall paradigm should address the structured context in which actors operate.

The Power Centre of British Government

Structural inequalities in British politics are reflected in governing institutions and practices (McAnulla, 2007; Sztompka, 1993). The policy-making community is co-located in the geographical realm of Whitehall and Westminster. Within this context, axioms of the BPT develop a material manifestation. For example, the centre of British government is Number Ten Downing Street:

> The power nexus at the middle of the British state, encompassing Number Ten, parts of the Cabinet Office, and the Treasury. It is here, in one small building, that the different strands of power collide: the ruling political party, the domestic civil service, and the nation's representatives abroad – all brought together, in theory, around one Cabinet table.
>
> (Seldon, 2010: 3)

The intimacy of the Whitehall village can be discerned in its policy-making style, alluding to accusations of *sofa government* (Powell, 2010; Rawnsley, 2005; Riddell, 2006; Seldon, 2006). This depicted Blair's inclination to ignore the views of departments, officials and the Cabinet, taking decisions through a closed circle of advisers (Powell, 2010). According to one minister: 'This was very much a prime ministerial system [...] [Blair] thought that the Cabinet and large swathes of the civil service would have blocked what he was trying to do.'[1]

Similarly, as prime minister Gordon Brown 'relied on small circles of people around him to get things done',[2] although 'he thought there was a status to Cabinet which he got and took seriously'.[3] Seldon (2010: 4) refers to 'the tense balance of power, inherent in Downing Street's few offices, between civil servants and political appointees'. Blair's Chief of Staff testified to the importance of physical proximity in Number Ten: 'One of the first rules of government is that proximity to power is more important than comfort. In the White House, senior staff will settle for a cupboard in the West Wing rather than a palatial suite in the Old Executive Office' (Powell, 2010: 15). This emphasises the relationship between institutions and ideas: axioms of the BPT such as 'strong, responsible government' are entrenched within the institutions and processes of the central British state.

Informal Rules and Practices

An implicit, but nevertheless pervasive, characteristic of institutional inequality is that actors should have the capacity to respond to rituals and practices embedded within the Westminster model (Barker, 2001; Finlayson, 2004). These capabilities are not distributed evenly, however, perpetuating structural inequality in the composition of political and bureaucratic elites. For example, Lovenduski (2005: 147) vividly describes how gender bias operates in the House of Commons:

> Requirements for masculine dress codes, provision for hanging up one's sword but not looking after one's child, admiration for demagoguery and conflict, adversarial styles of debate, a chamber whose acoustics favour loud voices, the frequent use of military metaphors [...] are all manifestations of the gender regime of the UK parliament.

Similarly, an adviser refers to 'the machismo culture in the Treasury. People would get credit for slapping down departments and giving them as hard a time as possible'.[4] Barker (2001) alludes to how rulers sustain their legitimacy drawing on a variety of 'rituals and rhetoric', from architecture to etiquette, through which identity is cultivated. It is important to observe 'the external trappings of governing' (Barker, 2001: 140). The relationship between gender bias and norms within political institutions is linked to other aspects of institutional inequality in Whitehall, namely the tendency of elites to be drawn from particular socio-economic groups and classes (Marsh, 2008; Waylen & Chappell, 2012). Marsh reiterates that policy networks are:

> Dominated by a combination of three sets of actors representing state, economic or professional interests. It will also surprise no one that few women or blacks were involved in the networks. Policy networks are thus political structures whose membership reflects, but again is not determined by, broader patterns of structured inequality in society.
>
> (Marsh, 2001: 32)

Although 'negotiated governance' alludes to policy-making through participation and deliberative democracy, policy networks are controlled by particular groups and interests (Newman, 2005). For instance, one special adviser remarked that the Treasury 'was undoubtedly very pro-City [...] There are lots of professional relationships and interests [...] This makes the ties and connections really very close.'[5]

Inequality in the UK Civil Service

Traditionally, the higher echelons of the British civil service have been dominated by officials from public school backgrounds. Until the mid-twentieth century, the majority of civil servants attended one of eleven 'leading' independent schools (Hennessy, 2000). Nonetheless, recent data indicates a shift in the educational background of the Whitehall mandarinate. In addressing class bias, surveys indicate three-quarters of senior officials attended state schools (Figure 8.1): according to Figure 8.2, fewer senior civil servants attend independent schools than in the past in comparison to other elite professions.

That said, Tables 8.1 and 8.2 powerfully emphasise that ethnic minority groups and women continue to be under-represented in the senior grades of the civil service. Although the proportion has doubled since the early 1990s, women and BME groups are more likely to be employed in clerical and administrative posts.

The conceptualisation of British politics offered by the Westminster model neglects the socio-economic context in which the political system is located. Marsh, Richards and Smith (2001) infer that political outcomes cannot be 'read-off' from a particular pattern of inequality. The data reinforces the argument that political institutions are imbued with power relationships based on gender, class and ethnicity. The effect of inequalities in gender, class and ethnicity is mediated by education, knowledge and influence over the structures of

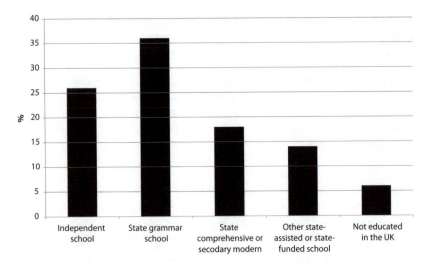

Source: Independent Reviewer on Social Mobility and Child Poverty (2012)

FIGURE 8.1 School background of top 200 civil servants 2010–11

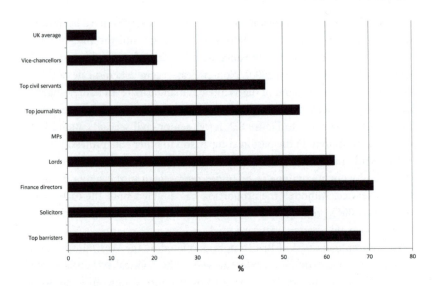

Source: The Sutton Trust (2009)

FIGURE 8.2 Proportion of independently schooled professionals

TABLE 8.1   Civil service employment – ethnic minority employees as a percentage of employees with known ethnic origin by responsibility level (31 March 2011)

Civil service grade	Headcount (per cent)
Senior Civil Service (SCS)	5.0
Grades 6–7	6.9
Senior and Higher Executive (SEO)	7.8
Executive Officers (EO)	11.0
Administrative Officers (AO)	9.4

Source: Office for National Statistics (2011)

TABLE 8.2   Civil service employment – female employees as a percentage of employees by responsibility level (31 March 2011)

Civil service grade	Headcount (per cent)
Senior Civil Service (SCS)	34.7
Grades 6–7	40.7
Senior and Higher Executive (SEO)	45.1
Executive Officers (EO)	56.7
Administrative Officers (AO)	57.1

Source: Office for National Statistics (2011)

decision-making and governmental power (Marsh, 2001). Inequalities impact on the resources available to political actors, reinforcing the asymmetric structures and processes through which policy-making is undertaken. In addition, structural inequalities constrain and facilitate the capacity of individuals and interest groups to achieve their goals within the policy process (Barberis, 1997; McAnulla, 2006).

This does not merely concern the under-representation of particular groups within the Whitehall system. Annesley and Gains (2010) demonstrate the links between women's location in the core executive and the potential for gender policy change, alluding to the agency and policy entrepreneurship of actors within the British polity. Their analysis emphasises that the greater prominence of women in Whitehall enables political power and resources to be wielded: 'In order to instigate policy change in a mainstream policy domain, it is essential for political actors to be positioned in the institutional sites' (2010: 67). This is a crucial backdrop to understanding the role of the BPT in shaping the contours of the British political system. The procedures and institutional norms of British politics are inscribed by an elitist, top-down view of democracy, which reflects and reinforces wider socio-economic inequalities in contemporary society (Marsh & Hall, 2007).

The British Political Tradition

This chapter substantiates the case for a dominant BPT, shaping the views and interpretations of actors. Of course, British politics has never been limited to a narrow, unchanging set of core ideas. Most writers acknowledge the fluid and contested nature of traditions. However, working within the framework of the BPT emphasises top-down government and asymmetries of power as major characteristics of the British tradition (Hall, 2011; Marsh, 2008; Marsh & Hall, 2007; Marsh & Tant, 1989; Smith, 2008; Tant, 1993). The essence of the BPT is the notion that Britain is ruled through the 'power-hoarding' structures of the central state. The hallmark of British democracy is a normative belief in the 'virtues' of political and territorial centralisation. There is no clear separation of powers and the legislature is invariably dominated by the executive (Flinders, 2010; Lijphart, 1999).

There is a paradox that New Labour was forced to confront on entering government in 1997, however. While the BPT enables the core executive to manipulate the levers of state power, hierarchical decision-making is increasingly contested in a multi-tiered polity where there are a myriad of institutions and actors (Bulpitt, 1983; McAnulla, 2006). The context in which governments determine policy has altered. Power is ceded from Westminster by devolution and European integration, and the principle of parliamentary sovereignty is eroding. In relation to delivery, New Labour ministers have decried the experience of governing with 'rubber levers'. While the central state has less discernible impact on the ground, 'Relatively trivial problems of implementation can threaten a minister's career' (Rhodes, 2012: 13).

This section examines how far ideas underpinning the BPT are narrated by actors, entrenching particular institutions and practices in the British state. The wider argument is that the BPT is composed of several strands of ideational 'DNA' which are encoded into the structures and institutions of British government. Ideas, norms, and traditions influence and shape the capacity for institutional reform and change. To reiterate, understandings of the BPT are generally organised around several prevailing, though not mutually exclusive, ideas:

- a top-down, leadership view of British democracy;
- a liberal concept of representation based on parliamentary democracy in which MPs act according to the national interest;
- a conservative notion of responsibility based on strong government;
- a commitment to secrecy in the conduct of government which determines the relationship between ministers and civil servants;
- an ethos in which 'central government knows best' (Birch, 1964; Marsh & Hall, 2007; McAnulla, 2006).

These ideas have drawn attention to the strategic context shaping British politics and the state. The 'critical wave' literature on the BPT in Chapter 1 examined the mutually supportive triangle of political practice, normative theories of government, and the ideational framework comprising the BPT. It is necessary to examine how ideas associated with the BPT shape the interpretations of ministers and officials, as well as legitimating key institutional relationships in the British polity. This chapter will do so by drawing in particular on political biographies and memoirs, underpinned by testimony from key actors through a series of lengthy semi-structured interviews.

The British Political Tradition and Elitism

The pre-eminent strand of the BPT concerns a top-down, leadership view of British democracy. The principle of strong, responsible government associated with the British model of democracy is firmly entrenched, emphasising debate and deliberation by 'the few' on behalf of 'the people' (Birch, 1964; Marsh & Tant, 1989). The Westminster model insists that ministers ought to take responsibility; hence politicians are often unwilling to delegate authority by devolving power to other institutions and actors (Stoker, 2006). Governments initiate change, projecting an image of strength, authority and resilience.

This elitist view of government's role during the New Labour era was most pronounced in relation to the reform of the state and public services. Blair (2010: 211) insisted the gap between expectations and delivery would be addressed through top-down change imposing 'a swathe of performance targets' on the state sector. Former Education Secretary David Blunkett argued:

> We were right to drive from the centre [...] once the foot had come off the accelerator, the whole results, and the attainment levels just plateaued again. I had toyed with the idea that if I had ten years in the job and we weren't losing whole generations, we could have adopted an entirely different approach which was all about nurturing Heads and leadership teams for the future. A cohort would eventually emerge that was so committed they'd drive it [...] That's not the real world.[6]

This impression is reinforced by Jonathan Powell, Blair's chief of staff (1997–2007), drawing on the insights of Machiavelli's treatise *The Prince*. Powell infers 'the great reformers in history were strong leaders [...] Only a strong leader can bring about such changes' (2010: 182). As a consequence:

> Blair came in with a much stronger Number Ten operation. He was very clear that he wanted that, and it lay behind stronger powers for Jonathan [Powell] and Alistair [Campbell], it lay behind the creation of a stronger policy unit, and stronger communications than had existed under Major. The Policy Unit in the Major years had focused on big picture policy development, but people now focused more on the day-to-day, monitoring what departments were doing for the Prime Minister.[7]

The Prime Minister assumed responsibility for driving this agenda from the centre: 'I was working flat out devising the direction of structural reform for schools, the NHS, criminal justice, welfare, and the Civil Service' (Blair, 2010: 302). Blair would not allow departments to compromise or dictate the pace of change: 'It is a feature of modern politics that nothing gets done unless it is driven from the top' (Blair 2010: 337). This led to the Prime Minister's controversial remarks about 'scars on my back',[8] as he believed the reform process meant confronting vested interests in the public sector:

> Once the framework is set, the departments know their direction and they know what they should do, but leaving it up to them to do it is highly risky, unless the individual ministers fully buy into the vision; and even then, they need to have the power of the centre behind them.
>
> (Blair, 2010: 337)

New Labour's strategy was eventually encapsulated in 'five-year plans' published by departments (Blair, 2010).[9] These were intended to get away from 'the endless stream of new initiatives' characterising Labour's first term (Barber, 2007: 47). Officials were encouraged to outline reform strategies emphasising choice, competition and public sector contestability (Barber, 2007; Seldon, 2007). The process of reform was driven by the Prime Minister and his team at the centre. As one Cabinet Office official observed: 'The role of the Prime Minister and his advisers was absolutely crucial in setting the direction and establishing a sense of ambition, giving permission to be radical.'[10] A senior ministerial figure added: 'I was conscious of the fact that if you didn't have a strong centre, you weren't going to be able to enforce the culture of New Labour throughout the system.'[11]

The top-down approach came to the fore during moments of crisis. Alistair Darling reflects on the importance of decisive leadership: 'For all the criticism a leader gets for appearing presidential and intolerant of dissent, people prefer that to a situation where there is no firm leadership or control' (2011: 222). Elsewhere, issues such as the street crime 'epidemic' after the 2001 election prompted demands for a 'COBRA-style' emergency response, bringing together departments and public agencies (Barber, 2007: 149). This was characterised by Michael Barber, head of the PMDU (2001–5), as a 'dramatic new process', galvanising the Whitehall machinery (2007: 153). The model of delivery was later applied to NHS Accident and Emergency waiting times (Barber, 2007). The capacity to tackle weak public sector performance is a crucial lever of strategic prime-ministerial leadership.

This indicates the on-going resonance of the strong leadership view: change occurs when driven from the centre as a manifestation of 'the top-down, directive tendency in Whitehall'.[12] Former Health Secretary Andy Burnham referred to the party's enthusiasm for centralised bureaucracy, 'The tendency of Labour to go straight to regulation, straight for the sledgehammer' (Behr, 2011). All three of Labour's paradigms of public service reform (Barber, 2007: 336–7) – top-down change, quasi-markets and 'earned autonomy' – reinforce rather than undermine strong, central government and the traditional 'power-hoarding' model. Although quasi-markets and devolution emphasise the dispersal of power, reforms were designed and overseen by the core executive.

This top-down, centralising style of government as a hallmark of the BPT is encapsulated by Nick Pearce, head of Policy in Number Ten under Brown (2008–10):

> The British state has the features of a centralised state [...] lots of fiscal power is exercised out of the centre. It has weaker local government than other countries. Local government can't raise money other than in London, so there are structural features of the British state which are more centralist than in comparable advanced economies.[13]

The 2001 PASC report concluded: 'Government in Britain is distinguished by a culture of administrative centralism' (House of Commons PASC report, 2001). Figure 8.3 below indicates that a relatively high proportion of public expenditure in the UK is administered through central government in comparison to other industrialised democracies.

According to a Home Office official, in the absence of:

> Strong social partners and strong local government [...] for the most part, the state can achieve a lot of what it wants, particularly if it has got money as New Labour did. They could smooth the path of contentious reforms [...] The House of Commons does not scrutinise how the state spends its money.[14]

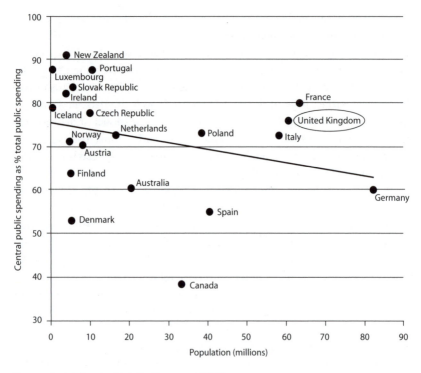

Source: adapted from Institute for Goverment (2010)

FIGURE 8.3   Administrative centralisation in OECD countries

This justifies the claim that responsible government means entrusting the elite to carry out decisions in the national interest (Tant, 1993). Various accounts examine how ministers' ideas and actions are shaped by, and in turn, shape the BPT. Moreover, an elitist, top-down approach is entrenched in the governing DNA of the Labour tradition, limiting the potential scope for Whitehall reform (Blair, 2010; Darling, 2011; Mandelson, 2010; Mullin, 2010; Powell, 2010; Prescott, 2008).

The British Political Tradition and a Liberal Notion of Representation

The top-down operating code at the core of the BPT is balanced by the normative commitment to a liberal notion of 'representative' democracy emphasising inclusion, participation and power-sharing (Birch, 1964; Flinders, 2010). The constitutional framework in which Britain's political institutions are anchored strikes a balance between responsible *and* representative democracy. The notion of elective representation avers that parliamentarians are chosen to make their own judgements: 'Thus by implication a minimal and largely passive role is envisaged for the British electorate, with wide discretion and independence for representatives and government' (Tant, 1993: 69). The governing process entails the implementation of contentious, even unpopular decisions in the national interest through a strong executive (Blair, 2010). One official noted: 'When a Prime Minister has a large majority, parliamentary scrutiny and accountability is reserved for big questions of war and peace.'[15]

British government is organised around the principle of collective responsibility (Birch, 1964; Hall, 2011; Tant, 1993). Powell (2010) disagrees with former Cabinet secretaries such as Lord Butler who insist that Blair replaced Cabinet government with 'presidentialism' (Foley, 2000). The Cabinet's constitutional role had not been significantly eroded. Similarly, Barber (2007) questions whether Britain was more effectively governed when the prime minister was merely 'first among equals'. A powerful premier can generally achieve more radical reforms: Barber insisted that Thatcher succeeded in reforming the education system where Callaghan manifestly failed. It was legitimate 'to give the Prime Minister much greater purchase over the policy development agenda'.[16] According to one adviser, 'The key influence was the health crisis in 1999–2000, people on trolleys in corridors. Blair realised you had to have much stronger policy at the centre.'[17]

Powell argues that the critique of 'sofa government' (Foster, 2005) trivialises how decisions are actually made: 'It doesn't matter whether decisions are made sitting on a sofa or round a coffin-shaped table [...] Those who suggest that it does are stuck in an old-fashioned mind-set that cannot distinguish between form and substance' (2010: 59–60). Nonetheless, Powell defends collective responsibility insisting 'the manifestation of ministerial government in Britain is the Cabinet' (2010: 57). Powell acknowledges that the prime minister does not govern alone, relying on the support of ministers and the parliamentary party. This underpins the power dependency model highlighted in Chapter 4 where power is not a zero-sum game: actors exchange resources through bargaining games (Dunleavy & Rhodes, 1990). Prime ministers risk losing office where they cease to command a Cabinet majority. British parliamentary democracy is predicated on the principle of collective responsibility.

In contrast, Darling and Prescott insist a strengthened role for the Cabinet would have eliminated apparently damaging decisions such as the Millennium Dome, military intervention in Iraq and the abolition of the 10p tax rate in

2006–7. As a departmental minister, Prescott reflected: 'Tony did at times seem to treat the Cabinet as a Shadow Cabinet, making his decisions with his chums on the sofa, with the Cabinet becoming less and less involved' (2008: 255). This is confirmed by Peter Mandelson, one of Blair's closest confidants:

> It is true, Tony [Blair] liked to take and form judgements, hear advice, take decisions, on the sofa as Robin Butler famously later said. He [Tony Blair] liked to do it with his own people not the civil servants; you know his political staff, Alistair, me, Pat [McFadden]. He liked to make sure his writ ran bilaterally to secretaries of state, not as it were, collectively. Cabinet committees were to all intents and purposes stood down.[18]

Darling attributed the centralisation of power to the trauma of defeat in the 1980s. Another departmental minister remarked:

> Tony [Blair] was not going to allow the gridlock, paralysis and stasis, and all the endless meetings and constant Cabinet sessions which he felt had benighted previous Labour administrations. He was of course thinking back to the 1970s [...] But that overhang of historical experience had a strong impact on New Labour in every sense.[19]

Consequently, Britain 'did not have effective cabinet government for the thirteen years we were in power. Cabinet government is a critical part of our constitution and it is being neglected' (Darling, 2011: 222). Mandelson concedes, 'I think that the government was the weaker for it.'[20] A retired senior official remarked:

> Jonathan Powell in his book, *The New Machiavelli*, is very disparaging. He says all these old farts kept telling me how to organise a proper meeting. It didn't matter whether it was an *ad hoc* meeting with the people in the room that mattered, or a meeting that was part of the Cabinet Office structure. But the answer was it did matter, it mattered a great deal. In a Cabinet Committee you have a structure, you have a membership of that committee. It's your right to turn up depending on your responsibilities. You couldn't just decide well, I don't want Clare Short there, she's a bloody nuisance. She was Secretary of State, she was entitled to be there [...] He had no patience. It was clear in the book [Peter] Mandelson wrote with Roger Liddle about how Labour would govern. And this, of course, becomes an issue in Iraq because all sorts of shortcuts are made [...] and who took the decision to make public that David Kelly was the 'leaker' of the report to the BBC? Of course that decision was taken in an *ad hoc* meeting [...] it wasn't part of any structure. And it turned out a lot of the preparation that had taken place was done by a very small team in the Prime Minister's office. A lot of [Blair's] Cabinet colleagues had no idea just how strongly he had committed himself to Bush. His view was that one of the problems with Cabinet committees is they slow you down and people will oppose you. Therefore the best thing is just to get on and do it. You don't get buy in to the decision and you may

actually get a worse decision because someone might be right to tell you this is a problem [...] war in Iraq would create other hostilities. So there was a philosophical difference all the way through.[21]

A senior minister, nevertheless, constructs an eloquent defence of Blair's approach:

> If Tony Blair had run the Cabinet in a way that gave any latter-day Jim Callaghan the opportunity to oppose what he was putting forward on schools, or universities, or health, or whatever, on the basis it was better these things were defeated in Cabinet than subsequently by the PLP [Parliamentary Labour Party], we'd never have had anything brought forward for consideration in the House of Commons. We'd always have had people saying, 'it's going too far, it's too dangerous, you won't get the PLP to support it'. In a sense it was only through sheer force of personality and operating the system in the way he did that he got anywhere at all. Some people believe he didn't get far enough. If there had been proper, functioning Cabinet government, how would Gordon [Brown] have used that against Tony to defeat what he was doing, probably very effectively? He would have got nowhere, so Tony tried to work through *force majeure*. That's why he treated the Cabinet in that way, it is why he treated the system in that way. Now it is hardly surprising that the Cabinet Secretary whose whole raison d'être is to operate a Cabinet system of government found all this very disagreeable and very disquieting.[22]

Numerous actors criticise Blair for underestimating the importance of ministers in departments: 'He thought that determination through Number Ten, his own speeches, his own arguments, his own weight of personality, his own advisers could carry it [...] actually, the story was they couldn't.'[23] Darling extolled the virtues of British representative democracy at the core of the BPT: 'The relationship between ministers and their fellow MPs [...] is vital, helping to sustain confidence in the government [...] and reinforcing the importance of the relationship between the Prime Minister and individual ministers' (2011: 84). The case for collegiality and ministerial government is emphasised:

> For government to work effectively, the Secretary of State of a particular department and the Prime Minister have to be able to work as close colleagues, sorting out differences and then issuing clear instructions to the civil service.
>
> (Darling, 2011: 170).

During the New Labour years, there was undoubtedly concern about an erosion of the collegiate style of government. This was directed particularly towards Gordon Brown, both as chancellor of the Exchequer (1997–2007) and prime minister (2007–10):

The way he behaved in government since 1997 was to rely on small circles of people around him to get things done. Not at all collegiate in the sense that he would not put himself into a room of Cabinet colleagues and have an open discussion about what should be done. He wanted to make up his own mind in his own way.[24]

Similarly, 'Blair didn't really understand the importance of getting hearts and minds.'[25] A senior ministerial figure such as Alistair Darling contextualises his experience by drawing on narratives from within the BPT. This illuminates the influence of past practices and conventions in British government on the present (McAnulla, 2007), recalling Rhodes' remark in *Everyday Life in British Government* (2011: 280): 'As I watched ministers and civil servants enact their everyday stories, I saw them re-enacting the nineteenth century constitution.' Rhodes examines how governance practices such as managerialism and marketisation are grafted onto the traditional Westminster model, leading to continuity *and* change rather than an inexorable shift towards the reconstituted Whitehall paradigm.

The British Political Tradition and a Conservative Notion of Responsibility

The liberal conception of representation informing Birch's work is balanced, and in practice outweighed, by a conservative notion of responsibility.[26] This infers that British democracy requires majoritarian governments acting decisively in the national interest, rather than governing consensually through a plurality of interest groups and actors (Flinders, 2010). The nation's well-being is entrusted to the custodianship of the ruling elite, while citizens have little reason to remain informed about the minutiae of policy (Tant, 1993). Indeed, putting too much information into the public domain is *irresponsible* according to the basic precepts of the BPT, since voters are generally viewed as incapable of reasoned judgement on matters of 'high' politics.

As we saw in Chapter 6, the novelty of the Labour government's approach in comparison to past historical epochs was arguably Number Ten's drive to intervene in the fine detail of implementation. Blair averred, 'you couldn't get the job done unless there were clear procedures and mechanisms in place' (2010: 338–9). The centre was required to challenge the Whitehall machinery operating in ways 'far more akin to the private sector'. Even so, Labour's Whitehall reforms such as centralising policy-making around Number Ten were 'wholly alien to the idea of departmental lines of command and stable departmental structures in Whitehall'.[27] As a result, 'By 2000, it had become too difficult to do. Blair was frightened it would be attacked as a huge centralisation of government under the Prime Minister.'[28] Nevertheless, the former Prime Minister remained on 'a collision course' with Whitehall mandarins (Blair, 2010: 688).

Powell and Barber as key Number Ten aides insist that the problem of prime-ministerial power in Britain is not that it is too strong, but too *weak*. The former Prime Minister himself remarked: 'One of the things I discovered was that the centre just wasn't powerful enough. In the modern world, this just doesn't work. You've got to have an agenda driven from the top.'[29] Powell maintained that Whitehall had numerous deficiencies: of greatest concern was the lack of delivery capability. Civil servants were trained as policy advisers rather than project managers (2010: 73). Powell compared the civil service to a 'monastic order' populated by 'cradle to grave careerists'. As a result, the Prime Minister increasingly relied on central units to generate ideas:

> Tony used to complain that all the new ideas came from Number Ten rather than departments. It was extraordinary how little capacity for original thought the departments seemed to have. Departments were almost as weak at policy-making as they were in terms of delivery, in part because that capacity had been effectively hollowed out during the Thatcher period.
>
> (Powell, 2010: 179–80)

This negative assessment of Whitehall's capabilities is captured in Darling's observation that the Treasury lacked the intellectual firepower to deal with the post-2008 crisis: 'Governments right across the world frequently boast about cutting civil service numbers. The Treasury had lost many of its staff over the preceding ten years, and the strains were now evident' (2011: 26). A Number Ten official concurred: 'Where departments have economic regulators, a lot of the capacity has been outsourced and it is not replicated in the department.'[30] Darling insisted that the Treasury continued to regard itself as 'a big beast of Whitehall patrolling the corridors of government', concluding that: 'Unlike most countries, the British Prime Minister has a very small staff' (2011: 169).

Indeed, Barber's concern is the lack of bureaucratic and political resources available to the prime minister. The Cabinet Office had not evolved as an enforcer of prime-ministerial power. One interviewee described the Cabinet Office as: 'the worst of all worlds. It doesn't actually serve the Cabinet, but it doesn't serve the Prime Minister either.'[31] The constraints on the centre remain formidable. The ability to wield influence over policy-making is weak, and there are too few change levers at the centre (Barber, 2007: 298–9). This corresponds with the findings in Chapter 5, emphasising that the centre rarely displaced departments in the policy-making process. Departments remained institutionally strong, as ministers 'control the flow of information to Number Ten and the access that the Prime Minister's people have to their departments. Indeed, decisions are often taken with minimal or no consultation with Number Ten' (Barber, 2007: 311).

Powell's enthusiasm for reforming the structures of the British state is concerned with strengthening the institutional power resources of the core executive. He is unwilling to contemplate changes to the top-down, centralised operating code underpinning the BPT. For example, Powell advocates breaking up the Treasury, but rarely acknowledges the limits of a power-concentrating model of statecraft. Similarly, Mandelson (2010) reveals that Brown developed proposals to restructure Whitehall, but never questioned the view that policy-making and implementation should be undertaken through centralising fiat. Of course, a range of actors have challenged the wisdom of this approach. An adviser in the Home Office lamented the lack of partnership between policy-makers at the centre and local government:

> Bringing in Jeremy Beecham [former Chair of the Local Government Association] for a half hour cup of tea is considered to be consulting local government [...] that idea mortifies me [...] these are the ideas that should be coming from local government and probably would be if we spent some time listening to them. It is mortifying that you have this really top-down approach which is considered consultation and engagement.[32]

This recalls Marsh's (2001) claim of 'plurality without pluralism' in the changing patterns of British governance. Although a wide range of actors are implicated in decision-making, the institutions of the central state remained dominant in the policy process. The British state continues to hoard power at the centre: local government has been 'hollowed out over the last fifteen years'.[33] In addition, weak planning in central government meant that 'funding streams force local government to work in silos'.[34] This was related to concerns about the capability and performance of the civil service. Another minister agreed: 'In a way, the civil service is the ministerial service, not the civil service [...] it serves ministers rather than serving the civic, and that's a problem. It is concerned with serving ministers, and even that didn't happen properly.'[35]

Barber (2007) emphasised the radicalism of Blair's agenda for Whitehall reform, overcoming the incrementalism of the first term. However, this raises the question of what might be defined as 'radical'. Indeed, one of the cornerstones of the Westminster model, that of ministerial accountability in which 'civil servants advise and ministers decide', is rarely questioned. One former civil service fast-streamer believes 'culturally, there is still a very long way to go':[36]

Everything you did had to be cleared through seven levels, there was a hierarchy around who went to meetings with ministers, who could comment on what, and I found the whole thing just frustrating. I went in with these high ideals of wanting to change the world and society and doing all these wonderful, idealistic things; and I found myself just a very small cog in a huge machine.[37]

This emphasises continuity in the state machinery, reinforced by officials who insist 'the core civil service at the centre of government'[38] has retained its traditional role. This is defined as 'working closely with ministers, having that interdependence in the relationship, giving really good policy advice when it was required'.[39] The role of officials in overseeing and steering policy-making continues, despite the emergence of an open 'market-place' of ideas: 'In the end, ministers still want really good, creative, innovative policy advice.'[40] As a result, there is a degree of scepticism about the academic commentary on change in the Whitehall model: 'Peter Hennessy is a bit wide of the mark in talking about the death of the traditional civil service. Dare I say it, it is quite a lazy thing to say from the outside.'[41] In fact, 'the civil service is alive and well', although:

It became much more outward-focused, much more interested in seeing the real world effects of what policy advice was given, and much more concerned about results and outcomes. It seems to me that this is a thoroughly good thing and even if the Coalition has got a view about targets and taking responsibility for all that, it has got a machine that is much more attuned to making things happen than in 1996–7.[42]

Mandelson (2010) is unusually complimentary about Whitehall and the civil service, implying that Blair was too casual about Number Ten's relationships with officials. According to Mandelson, Blair failed to draw sufficiently on the 'intelligence and insight' of his permanent staff.[43] A Home Office civil servant concurred that New Labour was reluctant to properly engage the civil service on key reforms: 'If you don't bring on board officials, it can destroy the idea at an early stage.'[44] Even Barber extols the 'restless excellence' of permanent secretaries (2007: 45). In opposition, Mandelson advocated a Prime Minister's Department, but relented having encountered the 'Rolls-Royce' service provided by the senior civil service, insisting that a strengthened centre would be more appropriate for the British system: 'What was needed was a mechanism for Tony to set the agenda, and ensure that every department was on the same page' (2010: 228). However, 'there was perceived to be a tension between the traditional role of the Cabinet Office, and the role of the Policy Unit in Number Ten'.[45] Barber (2007) advocated a hybrid structure akin to the Australian system, with a joint Department of the Prime Minister and Cabinet.

One permanent secretary insisted the willingness of the civil service to transform itself into a delivery agent was rarely appreciated: 'It is probably quite a success story for the British civil service that it adapted without too much pain to this implementation focus.'[46] As a result: 'Permanent Secretaries and senior officials were increasingly held to account, not just for the quality of policy advice, but for how much they could demonstrate their ability to implement things and to make change happen in the system.'[47]

It is striking that despite concerns about the crisis of political trust during the New Labour years (Flinders, 2012; Hay, 2006; Riddell, 2011; Stoker, 2007), actors in the core executive continued to emphasise the importance of strong, decisive government. The interest in responsive and participatory approaches was distinctly muted, and Labour's approach was generally underpinned by a strong leadership view (McAnulla, 2007; Stoker, 2002). Actors sought to protect the 'highly elitist, pre-democratic form of club government', encapsulated in the Westminster model (Flinders, 2010: 22). This ensured an informal code of operation based on high-trust relationships with few legal sanctions or rules, testimony to the enduring power of the BPT and closely related to the axiom of secrecy in British government.

The British Political Tradition and a Commitment to Secrecy

The operation of secrecy is compatible with notions of representative and responsible government. The BPT embraced the principle that 'good government is closed government' instilling a 'culture of secrecy' in Whitehall (Tant, 1993: 16). This upheld the convention that civil servants should provide ministers with 'full and frank advice' unencumbered by fear that it will be subsequently exposed to public scrutiny. According to Barberis, 'it is a prerequisite to free and frank exchange between officials and ministers' (1997: 148). The code of 'honourable secrecy' is underpinned by a system of informal, club regulation (Moran, 2003; Vincent, 1998).

Although the British state is now subject to the Freedom of Information Act (FOI), relative secrecy and the need for decisive, rather than responsive, government remains paramount. The code underpinning the British political system is one where ministers and officials in Whitehall 'know best'. Despite FOI, the Constitution Committee of the House of Lords insists:

> In general, policy advice given by civil servants to ministers is not disclosed to select committees or anyone else. This is said to be because disclosure would hinder the giving of free and frank advice in future. More importantly, it is in keeping with the general principle of ministerial responsibility. Civil servants give full and candid

advice to ministers, but it is for ministers to follow or disregard that advice as they choose.[48]

The confidentiality of policy advice to ministers is regarded by former Cabinet secretaries such as Lord Butler of Brockwell and Lord Wilson of Dinton as integral to the relationship between ministers, the civil service and Parliament. Ministers and civil servants are determined to defend the principle of secrecy. Blair regretted the passing of FOI legislation, insisting it played into the hands of a partisan media: 'For political leaders, it's like saying to someone who is hitting you over the head with a stick, "Hey, try this instead", and handing them a mallet.' Blair feared FOI would undermine the tradition of civil service neutrality which sustained the confidence of ministers, declaring: 'There really is no description of its stupidity, no matter how vivid, that is adequate. I quake at the imbecility of it' (Blair, 2010: 516–17). Blair insisted the civil service 'was and is impartial. It is, properly directed, a formidable machine' (2010: 205). Similarly, the Cabinet secretary, Gus O'Donnell, complained that FOI was having 'a very negative impact on the freedom of policy discussions' in Whitehall (cited in Stratton, 2011).

The ethos of honourable secrecy is reflected in the accounts of officials who argue 'you are there to serve ministers'.[49] One departmental official remarked: 'There is a very strong civil service culture. Deference to ministers and a sense of duty.'[50] This is at the core of the public service ethos:

> A sense of duty to serve the public interest […] that is ultimately the goal. You're not doing it for private financial gain and that's actually very strong in the British system. Ministers are the driving force of the department. It was at times a combination of *Yes, Minister* and *The Thick of It!* It is a very pragmatic system.[51]

The importance of the civil service tradition is emphasised:

> Many of the traditional civil service qualities – impartiality, objectivity – intelligently interpreted with an open mind remain as relevant to a very different world and can serve you incredibly well. One of the tragedies is that across generations of civil servants and policy-makers we constantly re-learn things we have forgotten.[52]

Interviewees concur that the 'end of Whitehall' perspective is inaccurate and overstated. Mulgan, for example, averred:

> There might have been a partial further shift towards a more open market, but it happened every bit as much in the early years of Margaret Thatcher, more than it did under New Labour. New Labour to some extent was more deferential to the civil service than the Tories had been in 1979 […] Whereas the Thatcherites, partly because they had a very ideological anti-government view, and because quite a few of

them had actually run large organisations [...] an obsession for them was completely bypassing civil service policy-making capacity.[53]

On the contrary, Mulgan's contention is that Blair's administration was too enamoured of the traditional machinery and excessively deferential to Whitehall. He found Blair to be 'quite disinterested in the reform of structures and systems'.[54] A Number Ten policy adviser agreed:

> Tony never really understood the point about the organisation of the civil service [...] he just didn't grasp the significance of this. It was thought that Richard Wilson [as Cabinet Secretary] would try to find a solution, but his innovations did very little to improve things.[55]

One adviser added that as New Labour entered government in 1997, 'what I didn't see was any thinking about the machinery of government'.[56] The critique that Mulgan espoused originated in the revolt against club government and institutional stagnation in the late 1960s and 1970s:

> The secrecy and lack of openness in government, the cult of amateurism, the magic circles of insiders, which once were celebrated as strengths and factors of cohesion, are now much more often denounced as handicaps and evils. The British governing class has long been under attack, but has never been in such disarray.
>
> (Gamble, 1984: 41)

This was scarcely acknowledged by Labour ministers, however. Blair dismissed the arguments of Crossman, Castle and Benn that 'the civil service is intent on suppressing radical change in support of a right-wing establishment agenda' (2010: 542). Nonetheless, some members of the Labour Cabinet in 1997 clearly adhered to the conspiratorial view.[57] The Prime Minister's dissatisfaction with Whitehall related to lack of responsiveness, rather than fear of ideological capture. The implicit bargain between ministers and civil servants, where officials pledge loyalty in return for anonymity, was sacrosanct (Richards and Smith, 2004). This contributed to the emphasis on secrecy emphasised by Tant (1993: 44):

> The people's representatives require to have a large measure of discretion and auton-omy in decision making 'on behalf of' the people and in their ultimate interests [...] In this view government is a specialised vocation; government must therefore be unfettered, free and independent, in order to make sometimes difficult decisions in the national interest.

Kate Jenkins similarly underlines the importance of the secret state:

> What is going on within the department is, to a large extent, unknown to a lot of people, and although we now have far greater openness and far greater freedom of information, I can tell you that the instincts of secrecy are in the blood of people who

have been in the civil service for any length of time. It took me four or five years after leaving the civil service before I felt I could really say what I thought because it was drummed into me.[58]

The relationship between the BPT, secrecy and the notion of responsible government is axiomatic. Alistair Darling led the British and American response to the financial crisis and the stabilisation of the banking system through the Troubled Assets Relief Programme (TARP) (Darling, 2011). While the Obama administration faced arduous congressional negotiations over TARP, Darling proceeded unencumbered by legislative scrutiny:

> I was struck by the fact that the US president, although frequently described as the most powerful man in the world, cannot automatically get what he wants at home. He has to horse-trade. In contrast, when I effectively wrote a cheque to buy £50 billion of bank shares in the UK, I did not even have to get specific parliamentary authority to do so. We could act overnight.
>
> (Darling, 2011: 118)

This reflects the power commanded by the core executive, while the balance between representative and responsible government at the heart of the Westminster model provides a powerful legitimating mythology. The secrecy compact is integral to the maintenance of the BPT. In the midst of the banking crisis, Darling could legitimately:

> Authorise the Bank of England to provide exceptional funds to keep HBOS going. I told John McFall, chairman of the Treasury select committee, but otherwise the facility was to be kept secret in case it created another wave of panic. RBS also needed exceptional funding to the tune of around £14 billion which I had to authorise.
>
> (Darling, 2011: 119)

Similarly, Andy Burnham spoke of the dilemmas concerning secrecy in the management of the NHS. Following the outbreak of swine flu in the summer of 2009, Burnham as secretary of state for health (2009–10) discussed with the chief medical officer, Liam Donaldson, how much information should be released into the public domain. The projected death rate from the pandemic was alarming, and ministers feared it might trigger widespread panic and public hysteria.[59] The ethos of secrecy underpinned by the claim that 'central government knows best' was invoked to protect the national interest. This public interest defence is epitomised by the Conservative minister, Kenneth Clarke:

> I think civil servants should be accountable through their ministers. I think the secrecy of their advice and therefore their ability to give frank and fearless advice

should be protected. It has been weakened. The Freedom of Information Act has raised all sorts of problems which we have not solved.[60]

It is clear that both sets of actors, politicians and civil servants, tenaciously defend the axiom of secrecy in the British state as a core premise of the BPT, underpinned by the notion that 'central government knows best'. The ethos of secrecy is hard-wired into the DNA of the British political system, limiting the potential and scope for reform of the structures and processes of Whitehall policy-making.

The British Political Tradition and an Ethos of 'Central Government Knows Best'

The emphasis on 'responsible' government, elitism and secrecy is further reinforced by the centralisation of power within the Whitehall model and the core executive. New Labour drew from its Fabian heritage, emphasising the potential for reform through strong, centralising government (Bevir, 2005; Driver & Martell, 2002; Marquand, 2008). The state is viewed as an agent of change through which ministers are able to progressively transform society. One interviewee reflected this benign view of what the levers of the central state can achieve: 'Power has visibly delivered results when you have put more money in and built things, expanding the numbers.'[61] Indeed, New Labour's goal was transformational change through the public sector:

> Standards were not good enough [...] there wasn't enough attention to the places round the country where children were being neglected and communities were poor. At the beginning, the Labour government saw it as its job to reverse that and the only way it could do it fast, it believed, was to run it from the centre.[62]

Blair characterised the socialist tradition in relation to the efficacy of state power: 'The state as benefactor, as provider for those who couldn't provide for themselves [...] Its power would regulate, restrain and tame the power of capital' (2010: 213). One thinktank analyst remarked that New Labour's centralising and technocratic approach was anchored in a commitment to social equity:

> I genuinely think that Blair wanted to have an impact on how the education system raises life-chances. He thought [...] 'how can I do it quickly'? And a lot of ideas were coming from Blair literally. This was seen as the quickest way to turn the ship around.[63]

Meanwhile, New Labour eschewed theory in favour of 'what works': a coherent conception of the state's role never emerged. Powell conceded that

Labour lacked an incisive governing philosophy: 'Prime Ministers in government don't have time to think about "isms". They are too busy governing [...] we had to make up our philosophy as we went along' (2010: 186). Prescott lists various New Labour initiatives that were designed to tackle deprivation. There is little evidence, however, they are underpinned by a coherent philosophical vision (Prescott, 2008). Similarly, David Miliband has insisted that New Labour was prone to 'strategic fallibility', lacking a clear view of the state's role: 'What's the role of central government, what's the structure of central government, what's the role of the civil service?'[64] A Number Ten adviser commented:

> In 1997, did New Labour understand what policy was? They'd never been in government, and they thought that making an announcement, making a speech, was a policy [...] a lot of our people didn't understand what policy was, nor indeed did Tony Blair. They saw government as they had done opposition, a kind of public relations exercise, a daily battle with the media, a continuous election campaign. There wasn't enough forward thinking on policy.[65]

A departmental official concurred:

> I found Number Ten in those early days entirely ineffective in understanding how to get things done. We were trying to do some pretty fundamental thinking about the pensions system, and Number Ten couldn't engage at all really. I think Blair started to realise quite early on he needed to pull things together across government.[66]

Similarly, Darling bemoaned an absence of ideas and strategic thinking during the Brown era: 'There was no sign of clarity or direction [...] it was all about tactics' (2011: 35). Barber comes closest to a concise definition of New Labour's strategic purpose: 'The belief that active government backed by rising public spending was necessary to address Britain's problems and to improve public services' (2007: 47). The absence of substantive reflection on New Labour's governing project is, nevertheless, revealing.

Much of the 'classical wave' BPT literature assumes the British political system is innately virtuous, conferring stability and governing authority (Hall, 2011). 'Critical' accounts highlight the inadequacy of a relatively closed and secretive form of government (Evans, 1993; Marsh, 1980; Marsh & Tant, 1991; Tant, 1991). However, the paradox of Britain's strong government tradition is rarely acknowledged. While the BPT conferred untrammelled power on the executive, ministers discovered they were operating with 'rubber levers', struggling to translate their policy aspirations into delivery on the ground (Lipsky, 1979; Riddell, 2006).

As one adviser remarked, 'the model of change which still distorts a lot of policy-making assumes that pulling a lever at the top through a law or a programme actually has a series of effects. Most of the time, it doesn't'.[67] The centre took responsibility for improving state-financed services while maintaining downward pressure on public expenditure and taxation. While spending on health and education rose significantly as a proportion of national income after 1998–9, Labour eschewed its historical reputation as a 'tax and spend' party. Nonetheless, it quickly became apparent that an implementation gap between Whitehall and the front-line had emerged. Moreover, a minister inferred that the coherence of the Thatcher government's reforms was weakened by New Labour's ambiguity about how to operate the Whitehall machinery: 'The simplicity and clarity of the purchaser/provider split of the Next Steps agencies was distorted by the complexity of the issues, and the demands for central action.'[68]

One official noted that while Britain has 'a politically strong centre', it is 'organisationally weak', leading to lack of alignment between programme budgets across departments. This produces 'a very fragmented treatment of issues'.[69] As a result, prime ministers grow:

> Very frustrated because there is an implementation gap when things don't happen and there is a lack of management information. So you see the emergence of a delivery or implementation unit [...] the centre has gone through a remarkable series of convulsions.[70]

Blair's response was to create the PMSU and the PMDU 'increasing the capacity of the centre to take a view on big policy issues which would involve a battle with departments'.[71] One observer insisted departments were reduced to the role of 'tweaker and implementer, consolidating the ideas'.[72] The emphasis on delivery led to numerous tensions, notably the contradiction between ministerial accountability, operational responsibility and parliamentary sovereignty, highlighted by former permanent secretaries such as Richard Mottram.[73] An official recalled the experience of being held to account for school performance: 'I think at times as a senior official, and I suspect as a minister, you felt in a rather awkward position.'[74] That said certain ministers welcomed the pressure applied through the PMDU:

> It was a very helpful boost to what I wanted to do anyway. The PMDU enables you to say, 'we've got to do this because the PMDU are on our backs and they'll be reporting to Tony, and the whole thing will be blown if you don't co-operate'. Where it falls apart is if ministers in a department don't agree with the direction.[75]

The pressure intensified as ministers were made to feel culpable for performance: 'The Secretary of State felt more responsible for what was happening out there.'[76] Since 1997, governments had taken a stronger interest in national test results in primary schools, particularly for 11-year-olds at Key Stage 2: 'The machinery of government was almost designed at this stage to make them feel twitchy about it [...] you had Michael Barber and the Delivery Unit really chasing them down hard.'[77] As Estelle Morris recalls, 'we'd put our political lives on the line over pedagogical policies.'[78] There had been a failure to resolve 'where accountability lies and who is responsible.'[79]

Burnham and Pyper (2008) attest that the operational accountability of the civil service grew as the result of parliamentary scrutiny, judicial oversight, and internal accountability to line managers and ministers. This ensures that staff heading divisions and agencies were more likely to answer directly on operational matters (Flinders, 2008). However, according to one minister, the Labour 1997–2010 administration 'was miles off resolving that. We have no idea who is accountable for anything anymore [...] everybody passing the bloody buck. There is still total confusion [...] sorting out where accountability lies and who is responsible.'[80] While the convention of ministerial responsibility has been undermined, Parliament was reluctant to concede that ministers are no longer responsible for each operational decision. This underlines the continuing confusion over accountability in the administrative structures of the central state.

This chapter has drawn on key elements of the BPT, examining how ideas associated with the British tradition shape the actions and attitudes of ministers and officials. This has sought to demonstrate how ideas, traditions and norms influence and shape the process of institutional reform. As such, the chapter illuminates the central paradox of this study: New Labour sought to adapt the levers of governance within the British state creating new steering capabilities, while retaining core elements of the traditional 'power-hoarding' Westminster model. The scope for structural change was limited, since axioms of the BPT were encoded in the institutions and processes of the British polity. The symbiotic relationship between ministers and officials is shaped by constitutional conventions that New Labour implicitly maintained. Inevitably, there was antagonism between *traditional* and *modernising* practices, encapsulated by the tension between managerialism and the Haldane model of minister-civil service relations (Flinders, 2008; Marquand, 2004).

As such, the structure of policy-making in the British state cannot be examined by referring only to the role of interests and institutions. It is necessary to pay attention to the role of *ideas*, and the relationship between institutions and ideas in the core executive. The previous section illuminated the resonance of key strands of the BPT among actors. As McAnulla (2007) attests, agents are attached to established institutions having a tendency to reproduce existing practices. Inherited wisdom and knowledge are not easily cast aside, as human agents inevitably seek to maintain connections with the past alluding to the on-going resonance of political traditions in British government (Shils, 2006).

This perspective reinforces the argument for institutional path dependency in the central British state. That said, it is crucial to assess how traditions reproduce institutional continuity *and* change over time. Traditions generate tensions and ambiguities which actors seek to resolve by initiating and embracing reform initiatives that lead to institutional change. The resonance and impact of traditions is, as ever, asymmetrical (Sztompka, 1993). The Whitehall paradigm is characterised by underlying continuities; however, institutional change has not been absent since 1997. The relationship between stability and change is always iterative, dynamic and mutually reinforcing.

Institutions and Ideas within the BPT

The interaction between continuity and change in the core executive and Whitehall paradigm is highlighted by the relationship between institutions and ideas. Within the BPT, there is an ongoing tension between 'Whitehall' and 'liberal' values, between contested notions of representation and responsibility, and between the impulse to devolve power and retain control over the central levers of the state. While New Labour has upheld a dynamic conception of the interventionist role and transformative capacities of central government, there was an implicit desire to maintain the traditional 'power-hoarding' structures of the centralised British state. This is the perennial paradox at the core of the Labour tradition.

The following section addresses how competing, even diametrically opposing, ideas inform New Labour's approach to governance and Whitehall. Greenleaf (1983a; 1983b) depicts British politics as an on-going conflict between collectivism and libertarianism. This drew on Dicey's (1982) account in which government's role is defined by the clash between constitutional doctrines of liberalism and conservatism (Bogdanor, 2010). Birch defines the political system in relation to the dispute between 'liberal pluralism' and 'Whitehall' as 'two competing and diametrically opposed sets of values' (Flinders, 2010: 73). Moreover, Greenleaf infers that there are 'cycles of influence' (Gamble, 1990): the domination of a particular ideological tradition is always contingent. Nonetheless, the strong, centralising state tradition is the dominant manifestation of the BPT (Gamble, 1988; Marquand, 2004).

The literature on the BPT explores the role of ideas and institutions in the practices of British government. Bevir and Rhodes (2006a: 8) argue that British politics was never limited to a narrow set of core traditions, dismissing 'classical' notions of the BPT as essentialist. Kerr and Kettell (2006) insist that Greenleaf and Birch maintain an emphasis on stability and continuity arising from their normative commitment to the institutional orthodoxies of the British political system: a dominant characteristic of the British tradition (Collini et al., 1984; Gamble, 1990; Kenny, 1999). The 'classical' wave BPT literature underlined how the interaction between institutions and ideas reinforced patterns of continuity over change. The dialectical and iterative relationship between institutions and ideas is highlighted in Table 8.3, drawing on the case studies elaborated in Chapter 5.

TABLE 8.3   Institutions, ideas and the BPT

Case Studies	BPT I: Representation (delegation, decentralisation and participative governance)	BPT II: Responsibility (strong and decisive government through the centre)
Academy Schools	Using policy leverage to encourage greater devolution to front-line providers, curtailing the role of local and central bureaucracy, making schools more responsive to parental 'voice'	Enforcing prime-ministerial power throughout Whitehall imposing decisions on departments through the centre. Reducing dependency on departments by strengthening the capacity of the core executive and Number Ten
Family-Nurse Partnerships	Policy approach intended to tackle social exclusion and strengthen citizen empowerment through innovative, health-led delivery in public services	Boosting Number Ten's capacity to initiate social policy and control implementation at the front-line; despite department's control over programme expenditure, the balance of dependency between departments and the core executive shifted further
National Economic Council	New policy-making structures dilute the power of the Treasury and emphasise the importance of working through departments and actors beyond Whitehall	Targets, initiatives and PSAs sustain a chain of command from the Treasury at the centre to departments and agencies at 'street-level', maintaining Treasury controls over aggregate expenditure in Whitehall

The Dialectical Relationship between Ideas and Institutions in the BPT

The conception of the BPT outlined in Table 8.3 enables the tension between governing practices and ideas to be more fully elaborated. The nostrums of representation and responsibility are concurrent and both are influential across time, although governmental responsibility has taken precedence as the core idea of the BPT. This further emphasises that inferring a fundamental shift in the distribution of power from departments to Number Ten is over-simplistic; it is necessary to reject, and move away from, such binary classifications. Greater analytical precision is needed to understand how change occurs within the context of continuity, through a set of institutions underpinned by a power-hoarding conceptualisation of British democracy. In summary:

- *Academy schools* are established by delegating authority to front-line providers, strengthening managerial discretion while ensuring that schools are responsive to parental voice. As one Number Ten adviser attested:

  > Part and parcel of this new type of contract was much greater managerial autonomy [...] the establishment of institutions that were intended to be self-governing. Local and central bureaucracies of all kinds are not good at managing schools. The best people to manage schools are successful managers.[81]

  Nonetheless, despite an emphasis on the role of 'negotiated governance', academies were usually imposed on localities replacing under-performing schools. The chain of command ran directly to the centre. This emphasised the on-going importance of centralisation and an ethos of 'Whitehall knows best'. According to one DfES official, 'Number Ten wanted to reproduce the advantages of City Academies across the system. These priorities were driven firmly from the centre.'[82]

- *Family-Nurse Partnerships* were intended to give citizens a voice in social exclusion programmes, operating through consortia of PCTs and local authorities. As one DoH practitioner described:

  > Intervention always sounds like you are doing something to somebody. Whereas the ethos of FNP is: 'you can do this, and together we are going to find out'. People only change themselves, we never change other people [...] with FNP we've always done it on the basis that people want to do it locally.[83]

  Nonetheless, FNPs were driven from the centre, and the SETF remained heavily involved in the design, implementation and monitoring of programmes. There was little scope for varying front-line delivery: the 'dosage' of intervention and clinical support was prescribed centrally, ensuring rigorous cross-national evaluation.[84] Evidence-based policy was created through strong, centralising government.

- The *National Economic Council* challenged the Treasury's control over economic policy, encouraging a more collegiate approach and working with actors beyond Whitehall to stimulate economic growth. A Number Ten adviser explained: 'The NEC put it [the Treasury] under a lot more pressure to defend itself [...] it was made to move much faster than it really wanted to.'[85] Another official confirmed:

> The NEC was a big shift for Gordon Brown because he didn't want the Treasury to dominate. He realised that departments with a supply-side input like BIS [Department of Business, Innovation and Science] had to have their say in the formation of key policies. This was a return to a more collegiate style of government which on the whole the civil service welcomed because it made their relationship with the Treasury more equal.[86]

Nevertheless, the Treasury continued to impose targets and initiatives on departments, thereby steering local authorities and agencies at 'street-level'. As one Number Ten adviser remarked: 'The Treasury still had the power as budgets were beginning to be cut.'[87] Another reiterated: 'The Treasury was still immensely powerful [...] the departments used to moan to Number Ten that the Treasury wasn't taking them seriously.'[88] The creation of the NEC reflected the core executive's search for administrative capacity, rather than any retreat from the centralising governance code.

The literature on the BPT illuminates the iterative and dialectical relationship between institutions and ideas. There is not a linear, inexorable, one-way shift to command-and-control in New Labour's statecraft: centralising tendencies co-exist alongside 'negotiated governance', devolution and reform. This point is reinforced by former Home Secretary Charles Clarke, insisting that New Labour's approach to governance involves an implicit tension between:

> The Webbite version of public sector reform, and the social entrepreneurship version of public sector reform. The Webbite version, which I characterise as Gordon Brown's, was based on the view of the Webbs that at the centre of Whitehall, you could push buttons and pull levers and change things throughout the country. That also had a defence of equity. Social entrepreneurship was foundation hospitals, trust schools [...] you mobilised people's energies and powers to make a difference. Those are the two models.[89]

Similarly, Peter Clarke (1978: 4) highlighted the distinction between 'moral' and 'mechanical' reform in early twentieth-century liberalism and social democracy. This envisaged a dual approach to reform within the Labour tradition:

> Moral reformers are essentially bottom-up reformers. Values can only be effective in politics when they are widely shared, and the task of the moral reformer is to take the long view and to try to transform the values by which people live in the direction that he wants to see. The mechanical reformer is a top-down reformer, who believes that there might be political, social and economic strategies available which would produce the desired results, without necessarily having to transform the underlying moral culture of citizens.
>
> (Plant, 1991: 43)

Charles Clarke insisted although there was a tension between such ideas, centralisation and the Westminster model remained the dominant governing code under New Labour. This was 'a serious intellectual flaw'.[90] The top-down model was encapsulated in the practices of the PMDU and the PMSU. While it was necessary to develop performance indicators and targets, Labour's reforms were inherently top-down and managerial, 'no longer owned by the professions themselves'.[91] The centralisation of power undermined the potential impact of structural reforms: 'Centralised control [...] made it almost impossible to use resources to help economies in different parts of the country according to the characteristics of those economies.'[92]

This tension is highlighted by New Labour's relationship with the BPT. The previous section affirmed that actors rationalised their approach drawing on ideas from within the BPT, operating through the dominant tradition of the Westminster model. At the same time, Labour sought to challenge central axioms of the Westminster model, notably the efficacy of 'club government' (Moran, 2003). The institutions associated with the 'self-regulated, good chaps' approach had been implicated in Britain's political stagnation and relative economic decline (Flinders, 2010; Gamble, 1984; Goodwin, 2011; Hennessy, 2000). This position is aptly summarised by Pollard: 'The peculiar strengths and weaknesses of the civil service and of the Treasury in particular, form a powerful contributory cause of our decline' (1982: 159).

According to Bulpitt, territorial political management in the UK meant granting autonomy to institutions, interest groups and actors beyond the central state. This made it more difficult to impose financial controls, while using executive power to enact reforms (Bulpitt, 1983; Campbell & Wilson, 1995; Lowe & Rollings, 2000). Ministers sought to strengthen the authority and autonomy of the core executive (Mandelson & Liddle, 1996). The New Labour project was influenced by notions of modernism based on a powerful, controlling state

(Bevir, 2005; Moran, 2003; Newman, 2001; Smith, 2009). Governance practices such as 'evidence-based' policy and 'joined up' government were mediated through the dominant paradigm of the BPT. Although apparently novel and innovative in the context of Whitehall policy-making, these practices were underpinned by an elitist and top-down conceptualisation of democracy within the core executive.

The Labour State Tradition

Such governing practices go to the heart of the Labour tradition, and the relationship between the party's conception of the state, Whitehall and the BPT. The claim is that actors in the Blair and Brown governments developed an interpretation of the BPT based on Labour's traditional view of bureaucracy and expertise outlined in Chapter 3. The content and meaning of party ideology continued to develop as New Labour 'represents a particular response to intellectual and political developments and pressures from within the core of its own tradition in the form of a refashioned or modernised social democracy' (Meredith, 2008: 110). The party's ideas draw on distinct notions of governance and power: first, the idea of a strong and 'indivisible' state anchored in the Westminster model. And second, the 'English pluralist' tradition focused on dispersing and decentralising power. Throughout the party's development, antagonism occurred between these ideological strands: Labour's statecraft was historically concerned with appealing to divergent traditions in order to justify and explain its programme to the party faithful.

The 'critical' account of the BPT infers that Labour's relationship to the BPT and the British state is based on acquiesce and deference (Evans, 1993; Marquand, 1988; Marsh & Tant, 1991). Mulgan remarked:

> This was always the critique of the Labour Party in general, that it was the deferential wing of the working class. And Ramsey MacDonald being the extreme, but part of a trend of fairly easy co-option. I made a lot of enemies writing a piece around the time that Tony Blair stood down saying that was a large part about his time in power. There was essentially not a single issue on which he challenged the establishment view. On every issue, he sided with what Cobbett called 'the thing', the London-based establishment.[93]

Mulgan insists that New Labour refused to address 'deeper structural issues and challenge power'.[94] Similarly, David Miliband contends there has been 'a historical problem in the Labour party persuading people that political reform is relevant to economic and social reform'.[95] Bevir and Rhodes aver: 'This socialist or Fabian lineage is so obvious it hardly needs explaining'

(2003: 152). The literature explores Labour's heritage in terms of 'the top-down, directive tendency' in domestic statecraft.[96] Indeed, there are parallels between New Labour and the Webbs' conception of the bureaucratic and elitist state (Bevir, 2011). The Labour government's commitment to delivering rapid improvements in outcomes meant 'quickly' was the theme. And the way to quick improvement was to tell people what to do. It had become so centralised [...] there was a strong thread of imperious evaluation and auditing. It was a 'government knows best' view.[97]

The motif of Fabianism is that central state power epitomised by the Whitehall model is benign and effective entailing 'practical activities to improve the life of the working people of the country [...] as Max Weber said, politics is the patient boring of hard boards, and the Fabians [...] practiced what Weber preached' (Rose quoted in Kandiah & Seldon, 1995: 182). The relationship between Fabianism and New Labour resides in the 'horrendously bureaucratic culture' characterising departments during the Blair and Brown governments.[98] The approach mirrors Marquand's characterisation of democratic collectivism in the Labour Party's history, with its faith in the redemptive powers of the rational, technocratic state. The purpose of British social democracy is 'to win control of the existing state in order to build a better society' (Marquand, 2008: 61). This is a point of continuity between New Labour and its past.

There is a vigorous debate about the relationship between British social democracy and the state. McCaig (2001: 201) demonstrates that Labour's education policy harnessed 'a vague, plural ideology' combining egalitarian meritocracy with authoritarian and libertarian sentiments. This enabled the leadership to manoeuvre around opposition to its reforms, notably in relation to academy schools.[99] The social democratic tradition, fashioned within the contours of the BPT, consisted of two interwoven elements: Fabian socialism and pluralist syndicalism. Fabianism was sympathetic to the notion of an indivisible, sovereign state predicated on the Westminster model, while syndicalism and guild socialism are integral to the 'English pluralist' tradition.

Fabian Social Democracy

The discussion in Chapter 3 emphasised that the Fabian strand of the British social democratic tradition is intrinsically elitist, assigning importance to the role of expertise in which the state acts as the primary agent of social justice (Bevir, 2012). This is explicitly stated in Douglas Jay's infamous work, *The Socialist Case* (1937): 'In the case of nutrition and health, just as in the case of education, the gentleman in Whitehall really does know better what is good for people than the people know themselves.' The pre-war 'new liberals' such as Charles Masterman had close links to the Fabian Society and spoke of the need for government 'by an aristocracy of intelligence, of energy, of character' (cited in Morgan, 2013: 77). This emphasis on governing through an elite who have the knowledge to make policy illustrates how British social democracy was infected by the dominant tradition in British politics conditioned by the precepts of the BPT.

Bevir (2012) contests subsequent interpretations which have unduly caricatured the Fabian strand of the British socialist tradition. In fact, the Webbs acknowledged the potentially negative implications of a centralised and coercive bureaucracy. This does not explain why the Labour Party so readily identified its interests with sustaining and consolidating the Whitehall model, however. Beatrice Webb (quoted in Barker, 1994: 34) envisaged a 'Jesuitical corps' of dedicated professionals building a planned society free of corruption and inefficiency. Howell (1981: 27) insists the influence of the Fabian Society on the Labour Party was significant:

> This was a consequence of key individuals, most notably Sidney Webb, occupying major positions at crucial times. Fabian beliefs provided major motifs in the party's development: the commitment to gradualism, the denial of inevitably opposed class interests, the faith in the neutrality of the existing state. These were central Fabian tenets and were to be basic beliefs of successive generations of Labour leaders. The Fabian doctrines provided an intellectual rationale for the instinctive attitudes of leaders.

Hood (1996) demonstrates that Fabian ideas about creating expert boards audited and overseen by the permanent bureaucracy were replicated in the notion of separating policy-making in public administration from delivery through *Next Steps* in the late 1980s. Indeed, empirical research was increasingly employed to enhance the system of depoliticised state management: a progenitor of 'evidence-based' policy.

The 'English Pluralist' Tradition

The alternative strand of British social democracy was 'English pluralism', focused on liberal notions of personal liberty, parliamentary government and democratic accountability. In contrast to Fabianism, pluralists and guild socialists feared the growth of unaccountable concentrations of public and private power. By drawing on ideological concepts such as liberty, community, democracy and the state, pluralist socialism promoted radical decentralisation of the economy and the political system (Cole, 1920; Laski & Gooch,

1954). More specifically, socialist theory led pluralists to advocate the state ownership of industry and management through trade-related workers guilds (Stears, 2002).

As such, various strands of the Labour Party tradition are encapsulated within New Labour's statecraft, as the case study of FNPs elucidates:

- Like the Fabians, New Labour emphasised the importance of expertise and the translation of social science into public policy. FNPs were 'evidence-based', drawing on evaluations of pilot programmes in the United States. They sought 'to identify early who is at risk of persistent exclusion and use this information to intervene' (Cabinet Office, 2006a: 22). The programme originated in the interaction between experts and practitioners, exemplified by social scientists such as David Olds from the University of Colorado and David Halpern in the PMSU.

- Similarly, New Labour's approach to social policy stressed the interconnect-edness of rights and duties. FNPs were not passive interventions delivering services to recipients, but required active parental engagement. According to one Number Ten adviser, the ethos of the programme was avowedly 'anti-liberal'. Many services traditionally demanded little of users, bequeathing a legacy of inaction. Welfare policy too often consisted of 'knocking on the door with a wet sponge'.[100] FNPs sought to redefine the relationship between rights and obligations: 'Our approach is framed by a clear understanding of the rights and responsibilities of citizens, services and communities' (Cabinet Office, 2006a: 22).

- In contrast, an alternative strand of Labour's programme entailed devolving power, forging a more participative model of governance akin to the ethos of syndicalism and guild socialism. One policy statement published in 2003 posed the following question:

> We ask how government can become truly enabling, not crowding out but drawing on the capacity of individuals and communities [...] it is at the most local level that people can best get involved in deciding priorities and shaping services.
>
> (Labour Party, 2003)

The SEU sought explicitly to involve citizens in policy design and implementation, translated into programmes such as the New Deal for Communities (NDC). As a senior official in the Home Office remarked:

> I think we forget how Big Society Blair was in those 1997 days. A lot of the rhetoric was around new ways for communities to be involved. If you think about how they used precious resources in the very constrained period for the first two years, they

used £400 million from the lottery to fund healthy living centres which was about new engagement between the health service and communities.[101]

Indeed, there was a commitment within FNPs to 'empower, where it is appropriate, excluded groups to make choices' (Cabinet Office, 2006a: 22). This placed the UK at the forefront of community-led initiatives,[102] encapsulated in Mulgan's critique of elite models of policy-making:

> The idea that simply putting a bunch of the great and the good together around a table will get you to the right and legitimate answer no longer works today for quite a few reasons. One is that it is not clear whether they would use the right methods for analysing a problem. Second, it is not clear that the public will see their views as legitimate just because they are the great and the good.[103]

Nonetheless, an alternative literature posits that programmes and instruments predicated on 'negotiated' governance are merely levers for disciplining and controlling the recipients of welfare services (Newman, 2001).

There are, inevitably, points of divergence between New Labour's governance code and the social democratic tradition. Fabianism is concerned with planning and the centralised administration of the economy. In contrast, New Labour eschewed attempts to control and manage the economy in favour of markets and neo-endogenous growth theory (Gamble & Kelly, 2001). Bevir and Rhodes (2006b: 83) insist 'Old' Labour was built on Fabianism, alluding to a shift within the socialist tradition to 'New' Labour, 'inspired in part by the New Right's concerns with market efficiency and choice'. However, this chapter has shown that both the Fabians and New Labour have sustained a commitment to state-centric policy-making and technocratic efficiency. Bevir and Rhodes (2006b: 82) have understated how far New Labour retained social democracy's faith in 'top-down, command-style bureaucracy' through centralising norms and rules. This approach was institutionalised through agencies in the core executive, notably the PMDU and the PMSU.

The social democratic tradition influenced and shaped the beliefs of New Labour actors within the parameters of the BPT. In this context, it is necessary to explore how the historical past continues to shape and influence the present. Marquand's work addresses 'the constraints that Labourism has placed on the actions, and even on the thinking, of individual Labour politicians and intellectuals' (1991: ix). The writings of Bevir and Rhodes are concerned with the contingency of traditions and governing practices. However, Bevir and Rhodes' interpretivism underplays the degree to which political traditions contain an essential body of ideas constraining the agency of actors. New Labour's approach to Whitehall was shaped by the strategic choices of agents drawing on traditions in order to resolve contemporary problems and dilemmas. It is the dominant tradition underpinned by a top-down and elitist conceptualisation of British democracy which so often appears most pervasive and influential (Marsh & Tant, 1989). This focus on the interpretation of core ideas emphasises interrogating and exploring the role of traditions in British politics.

The following section focuses on how political traditions manifest themselves in the practices and beliefs of agents. In drawing on cross-cutting ideas about governance, power and the role of the state, actors make particular forms of rule possible. Under New Labour, this leads to apparently innovative practices such as 'evidence-based' policy and 'joined-up' government. While 'evidence-based' policy and 'joined-up' government are integral to New Labour's statecraft, however, they are consistent with the dominant political tradition. For all the modernising rhetoric of Labour's governance reforms, the assumptions underpinning institutional change are compatible with the BPT, enhancing the pre-eminent role of the core executive within a power-hoarding polity.

Evidence-based Policy: Social Science and the Role of Expertise

The example of 'evidence-based' policy illustrates and reinforces this argument about New Labour's commitment to the traditional power-hoarding structures of the central state machine. By emphasising the importance of evidence and best practice in the structure and processes of policy-making, New Labour gave an enhanced role to social scientists and practitioners (Bevir, 2005; Fairclough, 2000; Newman, 2001; Saint-Martin, 1998). Contemporary expertise and political agency are powerfully intertwined. According to Eyerman, the period after World War I saw 'the formation of a new intellectual role – the professional expert', of whom Beveridge and Keynes were exemplary figures (2006: 194). Similarly, the Webbs believed that government should be conducted through 'the disinterested professional expert' (Sidney Webb quoted in Bevir, 2011: 191). This would reveal facts about the changing nature of society, informing governmental actors about public policy and the process of institutional reform.

The role of expertise in New Labour's statecraft acknowledges that social scientists are not merely observers of the political process, but actors helping to construct and reconfigure the state (Bevir, 2011). Bevir argues that shifting from neo-liberalism and the rational choice ontology of the New Right to New Labour's 'institutionalism' meant a renewed emphasis on partnership and the enabling state. This implies institutional continuity alongside change: the nature of the social democratic tradition meant Labour politicians remained attached to technocratic expertise and the elitist structures of the centralising state. 'Evidence-based' policy was consistent with the BPT.

The basis of expertise was arguably the epistemological commitment to positivism in public policy (Foucault, 1976; Wells, 2007). Positivism sought to uncover typologies, correlations and classifications through the practices and methodologies of social science, drawing on the legacy of Auguste Comte, Charles Darwin and Herbert Spencer (Bevir, 2011). Indeed, positivist approaches are evident in the contemporary literature on early intervention underpinning Family-Nurse Partnerships, emphasising predictive approaches that identify disruptive adolescents before they are born (Halpern, 2010). The PMSU sought to determine:

> Causal models of why some children thrive and some children don't [...] drawing on a lot of formal social scientific evidence, literature surveys and so on [...] a lot of people have engaged with some serious evidence and some of the deep questions that follow from it.[104]

The *Social Exclusion Action Plan* proposing FNP pilots draws on a model of 'heterotypic continuity', demonstrating how early problems are manifested in childhood among a population of 'at risk' individuals (Cabinet Office, 2006b: 47). The result is 'a shift to an unprecedented level of prediction and early supportive intervention' (Halpern, 2010: 156). In 2006, the Prime Minister gave an interview implying that teenage pregnancy and criminality could be predicted 'pre-birth'. This led to the term 'Fetal Anti-Social Behaviour Order' ('FASBO').[105] In a subsequent speech, Blair insisted:

> Where it is clear, as it is very often at a young age, that children are at risk of being brought up in a dysfunctional home where there are multiple problems, say of drug abuse or offending, then instead of waiting until the child goes off the rails, we should act early enough [...] to prevent it.[106]

The focus on early intervention linked rational choice theory with literature on behavioural economics and policy-making. This was the progenitor to 'nudge' and the philosophy of libertarian paternalism (Halpern, 2008; Thaler & Sunstein, 2007). Halpern affirmed that drawing on evidence to adjust programme design is more important than 'big set piece arguments about structural reforms':

> What you can do in any given programme is look at the marginal choices, if you keep experimenting and learning, you create a 'contest and learn' culture. You get huge improvements. People often think in health it is about major breakthroughs. But if you look beneath the surface, improvements in heart disease and cancer are about a combination of changes, very small refinements and dosages of drugs.[107]

This perspective on the link between evidence and policy-making is reinforced by Mulgan, appearing before the Public Administration Select Committee:

> It is generally wrong to look for the individual policies, it is where a cluster of policies, a strategy, has been pursued consistently over a long period of time and been adapted to different circumstances [...] The conventional wisdom of twenty years ago, which was that everything government does is futile, doomed, inefficient, just hand it over to business, that is absurd if you look at the real achievements of government on most of the outcomes the public judges them on.[108]

This emphasis on the role of evidence is affirmed by Stephen Aldridge, former Director of PMSU:

> We are expected to be analytically rigorous, we are expected to start with that blank sheet of paper and suggest, based on an analysis of evidence, what might be the right answers to the problems that need to be tackled. Ministers will decide what is politically possible, or not. We are asked to give the best analysis and advice that we can.[109]

Halpern's approach draws on empirical evidence of what works, alongside theoretical models from psychology and medical science. This implies a productive relationship between New Labour and the social science community,[110] manifested in early intervention strategies.[111] Like the early Fabians, Labour adopted a positivist epistemological world-view forging a modernist state overseen by professional managers and technocrats. Hennessy notes: 'There is a kind of continuity there, a passing on of tradition and knowledge.'[112] Of course, there is inevitably scepticism about the impact of 'evidence-based' policy. Governments lack the capacity to learn from evidence given the volume of research and pressure for results, while the use of empirical data is invariably limited and selective (Exley, 2012; Halpern, 2010).

In the New Labour years, the focus of state action shifted from regulating the national economy through the Keynesian welfare state to modifying individual lifestyles and behaviour (Smith, 2009). The welfare system was engaged in moral efforts to shape 'better' families and citizens among the socially excluded (Dodds, 2009; Newman, 2001). This was undertaken within the parameters of the BPT, centred on a top-down, elitist governing code. Power is predominantly located in the core executive, while central government enhances its role throughout the policy process. The BPT operates as: 'a system of power that both reflects and reinforces existing institutions and histories' (Marsh et al., 2003: 29).

In relation to institutional reform, the dominant political tradition runs through Northcote-Trevelyan (1854) and early twentieth century Fabianism to a series of subsequent inquiries, notably Haldane (1918), *The Administrators* (1964), the Fulton Report (1968) and the *Modernising Government* White Paper (Cabinet Office, 1999). While such reports emphasise the importance of bureaucratic modernisation, they do so by upholding fundamental tenets of the BPT focused on parliamentary sovereignty, top-down government and a neutral, permanent bureaucracy. The core ideas of the BPT remained a powerful influence in New Labour's statecraft: the scope for fundamental change and reform is necessarily circumscribed.

'Joining-up' Government: Networks and Institutionalism

While Labour's approach has been shaped by expertise and social science according to the tenets of 'evidence-based policy', institutionalism and networks have been similarly influential in promulgating 'joined-up' government (Bevir, 2005; McAnulla, 2007). Although 'joined-up' government appeared innovative and modernising in the late 1990s, it similarly drew upon and reinforced the dominant paradigm of the BPT. Institutionalism addressed problems of co-ordination and control bedevilling British government throughout the twentieth century (Mulgan, 2001). Labour sought to rebuild confidence in the state, strengthening the efficacy of the policy-making process while creating machinery to improve cross-departmental co-ordination (Driver & Martell, 2006; Gamble, 2003). Early in Blair's premiership, the *Modernising Government* White Paper set out the objectives of effective policy-making as strategic, holistic, focused on outcomes and delivery (Cabinet Office, 1999).

Bevir (2005) draws attention to the emphasis on 'joined-up' government in response to the pathology of fragmentation and failed steering across Whitehall (Bogdanor, 1997). The search for an effective governing strategy is encapsulated by Michael Bichard, permanent secretary at DfES (1997–2001):

> The time is coming when we need to move away from this preoccupation with services to a more strategic sort of government which is more about influencing behaviour, which is much better at joining up issues, which is agile, quick on its feet and innovative.[113]

The importance of a coherent statecraft was acknowledged by New Labour actors given the implementation failures of previous Labour governments, and the implausibility of resurrecting post-war corporatism (Barber, 2007;

Mandelson & Liddle, 1996; Miliband, 1994; Mulgan, 1996). In particular, networks emerged as an important plank of Labour's reforms. Halpern (2010: 207) insists:

> Larger networks have a number of advantages. They can achieve scale benefits around purchasing and service development. They can extend the reach of the best leaders, an expensive and precious resource. They can spread innovative practice more rapidly.

The influence of Demos on Labour's governance strategy has already been noted (Bevir, 2005). However, there were other relationships with the Centre for the Analysis of Social Exclusion (CASE), and more ideologically sympathetic thinktanks such as the IPPR. CASE focused on the scope for area-based policies in tackling social exclusion and poverty, and the importance of 'joined-up' policy-making (Glennerster, 2006). In 'joining-up government', Labour made more progress than has been acknowledged according to Mulgan:

> By the end of the Labour government, a third of all targets were shared across departments. There was lots of experiment with pooled budgets from post-conflict reconstruction to early years; a lot of cross-cutting teams such as rough-sleeping and climate change; and important experiments around data, particularly the children at risk data base.[114]

Nonetheless, departmental ministers were frustrated by the tendency of departments to work in isolation, and the difficulty this created in achieving their objectives:

> One of the reasons why New Labour found it difficult to get cross-departmental working right is because of the way departments are structured. We moved from a one year cycle to a three year cycle, and the money went to individual departments. The programme expenditure is where the power is, where the real power of decision making lies.[115]

While 'joined-up' government was initially the central pillar of New Labour's modernisation strategy, the approach fought to overcome a series of bureaucratic obstacles alongside the traditional commitment to departmentalism underpinning the Westminster model. Despite Labour's emphasis on institutional reform and modernisation, such approaches are consistent with, rather than a threat to, the dominant paradigm and the BPT. Indeed, 'evidence-based' policy and 'joined-up' government entail the re-imposition of centralised state control and core executive autonomy, encapsulating the British post-war modernist tradition of governing society and the polity from the 'commanding heights' of Whitehall.

Conclusion

This chapter addressed how far New Labour's attitude to the state and the administrative and political machinery of government were anchored in past ideas and practices mediated through the dominant political tradition. The chapter examined how the BPT influenced the beliefs and actions of agents, reinforced by New Labour's determination to acquire the capacity to authoritatively govern state-society relations. The analysis sought to highlight how traditions operate as an ideational 'DNA' hard-wired into Labour's conception of the state and the BPT. If the concept of political tradition is analogous to 'DNA', traditions do not pre-determine outcomes: instead, the argument is that tradition creates a 'genetic' pre-disposition towards stasis and inertia in Whitehall.

The focus on the role of tradition and institutional norms mediating how actors think and behave provides an antidote to the governance literature, which promotes a dynamic, path-breaking view of change. Traditions are not just about the force of inertia, however, since actors draw on traditions in resolving dilemmas. Tradition prompts change as well as reinforcing continuity, emphasising the dynamic and interactive relationship between continuity and change. This underlines the role of ideas and institutions in shaping stability and change in Whitehall. The chapter's key findings are:

- The emphasis on tradition draws attention to continuity in the Whitehall paradigm: the resonance of an enduring civil service culture, the axiom of secrecy, the claim that 'central government knows best', and the convention that 'officials advise and ministers decide'. Tradition alludes to the inertial power that persists in contemporary politics.
- New Labour's Whitehall reforms fulfil central nostrums of the BPT. These are predicated on a top-down and elitist conceptualisation of British democracy, shaping the beliefs and actions of agents within departments and the core executive.
- The BPT and the Westminster model emphasise the power of the ideational. Whether empirically accurate or not as representations of the political system, ideas associated with the BPT have an enduring impact on how actors think and act, shaping and influencing policy outcomes.
- The Labour tradition draws on conflicting notions of governance and power: the conception of a strong and indivisible state anchored in the Westminster model, overidding the commitment within the 'English pluralist' tradition to decentralisation and individual liberty.

- This offers an analytically rigorous approach to continuity and change. In drawing on tradition, governance practices develop and mutate across time. New Labour sought to promote 'evidence-based' policy and 'joined-up' government, anchored in administrative traditions such as Fabianism and the BPT.
- As such, there is never a fundamental rupture with the past. Instead, change is built up and accumulated on top of existing conventions and practices. Over time, this leads to tensions and dilemmas in the management of the central state.

Overall, the chapter argues that 'agent-orientated path dependency' has tended to characterise institutional reform in Whitehall. On the one hand, previous chapters demonstrate that changes beneath the surface are modest, shaped and mediated by actors. The dominant assumptions of the BPT have constrained the impact of modernising reforms. On the other hand, change occurs through the antagonism between traditional and modernising practices, which agents experience in the everyday life of British government. This leads to pathologies within the state's central operating code unleashing 'the sour law of unintended consequences'. That, in turn, prompts change as agents seek to resolve the dilemmas created by the putative conflict between new models of public management and the traditional Westminster model (Hennessy, 1995b: 453).

As discussed, 'classical' accounts of the BPT celebrate the virtues of the British polity, highlighting the stability afforded by representative and responsible government. By the 1970s, however, 'critical' interpretations emerged emphasising a crisis of legitimacy in the British state: 'British political institutions suddenly had as many critics as formerly they had admirers' (Gamble, 1990: 414). Dissatisfaction deepened according to one observer:

> The limitations of Whitehall and Westminster, and I think it is both sides, the political and the governmental, are very urgent and I do not think they are simply expressed in terms of overload and mission creep and competence. The centrifugal forces in the UK are related to this [...] in Scotland and Wales what people are expressing is not hostility to the idea of the United Kingdom, they are expressing hostility to the idea of being run from Whitehall and Westminster.[116]

This was acknowledged by New Labour prior to its 1997 victory. The conception of the British political system based on participative and inclusive 'liberal' values resonated with the party in opposition. Blair insisted New Labour's vision was about 'democratic renewal' and 'constitutional modernisation', strengthening the legitimacy of the Westminster model (Blair, 1996b). Similarly, Mandelson and Liddle (1996: 173) advocated 'a new politics', reversing centralised decision-making and deepening the relationship between citizen and state, promoting 'open government' and parliamentary reform.

Once in office, however, fashioning a governing strategy premised on a strong central executive proved irresistible, fulfilling New Labour's electoral mandate and implementing reforms by harnessing the central levers of the state. The capacity of the traditional 'power-hoarding' model to enable the party to deliver its manifesto commitments meant there was, in practice, little appetite for participatory reform. The leadership was able to draw deeply on the party's statecraft tradition in order to legitimise its approach to the machinery of the British state. As such, the chapter showed how Labour politicians and policy-makers derived inspiration from a variety of traditions and ideological resources in responding to the recurrent challenge of governing effectively.

CHAPTER 9

Conclusion: Power, Policy and the Modern State

It was all very well to adopt a more pluralist framework away from London, but not within the Palace of Westminster.

Bogdanor (2002: 719)

I know that it is easy to talk about pluralism when in opposition but much harder to give up power when in government. I am determined that we should do so.

Blair (1996: 262).

One of the great adjustments it is important for any government to make is to realise that much of the skill set that brings you to power is then redundant in government. Someone quoted Genghis Khan at me the other day who said [...] conquering the world on horseback was relatively easy, what was really hard was when he dismounted and had to govern.

Senior Labour minister[1]

Introduction

The history of New Labour is of a governing party relentlessly searching for instruments and levers that would enable politicians to govern authoritatively, restoring central administrative capacity within the state. What occurred, as a result, was not an inexorable decline in the hierarchical state, but a new effort to expand the institutional power resources of the core executive and the capability to control and steer the machinery of government. Of course, concerns about the capacity of political actors to govern are nothing new given the vast 'public choice' literature which examines the role of self-interested bureaucrats in allegedly stifling governments from implementing structural reforms (Peters, 2004). The challenge New Labour faced, however, was inheriting a governing apparatus that had already been segmented and dispersed among a variety of institutions and actors outside the centre of the state, weakening the capacity for strategic leadership. At the same time, whatever the debate about the apparent 'presidentialisation' of British politics, voters have increasingly challenged their leaders to solve practical problems, while articulating a persuasive vision for the country. As a consequence, politicians have searched intensively for ways of governing Britain more effectively from the centre.

After 1997, the constant and growing pressure for more efficient, 'outcome-driven' government made the leading protagonists in New Labour uneasy about the capacity of Whitehall to provide policy coherence and effective service delivery. The current debate about the Whitehall model relates to whether the civil service is considered competent, up to date and 'fit for purpose'. Many figures in the Blair and Brown governments increasingly believed that the Whitehall paradigm was the artefact of an outdated nineteenth-century constitution. Senior civil servants, in contrast, insisted that the long-standing constitutional principles overseeing the core executive had been undermined by the modernising zeal of Thatcherism and New Labour. The Blair administration sought to make departments and agencies more responsive to the centre, accumulating power in Number Ten and exposing the public sector to an ever more intrusive regime of 'command-and-control' (Foster, 2005; Foster & Plowden, 1998; Gray, 2000). The incoming Prime Minister in 1997 had exhorted the civil service to redefine its role, no longer providing ministerial policy advice and 'speaking truth to power', but driving improvement throughout Britain's public services as the agent of institutional reform.

These structural changes in the core executive are reflected in Michael Moran's claim that British government shifted 'from stability to hyper-innovation' (2003: 5). While an era of 'club' government had insulated the political elite from popular pressures, recent decades were marked by 'the invasion of hitherto enclosed policy communities by a wide range of new actors' (Moran, 2003: 9). According to Moran, the centre of government became increasingly hyperactive and politicised: 'permanent revolution' was the order of the day. The ethos of informal self-regulation and an 'amateur' policy-making style were replaced by formal oversight, a target regime, the audit culture, public sector restructuring, and evidence-based policy-making. The climate was apparently one of relentless innovation and change, uprooting many long-established features of the constitutional landscape in Whitehall and the core executive.

This reinforced a view of British central government as the object of waves of far-reaching and transformative change, promulgated both in journalistic commentary and the academic literature. Contrary to the received wisdom, however, this book has argued that Whitehall reform ought to be conceived as evolutionary and adaptive, rather than revolutionary. Indeed, there is a constant danger of overstating the impact and scale of institutional change. It is essential to address how key elements of the Whitehall paradigm have adapted and evolved within the parameters of the dominant political tradition. Labour's reforms did not represent a radical break with the past; instead, they sought to consolidate earlier, piecemeal attempts at change.

Other academic accounts are in keeping with this view having utilised a fluid, dynamic and incremental conception of change in relation to Whitehall and the core executive (Burnham & Pyper, 2008; Smith, 2011; Wrisque-Cline, 2008). They acknowledge that the structure of the civil service and British public administration continues to reflect the essential vision enshrined in Northcote-Trevelyan. According to Peters (1999: 65), 'There will always be change and evolution, but the range of possibilities for that development will have been constrained by the formative period of the institution.' New Labour's approach to the Whitehall model sought a shift in emphasis, rather than a fundamental overhaul of the status quo.

Despite the protestations of successive Cabinet secretaries, the role and function of the civil service in Whitehall has remained substantially unchanged. This reflected New Labour ministers' ambivalence about the mandarin class: they were irritated, annoyed and occasionally dismayed by the perceived failings of Whitehall, but ministers realised they could not achieve much without their officials. Similarly, despite rebuking departments for their lack of ideas and an apparently ineffectual style of implementation, both Blair and Brown as prime minister came to realise there was little they could deliver without the engagement of departments. The overarching claim of this book is that the key organising principle of British central government remains that of *mutual dependency*.

Moreover, the power relationship between ministers and officials, centre and departments, has been fashioned by constitutional rules of the game which, on the whole, New Labour judiciously maintained. As a result, the impact of structural reform in the core executive has been offset by inertia, departmental resistance and the weight of tradition in administrative procedures and practices. A pattern has been established in which the 'dynamic conservatism' of Whitehall can thwart numerous initiatives conceived by the centre. This concluding chapter provides a synoptic overview, outlining the contribution of the book to the wider literature on governance, power and the core executive.

Governance, Power and the State: Continuity and Change in the Core Executive

At the outset, this study posed a set of core empirical questions: how far did the centre in Number Ten bypass departments in the policy-making process? To what extent was the Whitehall model reshaped by politicisation and pluralisation, and how did that influence patterns of stability and change in the central state? And how far has the British state been characterised by institutional path dependency: do modernising practices such as 'evidence-based policy' and 'joined-up government' undermine or reinforce the hierarchical power-hoarding model? The study locates contemporary accounts of governance within the tension that has long existed in the British Labour tradition between a strong, 'indivisible' state anchored in the Westminster model, and an 'English pluralist' vision focused on the decentralisation of power, autonomy and the liberty of citizens. In practice, the Westminster model appears to have won out decisively in the New Labour era.

The party's statecraft was, nevertheless, predicated on an appeal to divergent 'socialist' and 'social democratic' traditions in order to justify its programme (Richards & Smith, 2010). While elements of Labour's discourse challenged a top-down, centralising view of British democracy, the dominant approach viewed the state as an instrument for governing society and the polity. This study has emphasised the role of the dominant political tradition in shaping the attitudes and actions of agents, capturing the essentially dialectical relationship between continuity and change, structure and agency, and institutions and ideas.

The New Labour Effect on Whitehall

As such, this book has highlighted the iterative and mutually reinforcing interaction between continuity and change: the trajectory of institutional reform has been gradual and evolutionary, conditioned and shaped by the dominant paradigm in British politics. This is captured in the study's empirical findings on the core executive set out below.

Policy-making in the Centre and Departments

New Labour's creation of the PMDU and the PMSU was potentially pathbreaking, enabling Number Ten to intervene throughout the policy implementation process. Ministers sought to emphasise their political accountability, enlarging core executive responsibility for the management of the state and its performance. There was an abiding faith in a strong executive anchored in the central precepts of the Westminster model. Nonetheless, departments have remained at the centre of policy-making: Britain continued to be ruled through ministerial government; departments are still the key agents of the policy process in the British political system. The relative autonomy of departments has been highlighted throughout this study. Number Ten is implicated in complex power and resource dependencies: actors work within structured networks negotiating policy outcomes through bargaining games.

The core executive adopts a collaborative approach which is intended to expand its influence across the institutions of the central British state. While the centre accumulated institutional power, its capacity to exploit bureaucratic resources depends on the competence and capability of key agents. Number Ten sought to extend its leverage over policy, but this was a contingent process and did not equate to central control. In addition, ministers invariably had little or no idea about what delivery meant in practice since they had rarely worked in, or even run, large-scale organisations. The mantra of 'the prime minister wants' galvanised officials in Whitehall, but struggled to reduce waiting times in NHS hospitals and improve standards in secondary education. This affirms that although power in Britain is tightly centralised and hoarded at the apex of the state, it is often difficult to wield that power effectively without alienating citizens – precisely why the critique of the centralised British state emerged with such force in the 1970s and 1980s.

Dynamics of Continuity and Change in the Whitehall Model

The nature of the interaction between *political* ministers and *permanent* civil servants has evolved markedly over the last quarter of a century. Some officials have been displaced from their role as the principal source of ministerial policy advice, increasingly marginalised and excluded from key policy decisions. Even so, the Haldane model, which was predicated on a relationship of mutual loyalty and 'serial monogamy' where officials advise but politicians decide, has retained its essential integrity and remains largely unbroken.

There was, undoubtedly, greater emphasis on the managerial capabilities of civil servants: New Labour subjected officials to a delivery regime enforced through the centre, making them accountable for the performance of public sector agencies beyond central government. However, the Whitehall paradigm had not been eclipsed by the time of New Labour's departure from office in 2010. The extent of politicisation and pluralisation in the policy-making process has been overstated: officials have retained significant influence over policy. The relationship between civil servants, ministers and political advisers in Whitehall remains collaborative and, in the main, non-adversarial.

Institutional Path Dependency and the Dominant Tradition of British Politics

This research highlights that the core executive, underpinned by a power-hoarding approach, has remained predominant in the British system of government, encapsulated by the Asymmetric Power Model and the 'critical wave' BPT literature. The centre of government is able to exercise wide-ranging influence over policy delivery and implementation. As such, while much changed in the Whitehall model, much remains the same: NPM and governance reform have not fundamentally weakened the dominant political tradition prevailing in Westminster and Whitehall. This study confirms that managerial reforms have been grafted onto a centralised operating code, reinforced by the Westminster model.

As such, a key conclusion of the book is that governing institutions are fundamentally resilient despite the potential for turning points and critical junctures: institutional path dependency emphasises that reforms occur in the context of previous attempts at change, leading to inertia in the organisational structure of Whitehall. The process of institutional change has more often been gradual, piecemeal and evolutionary – rather than revolutionary. Historical institutionalism attests that ad hoc and incremental change creates 'tipping points', however, leading to more far-reaching change. Thelen's (2003: 101) analysis of institutional stickiness is apposite:

> What we often see is, on the one hand, a remarkable resilience of some institutional arrangements even in the face of huge historic breaks, and, on the other hand, on-going subtle shifts beneath the surface of apparently stable formal institutions that, over time, can completely redefine the functions and political purposes they serve.

Moreover, the interpretation of stability and change in Whitehall is necessarily *positional*: opinions vary according to the structural status of actors. In other words, it depends on where agents sit within the system, the political salience of their role, and contingent factors such as the personality and leadership style of ministers. The perception of what has changed varies according to where individuals are located within the institutional hierarchy, and cannot be conclusively determined by looking 'top-down' from the centre:

- As such, *ministers* conveyed disappointment about the missed opportunities of the New Labour years, along with the frustration of attempting to steer the unwieldy and cumbersome Whitehall machinery. In their view, governance reform did not go too far, but was at times excessively cautious and incremental. Nonetheless, ministers remained mutually dependent on their officials and departments. Intriguingly, ministers were often as sceptical about Number Ten as their civil servants: they saw the political centre as naive, inexperienced and excessively concerned with short-term presentational initiatives.

- Politically appointed *advisers* in Number Ten were sceptical about Whitehall's performance and its capacity to ensure effective policy-making and implementation. They bemoaned the culture of hierarchy and lack of innovation in the civil service. In contrast, special advisers in departments usually saw themselves as engaged in a joint endeavour with officials, protecting and enhancing their minister's political reputation. The extent of open conflict between political advisers and officials has been overstated, while most had a similar view of Number Ten's limitations.

- *Civil servants* tended to rationalise and downplay conflict. They were liable to perceive change through an evolutionary prism, and were reluctant to concede that there have been significant changes in the status and authority of the civil service. Of course, senior civil servants still allude to the centralisation of the policy process around Number Ten, and its detrimental impact on the quality of decision-making and 'good government' in the British state. Nonetheless, more often than not officials have remained mutually dependent and loyal to ministers.

As well as disaggregating actors' views of structural change in Whitehall and the core executive, it is important to examine how New Labour's strategy evolved over time. This approach underlines the importance of the temporal dimension of institutional change. While core elements of the Whitehall model had seemingly eroded, fundamental tenets and principles have remained intact. The 'end of Whitehall' view fails to distinguish between where institutional change did, and did not, occur. For example, the widely aired critique of Number Ten 'micro-management' is principally focused on the early years of the New Labour administration. Labour's statecraft, its approach to the conduct of government, evolved sequentially, as Table 9.1 enunciates. Table 9.1 captures evolutionary and incremental change in New Labour's governance and Whitehall strategy.[2]

In *Phase I*, a high trust model was adopted, leaving civil servants, departments and the front-line to implement policy, while injecting limited additional resources into the public sector. Only in specific programmes such as the literary and numeracy strategy in primary education was a centralised regime

TABLE 9.1   New Labour's four phases of governance reform

Temporal phase (1997–2010)	Core executive	Departmental framework	Governance strategy
Phase I: 'Wiring Up' 1997–1999	Strengthening Number Ten through larger and more 'political' Policy Unit, the establishment of the SCU, and an increase in special advisers in Number Ten and the Treasury. Launch of PIU (1998)	Policy making arena driven by ministers; departmental autonomy strong, although less emphasis on Cabinet committees and collective responsibility; multitude of tsars and policy task forces created	'Joining-up' government and cross-departmental co-ordination through Number Ten and Cabinet Office, including creation of SEU
Phase II: 'Command-and-Control' 1999–2003	Expansion of Number Ten Policy Directorate which is merged with Private Office; launch of PMDU (2001) and PMSU (2002)	Departments subject to PSAs alongside reporting and monitoring regime at centre with greater managerial autonomy at front-line; search for alternative sources of policy advice beyond Whitehall	Implementation of central command through performance management, targets, regulation, and direct political control within increasingly fragmented delivery system
Phase III: 'Pluralising Delivery' 2004–2007	Slimming down and recalibration of Number Ten's role in policy and delivery. Launch of Social Exclusion Task force replacing SEU in Cabinet Office	Responsibility for reform agenda shifts back to departments through five-year plans	Quasi-markets, devolution and autonomy for front-line managers in public service delivery
Phase IV: 'Crisis Management' 2007–2010	Scaling back centre (partially reversed), revoking special advisers managerial powers over Whitehall, and launch of NEC (2008) following financial crisis	Cabinet government reasserts itself in Whitehall alongside curtailing of executive and prime-ministerial powers	Accountability in fragmented delivery structure through citizen 'guarantees' and 'voice', alongside dilution of market-based reform programme in public services

imposed. Nonetheless, events such as the 'winter flu crises' in the NHS underlined the limits of a 'hands-off' approach. As a result, *Phase II* reverted to a low trust model: a regime of 'targets and terror' in which centralised initiatives are imposed from Number Ten. Departmental officials were increasingly held to account for public sector performance by the centre. However, while improvements did undoubtedly occur, Number Ten acknowledged that the top-down reform model was unlikely to be sustainable in the long-term.

As a consequence, *Phase III* focused on pluralistic methods of public service delivery: consumer choice, competition, contestability, and bottom-up change entailing departmental autonomy and less intrusive intervention from Number Ten. Quasi-market reforms such as academy schools which encouraged greater competition between providers, nonetheless, remained controversial. This meant that in reaction to the unpopularity of Blair's reforms, the Brown administration in *Phase IV* adopted citizen's 'voice' rather than 'choice' as a lever of change, strengthening the mechanism of collective responsibility and Cabinet government through the creation of the National Economic Council.

Between 1997 and 2010, the New Labour administration adopted a diverse repertoire of approaches to policy-making and implementation. This entailed a dynamic conception of the interventionist role and capacities of central government, while safeguarding the traditional power-hoarding structures of the British state. The central state under New Labour sought to intervene pro-actively, reforming British society and the polity from the 'top-down'. Nonetheless, ministers and their advisers realised that the levers of power were diffuse and unwieldy, more often than not disconnected from anything outside. The new tools of governance such as PSA targets, delivery reviews and the audit culture notionally gave the centre of government greater control over policy, but outcomes depended on negotiation between multiple actors, institutions and centres of power. The Westminster model confers considerable influence and leverage on ministers, but within a more segmented and disaggregated policy-making arena where it is harder than ever for politicians 'to get things done'.

The Future Reform Agenda

An official making an assessment of Whitehall and the civil service at the end of the New Labour years remarked: 'The formal position has been entrenched in legislation, but the 'efficient' part of the constitution is actually developing in a way that goes beyond it.'[3] Whatever formal understandings are reached about the permanent bureaucracy, the civil service is being pushed and pulled in unpredictable directions, as the Blair and Brown governments have sought to re-cast the structures of Whitehall and the core executive. This has bequeathed a legacy of ambiguity and uncertainty about the trajectory of the central state in the aftermath of New Labour's reforms:

- *New Labour's governance strategy perpetuated confusion.* On the one hand, key relationships between ministers and officials integral to the Whitehall model were entrenched. On the other hand, structural changes in public management strained existing constitutional practices, underpinned by the putative shift from 'government' to 'governance'. Civil servants exist principally to serve ministers, but they can no longer operate in isolation imposing policy in an ordered, hierarchical fashion from Whitehall. The policy-making and delivery process occurs through a myriad of institutions and actors outside the direct authority of the central state, straining existing conceptions of accountability.

- *As such, emphasising the responsibility of officials for operational delivery has repercussions for ministerial and parliamentary oversight.* There is greater pressure to subject civil servants to parliamentary scrutiny, undermining the axiom of ministerial responsibility. NPM strains traditional understandings of accountability: ministers make officials responsible for achieving targets, yet retain the power of intervention where political pressures require it. Politicians claim the latitude to determine policy, while civil servants get on with the job of delivery. As the artificial distinction between 'policy-making' and 'implementation' has been further entrenched, it is clear that policy and delivery cannot be neatly separated. There is a 'feedback loop' between setting overarching objectives, selecting appropriate policy instruments, and implementing change on the ground. New Labour's reforms have done little to assuage the confusion. Indeed, there is a danger that policy-making and implementation are prised ever further apart.

- *Whitehall's struggle to co-ordinate the policy process has fuelled demands for institutional reform, in particular curtailing the autonomy of departments as ministerial fiefdoms.* Departmentalism and an absence of horizontal co-ordination has been a recurring problem in Whitehall since World War I. Nevertheless, New Labour remained ambivalent about the case for large-scale structural reform. There was an argument for removing departmental boundaries altogether, reducing horizontal and vertical fragmentation. Similarly, there were proposals for absorbing the civil service within an overarching structure combining central and local government, with a mandate to adopt a strategic approach to public service delivery. Until now, however, reform has been transposed onto the existing Whitehall model. The reluctance to embark on any fundamental overhaul of the organisation and management of the state has been striking indeed (HM Government, 2012).

- *Any reform programme has to acknowledge that Whitehall restructuring is in no way analogous to organisational and management change generally.* Institutional reform in central government is an inherently *political* exercise relating to the accountability of ministers and civil servants to Parliament, and the maintenance of existing constitutional arrangements. All programmes of reform have profound implications for the authority and legitimacy of the state: plans which merely seek to mimic private sector 'best practice' are inherently flawed.

However, the key problem arising from New Labour's statecraft is that while the British tradition of gradualism which shaped Labour's governing strategy has strengths, the state has too often lacked strategic oversight. Problems were addressed in an ad hoc fashion through the tacit principles of an uncodified constitution: an approach to governing premised on 'muddling through'. Rhodes (2012: 15) insists: 'Even today, ministers and civil servants act as if the nineteenth century liberal constitution sets the rules of the political game.' This arguably understates the seriousness of the challenge to beliefs and practices within the inherited traditions of Whitehall and Westminster: a coherent, overarching framework shaping the state's development appears to be absent.

This missing link echoes Matthew Flinders' argument about 'walking without order': under the New Labour regime, an explicit logic and rationale shaping the process of public management reform has been lost. The consequence is, 'widespread and fundamental confusion about the administrative structure of the state' (Flinders, 2008: 1). Indeed, Labour's initial aim was to rectify co-ordination weaknesses in the British state. In creating new institutions at the centre, however, the state has merely become even further fragmented. At the same time, the changes occurred without any explicit reference to the wider programme of constitutional reform. This has led to misrepresentation of the role played by actors and institutions within the British political system, underlined by the recent controversy over politicisation and increasing numbers of special advisers. Looking forward, if an alternative approach to state management was adopted that acknowledged the importance of coherent governing principles, it is necessary to address which institutional reforms ought to be prioritised in Whitehall and the UK core executive.

The first task is to clarify the role of Whitehall and the civil service in a more intricate governance and policy-making arena. The political terrain has opened up over the last thirty years through a critique of the centralised, bureaucratic and hierarchical nature of the British state (Ascherson, 1990; Bogdanor, 2009; Marquand, 1988). This implies the rejection of a centralised planning model epitomised by Jay's claim that 'the gentleman in Whitehall knows best'. This framework emphasises diversity, choice, decentralisation and pluralism: a new operating code for the British state. The emphasis is on the *enabling* role of government, rather than 'command-and-control' from on high.

Despite the strength of this critique, more often than not recent governments have fallen back by default on the practices and procedures of the predominantly English centralising state. The state machinery, especially the Whitehall model, has rarely been amenable to fundamental reform of the governing process. A democratic vision of a reformed British state more transparent, democratically representative and institutionally responsive anchored in a coherent conception of the public interest has so far been absent in British politics. It remains essential, however, as the precondition for a wide-ranging programme of civil service and Whitehall reform.

The second priority for institutional renovation entails adapting the current model of ministerial-civil service relations. The status quo, epitomised by the Haldane model, was forged nearly a century ago, overseeing the expansion of the state during and after World War I. Haldane envisaged a straightforward division of labour in which ministers confer authority, and officials provide expertise. Nonetheless, the problem of accountability in a more fragmented policy-making arena has never been adequately resolved. This results from underlying confusion about operational responsibility in the central state, the consequence of an expansion of 'arms-length' agencies and delegation as well as the secrecy underpinning the policy process. Ministers and officials have clung to the outmoded tenet that policy advice must remain confidential.

In contrast, a more transparent system of policy formulation would ensure that officials justified their advice, while ministers were subject to rigorous external appraisal and scrutiny. The aim must be to promote an informed debate about long-term strategic policy choices and trade-offs in an era of unprecedented fiscal strain. The pressure on the public finances is unlikely to dissipate in the near future: the consequences of demography and an ageing population, for example, will have a far greater long-term impact on state resources than even the post-2008 financial crisis. A major redrawing of the economic and political parameters of the state is underway. There are pivotal decisions for the United Kingdom that remain unresolved, from future aviation capacity and the funding of health and social care, to the future of the British state itself in the light of an imminent referendum on Scottish independence. In this context, improving the transparency of the policy-making process should, over time, resolve the ambiguity and confusion about accountability, while ensuring that policy is more robustly formulated and tested prior to implementation. There have been too many instances where civil servants' obedience to ministers has led to policy fiascos, most notoriously the Westland affair, the Poll Tax, and the intelligence failings which led to the Iraq war.

Rather than advocating an approach based on 'permanent revolution' in Whitehall, fundamental questions of constitutional legitimacy ought to be addressed, developing a transparent and publicly accountable role for the civil service (Savoie, 2008). Officials should share the advice given to ministers through parliamentary hearings, reinforcing the work of the civil service as a trusted arbiter of economic forecasting, statistical data, cost-benefit analysis and options appraisal. Senior civil servants should not regard their anonymity as sacrosanct, forging a public identity based on their trusted and independent status within the British political system. Officials ought to answer publicly for the evidence and analysis underpinning key ministerial decisions, exposing the policy-making process to far more wide-ranging scrutiny and debate.

In turn, the civil service will contribute to addressing the perceived legitimacy crisis afflicting the institutions of the UK polity, fuelled by the parliamentary expenses scandal, concerns about the use of intelligence material and the security state, and plummeting turnouts in recent British general elections. The quid pro quo for politicians is that the quality of policy analysis needs to take precedence over ministers' daily appetite for presentational initiatives and short-term headlines.

The third priority for reforming the Whitehall model entails deeper cultural changes in the institutions of the central state. This requires a shift in the core executive's operating code which remains heavily skewed towards working 'downwards' from the centre through departments, rather than 'outwards' through the public sector and civil society. The traditional 'command chain' has exacerbated weaknesses in the capacity of the civil service to effect change. Rather than applying the levers of the central state to every conceivable societal problem, governments must invest in the capacity of local citizens and communities to improve the quality of life themselves. The central state has to escape from the untenable position that it is responsible for everything, and able to solve everything. There is little central government can do without the consent of the public, alongside the active involvement of civil society.

Indeed, a balance will need to be struck between protecting the spirit of universalism and national community underpinning the post-1945 settlement, alongside a renewed commitment to decentralising and dispersing political power in Britain. This inevitably has an impact on the quality of governmental decision-making. The widely held view is that British public administration has been characterised by a 'silo mentality': powerful resistance to cross-departmental working, prominent failures in project management, defensiveness about collaborating with the private and voluntary sectors, and a counter-productive audit culture which rewards the status quo rather than officials prepared to take risks. Breaking this cycle entails distinct roles for public servants, redistributing and devolving power from political elites at the centre in Whitehall to local communities, agents and institutions.

Finally, any reform programme which redefines the relationship between civil servants and ministers has to take into account the constitutional arrangements shaping British government at the centre, particularly the doctrine of parliamentary and ministerial accountability. Traditionally, the Labour Party in government has focused on delivery, worrying less about the constitutional nature of the state and the vibrancy of British democracy. This was a historical pattern established by the post-war Attlee government, further entrenched by successive Labour leaders, from Wilson and Callaghan, to Blair and Brown. However, constitutional issues ought to remain of paramount importance. The state should remain accountable and transparent, subject to the will of the people, and capable of promoting democracy and self-government.

The case for a Royal Commission examining the fundamental constitutional issues relating to Whitehall and the civil service is compelling. What is more, it is necessary before any decision is taken to adopt an alternative system of public administration, such as the introduction of fixed-term contractual appointments for permanent secretaries. The Royal Commission ought to consider controversial questions about politicisation, the appointment process for special advisers, and proposals for ministerial *cabinet*, as these relate to long-standing constitutional principles. For example, further political appointments might be justified if candidates were required to appear before pre-appointment hearings of the Public Administration Select Committee, enhancing legislative oversight within the British polity.

Moreover, this discussion about the strategic purpose of Whitehall and the core executive is taking place in an era where there is arguably a shift back towards the public interest and the public domain, following two decades in which the dominant view has been that the private interest and market institutions should prevail in British society. There is greater cognisance of the limits to markets in the wake of the financial crisis, alongside the importance of the democratic state in creating the frameworks and incentives that sustain and uphold the ethos of public service in Britain. Nevertheless, it ought to be acknowledged that the institutional reforms discussed above, if adopted, would pose a serious challenge to the dominant tradition in British politics. This volume has underlined the importance of path dependency – a centralising, power-hoarding approach is intrinsic to the 'wiring' of British government, creating practical obstacles to any administration wishing to reform it. The question remains as to whether any of the major parties in the British polity is willing to mount a bolder and more imaginative challenge to the existing structures and practices of the central state.

Conclusion: New Labour's Governance Dilemmas

This book has addressed the subtle and incremental nature of change in the core executive during the New Labour years. The 'end of Whitehall view' has been overstated, having infected much popular commentary on the British system of government at the centre. There is a dominant tradition in British politics which enforces a top-down operating code and a power-hoarding approach, despite a decade of far-reaching constitutional reform. This power-concentrating instinct is at the core of the Whitehall model, creating contrary pressures towards stability, inertia and incrementalism, reinforced by the self-interested motivation of ministers and civil servants protecting their status and power within the British polity. Mandarins in particular have displayed an 'elegant genius' in thwarting embryonic reforms.

This relates to a key theoretical issue: the nature of power relations in the British central state. The dominant perspective in studies of post-war politics has been pluralism, underpinned by the recent emphasis in the differentiated polity on the disaggregation of power. This study revealed the extent to which power has remained heavily concentrated in the British polity, emphasised by the attempt to recreate governance capacity within the centre of the state. The institutions and practices of the British political system are underpinned by a view of representative democracy emphasising 'strong, decisive and responsible government' (Evans, 1993: 91). Despite a multitude of internal and exogenous pressures on the state, the British system of government retains a hierarchical structure: Whitehall and the centre continue to 'know best'.

After 1997, Tony Blair proclaimed: 'There is a fundamental change to Britain's constitution underway, devolving and decentralising power to the nations and the regions of the UK and revitalising local government.'[4] The governing party espoused its commitment to decentralising power, as New Labour sought to project an appeal based on pluralism and change. However, Labour intended to reform the constitution, the civil service and the machinery of government by utilising the levers of the central state. Its mode of statecraft meant devolving autonomy and control, while reinforcing the authority and power of the core executive. The central premise of the British political system predicated on 'elective dictatorship' remained firmly in place (Bogdanor, 2009).

This is the paradox of the Labour Party's approach to the state as depicted by Marquard (2008): Labour emerged from a dissenting tradition that was critical of orthodox notions of state legitimacy and authority. Once in government, however, the party eagerly embraced established constitutional principles of political representation and parliamentary sovereignty enshrined in the Westminster model. During the New Labour years, as if reaffirming this legacy, governing capacity and the strong state were reinforced, driving through policy implementation and reform from the centre. While Labour's constitutional agenda had the potential to redefine the Westminster model, the Whitehall paradigm was actually further entrenched.

According to Marquand, New Labour was 'oblivious of the long tradition of political and constitutional reflection [...] responding piecemeal and *ad hoc* to conflicting pressures.'[5] By retaining its attachment to the dominant political tradition, the ambition and reach of the party's programme was inevitably compromised. Britain has continued to be ruled through a political system in which power is distributed asymmetrically among ministers and civil servants, overwhelmingly concentrated at the centre of government. As such, the apparently contradictory forces of 'Old' and 'New' Labour are characterised by underlying continuities, and there is greater synergy than is commonly recognised between past and present.

In conclusion, this book insists that the effect of New Labour on Whitehall has been overstated. Nevertheless, the party's reforms have the potential to unleash a new set of dynamics forcing a wider renegotiation of dominant power relationships in the British core executive. The gap between the 'efficient' and 'dignified' elements of the political system has been stretched to breaking point, undermining long-established constitutional norms and governing principles. We may be witnessing only an initial phase in the on-going reconstruction of the British state, as political elites search for levers of power in a policy environment where they appear denuded of authority and control. This study emphasised that political actors turn to traditions as a guide to resolving the dilemmas of the present. Nearly two centuries ago, Marx exhorted that 'The tradition of all the dead generations weighs like a nightmare on the brain of the living.' Governing as New Labour, it seems, was no different.

Breakdown of Interviewees

Actor's location and role	Number interviewed within study
Number Ten ministers	2
Number Ten special advisers	10
Prime Minister's Policy Unit	*10*
Number Ten civil servants	9
Prime Minister's Policy Unit/Private Office	*1*
Prime Minister's Strategy Unit	*5*
Prime Minister's Delivery Unit	*3*
Departmental ministers	10
Department of Education	2
Department of Health	2
Department of Business	2
HM Treasury	2
Cabinet Office	2
Departmental special advisers	11
Department of Education	4
Department of Health	1
Department of Business	3
HM Treasury	2
Cabinet Office	1
Departmental civil servants	10
Department of Education	2
Department of Health	2
Department of Business	3
HM Treasury	2
Cabinet Office	1
Total	52

Policy Governance under New Labour: Delivery Fields in Academies, Family-Nurse Partnerships, and the National Economic Council[1]

A: Academy Governance under New Labour – the Policy Delivery Field

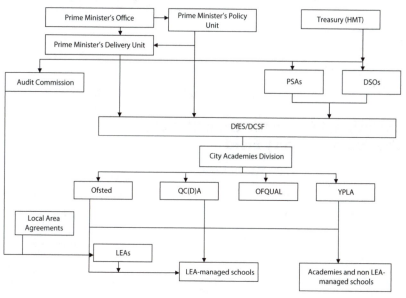

B: Family-Nurse Partnerships (FNPs) – the Policy Delivery Field

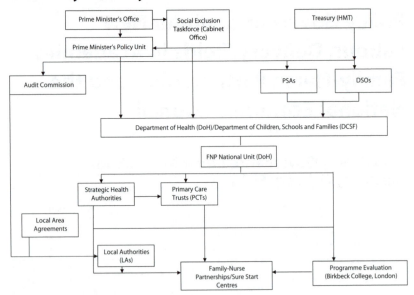

C: National Economic Council (NEC) – the Policy Delivery Field

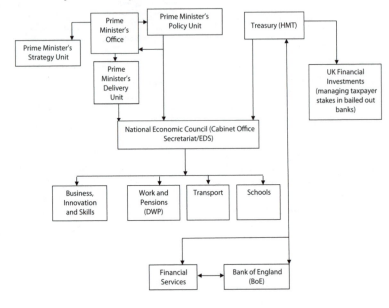

'Renewal and Strategic Audit': Memorandum to the Prime Minister[1]

Prime Minister

From: The Strategy Unit

June 2003

Personal

Renewal and Strategic Audit

1. This note provides some background and ideas on how to refocus and re-energise government and how to make the most of the various meetings on Strategic Audit.

2. The Audit exercise has confirmed that, overall, the record of the last 6 years is remarkably good in any long-term historical perspective: on the economy, education, crime, poverty, unemployment, northern Ireland, and Europe.

3. However, as you know, there is a widespread sense of energy dissipating and direction being lost – amongst ministers, the government's natural supporters at all levels in the public sector and amongst the public who believe that government has slowed down. Domestic policy seems to have lost much of its focus:

   • Although the strategies on health and education and well developed public service reform is not yet working as a unifying theme: although some of us in the centre have a clear view of where we are headed on public services (towards universal, diverse and personal services) many others inside and outside government are uncertain about the goals of reform, and the underlying principles. Ambiguities in presentation are partly to blame: it has sometimes appeared that current policies are intended to be a stepping stone to privatisation and marketisation;

decentralising rhetoric is still often matched by centralising actions; the targets regime has not been explained well.

- We are doing analysis which shows a sharp decline in public service productivity over the last 6 years. That means that more of the same won't be enough in a climate of more constrained resources. More radical reform will be essential. However, we are scarcely at first base in terms of selling that either to the Labour Party or to the wider public. In our view too much talk about choice doesn't help: it's absolutely right to go as fast as possible in opening up choice and contestability, but for the rhetoric to precede the reality by several years in most cases breaks every rule of good strategic communications.

- On social justice and poverty all the major steps were initiated in the first term (New Deal, minimum wage, WFTC &c). There is no second term agenda. Difficult issues (eg over disability or lone parents) have been fudged.

- Social mobility and opportunity, which could have been defining themes for this parliament, have not been given a clear enough shape – there have been many small initiatives but nothing resembling a strategy (and there are glaring holes – for example on the gender pay gap).

- On governance, after the major constitutional reforms of the first term, and the very welcome moves on LCD, there is no clear strategy on what happens next, whether in relation to the regions or local government or the Lords.

- 6 years in there is little clearly articulated philosophy of how government should work of the kind that the Conservatives successfully expounded in the 1980s (and sometimes it sounds as if we are either just a rather pale shadow of the 80s neoliberal reformers – and unaware of just how much went wrong with their plans in countries like New Zealand, or that we have an unnatural attachment to bureaucracy targets, inspectorates, and a continually rising head count in Whitehall).

4. Behind some of these problems is a problem at the centre. No 10's ability to synthesise politics, strategy and tactics is much weaker than a few years ago. The political inputs to decisions are now even more dominated by short-term communications or political management considerations than before; meanwhile, the people working on policy generally have far less political experience than was the case 5 years ago.

5. As a result, oddly for a mid-term, the mood is highly short-termist. The focus on short-medium term delivery is in almost every respect positive (though it often risks sliding into excessive micro-management). However, a great deal of time is being spent on issues which will have relatively little pay-off in 3–5 years time (like the Olympic bid, the Thames gateway, regional assemblies even Foundation Hospitals) while the bigger picture of where government is headed has been lost. Treasury, by contrast, have at least kept a firmer sense of medium term direction and a better synthesis of politics and policy, even though they too have lost momentum (on welfare reform, productivity etc).

6. This obviously matters a lot to the SU. Internationally we are coming to be seen as a model – and are being copied directly by countries as diverse as the Netherlands and Romania, and probably Japan and Australia. Our methods of project work are recognised within government as better than any of the alternatives and we have won the confidence of the ministers we work with, from Margaret Beckett and Patricia Hewitt to David Blunkett and John Prescott.

   However, our relations with No 10 are often less predictable: with a handful of exceptions there are fewer people with a clear sense of direction who can confidently commission and direct work from us, and, like others, we often suffer from the large numbers of people at No 10 giving conflicting steers.

7. Needless to say problems of this kind often happen to governments in mid-term. Equally obviously good ones take urgent action to address the problems. Over the last two years we have talked to senior people in several governments which remained in office for long periods of time – Labour in Australia, Social Democrats in Sweden, Christian Democrats in the Netherlands, Liberals in Canada, Tories in the UK – to clarify some of the keys to survival. Their experiences point to four essential conditions for renewal:

   - *new people:* this is the single most important source of renewal. It applies not only to ministers, but also to advisers and other key players. Often it is essential to have very visible – and brutal – changes of personnel. In the UK that means more people whose outlook is shaped by today's priorities not the battles of the 1970s or the 1980s. The virtual disappearance of the 40-something generation makes a change of this kind difficult, and the 30-something generation aren't yet ready. But a jump of generation will certainly be needed before the election.

- *sharper narrative:* Over time Governments' narratives tend to lose clarity. To listeners they become rote-like, as well as becoming more ambiguous and fudged. Much government rhetoric now sounds very tired. Renewed narratives are much clearer about dividing lines and relative priorities (we've attached some ideas on what these might be).

- deliberate cultivation of *new areas of policy energy.* New issues can generate new passions, and governments often find that renewal comes from identifying and develop [*sic*] promising fields which generate ideas, excitement and sense of mission.

- new ways of *engaging the public.* Governments need to repeatedly rethink how they talk to highly educated and sceptical publics. Sophisticated monologue is subject to a law of diminishing returns. Most of these governments innovated new styles of engagement (ranging from ministers learning to listen to the public, to the mass communication the Tories did around privatisation in the late 80s).

8. Some of these ingredients are now needed in the UK. As the Strategic Audit will confirm we are on the right track in many areas – but quite a few need a shift of direction or a change of gear. Some of this will be uncomfortable since it will question assumptions; inevitably most of the people involved in policy over the last 6 years have become very defensive. However the payoffs from a rigorous recharging of batteries will be big.

9. That is why over the next year you need to signal very clearly that the continued focus on delivery needs to be matched by equally serious attention to renewal. The aim should be that by the summer of 2004 the key decision makers around government share a clear view of the road ahead, the relative priorities, and the fields that offer most dividends in terms of definition and energy.

10. We now have a fairly clear view – agreed between No 10, CO and HMT – of how to get there – with exercises to clarify the key priorities in a handful of big areas; a smaller number of more classic SU type projects (eg on disability, police reform with HO and failing states with FCO/DfID); and some cross-cutting work (eg on stepping up the management of innovation in the public sector).

11. However, for these to have full impact they need your engagement – and they need to be driven forward by a leaner, more focused No 10 which has reconnected the politics, the strategy and the policy.

Ends/

Sharpening the narrative

Government needs to sharpen up its core narratives. There are at least three of these – political, governmental and national – which need to cohere:

There is a **political** narrative about the long history of expanding opportunity in the UK, promoting fairness and opening up institutions that were dominated by small elites, a story about traditions of reforming zeal – 1906, 1945. At the moment the government appears somewhat adrift in terms of its historical positioning. It is much more likely to be seen to leave a legacy if that legacy can be situated historically – ie as part of the broad progressive tradition.

There is a **government narrative** about tackling inherited problems (long-term unemployment, underinvestment, economic instability, overcentralisation, worsening inequality) and now moving into a new phase of widening opportunity, ensuring that Britain is ready for the future (science, education), moving public service from one-size-fits all to genuine choice and diversity, and facing up to the new insecurities (crime, ASB, WMD). Parts of this are in place – but too much focus on delivery and reform as ends in themselves drains the narrative of any passion.

There is a **national narrative** about Britain having come out of a long period of decline. We are now in a phase when perceptions understate our importance as one of the world's top five economic, military and cultural powers; the strengths which come from our links (US, Europe, diasporas); the imperative of moving quickly into higher value industries and occupations; how what is strategically necessary for the UK fits well with its own traditions.

Bringing these together we need **linking narrative** on the priorities for action. The best of various options could be summarised as: 'protect, empower and prepare'.

- A stronger story about **protecting** people from the risks they cannot handle on their own (crime, terrorism, climate change, WMD, recessions) – in some respects a return to the core role of the state, but defined in a social democratic way (ie covering economic risks as well as security ones)

- A stronger story about **empowering** people to take more control of their own lives – boosting social mobility, personal responsibility, devolution.

- A stronger story about **preparing** – getting ready – for the future: why the hallmark of progressive governments is investment in future people (children); future knowledge (science); and future environment (the shift to resource productivity, addressing climate change).

These three give a strong structure to narratives in a range of areas and have the virtue of closing off obvious vulnerabilities.

Energising policy areas

The following are some of the most likely policy areas that will generate new energy and momentum. Each of these needs to be deliberately cultivated – both with core strategies and with outriders – MPs, thinktanks, pilots – to test out the boundaries:

In relation to **public services** we need a better balance of topdown pressure and bottom up dynamism. Achieving that requires us to drive forward with contestability in all main public services, and steadily expanding choice in all its dimensions. This needs to be presented within a much stronger argument about equity and the virtues of universal systems. For similar reasons we need to develop new ideas around democracy and accountability (combining a more concerted approach to elected mayors with more direct public accountability and 'democratic contestability' for the services that matter most to the public – police, PCTs) recognising that this is key to driving up performance and answering charges of 'out of touch centralism'.

In relation to **personal responsibility** we need a clearer argument that once the basic problems of delivery are sorted the key advances in health, education, welfare and the environment depend on citizens taking greater responsibility for themselves (as Alan Milburn started tentatively doing with health).

In relation to **children**, we need to develop a more overt argument on the importance of raising the birthrate and the long-term benefits of better parenting: that could involve taking forward the trust fund, rolling out children's centres and developing a new deal for new parents (for example support for the first year). Despite a fair amount of investment, policy in this whole field has been underperforming.

On **opportunity and social mobility** we need to further develop practical policies to improve the UK's poor record on progression at work: turn learndirect into a much more visible national service; build up apprenticeships, including in the public sector; revive ILAs in a new form as part of a demand led learning system; and rigorously tackling all the barriers to opportunity (such as childcare, transport and time). A major hole in current strategy is the gender pay gap: we need to bring together new thinking on how to narrow it given the UK's particularly poor performance.

In relation to **welfare** we need a more overt argument for full employment: that means moving forward on WTW by tackling the other inactive groups: moderately disabled, lone parents, and over-50s.

In relation to **crime** we now have a clearer acknowledgement that the systems are antiquated, ineffective and need radical reform: we now need to systematically test out models that can sharply improve the prospects that criminals will be caught; tailor punishments to fit the person as well as the crime ('detect and punish' as an alternative to both overreliance on rehabilitation or continuing growth in prisons); and give the public a more direct say (as David Blunkett has floated).

In relation to diversity we need to continue going beyond multiculturalism: with a positive approach to high skill **migration** combined with recognition that migrants and minorities need to be more actively integrated into the mainstream society and economy.

In relation to **community** we need a more confident argument that the voluntary sector role will grow, both because of the need for new forms of public organisation and because public pressures on business will increase; transferring assets to community organisations and CICs; large-scale volunteering.

In relation to global issues we need to articulate a positive 'progressive internationalist' vision of global governance: preventing wars, genocides, famines; maintaining and enforcing rules; sharing wealth and opportunity.

In relation to **economic policy** we need to move beyond timidity in relation to business and markets with a more hard-nosed view of corporate governance, transparency and the importance of regulation for larger firms; a more confident and proactive industrial strategy to support key areas of new growth – such as nanotechnology, fuel cells, grid computing – (as followed in the most competitive economies including Bush's USA).

In the creative industries and **arts** we need radical ideas on what cities can do to create a sense of identity and excitement – national arts and cultural policy has been virtually frozen for a decade or more while it has rapidly progressed at a local level and in other countries.

In relation to **transport** we need to make a virtue of planning for the introduction of national road charging and reinvesting the proceeds as a symbol of a modernised society.

In relation to dialogue with the public we need to complement the classic topdown communications through the national media with other methods of **engaging the public**. A key opportunity here is the BBC charter renewal – the BBC could play a much bigger role in engaging the public on big long-term issues (pensions, Europe &c). Other countries (US, Sweden) have also shown the scope for mass participation in policy discussion – and how this can achieve wider buy in to targets and policies.

Finally, we need to think about **legacy institutions**. Despite devolution there are still relatively few institutions which clearly embody the values of this government – in the way that the NHS, Open University, privatised utilities &c did for previous governments (though some new institutions – from Learndirect to Community Interest Companies – could become so).

New Labour's Critique of Whitehall and Proposals for Reforming the Centre of Government: Memorandum to the Prime Minister June 2000[1]

CENTRAL GOVERNMENT PROBLEMS WE STILL FACE

- Insufficient focus on delivery priorities
- Perceived slow speed of response
- Poor innovative capacity

Government seen as highly centralised/control freaks – though reality very different

WHY THESE PROBLEMS?

- Inadequate performance management; departments unclear on who does what in centre; centre insufficiently clear at setting strategic direction and priorities and monitoring performance
- Departmental silos slow down cross boundary working
- Senior Civil Service insufficiently focused on delivery of priorities
- Hard to free up resources for new initiatives

Confusion about who is responsible for what

WHAT TO DO?

- Incremental improvements underway: <u>not enough</u> and too slow
- Need to communicate <u>clear vision of objective</u> in 5 years time
- Start <u>culture change now</u> to show we are for real
- Keep up pressure through <u>political commitment</u> and <u>milestones</u> to reach

OUR VISION OF THE SYSTEM IN 5 YEARS

- Ministers/officials focused on results, structures rapidly adaptable
- Clearly defined centre sets strategy: focuses on few issues, delegates management of others; access to quality information on progress
- Continual improvement through better knowledge of what works: performance influences strategy

REFORM THE CENTRE

- <u>Central strategy team</u>: Policy Unit, PIU, Secretariats, new Performance Evaluation function, Press Office, Political Office: <u>defines</u> and <u>communicates</u> policy priorities and future strategy
- <u>Streamline and clarify No 10/Treasury</u> working; increase information flows
- <u>Focus</u> on <u>delivery</u> of 3–4 immediate priorities; <u>delegate</u> others with regular report back
- <u>Jobs and objectives</u> of Ministers/senior officials <u>defined</u> in terms of <u>achieving</u> these <u>tasks</u>
- Head of Civil Service becomes <u>Chief Executive</u> with direct management responsibility for top 300 officials tasked to deliver priority outputs

Does this need a No 10/Cabinet Office Minister to lead/coordinate?

How to ensure that No 10/Cabinet Office works as one with HMT?

DEPARTMENTS: A NEW TASK-BASED SYSTEM

- End to primarily departmental Whitehall system; structures related explicitly to policy objectives/service delivery

- Jobs/rewards related explicitly to tasks and success in achieving them

- Some Ministers given task rather than formal departmental responsibilities; others work with two or more departments

- Permanent Secretary job able to be deconstructed into policy/personnel/propriety functions; these could be done by different people

DAY ONE HEADLINE CHANGES

1. New Chief Executive of Civil Service post, with direct management of top 300 posts to unify bureaucracy around key objectives. Reports to small Supervisory Board with 5–6 members, half from private sector

2. Abolish Permanent Secretary title and separate out roles; reshuffle to reduce average age; announce targets on gender, ethnic minorities and private sector experience for next 4 years

3. Make clear government strategy determined by the centre [?new No 10 Minister] with 3–4 key tasks highlighted; new central Performance Evaluation function

4. Initial restructure of departments to correspond with these priorities; appoint 10 junior Ministers with specific tasks to achieve, monitored by centre

5. Upgrade Whitehall IT to cutting edge standards for better knowledge management

EIGHTEEN MONTHS ON

1. Review of key priorities. Junior Ministers achieving objectives rewarded

2. Departmental structures evolve to meet new priorities/problems; list of tasks being dropped

3. Clear incentives for officials who deliver; removal of those who have not bought into task-based working; more senior executives in 30s and 40s

4. Range of management styles in departments: from part-time non-executive chair, through policy boards; end of Perm Sec club as senior officials work more flexibly

5. Mobility between departments and with private sector seen as key to promotion; all SCS promotions managed direct by the centre

THREE YEARS ON

1. Departments are convenient post addresses; work defined by tasks and objectives linked to centre's priorities

2. Injection of outside Human Resource expertise improves training of officials and Ministers; unlocks underused potential; clarity about job roles makes bringing in external talent easier

3. Culture of high IT literacy and regular exchange with private sector

4. Policy functions clearly separated from financial/propriety/personnel issues

QUESTIONS

1. Is the basic analysis right? We assume a <u>centralising system setting priorities</u>

2. Is change worth the <u>political pain</u>? The system will protest, accusation of political bias, some departmental Ministers unhappy. If it is not, don't start

3. Needs a <u>committed set of top officials</u>. Will not become self-perpetuating without culture change from the top, and sustained political pressure. What is the engine for sustained change?

4. <u>No 10-Treasury</u> division of responsibilities need <u>clarification</u>: higher quality of information exchange, understanding of who does what on resource allocation/efficiency issues; dispute resolution mechanism

SECOND ORDER DECISIONS

1. Which departments to change/Perm Sec reshuffle?

2. How to tighten structures at centre (separate note)?

3. Do we need a Chief Executive separate from Head of Civil Service to deliver this?

4. How to get key players to buy in – direct PM involvement, sustained political support?

Policy Unit
June 2000

Option One: Prime Minister creates Super Minister Executive Cabinet but retains direct link to other Ministers but with reduced Cabinet supervision

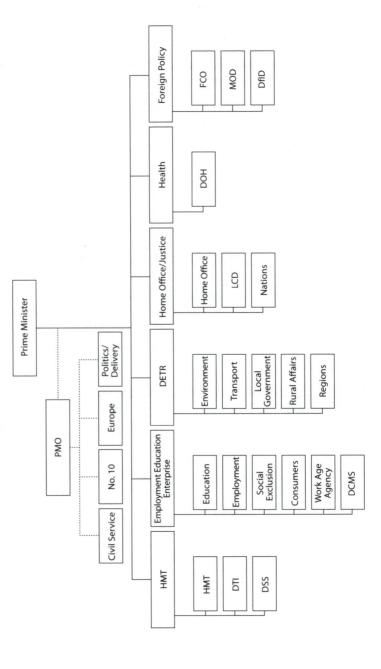

Option Two: Prime Minister manages five Super Ministers via an Executive Cabinet, all other Ministers report through a Super Minister. Tier 1 – more frequent Cabinets, monthly stock-take. Tier 2 – less frequent Cabinet, 3 monthly stock-take/bilateral.

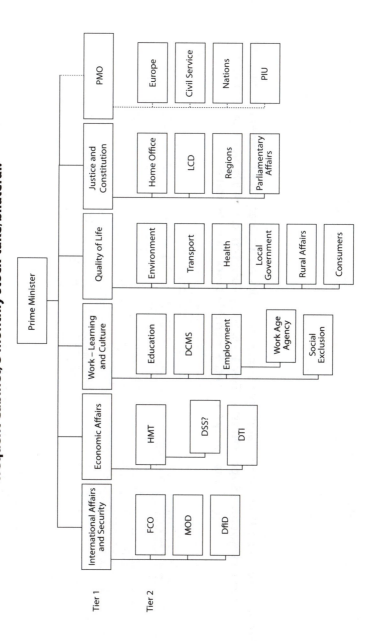

Option Two: Prime Minister manages five Super Ministers via an Executive Cabinet all other Ministers report through a Super Minister. Tier 1 – weekly Cabinets, quarterly stock-take. Tier 2 – quarterly Cabinet, 6 monthly stock-take/bilateral

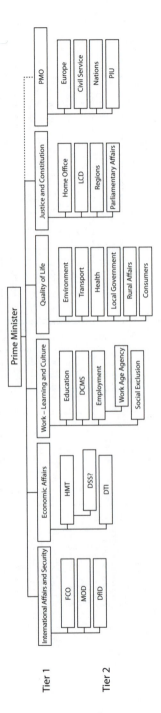

Option Three: we could strengthen the matrix approach by elevating the role and authority of key cross cutting responsibilities

		Economic Affairs	International Affairs	Work Learning and Culture	Quality of Life	Justice
1. Strategic Priority	Equality	✓			✓	✓
	Safer Communities			✓	✓	✓
	Europe	✓	✓	✓	✓	✓
	SEU	✓		✓	✓	✓
	Delivery					
2. Capability	Innovation/R&D & organisation capabilities	✓	✓	✓	✓	✓
3. User Focus	Nations and Devolution	✓	✓	✓	✓	✓
	Elderly			✓	✓	
	Working Age			✓	✓	
	Children			✓	✓	

Notes

Introduction

1. Quoted in Mount (1992).
2. Internal Cabinet Office memorandum to the Prime Minister, January 2000: see Appendix IV.
3. Internal memorandum from the Prime Minister to senior Number Ten staff, 22 April 2001.
4. The author served as a special adviser in the Northern Ireland Office (2000–1), the No.10 Policy Unit (2001–4), the Cabinet Office (2004–5), and as head of policy planning in 10 Downing Street (2009–10).
5. This phrase was first coined by the American political scientist, Harold Lasswell (1936), who famously argued politics is about 'who gets what, when, and how'.
6. The first edition of *The Private Government of Public Money* was published in 1974.
7. This volume adopts a 'historical institutionalist' perspective which emphasises that political institutions are structured by asymmetries of power, alongside the role of path dependency and unintended consequences (Hall & Taylor, 2001). Actors are those individuals including politicians, ministers, political appointees, advisers, permanent civil servants, and public service managers who seek to influence the policy and decision-making process within the state.
8. Christopher Foster is a former senior Whitehall official who has written among the most influential accounts. His recent book is *British Government In Crisis or the Third English Revolution?*, Oxford: Hart Publishing, 2005. Foster is a leading member of the Better Government Initiative (BGI), a group of retired mandarins formed 'as a response to widespread concerns about the practical difficulties which government today faces as it seeks to run the country against a background of rapid change'.
9. The practitioner's background may influence actor's perceptions and their interpretations of events. There is a 'double hermeneutic' operating here, since the concepts generated by political science re-enter the world they are

intended to explain. For example, the lexicon of 'new institutionalism' has subsequently shaped New Labour's approach to 'joining-up' government.

Chapter 1   The British Political Tradition and Whitehall Reform

1. On this point I am grateful to Dr Felicity Matthews, Department of Politics at the University of Sheffield.
2. Matthew Hall's recent volume, *Political Traditions and UK Politics* has closely informed the approach adopted in this chapter.
3. Idealism was a philosophical school influential in British intellectual life from the mid-nineteenth century; leading proponents included T.H. Green and Bernard Bosanquet. The aim of these theorists was to refute notions of 'atomistic individualism', and to assert that humans were fundamentally 'social beings'. The idealists were, however, reluctant to 'reify' the state in Hegelian terms. The state's role was only justified in so far as it helped individuals to realise their own purposes and values (Kenny, 1999).
4. The classical account of the British constitution refers to the 'balance' between monarchical, aristocratic and democratic forms of rule encompassed by the monarch, the House of Lords and the House of Commons (Bogdanor, 2009).
5. There is a striking similarity between Tant's account and Richard Hofstadter's work in *The American Political Tradition*, a point acknowledged by Hall (2011). Hofstadter sets out to dispel the dominant interpretation of American history as a continuing conflict between antagonistic forms of property. He shows how this produced an uncritical celebration of America's past and its political institutions, heralded by the eventual triumph of liberal progressivism. Such perspectives encouraged an unjustified, 'literature of hero worship and national self-congratulation' (1973: 37).
6. The concept of 'elective dictatorship' predates Thatcherism, however, popularised by Lord Hailsham in his 1976 Richard Dimbleby lecture at the BBC. 'Elective dictatorship' refers to the dominance of the legislature by the executive due to the majoritarian 'first-past-the-post' system for electing the House of Commons in the UK, and the dangers this posed to 'good government' and personal liberty (Bogdanor, 2010).
7. Tant's account of how the Labour Party in Britain was incorporated into the dominant political tradition is at risk of underplaying the strength of the participatory challenge. The work of G.D.H. Cole, R.H. Tawney and

the Guild Socialists is testimony to that questioning of the BPT and the theory of government it espoused. Gamble observed that ideas from the British left 'have produced a powerful anti-wing and anti-pluralist account of British politics but they base it not on a comparative political theory but on an alternative historical interpretation of the British political tradition, which continues to treat it as a unique historical formation' (1990: 410). There have also been major discontinuities in British constitutional history which tend to be downplayed, including the Tudor revolution under Henry VIII, and the republic of the 1650s which abolished the Monarchy and the House of Lords (Langan & Schwartz, 1985).

8.   Indeed, Bevir and Rhodes (2003) praise the historical and philosophical orientation of A.H. Birch and Samuel Beer's writings on British government, although they diverge from Birch and Beer who they insist 'reify' traditions, and fail to recognise that traditions only exist in so far as they are 'narrated' by individual subjects.

Chapter 2   The Westminster Model and the Whitehall Paradigm

1.   The model is derived from Haldane (1918).
2.   Sir Richard Wilson, Cabinet secretary, giving evidence to the Parliamentary Select Committee on Public Administration, 9 February 2000.

Chapter 3   Interpreting Continuity and Change in the Labour Party's Statecraft

1.   Interviews 4 (departmental minister) and 22 (No.10 special adviser) conducted for this study.
2.   Interviews 4 (departmental minister) and 42 (departmental minister) conducted for this study.
3.   Interview 4 (departmental minister) conducted for this study.
4.   Interview 14 (No.10 special adviser) conducted for this study.
5.   Interview 31 (Home Office civil servant) conducted for this study.
6.   Interview 31 (Home Office civil servant) conducted for this study.
7.   Interview with the author conducted for this study.
8.   Interview with the author conducted for this study.
9.   Interview 19 (No.10 special adviser) conducted for this study.
10.   Interview 42 (departmental minister) conducted for this study.
11.   Interview conducted for this study.

12. Interviews 38 (PMSU official) and 43 (No.10 special adviser) conducted for this study.
13. Interview 42 (departmental minister) conducted for this study.
14. Departmental five-year plans were published prior to the 2005 election covering major public service delivery priorities such as health, education, law and order, transport, and housing.
15. The assault on New Labour's approach, allegedly epitomised by an informal policy-making style that 'bypassed experienced officials and weakened departmental co-ordination', was led by an influential group of former mandarins, including Lord Butler of Brockwell and Sir John Chilcott, through a series of reports produced for the *Better Government Initiative*: www.bettergovernmentinitiative.co.uk (accessed 22 November 2012).

Chapter 4   The Core Executive, Governance and Power

1. Flinders legitimately questions whether governance narratives can be said to constitute a body of theory, giving an impression of coherence which may not exist in practice. Peters and Pierre (2000) emphasised that governance concepts require on-going refinement in the light of further theoretical and empirical research.

Chapter 5   Mapping the Case Studies of the 'Primeval Policy Soup'

1. Interview conducted for this study.
2. Interview 33 (Cabinet Office civil servant) conducted for this study.
3. Interview conducted for this study.
4. Interview 6 (DfES civil servant) conducted for this study.
5. Interview 15 (DoH civil servant) conducted for this study.
6. Interview 9 (Cabinet Office special adviser) conducted for this study.
7. Interview 9 (Cabinet Office special adviser) conducted for this study.
8. Interview conducted for this study.
9. Interview 15 (DoH civil servant) conducted for this study.
10. It was noteworthy that Brown and Alistair Darling still refused to countenance nationalisation of the failed banks, fearing this would reinforce an impression of the Labour government as shifting dramatically leftwards in the aftermath of the financial crisis (Thompson, 2010).
11. Interviews 20 (departmental minister) and 28 (No.10 official) conducted for this study.

12. Interview 22 (No.10 special adviser) conducted for this study.
13. Interview 14 (No.10 special adviser) conducted for this study.
14. Interview 22 (No.10 special adviser) conducted for this study.
15. Interview 22 (No.10 special adviser) conducted for this study.
16. Interview 26 (Treasury/No.10 special adviser) conducted for this study.
17. Interview 27 (Home Office special adviser) conducted for this study.
18. Interview 26 (Treasury/No.10 special adviser) conducted for this study.
19. Interview 27 (Home Office special adviser) conducted for this study.
20. Interview 28 (No.10 official) conducted for this study.
21. Interview 26 (Treasury/No.10 special adviser) conducted for this study.
22. See the writings of Lowndes (2010), Schmidt (2010) and Hay (2006).
23. See the path-breaking article by Rhodes (1997).
23. This is an expansive philosophical approach associated with the writings of Sandel (1998), Walzer (1995), Taylor (1992) and MacIntyre (1982).
25. This is an attempt to provide a microeconomic foundation to Keynesian macroeconomic theory associated with the writings of Reich (2002) and Blanchard (1998).
26. Interview 4 (departmental minister) conducted for this study.
27. Interview conducted for this study.
28. Interview 4 (departmental minister) conducted for this study.
29. Interview 6 (DfES civil servant) conducted for this study.
30. Interview 7 (departmental minister) conducted for this study.
31. Gordon Brown, 'A modern agenda for prosperity and social reform', Speech to the Social Market Foundation, 20 March 2002.
32. Interview 19 (DfES civil servant) conducted for this study.
33. Interview 35 (thinktank research fellow) conducted for this study.
34. Interview 7 (departmental minister) conducted for this study.
35. Interview 7 (departmental minister) conducted for this study.
36. Interview 6 (DfES civil servant) conducted for this study.
37. Interview conducted for this study.
38. Interview 31 (Home Office civil servant) conducted for this study.
39. Interview 31 (Home Office civil servant) conducted for this study.
40. Speech by Prime Minister Tony Blair, 'Bringing Britain Together', 8 December 1997.
41. Interviews 10 (Cabinet Office special adviser) and 11 (departmental minister) conducted for this study.
42. Preface to the Department of Social Security White Paper, *Modernising the Welfare State*, July 1998.
43. Interview 10 (Cabinet Office special adviser) conducted for this study.

44. Interview conducted for this study.
45. Interview conducted for this study.
46. Interview 10 (Cabinet Office special adviser) conducted for this study.
47. Interview 17 (PMSU official) conducted for this study.
48. Interview conducted for this study.
49. Interview 13 (PMSU official) conducted for this study.
50. Interview 13 (PMSU official) conducted for this study.
51. Interview 17 (PMSU official) conducted for this study.
52. The FNP pilot areas covered each of the Government Offices for the Regions: Durham, Manchester, Barnsley, Derby, Walsall, South-East Essex, Slough, Somerset, Southwark and Tower Hamlets.
53. Interview 14 (No.10 special adviser) conducted for this study.
54. Interview 13 (PMSU official) conducted for this study.
55. Interview 13 (PMSU official) conducted for this study.
56. Interview 9 (Cabinet Office special adviser) conducted for this study.
57. Interview 15 (DoH civil servant) conducted for this study.
58. The findings relate to a sample drawn from the 1970 British Cohort Survey based on tests of cognitive, emotional and behavioural development. The differences between the top and bottom quartiles at age 22 and 42 months are statistically significant.
59. Interview 9 (Cabinet Office special adviser) conducted for this study.
60. Interview 22 (No.10 special adviser) conducted for this study.
61. The phrase was attributed to Balls although it appeared in several of (the shadow chancellor) Gordon Brown's speeches between 1994 and 1997. It is referenced in Balls et al. (2004).
62. Interview 20 (departmental minister) conducted for this study.
63. Interview 26 (Treasury/No.10 special adviser) conducted for this study.
64. The DEA was abolished in 1969 as the primary instruments of macro-economic policy remained with the Treasury, while pressure on sterling (1966– 7) destroyed the prospects of the National Economic Plan. See Macpherson (2009).
65. Interview 22 (No.10 special adviser) conducted for this study.
66. Interview 22 (No.10 special adviser) conducted for this study.
67. Interview 21 (No.10 special adviser) conducted for this study.
68. Interview 22 (No.10 special adviser) conducted for this study.
69. This is confirmed in a recent report by the House of Commons Treasury Select Committee (2012).
70. Interview 23 (BIS special adviser) conducted for this study.
71. Interview 23 (BIS special adviser) conducted for this study.

72. Interview 23 (BIS special adviser) conducted for this study.
73. Interview 22 (No.10 special adviser) conducted for this study.
74. Interview 20 (departmental minister) conducted for this study.
75. Interview 22 (No.10 special adviser) conducted for this study.
76. Interview 23 (BIS special adviser) conducted for this study.
77. Interview 21 (No.10 special adviser) conducted for this study.
78. Interview 22 (No.10 special adviser) conducted for this study.

Chapter 6   The Centre and Departments in the Policy-making Process

1. Interview 29 (DfES civil servant) conducted for this study.
2. Interview 13 (PMSU official) conducted for this study.
3. Quoted in Evidence to the Public Administration Committee, p. 112, 15 January 2000.
4. Quoted in report on 'The Cabinet Office and the Centre of Government', House of Lords Constitution Committee, 2009.
5. Figures for the Prime Minister's Delivery Unit are available only up to 2009.
6. Quoted in Minutes of Evidence, House of Commons Public Administration Committee, 1 November 2001.
7. Quoted from Evidence to the Public Administration Committee, 15 January 2000.
8. Interview 37 (PMDU official) conducted for this study.
9. Interview 22 (No.10 special adviser) conducted for this study.
10. Interview 39 (Cabinet Office civil servant) conducted for this study.
11. Interview 38 (PMSU official) conducted for this study.
12. Interview 1 (DfES civil servant) conducted for this study.
13. Interview 1 (DfES civil servant) conducted for this study.
14. Interview 1 (DfES civil servant) conducted for this study.
15. Interview 1 (DfES civil servant) conducted for this study.
16. Interview 6 (DfES civil servant) conducted for this study.
17. The PMPU was reorganised as the PMPD in June 2001, then re-designated as the PMPU immediately after the 2005 election.
18. Interview 7 (departmental minister) conducted for this study.
19. Interview 29 (DfES civil servant) conducted for this study.
20. Interview 6 (DfES civil servant) conducted for this study.
21. Interview 8 (DfES civil servant) conducted for this study.
22. Interview 8 (DfES civil servant) conducted for this study.

23. Interview 5 (trade union general secretary) conducted for this study.
24. Interview 7 (departmental minister) conducted for this study.
25. This led to a flood of allegations in 2006 that peerages were being offered in return for donations to academy projects. For example, see BBC News (2006).
26. Interview 5 (trade union general secretary) conducted for this study.
27. Interview 7 (departmental minister) conducted for this study.
28. Interview 7 (departmental minister) conducted for this study.
29. Interview conducted for this study.
30. Interview 2 (departmental minister) conducted for this study.
31. Interview 1 (DfES civil servant) conducted for this study.
32. Interview conducted for this study.
33. Interview 6 (DfES civil servant) conducted for this study.
34. Interview 1 (DfES civil servant) conducted for this study.
35. Interview 29 (DfES civil servant) conducted for this study.
36. Interview 29 (DfES civil servant) conducted for this study.
37. Interview conducted for this study.
38. Interview 7 (departmental minister) conducted for this study.
39. Interview 7 (departmental minister) conducted for this study.
40. Interview 29 (DfES civil servant) conducted for this study.
41. Interviews 5 (trade union general secretary), 6 (DfES civil servant), 7 (departmental minister), 23 (BIS special adviser) and 29 (DfES civil servant) conducted for this study.
42. Interview 29 (DfES civil servant) conducted for this study.
43. Interview 7 (departmental minister) conducted for this study.
44. Interview 5 (trade union general secretary) conducted for this study.
45. Interview 14 (PMSU official) conducted for this study.
46. Interview 29 (DfES civil servant) conducted for this study.
47. Interview 5 (trade union general secretary) conducted for this study.
48. Interview conducted for this study.
49. Interview 21 (No.10 special adviser) conducted for this study.
50. Interviews 11 (departmental minister) and 36 (DCLG/Cabinet Office civil servant) conducted for this study.
51. Interview 38 (PMSU official) conducted for this study.
52. Interview 10 (Cabinet Office special adviser) conducted for this study.
53. Interview 10 (Cabinet Office special adviser) conducted for this study.
54. Interview 17 (PMSU official) conducted for this study.
55. Interview 10 (Cabinet Office special adviser) conducted for this study.
56. Interview 10 (Cabinet Office special adviser) conducted for this study.

57. Interview 13 (PMSU official) conducted for this study.
58. Interview 13 (PMSU official) conducted for this study.
59. Interview 10 (Cabinet Office special adviser) conducted for this study.
60. Interview 10 (Cabinet Office special adviser) conducted for this study.
61. Interview 15 (DoH civil servant) conducted for this study.
62. Interview 10 (Cabinet Office special adviser) conducted for this study also detailed in Cabinet Office (2006a: 8–11).
63. Interview 10 (Cabinet Office special adviser) conducted for this study.
64. Interview 22 (No.10 special adviser) conducted for this study.
65. Interview 10 (Cabinet Office special adviser) conducted for this study.
66. Interview 12 (DoH special adviser) conducted for this study.
67. Interview 10 (Cabinet Office special adviser) conducted for this study.
68. Interview 15 (DoH civil servant) conducted for this study.
69. Interview 9 (Cabinet Office special adviser) conducted for this study.
70. Interview 15 (DoH civil servant) conducted for this study.
71. Interview conducted for this study.
72. Interview 10 (Cabinet Office special adviser) conducted for this study.
73. Interview 31 (Home Office civil servant) conducted for this study.
74. Interview 31 (Home Office civil servant) conducted for this study.
75. Interviews 9 (Cabinet Office special adviser) and 14 (PMSU official) conducted for this study.
76. Interview 44 (No.10 special adviser) conducted for this study.
77. Indeed, in his All Souls College Lecture, Nick Macpherson did not make a single reference to the creation of the NEC (Macpherson, 2009).
78. Interview 30 (Treasury special adviser) conducted for this study.
79. Interview 28 (No.10 civil servant) conducted for this study.
80. Interview 26 (Treasury/No.10 special adviser) conducted for this study.
81. Interview 20 (departmental minister) conducted for this study.
82. Interview 21 (No.10 special adviser) conducted for this study.
83. Interview conducted for this study.
84. Interview conducted for this study.
85. Interview 20 (departmental minister) conducted for this study.
86. Interview 20 (departmental minister) conducted for this study.
87. Interview 28 (No.10 special adviser) conducted for this study.
88. Interview conducted for this study.
89. Interview 20 (departmental minister) conducted for this study.
90. Interview conducted for this study.
91. Interview 25 (BIS civil servant) conducted for this study.
92. Interview 30 (Treasury special adviser) conducted for this study.

93. Interview 30 (Treasury special adviser) conducted for this study.

94. Interviews 21 (No.10 special adviser) and 26 (Treasury/No.10 special adviser) conducted for this study.

95. Interview 44 (No.10 special adviser) conducted for this study.

96. Interview 20 (departmental minister) conducted for this study.

97. Interview 20 (departmental minister) conducted for this study.

98. Interview 23 (BIS special adviser) conducted for this study.

99. See the work of Dowding (1995), Dunleavy (1990) and Niskanen (1974) on public choice approaches to political science and rational choice theory.

100. Interview conducted for this study.

101. Quoted in Minutes of Evidence, House of Commons Public Administration Committee, 11 July 2002.

102. Quoted in Minutes of Evidence, House of Commons Public Administration Committee, 1 November 2001.

103. Interview 29 (DfES civil servant) conducted for this study.

104. Interviews 20 (departmental minster) and 21 (No.10 special adviser) conducted for this study.

105. Interview 5 (trade union general secretary) conducted for this study.

106. Interview 6 (DfES civil servant) conducted for this study.

107. Interview 41 (IfG research fellow) conducted for this study.

108. Interview conducted for this study.

109. Interview conducted for this study.

110. Interview 31 (Home Office civil servant) conducted for this study.

111. Interview 32 (departmental minister) conducted for this study.

112. Interview 32 (departmental minister) conducted for this study.

113. Interview 43 (departmental minister) conducted for this study.

114. Interview 32 (departmental minister) conducted for this study.

115. Interview 33 (Cabinet Office civil servant) conducted for this study.

116. Interview 33 (Cabinet Office civil servant) conducted for this study.

117. Interview 30 (Treasury special adviser) conducted for this study.

118. Interview 30 (Treasury special adviser) conducted for this study.

119. Interview 30 (Treasury special adviser) conducted for this study.

120. Interview 30 (Treasury special adviser) conducted for this study.

121. Interview 6 (DfES civil servant) conducted for this study.

122. Since their introduction in the 1998 CSR, 'Public Service Agreements (PSAs) played a role in public service delivery and driving improvements in outcomes. Each PSA is underpinned by a single Delivery Agreement, shared across all contributing departments and developed in consultation with delivery partners and front-line staff. They describe the basket

of national outcome-focused indicators that are used to measure progress towards each PSA. A subset of indicators had specific national targets or minimum standards attached.' (HM Treasury, 2000: 22).

123. Interview 41 (IfG research fellow) conducted for this study.
124. Interview 39 (Cabinet Office civil servant) conducted for this study.
125. Interview 16 (PMSU official) conducted for this study.
126. Interview 39 (Cabinet Office civil servant) conducted for this study.
127. Interview 43 (No.10 special adviser) conducted for this study.
128. Interview 5 (trade union general secretary) conducted for this study.
129. Interview 43 (No.10 special adviser) conducted for this study.
130. Interview 34 (departmental minister) conducted for this study.
131. Interview 2 (departmental minister) conducted for this study.
132. Interview 39 (Cabinet Office civil servant) conducted for this study.
133. Interview 44 (DfES/No.10 special adviser) conducted for this study.
134. Interview 4 (departmental minister) conducted for this study.
135. Interview 34 (departmental minister) conducted for this study.
136. Interview 1 (DfES civil servant) conducted for this study.
137. Interview conducted for this study.
138. Interview 37 (PMDU official) conducted for this study.
139. Interview 37 (PMDU official) conducted for this study.
140. Interview 2 (departmental minister) conducted for this study.
141. Interview 4 (departmental minister) conducted for this study.
142. Interview 3 (departmental minister) conducted for this study.
143. Interview 3 (departmental minister) conducted for this study.
144. Philip Gould, personal memorandum to the PM, April 2000.
145. Interview 19 (PMSU official) conducted for this study.
146. Interview 18 (PMSU official) conducted for this study.
147. Interview 38 (PMSU official) conducted for this study.
148. Quoted in Evidence to the House of Commons Public Administration Committee, 26 January 2006.
149. Interview conducted for this study.
150. Interview 38 (PMSU official) conducted for this study.
151. Interview 40 (PMSU official) conducted for this study.
152. Interview 38 (PMSU official) conducted for this study.
153. Interviews 2 (departmental minister) and 3 (departmental minister) conducted for this study.
154. Interview 16 (PMSU official) conducted for this study. See also Saint-Martin (2004).
155. Interview 13 (PMSU official) conducted for this study.

156. Interview 13 (PMSU official) conducted for this study.

157. Quoted in Evidence to the House of Commons Public Administration Select Committee, 26 January 2006.

158. Interview 31 (Home Office civil servant) conducted for this study. The FSU review of the criminal justice system undertaken by John Birt adopted a 'life-cycle' approach to how individual offenders negotiated the CJS, focusing on the lack of 'joining-up' with other agencies such as education, housing and employment.

159. Interview 31 (Home Office civil servant) conducted for this study.

160. Interview 31 (Home Office civil servant) conducted for this study.

161. Interview 31 (Home Office civil servant) conducted for this study.

162. Interview 38 (PMSU official) conducted for this study.

163. Interview 39 (Cabinet Office civil servant) conducted for this study.

164. Interview 42 (departmental minister) conducted for this study.

165. Interview 3 (departmental minister) conducted for this study.

166. Interview 3 (departmental minister) conducted for this study.

167. Quoted in Evidence to the Public Administration Select Committee, 17 July 2009.

178. Quoted in Evidence to the Public Administration Committee, 17 July 2009.

169. Interview 15 (DoH civil servant) conducted for this study.

170. The term 'Public Service Bargain' (PSB) is based on the analytical perspective of Hood and Lodge (2006) accounting for 'diverse bargains within systems of executive government'. Drawing on 'comparative experiences from various state traditions', Hood and Lodge examine ideas and 'contemporary developments' along three key dimensions of PSBs: 'reward', 'competency', and 'loyalty and responsibility'.

171. Interview 31 (Home Office civil servant) conducted for this study.

172. Interview 3 (departmental minister) conducted for this study.

173. Interview 14 (PMSU official) conducted for this study.

174. Interview 43 (No.10 special adviser) conducted for this study.

175. This memorandum to the Prime Minister is contained in Appendix III.

176. Interview 16 (PMSU official) conducted for this study.

177. Interview 49 (senior government minister) conducted for this study.

178. Interview 28 (Cabinet Office civil servant) conducted for this study.

179. Quoted in Evidence to the House of Commons Public Administration Committee, 15 January 2000.

180. Interview 35 (thinktank research fellow) conducted for this study.

181. Interview 35 (thinktank research fellow) conducted for this study.

182. Interview conducted for this study.
183. Interview 29 (DfES civil servant) conducted for this study.
184. Interview 14 (PMSU official) conducted for this study.
185. Quoted in Evidence to the House of Commons Public Administration Select Committee, 16 October 2008.
186. Interview conducted for this study.
187. Interview 37 (PMDU official) conducted for this study.

Chapter 7   Government and Governance: Patterns of Continuity and Change in the Whitehall Paradigm

1. Interview 49 (senior government minister) conducted for this study.
2. Quoted in evidence to the House of Commons Public Administration Select Committee, 1 April 2004.
3. Interview 16 (PMSU official) conducted for this study.
4. Interview 32 (departmental minister) conducted for this study.
5. Interview 16 (PMSU official) conducted for this study.
6. Interview 27 (Home Office/No.10 special adviser) conducted for this study.
7. Quoted in Evidence to the House of Commons Public Administration Select Committee, 23 October 2008.
8. Quoted in Evidence to the House of Commons Public Administration Select Committee, 23 October 2008.
9. Quoted in Evidence to the House of Commons Public Administration Select Committee, 16 December 2008.
10. Quoted in Evidence to the House of Commons Public Administration Select Committee, 16 December 2008.
11. Interview 14 (PMSU official) conducted for this study.
12. Interview 10 (Cabinet Office special adviser) conducted for this study.
13. Interview 7 (departmental minister) conducted for this study.
14. Interview 36 (DCLG/Cabinet Office civil servant) conducted for this study.
15. Interview 30 (Treasury special adviser) conducted for this study.
16. Interview 43 (No.10 special adviser) conducted for this study.
17. Interview 43 (No.10 special adviser) conducted for this study.
18. Interview 7 (departmental minister) conducted for this study.
19. Interview 15 (DoH civil servant) conducted for this study.
20. Interview 23 (BIS special adviser) conducted for this study.
21. Interview 22 (No.10 special adviser) conducted for this study.
22. Interview 25 (BIS civil servant) conducted for this study.

23. 'Smaller government: what do ministers do?', Memorandum from Professor Kevin Theakston, School of Politics and International Studies, University of Leeds, to the Public Administration Select Committee, October 2010.
24. Interview 41 (IfG research fellow) conducted for this study.
25. Interview 6 (DfES civil servant) conducted for this study.
26. Interview 25 (BIS civil servant) conducted for this study.
27. Interview 39 (Cabinet Office civil servant) conducted for this study.
28. This includes the Brown administration up until the General Election of 2010.
29. Michael Jacobs, written evidence to the House of Commons Public Administration Select Committee inquiry on 'Political Special Advisers', 12 June 2012.
30. Interview 14 (PMSU official) conducted for this study.
31. Interview 40 (PMSU official) conducted for this study.
32. Interview 1 (DfES civil servant) conducted for this study.
33. Interview 25 (BIS civil servant) conducted for this study.
34. Interview 26 (Treasury/No.10 special adviser) conducted for this study.
35. Interview 14 (PMSU official) conducted for this study.
36. Interview conducted for this study.
37. Quoted in Minutes of Evidence to the House of Commons Public Administration Select Committee, 18 October 2001.
38. Interview 14 (PMSU official) conducted for this study.
39. Interview 27 (Home Office/No.10 special adviser) conducted for this study.
40. Interview 24 (BIS civil servant) conducted for this study.
41. Interview 22 (No.10 special adviser) conducted for this study.
42. Interview 22 (No.10 special adviser) conducted for this study.
43. Quoted in Minutes of the Evidence to the House of Commons Public Administration Select Committee, 26 January 2006.
44. Interview 25 (BIS civil servant) conducted for this study.
45. Interview 22 (No.10 special adviser) conducted for this study.
46. Interview 41 (IfG research fellow) conducted for this study.
47. Interview 6 (DfES civil servant) conducted for this study.
48. Interview 10 (Cabinet Office special adviser) conducted for this study.
49. Interview 30 (Treasury special adviser) conducted for this study.
50. Quoted in Minutes of the Evidence to the House of Commons Public Administration Select Committee, 26 January 2006.
51. Interview 39 (Cabinet Office civil servant) conducted for this study.
52. Interview 39 (Cabinet Office civil servant) conducted for this study.
53. Interview 42 (departmental minister) conducted for this study.

54. Interview 38 (PMSU official) conducted for this study.
55. Interview 37 (PMDU official) conducted for this study.
56. Interview conducted for this study.
57. Interview 3 (departmental minister) conducted for this study.
58. Interview 21 (No.10 special adviser) conducted for this study.
59. Interview 28 (No.10 civil servant) conducted for this study.
60. Interview 37 (PMDU official) conducted for this study.
61. Interview 39 (Cabinet Office civil servant) conducted for this study.
62. Interview 29 (DfES civil servant) conducted for this study.
63. Interview 2 (departmental minister) conducted for this study.
64. Interview 35 (thinktank research fellow) conducted for this study.
65. Interview conducted for this study.
66. Interview 10 (Cabinet Office special adviser) conducted for this study.
67. Interview 33 (Cabinet Office civil servant) conducted for this study.
68. Interview 13 (PMSU official) conducted for this study.
69. Interview 13 (PMSU official) conducted for this study.
70. Interview 22 (No.10 special adviser) conducted for this study.
71. The papers in Appendix IV set out New Labour's critique of Whitehall, and proposals for reforming the machinery of government.
72. Interview 22 (No.10 special adviser) conducted for this study.
73. Interview 42 (departmental minister) conducted for this study.
74. Interview 18 (PMSU official) conducted for this study.
75. Interview 6 (DfES civil servant) conducted for this study.
76. Interview 27 (Home Office/No.10 special adviser) conducted for this study.
77. Interview 27 (Home Office/No.10 special adviser) conducted for this study.
78. Interview 6 (DfES civil servant) conducted for this study.
79. Interview 22 (No.10 special adviser) conducted for this study.
80. Interview 30 (Treasury special adviser) conducted for this study.
81. Interview 27 (Home Office/No.10 special adviser) conducted for this study.
82. Interview 10 (Cabinet Office special adviser) conducted for this study.
83. Interview 27 (Home Office/No.10 special adviser) conducted for this study.
84. Interview 10 (Cabinet Office special adviser) conducted for this study.
85. Interview 41 (IfG research fellow) conducted for this study.
86. Interview 14 (PMSU official) conducted for this study.
87. Interview 29 (DfES civil servant) conducted for this study.
88. Interview 14 (PMSU official) conducted for this study.
89. Interview 29 (DfES civil servant) conducted for this study.
90. Interview 22 (No.10 special adviser) conducted for this study.
91. Interview 27 (Home Office/No.10 special adviser) conducted for this study.

92. Interview 47 (departmental minister) conducted for this study.

93. Interview 1 (DfES civil servant) conducted for this study.

94. Interview 1 (DfES civil servant) conducted for this study.

95. Interview 10 (Cabinet Office special adviser) conducted for this study.

96. Interview 21 (No.10 special adviser) conducted for this study.

97. Interview 21 (No.10 special adviser) conducted for this study.

98. Interview 30 (Treasury special adviser) conducted for this study.

Chapter 8   The Role of Tradition and Path Dependency: New Labour in Power

1. Interview 42 (departmental minister) conducted for this study.

2. Interview 22 (No.10 special adviser) conducted for this study.

3. Interview 44 (No.10 special adviser) conducted for this study.

4. Interview 31 (Home Office civil servant) conducted for this study.

5. Interview 31 (Home Office civil servant) conducted for this study.

6. Interview 34 (departmental minister) conducted for this study.

7. Interview 22 (No.10 special adviser) conducted for this study.

8. Tony Blair, speech to the British Venture Capitalists Association, 6 July 1999 (see Assinder, 1999).

9. Interview 16 (PMSU official) conducted for this study.

10. Interview 28 (No.10 civil servant) conducted for this study.

11. Interview 49 (senior government minister) conducted for this study.

12. Interview 32 (departmental minister) conducted for this study.

13. Interview in *The New Statesman*, 9 November 2011.

14. Interview conducted for this study.

15. Interview 27 (Home Office/No.10 special adviser) conducted for this study.

16. Interview 27 (Home Office/No.10 special adviser) conducted for this study.

17. Interview 28 (No.10 civil servant) conducted for this study.

18. Interview 22 (No.10 special adviser) conducted for this study.

19. Interview conducted for this study.

20. Interview 42 (departmental minister) conducted for this study.

21. Interview conducted for this study.

22. Interview 39 (Cabinet Office civil servant) conducted for this study.

23. Interview 42 (departmental minister) conducted for this study.

24. Interview 3 (departmental minister) conducted for this study.

25. Interview 22 (No.10 special adviser) conducted for this study.

26. Interview 31 (Home Office civil servant) conducted for this study.

27. Birch considers several notions of representation in *Representative and Responsible Government* (1964), but it is the concept of 'elective' representation emphasising strong, initiatory and decisive government which is highlighted here.
28. Interview 22 (No.10 special adviser) conducted for this study.
29. Interview 22 (No.10 special adviser) conducted for this study.
30. Interview conducted for this study.
31. Interview 22 (No.10 special adviser) conducted for this study.
32. Interview 4 (departmental minister) conducted for this study.
33. Interview 10 (Cabinet Office special adviser) conducted for this study.
34. Interview 10 (Cabinet Office special adviser) conducted for this study.
35. Interview 10 (Cabinet Office special adviser) conducted for this study.
36. Interview 4 (departmental minister) conducted for this study.
37. Interview 10 (Cabinet Office special adviser) conducted for this study.
38. Interview 10 (Cabinet Office special adviser) conducted for this study.
39. Interview 1 (DfES civil servant) conducted for this study.
40. Interview 1 (DfES civil servant) conducted for this study.
41. Interview 1 (DfES civil servant) conducted for this study.
42. Interview 1 (DfES civil servant) conducted for this study.
43. Interview 1 (DfES civil servant) conducted for this study.
44. Interview conducted for this study.
45. Interview 31 (Home Office civil servant) conducted for this study.
46. Interview 22 (No.10 special adviser) conducted for this study.
47. Interview 12 (DoH special adviser) conducted for this study.
48. Interview 1 (DfES civil servant) conducted for this study.
49. Quoted in Evidence to the House of Lords Constitution Committee Report, 'The Accountability of Civil Servants', 7 November 2012.
50. Interview 24 (BIS civil servant) conducted for this study.
51. Interview 36 (DCLG/Cabinet Office civil servant) conducted for this study.
52. Interview 24 (BIS civil servant) conducted for this study.
53. Interview 38 (PMSU official) conducted for this study.
54. Interview conducted for this study.
55. Interview conducted for this study.
56. Interview 22 (No.10 special adviser) conducted for this study.
57. Interview 31 (Home Office civil servant) conducted for this study.
58. Interview 42 (departmental minister) conducted for this study.
59. Quoted in Evidence to the House of Commons Public Administration Select Committee, 17 July 2009.

60. Interview 32 (departmental minister) conducted for this study.

61. Quoted in Evidence to the House of Commons Public Administration Committee, 23 October 2008.

62. Interview 27 (Home Office/No.10 special adviser) conducted for this study.

63. Interview 6 (DfES civil servant) conducted for this study.

64. Interview 35 (thinktank research fellow) conducted for this study.

65. Interview conducted for this study.

66. Interview 22 (No.10 special adviser) conducted for this study.

67. Interview 31 (Home Office civil servant) conducted for this study.

68. Interview 14 (PMSU official) conducted for this study.

69. Interview 4 (departmental minister) conducted for this study.

70. Interview 13 (PMSU official) conducted for this study.

71. Interview 13 (PMSU official) conducted for this study.

72. Interview 27 (Home Office/No.10 special adviser) conducted for this study.

73. Interview 35 (thinktank research fellow) conducted for this study.

74. Richard Mottram, 'Fifteen years at the top in the UK Civil Service – some reflections', speech to MPA Capstone event, London School of Economics, 6 May 2008.

75. Interview 1 (DfES civil servant) conducted for this study.

76. Interview 34 (departmental minister) conducted for this study.

77. Interview 1 (DfES civil servant) conducted for this study.

78. Interview 1 (DfES civil servant) conducted for this study.

79. Interview conducted for this study.

80. Interview 34 (departmental minister) conducted for this study.

81. Interview 34 (departmental minister) conducted for this study.

82. Interview 7 (departmental minister) conducted for this study.

83. Interview 29 (DfES civil servant) conducted for this study.

84. Interview 15 (DoH civil servant) conducted for this study.

85. Interview 13 (PMSU official) conducted for this study.

86. Interview 26 (Treasury/No.10 special adviser) conducted for this study.

87. Interview 22 (No.10 special adviser) conducted for this study.

88. Interview 21 (No.10 special adviser) conducted for this study.

89. Interview 26 (Treasury/No.10 special adviser) conducted for this study.

90. Interview conducted for this study.

91. Interview conducted for this study.

92. Interview conducted for this study.

93. Interview 3 (departmental minister) conducted for this study.

94. Interview conducted for this study.

95. Interview conducted for this study.

96. Interview conducted for this study.

97. Interview 32 (departmental minister) conducted for this study.

98. Interview 35 (thinktank research fellow) conducted for this study.

99. Interview 5 (thinktank general secretary) conducted for this study.

100. Interview 3 (departmental minister) conducted for this study.

101. Interview 12 (DoH special adviser) conducted for this study.

102. Interview 31 (Home Office civil servant) conducted for this study.

103. Interview 14 (PMSU official) conducted for this study.

104. Evidence to the House of Common Public Administration Select Committee, 8 December 2005.

105. Interview 14 (PMSU official) conducted for this study.

106. Interview by Prime Minister Tony Blair with Mark Easton, BBC Home Affairs Editor, 5 September 2006.

107. Speech by Prime Minister Tony Blair to the Joseph Rowntree Foundation, 5 September 2006.

108. Interview conducted for this study.

109. Quoted in Evidence to the House of Commons Public Administration Committee, 16 October 2008.

110. Quoted in Evidence to the House of Commons Public Administration Committee, 26 January 2006.

111. This is somewhat at odds with Flinders' (2012) claim that social science has little practical impact on the politics of the policy-making process in the United Kingdom.

112. Interview 14 (PMSU official) conducted for this study.

113. Quoted in Minutes of Evidence, House of Lords Constitution Committee, Report on 'The Cabinet Office and the Centre of Government', January 2010.

114. Quoted in Evidence to the House of Commons Public Administration Committee, 15 January 2000.

115. Interview conducted for this study.

116. Interview 20 (departmental minister) conducted for this study.

117. Matthew Taylor, former chief political strategy adviser to the prime minister (2003–6), quoted in Evidence to the House of Commons Public Administration Committee, 16 October 2008.

Chapter 9   Conclusion: Power, Policy and the Modern State

1. Interview 49 (senior government minister) conducted for this study.

2. This analysis builds on interview 41 (IfG research fellow) conducted for this study.
3. Interview 39 (Cabinet Office civil servant) conducted for this study.
4. T. Blair, 'A Modern Britain in a Modern Europe', speech, 20 January 1998.
5. D. Marquand, 'Populism or Pluralism? New Labour and the Constitution', Mischon Lecture, University College London, 1999.

Appendix II   Policy Governance under New Labour

1. The diagram of Academy Governance under New Labour is based on Goodwin (2011).

Appendix III   'Renewal and Strategic Audit'

1. Private papers provided to the author by colleagues in the Prime Minister's Policy Unit.

Appendix IV   New Labour's Critique of Whitehall and Proposals for Reforming the Centre of Government: Memorandum to the Prime Minister June 2000

1. Private papers provided to the author by colleagues in the Prime Minister's Policy Unit.

Bibliography

6, P. (1998) 'Holistic government', London: Demos.

Aberbach, J.D. & Rockman, B.A. (2002) 'Conducting and coding elite interviews', *Political Science and Politics*, 35 (4): 673–6.

Adcock, P. & Bevir, M. (2005) 'The history of political science', *Political Studies Review*, 3 (1): 1–16.

Adonis, A. (2012) *Education, Education, Education: Reforming England's Schools*, London: Biteback Publishing.

Adonis, A. & Hames, T. (eds) (1994) *A Conservative Revolution? The Thatcher-Reagan Decade in Perspective*, Manchester: Manchester University Press.

Adonis, A. & Pollard, S. (1996) *A Class Act: The Myth of Britain's Classless Society*, London: Hamish Hamilton.

Addison, P. (1976) *The Road to 1945: British Politics and the Second World War*, London: Jonathan Cape.

Akerlof, G. & Shiller, R. (2009) *Animal Spirits: How Human Psychology drives the Economy*, Princeton: Princeton University Press.

Albrow, M. (1996) *The Global Age: State and Society Beyond Modernity*, Cambridge: Polity Press.

Alexander, R. (1997) 'Basics, cores and choices: prospects for curriculum reform', in Soler, J., Craft, A. & Burgess, H. (eds) *Teacher Development: Exploring Our Own Practice*, London: Paul Chapman.

Annesley, C. (2001) 'New Labour and welfare' in Ludlam, S. & Smith, M. (eds) *New Labour in Government*, Basingstoke: Palgrave Macmillan.

Annesley, C. & Gains, F. (2010) 'The Core executive: gender, power and change', *Political Studies*, 58 (5): 909–29.

Annesley, C., Gains, F. & Rummery, K. (2010) 'Engendering politics and policy: the legacy of New Labour', *Policy and Politics*, 38 (3): 389–406.

Archer, M. (1990) 'Human agency and social structure: a critique of Giddens', in Clark, J., Modgil, C. & Modgil, S. (eds), *Anthony Giddens: Consensus and Controversy*, London: Falmer Press.

Archer, M. (1995) *Realist Social Theory: The Morphogenetic Approach*, Cambridge: Cambridge University Press.

Arestis, P. & Sawyer, M.C. (1998) 'Keynesian economic policies for the New Millennium', *Economic Journal*, 108 (1): 181–95.

Ascherson, N. (1989) *Games With Shadows*, London: Radius.

Assinder, N. (1999) 'Blair risks row over public sector', *BBC News*, 7 July, available at http://news.bbc.co.uk/1/hi/uk_politics/388528.stm (accessed 5 August 2013).

Attlee, C. (1948) House of Commons Debate (Hansard), Column 3418.

Attlee, C. (1965) *As It Happened*, London: Odhams Press.

Bache, I. & Flinders, M. (eds) (2004) *Multi-level Governance*, Oxford: Oxford University Press.

Bagehot, W. (1864) *The English Constitution*, Oxford: Oxford University Press.

Bale, T. (2010) *The Conservative Party: From Thatcher to Cameron*, Cambridge: Polity Press.

Ball, S. (2009) 'Academies in context: politics, business and philanthropy and heterarchical governance', *Management in Education*, 23 (3): 100–3.

Ball, T. (1992) 'New faces of power', in Wartenberg, T.E. (ed.), *Rethinking Power*, New York: State University of New York Press.

Balls, E., Grice, J. & O'Donnell, G. (2004) *Microeconomic Reform in Britain: Delivering Opportunities for All*, Basingstoke: Palgrave Macmillan.

Balogh, T. (1959) 'The Apotheosis of the Dilettante', in Thomas, H. (ed.) *The Establishment: A Symposium*, London: Allen Lane.

Barber, M. (1997) *The Learning Game: Arguments for an Education Revolution*, London: Phoenix.

Barber, M. (2007) *Instruction to Deliver: Tony Blair, Public Services and the Challenge of Achieving Targets*, London: Politicos.

Barberis, P. (1997) *The Civil Service in an Era of Change*, Sudbury, MA: Dartmouth Press.

Barker, R. (1994a) *Political Ideas in Modern Britain*, London: Routledge.

Barker, R. (1994b) *Politics, Peoples and Government: Themes in British Political Thought Since the Nineteenth Century*, Basingstoke: Palgrave Macmillan.

Barker, R. (2001) *Legitimating Identities: The Self-Presentations of Rulers and Subjects*, Cambridge: Cambridge University Press.

Barnett, A. (1997) *This Time: Our Constitutional Revolution*, London: Vintage Books.

Barnett, A., Ellis, C. & Hirst, P. (1993) *Debating the Constitution: New Perspectives on Constitutional Reform*, Cambridge: Polity Press.

Bauman, Z. (1991) *Thinking Sociologically*, Oxford: Blackwell.

Becker, G. (1992) 'The economic way of looking at life', New York: Nobel Prize Lecture.

Beer, S. (1965) *Modern British Politics*, London: Faber.

Beer, S. (1982) *Britain Against Itself: The Political Contradictions of Collectivism*, New York: Norton.

Behr, R. (2011) 'Andy Burnham on the NHS, school freedom and working with the Lib Dems', *New Statesman*, 9 November.

Bell, S. (2011) 'Do we really need a new constructivist institutionalism to explain institutional change?', *British Journal of Political Science*, 41 (4): 883–906.

Bell, S. & Hindmoor, A. (2009) *Rethinking Governance: The Centrality of the State in Modern Society*, Cambridge: Cambridge University Press.

Benn, T. (1981) *Against the Tide: Diaries 1973–76*, London: Arrow.

Bennister, M. (2012) *Prime Ministers in Power: Political Leadership in Britain and Australia*, Basingstoke: Palgrave Macmillan.

Bennett, A. & George, A.L. (2005) *Case Studies and Theory Development in the Social Sciences*, Boston: Massachusetts Institute of Technology Press.

Benson, J. K. (1975) 'The inter-organisational network as a political economy', *Administrative Science Quarterly*, 20 (2): 229–49.

Berman, S. (1998) *The Social Democratic Moment: Ideas and Politics in the Making of Inter-War Europe*, Harvard: Harvard University Press.

BERR (2009) 'Building Britain's Future: New Industry, New Jobs', Department for Business, Enterprise and Regulatory Reform, April, p. 3.

Berrill, K. (1985) 'Strength at the centre: the case for a Prime Minister's Department', in King, A. *The British Prime Minister*, London: Macmillan.

Better Government Initiative (2010) 'Good government: reforming Parliament and the executive', London: BGI.

Bevan, A. (1952) *In Place of Fear*, London: Kessenger.

Bevir, M. (1999) *The Logic of the History of Ideas*, Cambridge: Cambridge University Press.

Bevir, M. (2005) *New Labour: A Critique*, London: Sage.

Bevir, M. (2007a) *Modern Political Science: Anglo-American Exchanges since 1880* (with Adcock, R. & Stimson, S.), Princeton: Princeton University Press.

Bevir, M. (2007b) 'Socialism and Democracy: New Labour and the Constitution', *Observatoire de la société britannique* (3), University of Sud-Toulon-Var.

Bevir, M. (2011) *The Making of British Socialism*, Princeton: Princeton University Press.

Bevir, M. & Gains, F. (2011) 'Ideas into policy: governance and governmentality', *Policy and Politics*, 39 (4): 485–98.

Bevir, M. & Rhodes, R.A.W. (2003) *Interpreting British Governance*, London: Routledge.

Bevir, M. & Rhodes, R.A.W. (2006a) 'Disaggregating structures as an agenda for critical realism: a reply to McAnulla', *British Politics*, 1 (1): 367–403.

Bevir, M. & Rhodes, R.A.W. (2006b) *Governance Stories*, London: Routledge.

Bevir, M. & Rhodes, R.A.W. (2008) 'The differentiated polity as narrative', *British Journal of Politics and International Relations*, 10 (4): 729–34.

Bevir, M. & Rhodes, R.A.W. (2010) *The State as Cultural Practice*, Oxford: Oxford University Press.

Bevir, M. & Richards, D. (2009) 'Decentring policy networks: a theoretical agenda', *Public Administration*, 87 (1): 3–14.

Bhaskar, R. (2008) *A Realist Theory of Science* (with a new introduction), London: Routledge.

Birch, A.H. (1964) *Representative and Responsible Government*, London: Allen & Unwin.

Birch, A.H. (1967) *The British System of Government*, London: Routledge.

Blackstone, T. & Plowden, W. (1988) *Inside the Think-Tank: Advising the Cabinet 1971–83*, London: Heinemann.

Blair, T. (1996a) *New Britain: My Vision of a Young Country*, London: Fourth Estate.

Blair, T. (1996b) 'The Constitution: British democracy's second age', *The Economist*, 14 September.

Blair, T. (2010) *A Journey*, London: Hutchinson.

Blakey, H. (2011) 'Democratic governance: a review of Mark Bevir', *Parliamentary Affairs*, 64 (4): 628–30.

Blanchard, O. (1998) 'Revisiting European unemployment: unemployment, capital accumulation, and factor prices', *NBER Working Papers*, National Bureau of Economic Research (US).

Blick, A. (2004) *People Who Live in the Dark: The History of the Special Adviser in British Politics*, London: Politicos.

Blick, A. & Jones, G. (2010) *Premiership: the Development, Nature and Power of the Office of the British Prime Minister*, Exeter: Imprint Academic.

Blunkett, D. & Richards, D. (2011) 'Labour in and out of government: political ideas, political practice and the British Political Tradition', *Political Studies Review*, 9 (2): 180–92.

Blyth, M. (2002) 'Institutions and ideas', in Marsh, D. & Stoker, G. *Theory and Methods in Political Science*, Basingstoke: Palgrave Macmillan.

Bogdanor, V. (1998) *Devolution in the United Kingdom*, Oxford: Oxford Paperbacks.

Bogdanor, V. (1999) 'Devolution: decentralisation or disintegration?', *Political Quarterly*, 70 (2): 185–94.

Bogdanor, V. (2009) *The New British Constitution*, London: Hart Publishing.

Bovaird, T. & Russell, K. (2007) 'Civil service reform in the UK, 1999–2005: revolutionary failure or evolutionary success?', *Public Administration*, 85 (2): 301–28.

Bradbury, J. (2008) *Devolution, Regionalism and Regional Development: The UK Experience*, London: Routledge.

Brivati, B. & Jones, H. (1995) *What Difference Did The War Make? Themes in Contemporary British History*, London: Frances Pinter.

Brown, G. (1972) *In My Way: The Political Memoirs of Lord George Brown*, London: Littlehampton Books.

Brown, G. (1999) 'Modernising the British economy: the new mission for the Treasury', *Institute of Fiscal Studies*, 27 March.

Bryman, A. (2001) *Social Research Methods*, Oxford: Oxford University Press.

Buchanan, J. (1986) *The Demand and Supply of Public Goods*, Indianapolis: Liberty Fund.

Buller, J. (1999) *National Statecraft and European Integration: The Conservative Government and the European Union, 1979-97*, London: Cassell.

Bulpitt, J. (1983) *Territory and Power in the United Kingdom*, Manchester: Manchester University Press.

Bulpitt, J. (1986) 'The discipline of the new democracy: Mrs Thatcher's domestic statecraft', *Political Studies*, 34(1): 19–39.

Burch, M. & Holliday, I. (1996) *The British Cabinet System*, London: Harvester Wheatsheaf.

Burch, M. & Holliday, I. (2000) 'New Labour and the machinery of government', in Coates, D. & Lawler, P. *New Labour in Power*, Manchester: Manchester University Press.

Burchardt, T., Le Grand, J. & Piachaud, D. (2001) *Social Exclusion: An Introduction*, Oxford : Oxford University Press.

Burke, E. (1981) *The Writings and Speeches of Edmund Burke*, Oxford; Clarendon Press.

Burnham, P. (2002) 'New Labour and the politics of depoliticisation', *British Journal of Politics and International Relations*, 3 (2): 127–49.

Burnham, P. & Pyper, J. (2008) *Britain's Modernised Civil Service*, Basingstoke: Palgrave Macmillan.

Burnham, P., Grillard, K., Grant, W. & Layton-Henry, Z. (2004) *Research Methods in Politics*, Basingstoke: Palgrave Macmillan.

Burnham, P., Jones, L. & Lee, J. (1998) *At the Centre of Whitehall: Advising the Prime Minister and Cabinet*, Basingstoke: Palgrave Macmillan.

Butler of Brockwell, Rt. Hon. Lord (2004) *Review of Intelligence on Weapons of Mass Destruction: Report of a Committee of Privy Counsellors*, House of Commons (HC 898), 14 July.

Butler, D. & Seldon, A. (2000) *The Powers Behind the Prime Minister: The Hidden Influence of Number 10*, London: Harper Collins, 2000.

Cabinet Office (1999) *Modernising Government White Paper*, Cm 4310, London: The Stationery Office.

Cabinet Office (2003) Prime Minister's Strategy Unit, 'Strategic Audit', available at www.cabinetoffice.gov.uk/strategy/work_areas/strategic_audit (accessed 20 June 2011).

Cabinet Office (2006a) *Reaching Out: An Action Plan on Social Exclusion*, London: Cabinet Office.

Cabinet Office (2006b) Social Exclusion Task Force Press Notice, 'Tackling deep-seated social exclusion: Hilary Armstrong announces next steps and new arrangements in government', 13 June, London: Cabinet Office.

Cabinet Office (2008) Social Exclusion Task Force, 'Think Family: Improving the Life-Chances of Children at Risk', London: Cabinet Office.

Cairney, P. (2011) 'The new British policy style: from a British to a Scottish political tradition?', *Political Studies Review*, 9 (3): 208–20.

Cairney, P. (2012) *Understanding Public Policy: Theories and Issues*, Basingstoke: Palgrave Macmillan.

Callaghan, J. (2000) *The Retreat of Social Democracy*, Manchester: Manchester University Press.

Callaghan, J. (2006) *Time and Chance*, London: Methuen Politicos.

Callaghan, J., Fielding, S. & Ludlum, S. (eds) (2003) *Interpreting the Labour Party: Approaches to Labour Politics and History*, Manchester: Manchester University Press.

Cameron, S. (2009) 'Wither Whitehall', *The Hidden Wiring*, Mile End Group Newsletter, pp. 7–8, Autumn.

Campbell, C. & Wilson, G. (1995) *The End of Whitehall: Death of a Paradigm*, Oxford: Blackwell.

Chapman, R. (1988) *Ethics in the British Civil Service*, London: Routledge.

Chester, D.N. & Wilson, F.M.G. (1968) *The Organisation of British Central Government 1914– 64*, London: Allen & Unwin.

Chowdry, H., Muriel, A., & Sibeita, L. (2010) 'Radical or just radically vague? Manifesto proposals for education reform', *Institute of Fiscal Studies*, April.

Clarke, P. (1978) *Liberals and Social Democrats*, Cambridge: Cambridge University Press.

Clarke, P. (1989) *The Keynesian Revolution In The Making 1924–36*, Oxford: Oxford University Press.

Coates, D. (1975) *The Labour Party and the Struggle for Socialism*, Cambridge: Cambridge University Press.

Coates, D. (2005) *Prolonged Labour: The Slow Birth of New Labour Britain*, Basingstoke: Palgrave Macmillan.

Coates, D. & Krieger, J. (2004) *Blair's War*, Cambridge: Polity Press.

Cockett, R. (1995) *Thinking the Unthinkable: Think-tanks and the Economic Counter-revolution, 1931–1986*, London: Harper Collins.

Cole, G.D.H. (1920) *Guild Socialism Restated*, London: Leonard Parsons.

Collini, S., Winch, D., & Burrow, J.W. (1984) *That Noble Science of Politics: A Study in Nineteenth Century English History*, Cambridge: Cambridge University Press.

Collins, P. (2011) 'The man in Whitehall faces an uncivil future', *The Times*, 17 March, available at www.thetimes.co.uk/tto/opinion/columnists/philipcollins/article2948836.ece (accessed 14 October 2013).

Constitution Unit, The (2012) 'Special advisers: numbers, tenure and distribution – interim findings', September, London: University College, London.

Converse, P. (1964) 'The nature of belief systems', in Apter, D., *Ideology and Discontent*, New York: Free Press.

Corry, D. (2011) 'Power at the centre: is the National Economic Council a model for a new way of organising things?', *Political Quarterly*, 82 (3): 459–68.

Cortell, A.P. & Peterson, S. (2004) *Altered States: International Relations, Domestic Politics and Institutional Change*, Michigan: Lexington Press.

Crespi, F. (1992) *Social Action and Power*, Oxford: Blackwell.

Cronin, J.E. (1988) 'The British state and the structure of political opportunity', *Journal of British Studies*, 27 (3): 199–231.

Cronin, J.E. (1991) *The Politics of State Expansion: War, State and Society in Twentieth Century Britain*, London: Routledge.

Cronin, J.E. (2005) *New Labour's Pasts: The Labour Party and its Discontents*, London: Pearson Education.

Crosland, C.A.R. (1956) *The Future of Socialism*, London: Jonathan Cape.

Crossman, R. (1972) *The Myths of Cabinet Government*, Cambridge: Harvard University Press.

Crossman, R. (1975) *The Crossman Diaries*, London: Mandarin.

Crouch, C. (2010) *The Strange Non-Death of Neo-Liberalism*, Cambridge: Polity Press.

Cuomo, M. (1996) *Reason to Believe*, New York: Simon & Schuster.

Dahl, R. (1965) *Who Governs?*, New York: Yale University Press.

Dahl, R. (1976) *Modern Political Analysis*, New York: Prentice-Hall.

Daniel, C. (1997) 'May the taskforce be with you', *New Statesman*, 1 August.

Darendorf, R. (2000) *Modern Social Conflict*, Berkeley: University of California Press.

Darling, A. (2011) *Back From the Brink: One Thousand Days at Number 11*, London: Atlantic Books.

Davies, H. & Nutley, S. (2002) "Evidence-based policy and practice: moving from rhetoric to reality", University of St Andrews, Research Unit for Research Utilisation, Discussion paper 2.

Davies, J. (2000) 'The hollowing-out of local democracy and the "fatal conceit" of governing without government', *British Journal of Politics and International Relations*, 2 (3): 414–28.

Davies, P.H.J. (2001) 'Spies as informants: triangulation and the interpretation of elite interview data in the study of the intelligence and security services', *Politics*, 21 (1): 73–80.

Deakin, N. & Parry, R. (2000) *The Treasury and Social Policy: The Contest for Control of Welfare Strategy*, Basingstoke: Palgrave Macmillan.

Denham, A. (1996) *Think-Tanks of the New Right*, Aldershot: Dartmouth Publishing.

Denham, A. & Garnett, M. (1998) 'Think-tanks, British politics, and the "climate of opinion"', in Denham, A & Garnett, M. (eds), *Think-tanks Across Nations: A Comparative Approach*, Manchester: Manchester University Press.

Devine, F. (2002) 'Qualitative methods', in Marsh, D. & Stoker, G., *Theory and Methods in Political Science*, Basingstoke: Palgrave Macmillan.

Devine, F. & Heath, S. (2000) *Sociological Research Methods in Context*, Basingstoke: Palgrave Macmillan.

Dexter, L.A. (2006) *Elite and Specialist Interviewing*, New York: ECPR Press.

Dicey, A.V. (1982) *Introduction to the Study of the Law of the Constitution*, Liberty Fund INC.

Dodds, A. (2009) 'Families "at risk" and the Family-Nurse Partnership: the intrusion of risk into social exclusion policy', *Journal of Social Policy*, 38 (3): 499–514.

Dolowitz, D., Greenwold, C. & Marsh, D. (1999) 'Policy transfer: something old, something new, something borrowed, but why red, white and blue?' *Parliamentary Affairs*, 52 (4): 719–30.

Dolowitz, D., Marsh, D., O'Neill, M. & Richards, D. (1996) 'Thatcherism and the 3Rs: radicalism, realism and rhetoric: the third term of the Thatcher government', *Parliamentary Affairs*, 49 (3): 455–70.

Donoughue, B. (1987) *The Prime Minister: The Conduct of Policy under Harold Wilson and Jim Callaghan*, London: Jonathan Cape.

Dorpe, K. van & Horton, S. (2011) 'The public service bargain in the United Kingdom: the Whitehall model in decline?', *Public Policy and Administration*, 26 (2): 233–52.

Dowding, K. (1991) *Rational Choice and Political Power*, London: Edward Elgar.

Dowding, K. (1995) *The Civil Service: Theory and Practice in British Politics*, London: Routledge.

Dowding, K. & James, O. (2004) 'Analysing bureau-shaping models: comments on Marsh, Smith and Richards', *British Journal of Political Science*, 34 (2): 183–9.

Driver, S. & Martell, L. (2004) *New Labour: Continuity and Change*, Cambridge: Polity Press.

DTI (1998) 'Our Competitive Future: building the knowledge driven economy', Department of Trade and Industry, July.

Dunleavy, P. (1991) *Democracy, Bureaucracy and Public Choice*, London: Harvester Wheatsheaf.

Dunleavy, P. (2000) 'Elections and party politics', in Dunleavy, P. et al. (ed.) *Developments in British Politics 6*, Basingstoke: Palgrave Macmillan.

Dunleavy, P. & Rhodes, R.A.W. (1990) 'Core executive studies in Britain', *Public Administration*, 68 (4): 29–60.

Durbin, E. (1948) *The Politics of Democratic Socialism*, London: G.W. Routledge.

Economist, The (1999) 'The cafetiere theory of government', *The Economist*, 19 August, available at www.economist.com/node/233455 (accessed 18 September 2013).

Economist, The (2010) 'Empty shelves', *The Economist*, 27 April, available at www.economist.com/node/15996751 (accessed 27 April 2010).

Elgie, R. (2011) 'Core executive studies two decades on', *Public Administration*, 89 (1): 64–77.

Etzioni, A. (1995) *The Spirit of Community: Rights, Responsibilities, and the Communitarian Agenda*, New York: Crown Publishing.

Evans, M. (1993) *Charter 88: A Successful Challenge to the British Political Tradition?*, Glasgow: University of Strathclyde.

Evans, M. (1995) *Charter 88: A Successful Challenge to the British political Tradition?*, Dartmouth: Dartmouth Press.

Evans, M. (2003) *Constitution-Making and the Labour Party*, Basingstoke: Palgrave Macmillan.

Evans, M. (2008) 'New Labour and the rise of new constitutionalism', Paper to the *Political Studies Association Annual Conference*, University of Manchester, 8–11 April.

Exley, S. (2012) 'The politics of educational policy making under New Labour: an illustration of shifts in public service governance', *Policy and Politics*, 40 (2): 227–44.

Eyerman, R. (1994) *Between Culture and Politics*, Cambridge: Polity Press.

Fairclough, N. (2000) *New Labour, New Language*, London: Routledge.

Faucher-King, F. & Le Gales, P. (2010) *The New Labour Experiment: 1997–2009*, Stanford: Stanford University Press.

Fawcett, P. (2010) 'Metagovernance: the Treasury's evolving role within the British core executive, 1997–2007', *Paper presented at the 2010 PSA Annual Conference*, University of Edinburgh.

Fawcett, P. (2011) 'The core executive in New South Wales: 1995–2011', *Paper presented at the 2011 Australian Political Studies Association Annual Conference*, 26–28 September, ANU Canberra: Australia.

Fawcett, P. & Gay, O. (2005) 'The centre of government: the Prime Minister's Office, the Cabinet Office, and HM Treasury', *House of Commons Research Paper*, 5/12.

Fawcett, P. & Rhodes, R.A.W. (2007) 'Central government', in Seldon, A. (ed.), *Blair's Britain 1997– 2007*, Cambridge: Cambridge University Press.

Feinstein, L. (2003) 'How early can we predict future educational achievement?', *Centrepiece*, London: London School of Economics.

Feinstein, L. (2011) 'Inequality in the early cognitive development of British children in the 1970 cohort', *Economica*.

Ferlie, E., Fitzgerald, L., McGivern, G., Dopson, S. & Bennett, C. (2011) 'Public policy networks and "wicked problems": A nascent solution?' *Public Administration*, 89 (2): 307–24.

Finer, S.E. (1958) *Private Industry and Political Power*, London: Pall Mall.

Fielding, S. (2002) *The Labour Party: Continuity and Change in the making of 'New' Labour*, Basingstoke, Palgrave Macmillan.

Fielding, S. (2003) *The Labour Governments 1964– 70 Volume 1: Labour and Cultural Change*, Manchester: Manchester University Press.

Finlayson, A. (2004) 'The interpretative approach in political science: a symposium', *British Journal of Politics and International Relations*, 6 (2): 129–64.

Flinders, M. (2000) 'The enduring centrality of individual ministerial responsibility within the British constitution', *Journal of Legislative Studies*, 6 (1): 73–92.

Flinders, M. (2002) 'Governance in Whitehall', *Public Administration*, 80 (2): 51–64.

Flinders, M. (2008) *Delegated Governance and the British State: Walking Without Order*, Oxford: Oxford University Press.

Flinders, M. (2009) *Democratic Drift*, Oxford: Oxford University Press.

Flinders, M. (2010) 'Bagehot smiling: Gordon Brown's new constitution', *Political Quarterly*, 81(1): 57–74.

Flinders, M. (2012) *Defending Politics*, Oxford: Oxford University Press.

Flinders, M. & Curry, D. (2008) 'Bi-constitutionality: unravelling New Labour's constitutional orientations', *Parliamentary Affairs*, 61 (1): 99– 21.

Flinders, M. & Matthews, F. (2007) 'Rebuilding strategic capacity? Multi-level governance, leadership and public service agreements in Britain', in Koch, R. (ed.) *Public Governance and Leadership*, Berlin: Gabler Verlag.

Flyvbjerg, B. (2011) 'Case study', in Denkin, N.K. & Lincoln, Y.S. (eds), *The Sage Handbook of Qualitative Research*, Thousand Oaks, CA: Sage.

Foley, M. (2000) *The British Presidency*, Manchester: Manchester University Press.

Foster, C. (2005) *British Government in Crisis: or the Third English Revolution*, Oxford: Hart.

Foster, C. & Plowden, W. (1998) *The State Under Stress*, Buckingham: Open University.

Foucault, M. (1976) *Discipline and Punish: The Birth of the Prison*, London: Vintage.

Freeden, M. (1999) 'The ideology of New Labour', *Political Quarterly*, 70 (1): 42–51.

Fry, G. (1981) *The Administrative Revolution in Whitehall: A Study of the Politics of Administrative Change in British Central Government since the 1950s*, London: Croom Helm.

Gains, F. (2013) 'Observational Analysis', in Rhodes, R.A.W. & t'Hart, P. (eds) *The Oxford Handbook of Political Leadership*, Oxford: Oxford University Press.

Gains, F. & Stoker, G. (2011) 'Special advisers and the transmission of ideas from the policy primeval soup', *Policy and Politics*, 39 (4): 485–98.

Galbraith, J.K. (1992) *The Culture of Contentment*, London: Penguin Books.

Gamble, A. (1984) *Britain in Decline*, Basingstoke: Palgrave Macmillan.

Gamble, A. (1990) 'Theories of British politics', *Political Studies*, 38 (3): 404–20.

Gamble, A. (1994) *The Free Economy and the Strong State*, Basingstoke: Palgrave Macmillan.

Gamble, A. (2000) *Politics and Fate*, Cambridge: Polity Press.

Gamble, A. (2002) 'Policy agendas in a multi-level polity', in Dunleavy, P., Gamble, A., Heffernan, R., Holliday, I. & Peele, G. (eds), *Developments in Britush Politics* 6, Basingstoke: Palgrave Macmillan.

Gamble, A. (2003) *Between Europe and America: The Future of British Politics*, Basingstoke: Palgrave Macmillan.

Gamble, A. (2006) 'The European disunion', *British Journal of Politics and International Relations*, 8 (1): 34–49.

Gamble, A. (2009) *The Spectre at the Feast: Capitalist Crisis and the Politics of Recession*, Basingstoke: Palgrave Macmillan.

Gamble, A. (2010) 'New Labour and political change', *Parliamentary Affairs*, 63 (4): 639–52.

Gamble, A. (2012) 'Inside New Labour', *British Journal of Politics and International Relations*, 14 (3): 492–502.

Gamble, A. & Kelly, G. (2001) 'Labour's new economics', in Ludlam, S. & Smith, M. (eds), *New Labour in Government*, Basingstoke: Palgrave Macmillan.

Gamble, A. & Wright, A. (2004) *Restating the State (Political Quarterly Special Edition)*, Oxford: Wiley.

Geddes, A. (2004) *The European Union and British Politics*, Basingstoke: Palgrave Macmillan.

Geddes, A. & Tongue, J. (1997) *Britain Votes 1997*, Oxford: Oxford University Press.

Geddes, A. & Tongue, J. (2010) *Britain Votes 2010*, Oxford: Oxford University Press.

Geertz, C. (1973) *The Interpretation of Cultures: Selected Essays*, New York: Basic Books.

Giddens, A. (1984) *The Constitution of Society*, Cambridge: Polity Press.

Giddens, A. (1994) *Beyond Left and Right: The Future of Radical Politics*, Cambridge: Polity Press.

Giddens, A. (1998) *The Third Way*, Cambridge: Polity Press.

Giddens, A. (2007) *Where Now for New Labour?*, Cambridge: Polity Press.

Glaister, S. (2012) 'Major errors in West Coast mainline deal debacle', *BBC News*, 3 October, available at www.bbc.co.uk/news/business-21274903 (accessed 3 October 2012).

Glennerster, H. (2006) *British Social Policy: 1945 to the Present*, Oxford: Blackwell.

Goldstein, K. (2002) 'Getting in the door: sampling and completing interviews', in *Politics and Political Science*, 35 (4): 669–72.

Goodwin, M. (2011) 'Education governance, politics and policy under New Labour', Unpublished PhD, University of Birmingham.

Gould, P. (1996) *The Unfinished Revolution*, London: Random House.

Grant, W. (2003) *Economic Policy in Britain*, Basingstoke: Palgrave Macmillan.

Gray, J. (1996) *After Social Democracy*, London: Demos.

Gray, J. (2000) 'A hollow state', in Pyper, R. & Robins, L. (eds), *United Kingdom Governance*, Basingstoke: Palgrave Macmillan.

Greenaway, J. (1995) 'Having the bun and the halfpenny: can old public service ethics survive in the new Whitehall', *Public Administration*, 73: 357–74.

Greenleaf, W.H. (1974) 'The character of modern British politics', *Parliamentary Affairs*, 28 (2): 368–85.

Greenleaf, W.H. (1983a) *The British Political Tradition Volume I: The Rise of Collectivism*, London: Methuen.

Greenleaf, W.H. (1983b) *The British Political Tradition Volume II: The Ideological Heritage*, London: Methuen.

Greenleaf, W.H. (1987) *The British Political Tradition Volume III: A Much Governed Nation*, London: Methuen.

Grix, J. & Goodwin, M. (2010) 'Bringing structures back in: the "governance narrative", the "decentred approach" and "asymmetrical network governance" in the education and sport policy communities', *Public Administration*, 89 (2): 537–56.

Haldane, Lord (1918) *Report of the Machinery of Government Committee: Ministry of Reconstruction*.

Hall, M. (2011) *Political Traditions and UK Politics*, Basingstoke: Palgrave Macmillan.

Hall, P. (1985) *Governing the Economy: The Politics of State Intervention*, New York: Yale University Press.

Hall, P. & Taylor, R. (2001) 'Political science and the three new institutionalisms', *Political Studies*, 44 (3): 936–57.

Hall, S. (1988) *The Hard Road to Renewal: Thatcherism and the Crisis of the Left*, London: Verso.

Halpern, D. (2008) *Social Capital*, Cambridge: Polity Press.

Halpern, D. (2010) *The Hidden Wealth of Nations*, Cambridge: Polity Press.

Hammersley, M. (2005) 'Should social science be critical?', *Philosophy of the Social Sciences*, 35 (2): 175–95.

Harris, J. (1978) *William Beveridge: A Biography*, Oxford: Clarendon Press.

Harrison, B. (2009) *Seeking a Role: The United Kingdom 1951-70*, Oxford: Oxford University Press.

Hay, C. (1996) *Restating Social and Political Change*, Buckingham: Open University Press.

Hay, C. (2002) *Political Analysis*, London: Palgrave Macmillan.

Hay, C. (2003) 'How to study the Labour Party: contextual, analytical and theoretical issues', in Callaghan, J., Fielding, S. & Ludlum, S., *Interpreting the Labour Party*, Manchester: Manchester University Press.

Hay, C. (2006) *Why Do People Hate Politics?*, Cambridge: Polity Press.

Hay, C. (2010) 'Pathology without crisis: the strange demise of the neo-liberal growth model', *Government and Opposition*, 46 (1): 1–31.

Hay, C. (2011) 'Interpreting interpretivism interpreting interpretations: the new hermeneutics of public administration', *Public Administration*, 89 (1): 167–82.

Hay, C. & Rosamond, B. (2001) 'Globalisation, European integration and the discursive construction of economic imperatives', Queen's University Belfast, *Queen's Papers on Europeanisation*, 1.

Hay, C. & Wincott, D. (1998) 'Structure, agency and historical institutionalism', *Political Studies*, 46 (5): 951–7.

Hazell, R. & Yong, B. (eds) (2012) *The Politics of Coalition: How the Conservative-Liberal Democrat Government Works*, London: Hart Publishing.

Headey, B.W. (1974) 'The role skills of cabinet ministers: a cross national review', *Political Studies*, 21 (1): 66–85.

Healey, D. (1990) *The Time of My Life*, London: Penguin.

Heclo, H. & Wildavsky, A. (1981) *The Private Government of Public Money*, London: Macmillan.

Heffernan, R. (2000) *New Labour and Thatcherism: Political Change in Britain*, Basingstoke: Palgrave Macmillan.

Heffernan, R. (2003) 'Prime ministerial predominance: core executive politics in the UK', *British Journal of Politics and International Relations*, 5 (3): 347–72.

Heffernan, R. (2005) 'Exploring (and explaining) the British prime minister', *British Journal of Politics and International Relations*, 7 (4): 605–20.

Heffernan, R. & Webb, P. (2007) 'The British prime minister: more than first among equals', in Poguntke, T. & Webb, P. (eds), *The Presidentialization of Politics: A Comparative Study of Modern Democracies*, Oxford, UK: Oxford University Press.

Held, D. (2005) *Global Covenant: The Social Democratic Alternative to the Washington Consensus*, Cambridge: Polity Press.

Hennessy, P. (1986) *The Great and the Good: An Enquiry into the British Establishment*, London: Policy Studies Institute.

Hennessy, P. (1995a) 'Searching for the great ghost: the palace, the premiership, the cabinet, and the constitution in the post-war period', *Journal of Contemporary History*, 30 (2): 211–31.

Hennessy, P. (1995b) *The Hidden Wiring: Unearthing the British Constitution*, London: Phoenix.

Hennessy, P. (1997) *Whitehall*, New York: The Free Press.

Hennessy, P. (2000) *The Prime Minister: The Office And Its Holders Since 1945*, London: Penguin.

Hennessy, P. (2005) 'Rulers and servers of the state: the Blair style of government 1997–2004', *Parliamentary Affairs*, 58 (1): 6–16.

Hill, M. (2005) *The Public Policy Process*, London: Longman.

Hills, J. & Stewart, K. (eds) (2005) *A More Equal Society? New Labour, Poverty, Inequality and Social Excusion*, Bristol: Policy Press.

Hirschman, A.O. (1982) *Shifting Involvements: Private Interest and Public Action*, Princeton: Princeton University Press.

Hirschman, A.O. (1991) *The Rhetoric of Reaction: Perversity, Futility, Jeopardy*, New York: Belknap Press.

Hirst, P. & Thompson, G. (1996) *Globalisation In Question*, Cambridge: Polity Press.

HM Government (2012) 'The Civil Service Reform Plan', June, available at www.civilservice.gov.uk/wp-content/uploads/2012/06/Civil-Service-Reform-Plan-acc-final.pdf (accessed 8 April 2012).

HM Treasury (2000) *2000 Spending Review: Public Service Agreements White Paper*, London: The Stationery Office.

Hofstader, R. (1973) *The American Political Tradition and the Men Who Made It*, New York: Vintage.

Hogwood, B. (1987) *From Crisis to Complacency: Shaping Public Policy in Britain*, Oxford: Oxford University Press.

Holliday, I. (2000) 'Is the British state hollowing out?', *Political Quarterly*, 71 (2): 167–76.

Holliday, I. (2002) 'Executives and administrations', in Dunleavy, P., Gamble, A., Heffernan, R., Holliday, I. & Peele, G. (eds), *Developments in British Politics 6*, Basingstoke: Palgrave Macmillan.

Hood, C. (1996) *The Art of the State: Culture, Rhetoric and Public Management*, Oxford: Clarendon Press.

Hood, C. (2010) 'Accountability and transparency: Siamese twins; matching pairs; awkward couple?', *West European Politics*, 33 (6): 989–1009.

Hood, C. & Dunsire, A. (1981) *Bureaumetrics*, Farnborough: Gower.

Hood, C. & Lodge, M. (2006) *The Politics of Public Service Bargains: Reward, Competency, Loyalty – and Blame*, Oxford: Oxford University Press.

House of Commons PASC (2001) 'Making government work: The emerging issues: Report and proceedings of the committee', 28 March, London: The Stationery Office.

House of Commons Treasury Select Committee (2012) 'Financial Conduct Authority', 12 January.

House of Lords Constitution Committee (2009) 'The Cabinet Office and the centre of government', London: The Stationery Office.

Howell, D. (1971) *The Conservative Opportunity*, Basingstoke: Palgrave Macmillan.

Howell, D. (1981) *British Social Democracy: A Study in Development and Decay*, Basingstoke: Palgrave Macmillan.

Howlett, M. & Ramesh, M. (1995) *Studying Public Policy: Policy Cycles and Policy Subsystems*, Oxford: Oxford University Press.

Hutton, W. (1995) *The State We're In*, London: Harper Collins.

Hyman, P. (2004) *One in Ten: From Downing Street to Classroom Reality*, London: Random House.

Independent Reviewer on Social Mobility and Child Poverty (2012) *Fair Access to Professional Careers*, available at www.gov.uk/government/uploads/system/uploads/attachment_data/file/61090/IR_FairAccess_acc2.pdf (accessed 16 September 2013).

Institute for Government (2010) 'Shaping up: a Whitehall for the future', January, London: IfG.

IPPR (1995) The Commission on Social Justice Report, 'Strategies for National Renewal', London: Institute for Public Policy Research.

James, O. (2003) *The Executive Agency Revolution in Whitehall: Public Interest versus Bureau-shaping Perspectives*, Basingstoke: Palgrave Macmillan.

James, S. (1985) *British Cabinet Government*, London: Routledge.

James, S. (1995) 'Relations between the Prime Minister and Cabinet: from Wilson to Thatcher', in Rhodes, R.A.W. & Dunleavy, P., *Prime Minister, Cabinet and Core Executive*, Basingstoke: Palgrave Macmillan.

Jessop, B. (1999) 'The dynamics of partnership and governance failure', in Stoker, G. (ed.), *The New Politics of Local Governance in Britain*, Oxford: Oxford University Press.

Jessop, B. (2002) 'Globalisation and the national state', in Aaronwitz, S. & Bratsis, P. (eds), *Rethinking the State: Miliband, Poulantzas and State Theory*, Minneapolis: University of Minnesota Press.

Jessop, B. (2007) *State Power: A Strategic-relational Approach*, Cambridge: Polity Press.

John, P.C. (2009) 'Why study urban politics?' in Davies, J. & Imbroscio, D. (eds), *Theories of Urban Politics*, London: Sage.

John, P. (2011) *Making Policy Work*, London: Routledge.

Johnson, N. (1989) *The Limits of Political Science*, Oxford: Clarendon Press.

Johnston, J. (1998) 'The structure-agency debate and its historiographical utility', *Political Studies Association Annual Conference*, 'Questions of Theory and Method in Political Science', 27 March, University of Manchester.

Johnston, P. (2009) 'Yes, minister, we can get out of the thick of it', *Telegraph*, 14 December, available at www.telegraph.co.uk/comment/columnists/philip johnston/6807347/Yes-minister-we-can-get-out-of-the-thick-of-it.html (accessed 22 March 2013).

Johnston, W. (1965) *The Inland Revenue: New Whitehall Series No. 13*, London: Allen & Unwin.

Jones, B. & Keating, M. (1985) *Labour and the State*, Oxford: Oxford University Press.

Jones, G.W. (1985) 'The prime minister's aides', in King, A. *The British Prime Minister*, Basingstoke: Palgrave Macmillan.

Jones, G.W. (1995) 'The downfall of Margaret Thatcher', in Rhodes, R.A.W. & Dunleavy, P., *Prime Minister, Cabinet and Core Executive*, Basingstoke: Palgrave Macmillan.

Jones, T. (1996) *Remaking the Labour Party: From Gaitskell to Blair*, London: Routledge.

Joseph, K. (1975) 'Stranded on the middle-ground: reflections on circumstances and policies', *Centre for Policy Studies*, London: CPS, October.

Judge, D. (1993) *The Parliamentary State*, London: Sage.

Judge, D. (2004) 'Whatever happened to parliamentary democracy in the UK?', *Parliamentary Affairs*, 53 (3): 682–701.

Judge, D. (2006) '"This is what democracy looks like": New Labour's blind spot and peripheral vision', *British Politics*, 1 (1): 367–92.

Kaletsky, A. (2010) *Capitalism 4.0: The Birth of a New Economy in the Aftermath of Crisis*, New York: Perseus.

Kandiah, M. & Seldon, A. (1995) *Ideas and Think-Tanks in Contemporary Britain*, London: Routledge.

Kavanagh, D. (1986) *Thatcherism and British Politics: The End of Consensus?*, Oxford: Oxford University Press.

Kavanagh, D. (2001) *British Politics: Continuities, Changes and Flamboyant Behaviour*, Oxford: Oxford University Press.

Kavanagh, D. (2004) 'Introduction', in Kavanagh, D. & Jones, B. (eds) *British Politics Today*, Manchester: Manchester University Press.

Kavanagh, D. & Seldon, A. (2001) *The Powers Behind the Prime Minister*, London: Harper Collins.

Keir, D.L. (1969) *Constitutional History of Modern Britain Since 1485*, Edinburgh: A & C Black.

Kenis, P.N. & Schneider, V. (1991) 'Policy networks and policy analysis: scrutinizing a new analytical toolbox', in Marin, B. & Mayntz, R. (eds), *Policy Networks: Empirical Evidence and Theoretical Considerations*, Boulder, Colorado: Westview Press.

Kenny, M. (1999) 'Ideas, ideologies and the British tradition', in Holliday, I., Gamble, A. & Parry, G. (eds), *Fundamentals in British Politics*, Basingstoke: Palgrave Macmillan.

Kenny, M. (2009) 'Politics as an academic vocation', in Flinders, M., Gamble, A., Hay, C. & Kenny, M. (eds), *The Oxford Handbook of British Politics*, Oxford: Oxford University Press.

Kenny, M. & English, R. (2000) *Rethinking British Decline*, Basingstoke: Palgrave Macmillan.

Kenny, M. & Smith, M. (2001) 'Interpreting New Labour: constraints, dilemmas and political agency', in Ludlam, S. and Smith, M. (eds), *New Labour in Government*, Basingstoke: Palgrave Macmillan.

Kerr, P. (2001) *Post-War British Politics: From Conflict to Consensus*, London: Routledge.

Kerr, P. & Kettell, S. (2006) 'In defence of British politics: the past, present and future of the discipline', *British Politics*, 1 (1): 3–25.

Keynes, J.M. (1926) *The End of Laissez-Faire*, London: Hogarth Press.

Kilfoyle, P. (2000) *Left Behind: Winning Back a Labour Heartland and the Defeat of Militant*, London: Politico Publishing.

King, A. (1975) 'Overload: problems of governing in the 1970s', *Political Studies*, 23 (2–3): 284–96.

King, A. (1985) *The British Prime Minister*, Basingstoke: Palgrave Macmillan.

Kingdom, J. (2013) *Government and Politics: An Introduction*, Cambridge: Polity Press.

Kingdon, J. (1984) *Agendas, Alternatives and Public Policies*, Boston: Little, Brown.

Kingdon, J. (1995) *Agendas, Alternatives and Public Policies*, Boston: Little, Brown (second edition).

Kochan, N. & Pym, H. (1998) *Gordon Brown: The First Year in Power*, London: Bloomsbury.

Krasner, S. (1982) 'Structural causes and regime consequences: regimes as intervening variables', in Krasner, S. (ed.), *International Regimes*, Ithaca: Cornell University Press.

Krugman, P. (2009) *The Return of Depression Economics and the Crisis of 2008*, New York: Norton & Company.

Labour Party (1989) 'Meet the challenge, make the change: a new agenda for Britain', Final Report of Labour's Policy Review for the 1990s, London: The Labour Party.

Labour Party (1997) 'New Labour: Because Britain Deserves Better', The Labour Party Manifesto, London: The Labour Party.

Labour Party (2003) 'The Big Conversation: A Future Fair for All', 28 November, London: The Labour Party.

Labour Party (2005) *Forward Not Back*, Preface to the Labour Party General Election Manifesto, London: The Labour Party.

Langan, M. & Schwartz, B. (eds) (1985) *Crises in the British State 1880–1930*, London: Hutchinson.

Laski, H. & Gooch, G.P. (1954) *English Democratic Ideas in the Seventeenth Century*, Cambridge: Cambridge University Press.

Lasswell, H.D. (1936) *Politics: Who Gets What, When, How*, New York: P. Martin.

Lawson, N. (1992) *The View From Number Eleven: Memoirs of a Tory Radical*, London: Bantam Press.

Layder, D. (1994) *Understanding Social Theory*, London: Sage.

Le Gales, P. (2012) 'States in transition, research about the state in flux', in Burroni, L, Keune, M. & Meardi, G. (eds), *Economy and Society in Europe: A Relationship in Crisis*, Cheltenham: Edward Elgar.

Le Grand, J. (2005) *Motivation, Agency, and Public Policy: of Knights and Knaves, Pawns and Queens*, Oxford: Oxford University Press.

Le Grand, J. (1982) *The Strategy of Equality: Redistribution and The Social Services*, London: Allen & Unwin.

Lee, S. (2009) *Best for Britain: The Politics and Legacy of Gordon Brown*, London: One World.

Leech, B.L. (2002) 'Interview methods in political science', *Political Science and Politics*, 35 (4): 663–4.

Lemke, T. (2007) 'An indigestible meal? Foucault, governmentality and state theory', *Scandinavian Journal of Social Theory*, 15 (3): 43–66.

Leonard, D. (1997) *Crosland and New Labour*, Basingstoke: Palgrave Macmillan.

Levitas, R. (1998) *The Inclusive Society? Social Exclusion and New Labour*, Basingstoke: Palgrave Macmillan.

Levitt, R. & Solesbury, W. (2005) 'Evidence-informed policy: what difference do outsiders in Whitehall make?', *University of Bristol Working Paper 23*.

Leys, C. (2001) *Market Driven Politics: Neo-liberal Democracy and the Public Interest*, London: Verso.

Lijphart, A. (1999) *Patterns of Democracy: Government Forms and Performance in Thirty Six Countries*, New Haven: Yale University Press.

Lindblom, C. (1979) 'Still muddling not yet through', *Public Administration Review*, 39 (6): 517–26.

Lindblom, C. (1984) *The Policy-Making Process*, New Jersey: Prentice Hall.

Ling, T. (1998) *The British State since 1945*, Cambridge: Polity Press.

Lipsey, D. (2001) *The Secret Treasury*, London: Viking.

Lipsky, M. (1980) *Street-Level Bureaucracy: Dilemmas of the Individual In Public Services*, New York: Russell Sage Foundation.

Lister, M. & Marsh, D. (2006) *The State: Theories and Issues*, Basingstoke: Palgrave Macmillan.

Lodge, M. (2013) 'Crisis, resources and the state: executive politics in the age of the depleted state', *Political Studies Review*, published online 26 February 2013.

Lovenduski, J. (2005) *Feminising Politics*, Cambridge: Polity Press.

Lowe, R. & Rollings, N. (2000) 'Modernising Britain: 1957–64: a classic case of centralisation and fragmentation?', in Rhodes, R.A.W. (ed.) *Transforming British Government, Volume 2: Changing Roles and Relationships*, Basingstoke: Palgrave Macmillan.

Lowi, T. (1979) *The End of Liberalism: The Second Republic in the United States*, New York: WW Norton.

Lowndes, V. (2010) 'The institutional approach', in Marsh, D. & Stoker, G. (eds), *Theories and Methods in Political Science*, Third edition, Basingstoke: Palgrave Macmillan.

Ludlum, S. & Smith, M.J. (2001) *New Labour in Government*, Basingstoke: Palgrave Macmillan.

Lukes, S. (1974) *Power: A Radical View*, Basingstoke: Palgrave Macmillan.

Mackintosh, J.P. (1963) *The British Cabinet*, London: Steven & Sons.

Mackintosh, J.P. (1978) *The Devolution of Power*, London: Penguin.

MacIntyre, A. (1985) *After Virtue: A Study in Moral Theory*, Oxford: Oxford University Press.

Macpherson, N. (2009) 'Evolution of the Modern Treasury', Economic and Social Research Council Seminar, All Souls College Oxford, 9 December.

Madgwick, P.J. (1991) *The Central Executive Territory*, London: Phillip Allan.

Magee, B. (1985) 'Schopenhauer and Professor Hamlyn', *Philosophy*, 60 (2): 389–91.

Mandelson, P. (2010) *The Third Man: Life at the Heart of New Labour*, London: Harper Collins.

Mandelson, P. & Liddle, R. (1996) *The Blair Revolution: Can New Labour Deliver?*, London: Faber & Faber.

Marinetto, M. (2003) 'Governing beyond the centre: a critique of the Anglo-Governance School', *Political Studies*, 51 (3): 592–608.

Marquand, D. (1988) *The Unprincipled Society*, London: Jonathan Cape.

Marquand, D. (1996) *The Progressive Dilemma*, London: Palgrave Macmillan.

Marquand, D. (2004) *The Decline of the Public*, Cambridge: Polity Press.

Marquand, D. (2008) *Britain Since 1918: The Strange Career of British Democracy*, London: Weidenfeld & Nicholson.

Marr, A. (2000) *The Day Britain Died*, London: Profile Books.

Marsh, D. (1980) 'The British political tradition', *University of Essex Department of Politics Occasional Papers*, Mimeo.

Marsh, D. (2002) 'Pluralism and the study of British politics: it's always the happy hour for men with money, knowledge, and power', in Hay, C. (ed.), *British Politics Today*, Cambridge: Polity.

Marsh, D. (2010) 'Stability and change: the last dualism?', *Critical Policy Studies*, 4 (1): 86–101.

Marsh, D. (2011) 'The new orthodoxy: the differentiated polity model', *Public Administration*, 89 (1): 32–48.

Marsh, D. (2012) 'British politics: a view from afar', *British Politics*, 7 (4): 43–54.

Marsh, D. & Furlong, P. (2002) 'A skin, not a sweater: ontology and epistemology in political science', in Marsh, D. & Stoker, G. (eds), *Theory and Methods in Political Science*, Basingstoke: Palgrave Macmillan.

Marsh, D. & Hall, P. (2007) 'The British political tradition: explaining the fate of New Labour's constitutional reform agenda', *British Politics*, 2 (2): 215–38.

Marsh, D. & Rhodes, R.A.W. (1992) *Policy Networks in British Government*, Oxford: Clarendon Press.

Marsh, D. & Tant, T. (1989) 'There is no alternative: Mrs Thatcher and the British political tradition', *Department of Government working papers*, No. 69, University of Essex.

Marsh, D., Buller, J., Hay, C., Johnston, J., Kerr, P., McAnulla, S. & Watson, M. (1999) *Postwar British Politics in Perspective*, Cambridge: Polity Press.

Marsh, D., Richards, D. & Smith, M.J. (2001) *Changing Patterns of Governance Within the UK*, Basingstoke: Palgrave Macmillan.

Marsh, D., Richards, D. & Smith, M.J. (2003) 'Unequal power: towards an asymmetric power model of the British polity', *Government and Opposition*, 38 (3): 306–22.

Marx, K. (1852) *The Eighteenth Brumaire of Louis Napoleon*, Chapters 1 and 7 translated by Saul K. Padover from the German edition of 1869; Chapters 2 to 6 based on the third edition, prepared by Friedrich Engels (1885), translated and published by Progress Publishers, Moscow, 1937.

Marx, K. (1994) *The 18th Brumaire of Louis Napoleon*, London: International Publishers (revised edition).

Matthews, F. (2009) 'Developing delivery – the evolution of the PSA framework and its response to emergent societal and geopolitical challenges', *Paper presented to the PSA Conference*, University of Manchester, 7–9 April.

McAnulla, S. (1998) 'The utility of structure, agency and discourse as analytical concepts', *Department of Politics and International Relations*, University of Birmingham, unpublished paper.

McAnulla, S. (2002) 'Structure and agency', in Marsh, D. & Stoker, G., *Theory and Methods in Political Science*, Basingstoke: Palgrave Macmillan.

McAnulla, S. (2006) *British Politics: A Critical Introduction*, London: Continuum.

McAnulla, S.D. (2007) 'New Labour, old epistemology? Reflections on political science, new institutionalism and the Blair government', *Parliamentary Affairs*, 60 (2): 1–31.

McCaig, C. (2001) 'New Labour and education, education, education', in Ludlum, S. & Smith, M.J. (eds), *New Labour in Government*, London: Palgrave Macmillan.

McEvoy, J. (2006) 'Elite interviewing in a divided society: lessons from Northern Ireland', *Politics*, 26 (3): 184–91.

McNay, L. (1992) *Foucault and Feminism: Power, Gender and the Self*, Cambridge: Polity Press.

Meredith, S. (2002) 'Always New Labour? New Labour in historical perspective', *Paper presented to the PSA Conference*, University of Aberdeen, 5–7 April.

Meredith, S. (2008) *Labours Old and New: The Parliamentary Right of the British Labour Party 1970–1979 and the Roots of New Labour*, Manchester: Manchester University Press.

Middlemas, K. (1979) *Politics in Industrial Society*, London: Andre Deutsch.

Miliband, D. (1994) *Reinventing the Left*, Cambridge: Polity.

Miliband, R. (1972) *Parliamentary Socialism*, London: Merlin.

Milmo, D. & Topham, G. (2012) 'West coast rail debacle blamed on Whitehall brain drain', *Guardian*, 4 October, available at www.guardian.co.uk/uk/2012/oct/04/west-coast-rail-whitehall-brain-drain (accessed 4 October 2012).

Mitchell, J. (2009) 'The narcissism of small differences: Scotland and Westminster', *German Politics*, 63 (4): 98–116.

Moran, M. (2001) 'Not steering but drowning: policy catastrophes and the regulatory state', *Political Quarterly*, 72 (4): 414–27.

Moran, M. (2003) *The British Regulatory State: High Modernism and Hyper-Innovation*, Oxford: Oxford University Press.

Morgan, K.O. (2010) *Ages of Reform*, London: I.B.Tauris.

Morgan, K.O. (2013) 'The Left and constitutional reform: Gladstone to Miliband', *Political Quarterly*, 84 (1): 71–9.

Morrison, J. (2002) *Reforming Britain: New Labour, New Constitution?*, London: Reuters.

Mount, F. (1992) *The British Constitution Now*, London: Heinemann.

Mowlam, M. (2002) *Momentum: The Struggle for Peace, Politics and the People*, London: Coronet.

Moyser, G. & Wagstaffe, M. (eds) (1987) *Research Methods for Elite Studies*, London: Allen and Unwin.

Mulgan, G. (1996) *Connexity: How to Live in a Connected World*, Cambridge, MA: Harvard Business Press.

Mulgan, G. (2001) 'Joined up government: past, present and future', in Bogdanor, V. (ed.), *Joined Up Government*, Oxford: Oxford University Press.

Mulgan, G. (2006) *Good and Bad Power: The Ideals and Betrayals of Government*, London: Penguin.

Mulgan, G. (2008) *The Art of Public Strategy: Mobilising Knowledge and Power for the Common Good*, Oxford: Oxford University Press.

Mullin, C. (2010) *Decline and Fall: Diaries 2005–2010*, London: Profile Books.

Murray, C. (1985) *Losing Ground: American Social Policy, 1950–1980*, New York: Basic Books.

Naim, M. (2013) *The End of Power: From Boardrooms to Battlefields and Churches to States, Why Being In Charge Isn't What It Used to Be*, New York: Basic Books.

Nairn, T. (1980) *The Break-up of Britain: Crisis and Neo-nationalism*, London: New Left Books.

Nairn, T. (2000) *After Britain: New Labour and the Return of Scotland*, Edinburgh: Granta.

Naughtie, J. (2005) *The Rivals: The Intimate Story of a Political Marriage*, London: Fourth Estate.

Navari, C. (1996) *British Politics and the Spirit of the Age*, Keele: Keele University Press.

Newman, J. (2001) *Modernising Governance: New Labour, Policy and Society*, London: Sage.

Newman, J. (2005) *Remaking Governance: Peoples, Politics and the Public Sphere*, Bristol: Policy Press.

NISER (2012) 'Monthly Estimates of GDP', National Institute of Economic and Social Research, 10 May.

Niskanen, W.A. (1971) *Bureaucracy and Representative Government*, New York: Transaction Publishers.

Niskanen, W. (1974) *Bureaucracy and Representative Government*, New York: Aldine Atherton.

Norton, P. (1999) *The British Polity*, London: Longman.

Oakeshott, M. (1962) *Rationalism in Politics and Other Essays*, London: Methuen.

Office for National Statistics (2011) *Annual Civil Service Employment Survey*, London: ONS.

Olds, D.L., Robinson, J., Pettitt, L., Luckey, D.W., Holmberg, J.,Ng, R.K., Isacks, K., Sheff, K. & Henderson, C.R. (2004) 'Effects of home visits by paraprofessionals and by nurses: age 4 follow-up results of a randomized trial', *Pediatrics*, 114 (6): 1560–8.

Oppenheim, C. (ed.) (1998) *An Inclusive Society: Strategies for Tackling Poverty*, London: Institute for Public Policy Research.

Osbourne, D. & Gaebler, T. (1990) *Reinventing Government: How the Entrepreneurial Spirit is Transforming the Public Sector*, New York: Addison-Wesley.

Page, E. (2010) 'Has the Whitehall model survived?', *International Review of Administrative Sciences*, 76 (3): 407–23.

Page, E. & Jenkins, B. (2005) *Policy Bureaucracy: Government with a Cast of Thousands*, Oxford: Oxford University Press.

Parry, R. (2003) 'The influence of Heclo and Wildavsky's *The Private Government of Public Money*', *Public Policy and Administration*, 18: 3.

Parker, S., Paun, A., McClory, J. & Blatchford, K. (2010) 'A Whitehall for the future', *Institute for Government*, January.

Peck, E. & 6, P. (2006) *Beyond Delivery: Policy Implementation as Sense-Making and Settlement*, Basingstoke: Palgrave Macmillan.

Perry, A., Amadeo, C., Fletcher, M. & Walker, E. (2010) *Instinct or Reason: How Education Policy is Made and How We Might Make it Better*, Reading: CfBT Education Trust.

Peters, B.G. (1999) *Institutional Theory in Political Science: The New Institutionalism*, London: Pinter.

Peters, B.G. (2004) 'Back to the centre: rebuilding the state', *Political Quarterly*, 75: 130–40.

Peters, B.G. (2008) *Governance, Politics and the State*, Basingstoke: Palgrave Macmillan.

Peters, B.G. (2010) 'Democracy and bureaucracy in the modern state', *Public Administration Review*, 70 (4): 642–3.

Peters, B.G. & Pierre, J. (2000) *Politics, Governance and the State*, Basingstoke: Palgrave Macmillan.

Peterson, J. (2003) *Policy Networks, IHS Political Science Series*, Working Paper No. 90.

Peterson, R.A. (1983) 'Patterns of cultural choice', *American Behavioural Scientist*, 26 (4): 422–38.

Pierre, J. (ed.) (2000) *Debating Governance: Authority, Steering and Governance*, New York: Oxford University Press.

Pierson, P. (2004) *Politics in Time: History, Institutions, and Social Analysis*, Princeton: Princeton University Press.

Plant, R. (1991) *Modern Political Thought*, Oxford: Wiley.

Platt, S. (1998) *Government by Taskforce: A Review of the Reviews*, London: Catalyst Trust.

Poguntke, T. & Webb, P. (eds) (2007) *The Presidentialization of Politics: A Comparative Study of Modern Democracies*, Oxford: Oxford University Press.

Pollard, S. (1982) *Britain's Prime and Britain's Decline: The British Economy 1870–1914*, New York: Edward Arnold.

Pollitt, C. & Bouckaert, G. (2009) *Continuity and Change in Public Policy and Management*, London: Edward Elgar.

Pollitt, C. & Bouckaert, G. (2011) *Public Management Reform: A Comparative Analysis - New Public Management, Governance and the Neo-Weberian State*, Oxford: Oxford University Press.

Ponting, C. (1986) *Whitehall: Tragedy and Farce: The Inside Story of how Whitehall Really Works*, London: Hamish Hamilton.

Powell, J. (2010) *The New Machiavelli: How to Wield Power in the Modern World*, London: Bodley Head.

Power, A. (2001) 'Social exclusion and urban sprawl: is the rescue of cities possible?', *Regional Studies*, 35 (8): 731–42.

Power Inquiry (2004) 'Power to the people: an independent inquiry into Britain's democracy', York: York Publishing.

Prabhakar, R. (2004) *Rethinking Public Services: Government beyond the Centre,* Basingstoke: Palgrave Macmillan.

Prescott, J. (2008) *Prezza – My Story,* London: Headline Review.

Prideaux, S.J. (2005) *Not So New Labour: A Sociological Critique of New Labour's Policy and Practice,* Bristol: Policy Press.

Punnett, R. M. (1976) *British Government and Politics,* London: Heinemann.

Purnell, J. & Lewis, L. (2012) 'Leading a government department – the first 100 days', *Institute for Government,* September.

Pym, F. (1984) *The Politics of Consent,* London: Hamish Hamilton.

Pyrce, S. (1997) *Presidentializing the Premiership,* Basingstoke: Palgrave Macmillan.

Raadschelders, J. & Rutgers, M. (1991) 'The evolution of civil service systems', in Bekke, H., Perry, J.L. & Toonen, T.A.J. (eds) *Civil Service Systems in Comparative Perspective,* Bloomington: Indiana University Press.

Radice, G. (ed.) (1996) *What Needs to Change: New Visions for Britain,* London: Harper Collins, 1996.

Rafferty, F. (1998) 'Action zones will pilot new ideas', *Times Educational Supplement,* 6 February.

Rawnsley, A. (2006) *Servants of the People: The Inside Story of New Labour,* London: Penguin.

Rawnsley, A. (2010) *The End of the Party: The Rise and Fall of New Labour,* London: Penguin.

Read, M. & Marsh, D. (2002) 'Combining qualitative and quantitative methods', in Marsh, D. & Stoker, G., *Theory and Method in Political Science,* Basingstoke: Palgrave Macmillan.

Reich, R. (2002) *The Future of Success,* New York: Vintage.

Rentoul, J. (2009) 'No. 10 from Blair to Brown', *The Hidden Wiring,* Mile End Group Newsletter: 5–6, Autumn.

Rhodes, R.A.W. (1988) *Beyond Westminster and Whitehall: The Sub-Central Governments of Britain,* London: Allen & Unwin.

Rhodes, R.A.W. (1994) 'The hollowing-out of the state: the changing nature of the public service in Britain', *Political Quarterly,* 65 (2): 138–51.

Rhodes, R.A.W. (1995) 'From prime ministerial power to core executive', in Rhodes, R.A.W. & Dunleavy, P., *Prime Minister, Cabinet and Core Executive,* London: Macmillan.

Rhodes, R.A.W. (1997) 'From marketisation to diplomacy: it's the mix that matters', *Public Policy and Administration,* 12 (2): 31–50.

Rhodes, R.A.W. (2001) 'The civil service', in Seldon, A. (ed.), *The Blair Effect,* London: Little Brown.

Rhodes, R.A.W. (2011) *Everyday Life in British Government*, Oxford: Oxford University Press.

Rhodes, R.A.W. (2012) 'Political anthropology and public policy: prospects and limits', Keynote address to the conference on 'Forty years of *Policy and Politics*: Critical reflections and strategies for the future', University of Bristol, 19 September.

Rhodes, R.A.W., Carmichael, P., Macmillan, J. & Massey, A. (2003) *Decentralising the UK Civil Service: From Unitary State to Differentiated Polity*, Buckingham: Open University Press.

Richards, D. (2008a) *New Labour and the Civil Service: Reconstituting the Westminster Model*, London: Palgrave Macmillan.

Richards, D. (2008b) 'Sustaining the Westminster model: a case study of the transition in power between political parties in British government', *Parliamentary Affairs*, 62 (1): 108–28.

Richards, D. & Kavanagh, D. (2001) 'Departmentalism and joined-up government: back to the future?', *Parliamentary Affairs*, 54 (1): 1–18.

Richards, D. & Mathers, H. (2010) 'Political memoirs and New Labour: interpretations of power and the "club rules"', *British Journal of Politics and International Relations*, 12 (4): 498–522.

Richards, D. & Smith, M.J. (1997) 'How departments change: windows of opportunity and critical junctures in three departments', *Public Policy and Administration*, 12 (2): 62–79.

Richards, D. & Smith, M.J. (2002) *Governance and Public Policy in the UK*, Oxford: Oxford University Press.

Richards, D. & Smith, M.J. (2004) 'Interpreting the world of political elites: some methodological issues', *Public Administration*, 82 (4): 777–800.

Richards, D. & Smith, M.J. (2005) 'The hybrid state: Labour's response to the challenge of governance', in Ludlum, S. & Smith, M.J. (eds), *Governing as New Labour*, London: Palgrave Macmillan.

Richards, D. & Smith, M.J. (2010) 'Back to the future: New Labour, sovereignty and the plurality of the party's ideological tradition', *British Politics*, 5: 239–64.

Richards, D., Mathers, H. & Blunkett, D. (2008) 'Old and New Labour narratives of Whitehall: radicals, reactionaries and defenders of the Westminster model', *Political Quarterly*, 79 (4): 488–98.

Richards, S. (2010) *Whatever It Takes: The Real Story of Gordon Brown and New Labour*, London: Fourth Estate.

Richardson, J. & Jordon, G. (1979) *Governing Under Pressure: The Policy Process in a Post-Parliamentary Democracy*, Oxford: Martin Richardson.

Riddell, P. (2006) *The Unfulfilled Prime Minister*, London: Politicos.

Riddell, P. (2011) *In Defence of Politicians*, London: Biteback.

Rittel, H. & Webber, M. (1973) 'Dilemmas in a general theory of planning', *Policy Sciences*, 4 (2): 155–69.

Rose, R. (1971) *Governing Without Consensus*, London: Faber.

Rose, R. & Davis, P. (1994) *Inheritance in Public Policy*, New Haven: Yale University Press.

Rosenbloom, D. (2011) 'The politics-administration dichotomy in U.S historical context', *Public Administration Review*, January/February.

Rosenburg, A. (1988) *Philosophy of Social Science*, Oxford: Clarendon Press.

Rutter, J. (2011) 'Was Gordon Brown's "Economic War Council" a new model for driving the PM's agenda?', June, available at www.instituteforgovernment.org.uk/blog/2728 (accessed 14 September 2011).

Rutter, M. (1998) 'Introduction', in Rutter, M. (ed.), *Anti-Social Behaviour by Young People*, Cambridge: Cambridge University Press.

Saint-Martin, D. (2004) *Building the New Managerialist State: Consultants and the Politics of Public Sector Reform in Comparative Perspective*, Oxford: Oxford University Press.

Sandel, M. (1998) *Liberalism and the Limits of Justice*, Cambridge: Cambridge University Press.

Sanders, D. (2002) 'Behaviourism', in Marsh, D. & Stoker, G. (eds), *Theory and Methods in Political Science*, Basingstoke: Palgrave Macmillan.

Savoie, D.J. (2008) *Court Government and the Collapse of Accountability in Canada and the United Kingdom*, Toronto: University of Toronto Press.

Savoie, D.J. (2010) *Power: Where Is It?*, Montreal: McGill-Queens University Press.

Saward, M. (1997) 'In search of the hollow crown', in Weller, P., Bakvis, H. & Rhodes, R.A.W. (eds), *The Hollow Crown: Countervailing Trends in Core Executives*, Basingstoke: Macmillan.

Saward, M. (2001) 'Reconstructing democracy: current thinking and new directions', *Government and Opposition*, 36: 559–81.

Saward, M. (2011) 'The wider canvas: representation and democracy in state and society', in Alonso, S., Keane, J. & Merkel, W. (eds) *The Future of Representative Democracy*, Cambridge: Cambridge University Press.

Sayer, A. (1999) *Realism and Social Science*, London: Sage.

Sayer, A. (2001) *Method in Social Science: A Realist Approach*, London: Routledge.

Scharpf, F.W. (1991) *Crisis and Choice in European Social Democracy*, Ithaca: Cornell University Press.

Schmidt, V. (2005) 'Institutionalism and the state', in Hay, C., Marsh, D. & Lister, M. (eds), *The State: Theories and Issues*, Basingstoke: Palgrave Macmillan.

Schmidt, V. (2010) 'Taking ideas and discourse seriously: explaining change through discursive institutionalism as the fourth "new institutionalism"', *European Political Science Review*, 2 (1): 1–25.

Scott, J. (1998) *Seeing Like a State: How Certain Schemes To Improve Our Human Condition Have Failed*, New Haven: Yale University Press.

Seldon, A. (1988) *Contemporary History Practice and Method*, Oxford: Blackwell.

Seldon, A. (1995) 'The influence of ideas on social policy: interview with Rodney Lowe', in Kandiah, M. & Seldon, A., *Ideas and Think Tanks in Contemporary Britain*, London: Frank Cass.

Seldon, A. (2006) *Tony Blair*, London: Harper Collins.

Seldon, A. (2010) 'The heart of power', *Prospect*, 28 April.

Seldon, A. & Pappworth, J. (1983) *By Word of Mouth: Elite Oral History*, London: Methuen.

Seldon, L. & Lodge, G. (2010) *Brown at 10*, London: Biteback Publishing.

Shaw, E. (1996) *The Labour Party Since 1945*, Oxford: Blackwell.

Shaw, E. (2008) *Losing Labour's Soul? New Labour and the Blair Government 1997–2007*, London: Routledge.

Shils, E. (2006) *Tradition*, Chicago: University of Chicago Press.

Shore, C. & Wright, S. (eds) (1997) *Anthropology of Policy: Critical Perspectives on Governance and Power*, London: Routledge.

Short, C. (2008) *An Honourable Deception: New Labour, Iraq and the Misuse of Power*, London: Free Press.

Skinner, Q. (1978) *The Foundations of Modern Political Thought: Volume I, The Renaissance*, Cambridge: Cambridge University Press.

Skopol, T. (1979) *States and Social Revolutions: A Comparative Analysis of France, Russia, and China*, New York: Cambridge University Press.

Smith, M.J. (1995) 'Interpreting the rise and fall of Margaret Thatcher: power dependence and the core executive', in Rhodes, R.A.W. & Dunleavy, P., *Prime Minister, Cabinet and Core Executive*, London: Macmillan.

Smith, M.J. (1998) 'Reconceptualizing the British state: theoretical and empirical challenges to central government', *Public Administration*, 76 (1): 45–72.

Smith, M.J. (1999) *The Core Executive in Britain*, London: Palgrave Macmillan.

Smith, M.J. (2008) 'Re-centring British government: beliefs, traditions and dilemmas in political science', *Political Studies Review*, 6 (2): 146–54.

Smith, M.J. (2009) *Power and the State*, Basingstoke: Palgrave Macmillan.

Smith, M.J. (2010) 'From big government to big society: changing the state–society balance', *Parliamentary Affairs*, 63 (4): 818–33.

Smith, M.J. (2011) 'Tsars, innovation and leadership in the public sector', *Policy and Politics*, 39 (3): 343–59.

Smith, M.J., Geddes, A., Richards, D. & Mathers, H. (2011) 'Analysing policy delivery in the United Kingdom: the case of street crime and anti-social behaviour', *Public Administration*, 89 (3): 985–1000.

Smithers, A. (2001) 'Education policy', in Seldon, A., *The Blair Effect: The Blair Government 1997– 2001*, London: Little Brown.

Sorenson, G. (2004) *The Transformation of the State: Beyond the Myth of Retreat*, London: Palgrave Macmillan.

Stears, M. (2002) *Progressives, Pluralists, and the Problems of the State: Ideologies of Reform in the United States and Britain*, Oxford: Oxford University Press.

Stedman-Jones, G. (1983) *Languages of Class: Studies in English Working-Class History 1832–1982*, Cambridge: Cambridge University Press.

Steinmo, S. (1996) *Taxation and Democracy: Swedish, British and American Approaches to Financing the Modern State*, Yale: Yale University Press.

Stoker, G. (2004) *Transforming Local Governance*, Basingstoke: Palgrave Macmillan.

Stoker, G. (2006) 'Public value management: a new narrative for networked governance?', *American Review of Public Administration*, 36 (1): 41–7.

Stoker, G. (2007) *Why Politics Matter*, Basingstoke: Palgrave Macmillan.

Strange, S. (1998) 'The new world of debt', *New Left Review*, Issue 230, July.

Stratton, A. (2011) 'FOI has Hamstrung Government', *Guardian*, 23 November.

Streeck, W. & Thelen, K. (eds) (2005) *Beyond Continuity: Institutional Change in Advanced Political Economies*, Oxford: Oxford University Press.

Sutton Trust (2009) *The Educational Backgrounds of Leading Lawyers, Journalists, Vice-Chancellors, Politicians, Medics, and Chief Executives, Submission of Evidence to the Milburn Commission on Access to the Professions*, London: Sutton Trust.

Sztompka, P. (1993) *The Sociology of Social Change*, Oxford: Oxford University Press.

Tansey, O. (2007) 'Process-tracing and elite interviewing: a case for non-probability sampling', *Nuffield College Oxford Politics Papers*.

Tant, T. (1993) *British Government: The Triumph of Elitism*, London: Dartmouth.

Tawney, R.H. (1952) *The Attack and Other Papers*, London: Penguin.

Taylor, A.J.P. (1965) *English History 1914–45*, London: Penguin.

Taylor, C. (1992) *Sources of the Self: The Making of Modern Identity*, Cambridge, MA: Harvard University Press.

Thain, C. (2004) 'Treasury rules OK? The further evolution of a British institution', *British Journal of Politics and International Relations*, 6 (1): 121–8.

Thain, C. (2009) 'A very peculiar British crisis? Institutions, ideas and policy responses to the credit crunch', *British Politics*, 4 (4): 434–49.

Thain, C. & Wright, M. (1995) *The Treasury and Whitehall: The Planning and Control of Public Expenditure: 1976–1993*, Oxford: Oxford University Press.

Thaler, R. & Sunstein, C. (2007) *Nudge: Improving Decisions about Health, Wealth and Happiness*, London: Penguin.

Theakston, K. (1987) *Junior Ministers in British Government*, Oxford: Blackwell.

Theakston, K. (1992) *The Labour Party and Whitehall*, London: Routledge.

Theakston, K. (1995) *The Civil Service Since 1945*, Oxford: Blackwell.

Theakston, K. (1998) *Leadership in Whitehall*, Basingstoke: Palgrave Macmillan.

Theakston, K. (2006) 'Whitehall reform', in Dorey, P. (ed.), *The 1964–70 Labour Governments*, London: Routledge.

Theakston, K. (2010) *After Number Ten: Former Prime Ministers in British Politics*, Basingstoke: Palgrave Macmillan.

Theakston, K. (ed.) (1999) *Bureaucrats and Leadership*, Basingstoke: Palgrave Macmillan.

Thelen, K. (2003) 'How institutions evolve' in Mahoney, J. & Rueschemeyer, D. (eds), *Comparative Historical Analysis in the Social Sciences*, Cambridge: Cambridge University Press.

Thompson, H. (1996) *The British Conservative Government and the Exchange Rate Mechanism 1979–1994*, London: Pinter.

Thompson, H. (2008) *Might, Right, Property and Consent: Representative Democracy and the International Economy*, Manchester: Manchester University Press.

Thompson, H. (2010) 'National economic policy', in Kenny, M., Hay, C., Gamble, A. & Flinders, M. *The Oxford Handbook of British Politics*, Oxford: Oxford University Press.

Tilly, C. (ed.) (1975) *The Formation of National States in Western Europe*, Princeton: Princeton University Press.

Tivey, L. (1988) *Interpretations of British Politics: The Image and the System*, London: Harvester Wheatsheaf.

Tivey, L. (1999) 'Constitutionalism and the political arena', *Political Quarterly*, 70 (2): 175–84.

Trilling, L. (1954) *The Liberal Imagination: Essays on Literature and Society*, New York: Harcourt.

Tsebelis, G. (2002) *Veto Players: How Political Institutions Work*, Princeton, New Jersey: Princeton University Press.

Tucker, K. (1998) *Anthony Giddens and Modern Social Theory*, London: Sage.

Van Maanen, J. (1988) *Tales of the Field: On Writing Ethnography*, Chicago: Chicago University Press.

Vickers, R. (2004) *The Labour Party and the World: Volume I*, Manchester: Manchester University Press.

Vincent, D. (1998) *The Culture of Secrecy in Britain 1832–1998*, Oxford: Oxford University Press.

Walter, J. (2010) 'Elite decision processes and the perception of global imperatives', *Paper to ISPP Annual Meeting*, San Francisco, July 7.

Walzer, M. (1995) *Pluralism, Justice and Equality*, Oxford: Oxford University Press.

Walzer, M. (1995) *Spheres of Justice: A Defence of Pluralism and Equality*, New York: Basic Books.

Watt, N. (2002) 'Mandarin cries foul over Byers lifeline', *Guardian*, 8 March, available at www.guardian.co.uk/society/2002/mar/08/localgovernment (accessed 8 November 2012).

Waylen, G. & Chappell, L. (2012) 'Gender matters in politics', *Political Quarterly*, 38 (1): 24–32.

Webb, B. & Webb, S. (1913) 'What is Socialism?', *New Statesman*, 21 June.

Weir, M. & Skocpol, T. (1985) 'State structures and the possibilities for "Keynesian" responses to the Great Depression in Sweden, Britain, and the United States', in Evans, P. B., Rueschemeyer, D. & Skocpol, T. (eds), *Bringing the State Back In*, Cambridge: Cambridge University Press.

Weiss, C.W. (1979) 'The many meanings of research utilisation', *Public Administration Review*, 3 (5): 426–31.

Weissert, C. (1991) 'Policy entrepreneurs, policy opportunists and legislative effectiveness', *American Politics Quarterly*, 19 (2): 262–74.

Wells, P. (2007) 'New Labour and evidence-based policy making', *People, Place and Policy* (online), 1 (1): 22–9.

Westrup, J. (2005) 'The politics of financial regulatory reform and the privatisation of risk', Paper to the Carr Conference, London School of Economics, 15–16 September.

Wiborg, S. (2010) 'Swedish free schools: do they work?', *LLAKE*, Research paper 18.

Wiborg, S. (2011) 'Learning lessons from the Swedish model', *Forum*, 52(3): 279–84.

Wiener, M. (1981) *English Culture and the Decline of the Industrial Spirit 1850–1980*, Cambridge: Cambridge University Press.

Willets, D. (1988) 'The role of the Prime Minister's Policy Unit', *Public Administration*, 65 (4): 444–59.

Williams, R. (1977) *Marxism and Culture*, Oxford: Oxford University Press.

Wilson, H. (1986) *Harold Wilson Memoirs: The Making of a Prime Minister 1916–1964*, London: Weidenfeld & Nicholson.

Wright, A. (1979) *G.D.H. Cole and Socialist Democracy*, Oxford: Oxford University Press.

Wright, T. (2004) 'A new social contract: from targets to rights in public services', *The Fabian Society*, Fabian Ideas 610.

Wrisque-Cline, A. (2008) 'The modernisation of British government in historical perspective', *Parliamentary Affairs*, 61 (2): 144–59.

Yanow, D. (2003) 'Accessing local knowledge: policy analysis and communities of meaning', in Hajer, M.A. & Wagenaar, H. (eds), *Deliberative Policy Analysis*, New York: Cambridge University Press.

Yin, R. (1994) *Case Study Research: Design and Methods*, Beverly Hills, CA: Sage Publishing.

Yin, R. (1981) 'The case study crisis: some answers', *Administrative Science Quarterly*, 26: 58–65.

Young, D.I. (1990) *The Enterprise Years: A Businessman in the Cabinet*, London: Headline Publishing.

Young, H. (1991) *One of Us: A Life of Margaret Thatcher*, London: Pan Books.

Yutchtman, E. & Seashore, S.E. (1967) 'Factorial analysis of organizational performance', *Administrative Science Quarterly*, 12: 891–903.

Index